25 ×4

CHANNEL 4 AT 25

First published in Great Britain in 2008 by Cultureshock Media Ltd on behalf of Channel 4

Cultureshock Media
27b Tradescant Road
London SW8 1XD
T +44 (0)20 7735 9263
F +44 (0)20 7735 5052
www.cultureshockmedia.co.uk

ISBN 10: 0-9546999-4-7
ISBN 13: 978-0-9546999-4-9

A CIP catalogue record for this book is available from the British Library

Editors: Rosie Boycott & Meredith Etherington-Smith
Deputy Editor: Edward Behrens
Editorial Assistant: Delilah Khomo
Sub editor: Miles Chapman

Design: Spin www.spin.co.uk
Colour Reproduction: DawkinsColour
Printed in Italy by Graphicom

Production manager: Nicola Vanstone
Publisher: Phil Allison

Thanks and acknowledgements: 4 Creative, Channel 4 Picture Publicity, Season Butler, Cath Clarke, Pamela Dear, Emily Dixon, Louise Ellwood, Alfonso Iacurci, Kate Jazwinski, Chloe Kinsman, Jessica Lack, Ian Massey, John Newbigin, Thomas Phongsathorn, David Redhead & Anna Robinson. And to everyone who made this book possible.

Distributed by:
Thames & Hudson
181A High Holborn
London WC1V 7QX
T +44 (0)20 7845 5000
F +44 (0)20 7845 5050

cultureshock

25 × 4
CHANNEL 4 AT 25

Contents

Preface

Strip away the physical manifestations of Channel 4 – the steel and glass of its Richard Rogers-designed headquarters, its modish dissolving logo, its staff, the edit suites and satellite dishes and fibre optics – and what you are left with, at its most basic, is a creative space.

Prohibited from making its own programmes, for the past 25 years the channel has been a powerful platform for independent voices and ideas, a commissioning fund available to artists, performers, journalists and producers whose work demonstrates adherence to the channel's founding principles of innovation, diversity, education and distinctiveness.

As a result of this unique commissioning system, Channel 4 is rarely, if ever, committed to a fixed and final viewpoint on any subject matter. The first instinct of Channel 4 is always to question, to challenge orthodoxies and received wisdoms, to find and amplify the voices querying the status quo, however uncomfortable the reaction that provokes. In its mind's eye, at its best, Channel 4 remains quirky, counter-intuitive and oppositional in pursuit of a more informed national debate: alternative, often contradictory perspectives jostle each other for airtime; the ridiculously trivial can be comfortably accommodated alongside the intellectually sublime.

This book, on a small scale, attempts to replicate this creative approach that has guided Channel 4's editorial decision making in the past quarter century. It is a deliberately eclectic collection of essays, articles and interviews, photographs and visuals, loosely grouped around 25 social, political and cultural themes; issues that have never been far

from the centre of national debate in the time Channel 4 has been on air and about which the channel can claim to have raised awareness.

None of the contributors featured here is employed by Channel 4, although many of them have crossed paths with the channel both past and present, some merely as viewers, others as on and off screen participants in its creative story. They have been selected to represent the independent, original voices that the channel has prided itself on identifying and nurturing since its launch in 1982.

This book was commissioned to coincide with the launch of a new vision for Channel 4, which will explain how Channel 4 sees its public service role developing in the emerging digital media landscape. As other broadcasters reduce their contribution in key public service genres, such as news and children's programming, Channel 4 aspires to create public value in new ways, delivering the innovative and inspiring programmes that have always defined it in new forms and via new digital platforms.

Any vision for the organisation's future must first understand its past and this is what this book sets out to do. It is not, however, intended as a definitive record of Channel 4's achievements (and not so occasional failures). Many of the channel's more influential programmes and contributors are mentioned both in detail and in passing, but many others do not feature at all. There has been no systematic policy of inclusion and omission; just the subjectivity (sometimes infuriating, seldom predictable) that results when independent voices are let loose in a creative space.

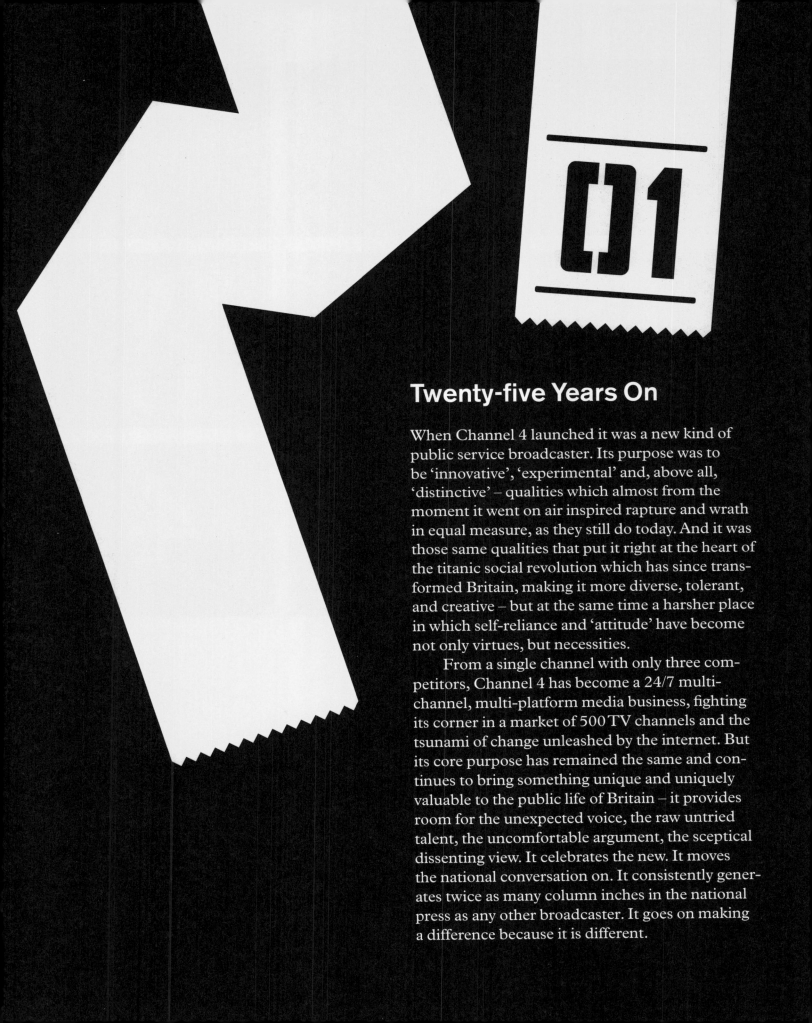

Twenty-five Years On

When Channel 4 launched it was a new kind of public service broadcaster. Its purpose was to be 'innovative', 'experimental' and, above all, 'distinctive' – qualities which almost from the moment it went on air inspired rapture and wrath in equal measure, as they still do today. And it was those same qualities that put it right at the heart of the titanic social revolution which has since transformed Britain, making it more diverse, tolerant, and creative – but at the same time a harsher place in which self-reliance and 'attitude' have become not only virtues, but necessities.

From a single channel with only three competitors, Channel 4 has become a 24/7 multi-channel, multi-platform media business, fighting its corner in a market of 500 TV channels and the tsunami of change unleashed by the internet. But its core purpose has remained the same and continues to bring something unique and uniquely valuable to the public life of Britain – it provides room for the unexpected voice, the raw untried talent, the uncomfortable argument, the sceptical dissenting view. It celebrates the new. It moves the national conversation on. It consistently generates twice as many column inches in the national press as any other broadcaster. It goes on making a difference because it is different.

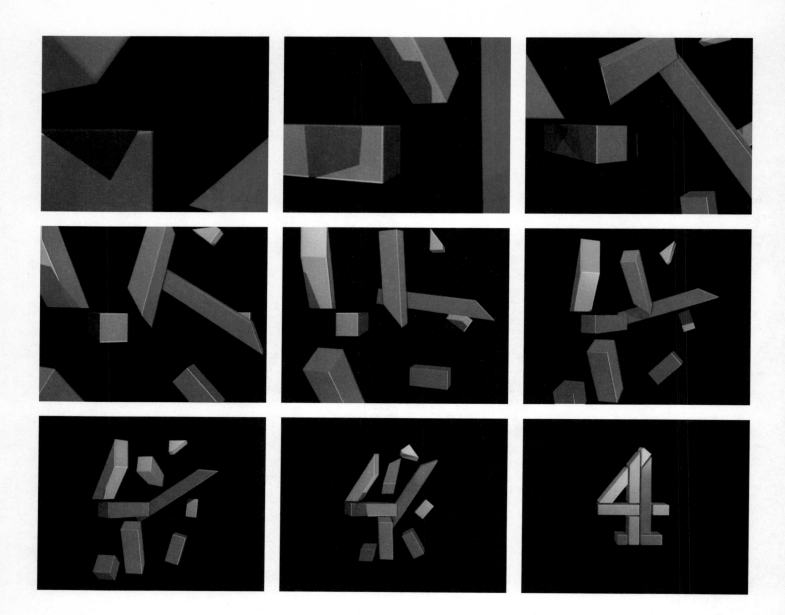

Channel 4 ident, 1982

Niall Ferguson on how life has
changed since Channel 4 went
on air

25 Years On:
How Life Got Shuffled

What were the historical turning points of the past 25 years?

The obvious answer is that there were two: first, the collapse of
Communism and the end of the Cold War; then, the rise of militant Islamism and the advent of the 'war on terror'. In a quarter
of a century, we went from a world of superpower tensions to a
world of clashing civilisations. The key dates were 9 November
1989 and 11 September 2001. The leading roles were played by
Margaret Thatcher and Ronald Reagan in the 1980s and Tony
Blair and George Bush after 2001. The main supporting actors
in the drama were Mikhail Gorbachev and Osama bin Laden.

But did any of this really alter the way we lived? Was the
average Briton's daily life fundamentally altered by either the
fall of the Berlin Wall or the fall of the World Trade Center?
Apart from longer lines at airport security and shorter waits for
plumbers (thanks to Polish migrant workers), the answer must
surely be no. Right now, most of us are about as worried about
terrorists today as we were by Soviet nuclear missiles in 1982.
Which is to say hardly at all.

So what did change our lives between 1982 and now? One
way of answering that question is to look at the way we lived then
and the way we live now. Make that comparison and you begin
to discern some real changes. Call it the difference between an
old stereo system and an iPod. Call it the difference between a
predictable world and a randomised world. Or let's just say:

We got shuffled.

The world of 1982 was boringly (or was it reassuringly?) bipolar:
US/USSR, Right/Left, Boy/Girl, Posh/Naff, Protestant/Catholic,
Rangers/Celtic. You were either on one side or the other. The
world of 2007 is chaotic by comparison. It is as if our very identities have become dazed and confused.

To begin with, we no longer spend so much time in a single
nuclear family. In fact, the family itself went nuclear at some
point between 1982 and now. Back in the early Eighties a third
of all households consisted of married couples with one child or
more. Today that proportion is down to 22 per cent. Meanwhile,
the number of single-person households has risen from 22 per
cent to 29 per cent. The nuclear family is now officially outnumbered by social atoms.

Marriage itself matters less. In 1982, twelve per cent of
babies were illegitimate. Today it's 42 per cent, and in Wales it's
more than 50 per cent. Marriages, if couples ever get around to
tying the knot, are less likely to last, while divorce appears to be
habit-forming. In 1981 just over one in ten men and women divor-
cing had already been divorced at least once. Today it's one in five.

Families form and fragment; households are in a state of
unprecedented flux. Lovers, spouses, offspring and even friends
move in. High property prices mean a substantial proportion of
children live with their parents into their twenties. But overall,
more people move out than move in. In old age we have a much
higher probability of ending up alone, often for many years.

Our increased mobility manifests itself in many other
ways. Only a quarter of us are still living in the same place where
we first watched Channel 4. And even those of us who haven't
moved house are peripatetic as never before. When Margaret
Thatcher was elected Prime Minister more than two-fifths of
households had no car, and those of us who did notched up just
over 400 billion passenger kilometres a year. The equivalent
figure in 2005 was 678 billion, a 70 per cent increase.

Channel 4 ident, 2004

One　　　　　　　　Twenty-five Years On

Wanderlust is a German word, but a British condition. Globalisation is a word with many meanings, but the most tangible is how much more we travel abroad than we used to. In 1982, the typical Briton worked in Grimy Town and spent his holidays in Sandy Bay. Only a quarter of British holidays were foreign. In 1981, UK residents made nineteen million trips abroad, of which just over eleven million were by air. Since then, the number of foreign trips we take has increased by a factor of three-and-a-half, and the share of journeys by air has risen from 60 per cent to more than 80 per cent. (The volume of domestic air travel has also increased more than three times. That's why de-industrialisation has done so little to reduce our carbon footprint.)

Our society, in short, has become manically mobile. I started writing this in my study in Oxfordshire, but finished it in a hotel room in Montreaux. By Monday night I shall be in Boston, Massachusetts. The next few weeks will take me to New York, Portofino and Barcelona. My next holiday will be in South Africa.

But it's not just that we love to see the world. The world has also come to Britain in unprecedented numbers – and not just as tourists. In the early 1980s, official statisticians assumed that net migration would remain negative as it had been in every decade since the 1960s. Government projections were for an annual net outflow of 30,000 a year in the 1990s. In fact, there was an average annual net *in*flow, rising from 5,000 in the 1980s, to 68,000 in the 1990s, to 182,000 between 2001 and 2005. A substantial proportion of this immigration was permanent. Grants of settlement to Africans and Asians have risen by a factor of roughly three.

In 1982, New Commonwealth and Pakistani immigrants accounted for less than four per cent of the British population. Today, according to the 2001 census, only 87.5 per cent of the population identify themselves as 'white British'. If you live in a big city, your neighbour is now significantly more likely to be of foreign origins, whether from Bangladesh, Bosnia or Burundi.

At the same time, however, there has been an upsurge in temporary migration, as Poles and other new members of the European Union have taken advantage of employment opportunities in the British Isles. This is one of the very few ways in which the great geopolitical events of the past quarter century have directly impacted on daily life in Britain.

Meanwhile, thanks to Scottish and Welsh devolution, the very meaning of being British has changed. The Scottish National Party rules in Edinburgh. Even in Northern Ireland, the Union no longer seems worth killing for. Perhaps the term 'British' is itself an anachronism. Perhaps the same could be said of that strange historical confection we call the United Kingdom of Great Britain and Northern Ireland – though premature predictions of its break-up were already being made when Channel 4 was born.

If our national identity has become more fragmented, so too has our religious identity. If your parents were 'C of E', so were you, and so were most people. Not any more. Perhaps the biggest change of the past quarter of a century has been the headlong collapse of Christianity in Europe. On an average Sunday in 1979, just under 4 million Britons attended one form of Christian worship or another, 1.4 million being children under fifteen. Since then church attendance has plummeted, more than halving among younger age groups. Just under two-fifths of British residents now say they belong to 'no religion'

whatever, though this should not be interpreted as a victory for atheism. Survey evidence suggests that we prefer to pick and mix our beliefs, confirming G K Chesterton's observation that, when people stop believing in God, they don't believe in nothing – they believe in anything.

It used to be fairly easy to predict what you'd do with your life. If your father was working class, so (probably) were you. A very large proportion of school-leavers in 1982 still assumed that they would follow their fathers into the manufacturing industry, which even after the recession of 1980–81 accounted for 30 per cent of all employment. Trade union membership remained high: two out of three manual workers (including the unemployed) were members of a trade union. People expected to be part of the union until they died. They were ready to strike at the drop of a flat cap: at the height of labour unrest in the early Eighties, more than 25 million working days a year were being lost. In 2005, the figure was just 157,400.

The shift from industry to services, plus the simultaneous expansion of higher education since 1982, has scrambled the class system. In the early Eighties, there were just over 800,000 full-time students in higher education, and 1.7 million in further education. Today it's 1.5 million and 5 million. University degrees are no longer for the elite of school-leavers. Soon they will be for everybody. On radio and television, meanwhile, estuary English has become the norm. It's not so much that social mobility has increased; it probably hasn't. It's more that social mobility matters less. The visible and audible differences between the classes have faded.

In short, our very identities have been shuffled. What's more, the same goes for the predictability of what we actually get up to.

Far more than the collapse of Communism or the rise of Islamism, it has been technological change that has really transformed our lives in the last 25 years. And by far the most profound changes have been in the field of telecommunications. Back in the early Eighties, a third of households still didn't have a telephone. (The same proportion didn't have a colour television.) Today, nearly 80 per cent of households have at least one mobile phone, more than 60 per cent have at least one home computer and more than half have Internet access.

We spend vastly more time and money than we used to on electronic communication: mobile phones, the Internet and email have transformed the way we relate to one another. In 1980–81 Britons made 20 billion domestic phone calls, most of them local, and 117 million calls abroad. Today, by contrast, we phone, text and email compulsively. You never know who's going to contact you and when.

Fun took a fairly limited range of forms. For two-thirds of men, going out meant going out for a drink, i.e. down the pub. The most popular forms of exercise were the least physically demanding. According to the 1982 edition of *Social Trends*, the most popular sports among teenage and adult males were billiards and darts. In addition, there were nearly 3.7 million anglers. When it came to spectator sports, toffs favoured the turf; yobs watched the footie or went to the dogs. Old ladies went to the bingo.

Back in 1982 boys played football or, if they were middle class or Welsh, rugby. In the summer, the upper and middle classes played cricket and tennis. Ordinary lads just kept playing footie, but with their shirts off. And a few nerds played Space

Invaders. But the most striking thing about the youth of the early Eighties (contrary to the folk memory of the punk generation) is how regimented they were. No fewer than 2.8 million young people belonged to one kind of organisation or another – the Boy Scouts, the Boys' Brigade or some kind of youth club. Today, it's precisely half that.

Organisation is superfluous to the Game Boy generation. The last generation of boys used to kick footballs compulsively. Now my sons can play umpteen electronic games from morning until night without so much as shifting from their desks. They do not even need to play together. Nevertheless, it would be a mistake to label this the 'couch potato' generation, despite the clear evidence that childhood obesity is on the rise. According to *Social Trends*, a much higher proportion of young men play outdoor football than did back in the early Eighties. A fifth of young men and women (aged sixteen to 24) regularly visit a gym or health club, institutions that were virtually unknown 25 years ago.

People still watch a lot of television, it's true. But the old, small-screen world was passive; ours is interactive. The small-screen world offered either BBC or ITV; our plasma-screen world offers nearly infinite choice. (Even Channel 4 itself has sub-divided to produce E4 and More4.) People in the 1980s also spent a remarkably large amount of time listening to the radio or to records and tapes. By our standards they were stunningly inert. This generation, by contrast, hyperactively taps at keyboards, changes channels and skips tracks. People used literally to do nothing. Now they multi-task.

One simple way to track the shifts in our behaviour is to look at changes in household expenditure. The biggest increase in expenditure has been on communication (up nearly five times since 1981), closely followed by tourist expenditure abroad (up fourfold) and clothing and footwear (also up fourfold). For pleasure, Eighties families drank and smoked. This generation chats, travels and shops. What we do has been revolutionised almost as much as who we are. A quarter of a century ago we bought singles with an A side and a (usually terrible) B side. Now we have a veritable playlist of pleasures and pastimes.

Not everything in the world has changed since 1982, to be sure. America is still Top Nation. Russia is back to being a menacing bear. Africa is still dirt poor. The Middle East is still bloody violent. It's still a world that runs on hydrocarbons.

But what we fear when we look to the future has changed profoundly. Our biggest nightmare in 1982 was nuclear war. We knew exactly what that would be like, right down to the fallout. Today, by contrast, we have the ultimate random nightmare: climate change. It would be bearable if it were predictable (e.g. Britain gets warmer). But it's more likely to mean chaos: more snowstorms, hurricanes, floods and – who knows – plagues of locusts?

Some people still worry about poverty in Africa, just as they did in 1982. But we now know from the experience of Asia how to cure poverty. Unleash the market. Go for growth. Flood the world with cheap exports. The problem is that the breakneck growth since 1982 of South and East Asia, especially China, is simultaneously reducing poverty… and accelerating climate change.

You have to ask yourself: How much more chaotic will life be when Channel 4 celebrates its fiftieth anniversary? Will Britain be a society of multicultural, multi-tasking metrosexuals living in co-ed condominiums, constructed on stilts to deal with rising sea levels? Or will there be a backlash against this iPod existence, a yearning to return to the simple vinyl verities that governed our lives back in 1982?

Will history suddenly reverse itself, as it does in Kurt Vonnegut's great novel, *Slaughterhouse Five*? Will repentant Islamists rebuild the Twin Towers in New York? Will contrite East Germans reconstruct the Wall through Berlin? Will the Russian economy flourish and the Soviet Union reconstitute itself? Will the British and American economies contract, dragging us back to the recession conditions of 1982? And will British society somehow revert to its old, rigid, predictable ways?

Stereo? Or iPod? Double-sided vinyl? Or shuffled playlist? When you put it like that, there isn't the slightest chance of returning to the good old, bad old days. History really has turned a corner – the sort that can't be reversed around. But it did not do so when and where we imagine. While walls and towers were tumbling down, our lives were imperceptibly but irrevocably changing. The shuffling may one day stop. But the old order will never be restored.

02

Making the News

In the world of 24-hour news on-screen, on-air and online, where every development is a news flash and a minute's head start is an exclusive, *Channel 4 News* retains an unrivalled distinctiveness as a source of news and in-depth analysis. While other channels have bounced their main evening bulletin around the schedule, *Channel 4 News* has always aired at 7pm, a cornerstone of the schedule and the only long-form news programme during peak viewing hours. Alongside *Dispatches* and *Unreported World*, *Channel 4 News* exemplifies the channel's commitment to broadening its viewers' understanding of the world around them, devoting a significant proportion of its airtime to foreign affairs and alternative voices. Its agenda helps attract a more diverse and younger audience for news, which it also seeks to serve by expanding onto new digital platforms.

Jon Snow's seminal moments
The fall of the Berlin Wall, 1989

© Magnum

Two   Making the News

Jon Snow looks at the history and development of the technology that makes *Channel 4 News* possible

The Snow Report: Making the News

The vast spools of the old two-inch format videotape were still the staple of the news film library. And, of course, there was film itself – requiring telecine apparatus to view it. But the birth of Channel 4 also coincided with the brief life span of one-inch video and the video cassette. The entire career of *Channel 4 News* has coincided with the most complex and rapid, but jerky, technical revolutions known to humankind. We have seen it all: from the death of the CP16 film camera, the black film-changing bag and three-hour film processing to the ongoing, tumultuous and tapeless digital revolution that we are suffering today.

And as the formats were evolving, the methodology for getting material from event to screen was changing equally rapidly: from shipping unprocessed film on aircraft to the present-day FTP e-mail package. In between, there was the period in the mid-Eighties when we would battle with other broadcasters to 'get onto' one of the few satellite paths across the Atlantic or Indian Oceans – paying thousands of dollars to do so.

Then came the birth of (the entirely undreamt of) 24-hour news, with mainstream news online and rolling channels. This had a huge impact on every aspect of what we did. But far from putting our conventional one-hour terrestrial news out of business, it made it the very cornerstone of Channel 4's output. This came exactly when our competitors were pushing national and regional news to the margins – or rushing to fuse their terrestrial output with their 24-hour channels – which, despite talk of trying to reboot their news operations, looked to me like a retreat.

What some prophets called the beginning of the end for 'appointment-

The technology revolution vastly increased the range of what *Channel 4 News* could do

to-view' news such as ours couldn't have been further from the truth. For all the media focus on 24/7 news during the 2003 Iraq War, *Channel 4 News* secured its best audiences ever, demonstrating the value of a programme that could make sense of the babble of truths, half-truths, propaganda, rumour and speculation that characterised the multi-channel, multi-media world.

Actually, the technology revolution vastly increased the range of what *Channel 4 News* could do. Channel 4 increased its expenditure to add *News at Noon* (2003), then *More 4 News* (2005), and increased its online news (2006). The channel also extended its current affairs coverage as a whole.

Still, the impact of the 24-hour-news culture has been intriguing. For politicians, the births of Rupert Murdoch's Sky News and BBC News 24 provided instant coverage for their every pronouncement. But for viewers it often proved a repetitive diet of sound bites and endlessly recycled reports. When a massive live news event kicks in, 24-hour news comes into its own – the problem is there are very few 'whens'.

So who watches 24-hour news? The answer is very few people watch it at any one time. Together, Sky News and BBC News 24 attract around 83,000 viewers at 7pm on weekdays. At this time *Channel 4 News* is steady at around a million. But the quality of those watching 24-hour news is creamy – MPs, business leaders and, critically, the rest of the media.

....

Channel 4 News still makes a conscious decision to remain based in reality

....

Worse, we may ourselves be influenced by the 24-hour output: concerning priorities, concerning who to interview and, even worse, concerning what to leave out. Stories are recycled so often on the 24-hour stations that we can find ourselves believing that most viewers know about it and that it will be 'old news' by the time we go on air. It can be nothing of the sort. Almost no one outside the City, the Commons and what we used to call Fleet Street will have seen it.

This said, I still confess I have Sky News or BBC News 24 on at my desk throughout the working day, yet I am horribly aware that in spite of audience figures almost too small to measure, they have a disproportionate impact on the daily news agenda. It pains me to say it, but the Prime Minister of the day may feel better rewarded by issuing a sound bite to a 24-hour news channel than by facing the rigours of a terrestrial evening news bulletin – despite *Channel 4 News* reaching around seven million per week, having a younger age profile than any other evening news bulletin and retaining its audience in an age of falling ratings across all channels – which is pretty remarkable.

Plus, these days, *News at Noon* adds up to 350,000 extra viewers every lunchtime, and *More 4 News* is the most-watched non-terrestrial news programme at 8pm.

Technological advances continue to allow the transformation of delivery platforms. Yet *Channel 4 News* still makes

a conscious decision to remain firmly based in reality. The current set and graphics style, originally conceived in 2001 and re-developed in 2005, is deliberately 'what you see is what you get'. The theory being that if the set is 'made up' using digital technology, who's to say that the content isn't the same? Our choices have continued to stand the test of time, and away from the studio *Channel 4 News* has increasingly invested in production on the road.

In 2001 we inaugurated the News from... format with News from India: transmitting from two locations, mixing on-the-day reports and filmed investigations put together by a director and programme editor, with me anchoring most of the programme for a full week. Many expected viewing figures to suffer. They didn't, and the experiment was judged a huge success, enabling us to look at the world from an entirely new perspective. News from Iraq followed in October 2003, with a second stint during the hand-over of sovereignty the following year. Then came News from Africa, anchored from Uganda, to coincide with the Gleneagles G8 summit in 2005 and the spectacular News from Iran in 2006. More recently, we anchored out of the High Arctic in 2007.

....

Channel 4 News continues to invest where others are cutting costs

....

And still we continue to invest where others are cutting costs. Channel 4 has invested in a larger and better newsroom, bringing together all Channel 4 news journalism into one space, and using the latest production and graphics technology. In 2008, we move into our new, enlarged, multi-media newsroom, and as the year progresses, we'll be joined by a radio team as Channel 4 rolls out what we do onto the radio airwaves. Innovative, authoritative and in-depth: thank heavens for the people, the channel and the technology that make it all possible.

When *Channel 4 News* made the news

<u>Michael Heseltine Storms Out</u>, 1986 Heseltine left the set when he saw that Clive Ponting, a former civil servant from the Ministry of Defence acquitted of leaking official secrets, was to be on the programme.

Novelist Edward Docx confronts the 'anything, everything for anyone at any time' that makes up our news today

Anything, Everything for Anyone

The news surrounds us, accompanies us, unites us as never before. We wake to the news-magazines of our radio and television, we fall asleep to round-up and special report. Our car journeys are marked out in bulletins. Our train trips swamped in endless pages of print – free, daily, weekly, monthly. Throughout the day, Comment and Analysis shoulder along beside us like twin shaven-headed bodyguards, forcing a path through the jostling hours, hanging around outside the door whenever something else requires our attention.

Then there's all the specialist news – sport, economics, politics, arts and science. Not to mention the media pages: the news about the news. And (deep breath) the news about not the news at all: the celebrity news. Underneath and over all this there's 24-hour news – all of the above and more, continually, from a choice of broadcasters, on a choice of media. Plus news in brief. Not forgetting the news reviews – jokes about the news, satires, send-ups, knock-downs.

And when all this news is done there is… all of it again. This time from a different outlet. The internet. To which we turn when we need to know the absolute latest or – a curious modern paradox this – when we have missed something from weeks ago and need to check back.

In short, the news and our experience of the news has changed more in the last 25 years than in the entire six and a half centuries since Gutenberg came grinning and jigging from his workshop with news of his printing press. Like Keanu Reeves when at last he beholds The Matrix, we have come to understand that the news is ubiquitous. The common fabric of our world.

Taking the longer view, this recent progress – if that is what we choose to call it – has been nothing short of extraordinary. We can be fairly sure that the fastest that news (or, indeed, anything) travelled in the days of the old civilisations – Egyptian, Assyrian, Babylonian – was at the gallop of an Arabian horse. Maximum. Which is precisely the same speed that news travelled in Europe in the early 1800s, until the railways and the telegraphs arrived. In other words, nothing much changed news-delivery-wise for 4,000 years. In this context, it seems truly incredible what homo sapiens has been up to in the last century – and absolutely staggering what the last few decades have witnessed. And four thousand years hence, historians will surely look back on the times in which we live – these decades, these very minutes – as wholly and utterly remarkable. 'How did they keep up with themselves?' they will ask. 'How did their barely understood psychologies cope with all this accelerating transformation? No wonder the poor bastards had a few issues. And that stupid business with oil – what the hell was that about?'

But even in the short view, the rate of change is breathtaking. When Channel 4 launched, I was nine. Nobody had a computer. Nobody had a mobile phone. Simple and bald and basic as that. Now, I am incandescent if the wireless network doesn't work or the broadband is slow. Outraged by diminished GPS coverage. I cannot endure a day without texts from around the world, calls, picture messages and rare Bob Dylan tracks downloaded to my phone-MP3player-camera-web-browser. And I expect total information about any subject on earth immediately – wherever I am – whenever I want it.

The digital age has revolutionised

NCB
Penrikyber Colliery
South Wales Area

The Picket Line,
Penrikyber
photograph by
Martin Shakeshaft

Pregnant Prisoner Revelation, 1996
Channel 4 News revealed that pregnant prisoners in Holloway were kept shackled to their hospital beds to give birth.

Alastair Campbell Storming In, 2003
Campbell unexpectedly arrived on set in order to defend his position over the BBC's now infamous reporting on the Iraq war.

more than the sheer speed of the news though. Perhaps an even more significant change is the manner in which we have all become participants in the news – gatherers, purveyors, disseminators. Because now we can all ring anywhere, from anywhere else; we can all take pictures of anything and send them wherever we please; we can all film anything, everything, for anyone, at any time.

What this means is that the news is no longer the authoritative and mildly mysterious totem of our childhoods. No more the lone reporter jammed into the only phone box in the village whispering his magic to some ancient and half-deaf copy-taker; no longer the half-forgotten foreign correspondent speaking to his equipment-laden crew on the outskirts of some distant township. Instead, the 'amateur's' camera-phone picture appears boldly on the front of the paper and the home-video features on the six-o-clock. We can all shoot footage. We can all be paparazzi. We are all *au fait* and happily involved at the front end. Just watch the phones come out next time you are on holiday and something of interest occurs; actress, tornado, accident, thief... Captured. Instantly.

Meanwhile, at the back end, we have all become broadcasters – or broadcasters of a sort. If none of the established news organisations will pay for our snaps or our videos, then we simply hit 'send-all' and mail them to everyone in the inbox; or better still, we put them up on our website, our blog, on YouTube, or throw them against a million unknown FunWalls.

Thus we now live. But these new gods of speed and ubiquity have also fostered some awkward new paradoxes. While we seem to care a lot more, for example, we also seem to care a lot less. Certainly, we engage with (or are at least aware of) a greater number of issues, events, crises at any one time; but we engage with them in much less depth and for a shorter time. This, I suspect, is something to do with the age-old problem that the more one apprehends the less one comprehends. And that which is instantly received tends to be instantly forgotten.

A second and related paradox arises from the dislocation between our very local physical lives and our very global mental lives. Being but grimly bound by time and space, our physical selves are unable to do much but breathe and eat wherever they find themselves breathing and eating... and yet our mental selves range the planet. In the gap between the two, a new form of anxiety breeds. Because while our cognitive self is forever in the business of connection, downloading news from around the teeming world, our corporeal self feels ever more strongly that there is no local endeavour sufficient to address or rectify the catalogue of concerns it is receiving. We are dislocated and disquieted; we suffer a persistent and untreatable news anxiety.

As a fosterer of community, the news is itself a force for good

And yet, taking the long view again, it is possible that the age of anxiety and instant news will eventually come to be seen as the birth pangs of our proper global consciousness. Because, to return to the first sentence, the other thing that the news very definitely does is... unite us. Not in our views, of course, but in our knowledge of the event. A disaster in Africa, an abduction in Europe, a bomb in America or the Olympics in China – increasingly, people know. By no means everyone, and by no means on every level, but to a greater and greater extent each day, there are more who know more about what is happening. Or at least what appears to be happening. And the biggest news items of all – global warming and the gang – are pretty much wholly unavoidable to anyone with a carbon footprint big enough to be contributing to the problem.

In this sense, as a fosterer of community, a centre of common concern and destiny, the news is itself a force for good. Because clearly, the best chance we have is to realise and to agree that, regardless of the medieval religions or the febrile nation states, there is but one small blue ball and it spins in a dark and thoroughly airless universe that is all the while colossally indifferent. And finally, that we are the first species, on this blue ball at least, to have its own destiny in its own hands.

Jon Snow's seminal moments
The impact of the Internet, Shanghai 2006

© Magnum

Jon Snow's seminal moments
The release of Nelson Mandela, 1990

Stewart Purvis, former CEO and Editor in Chief of ITN, explains how, after what might have seemed a rocky beginning, *Channel 4 News* has evolved into top quality TV journalism

Last Laugh

In its first two decades, television news in Britain had one thing you could count on – the news was read by a man at a desk. By the 1980s, the format had developed just a little. On BBC1 and BBC2, the news was read by a man or a woman at a desk, and on ITV the flagship news programme was read by a man and a woman at a desk. The arrival of Britain's fourth channel in 1982 brought something new and different. *Channel 4 News* was to be presented by three men and one woman – with no desks.

It was not a success.

In the opening shot of the opening night the four sat uneasily, trying to control the pile of scripts in their laps. Within a few months, it was back to a man or a woman at a desk and it was many years before any network tried anything like that again. The four presenters all went on to considerable success: Peter Sissons and Trevor McDonald in broadcasting, Sarah (now Baroness) Hogg as head of John Major's policy unit at Downing Street, and Godfrey Hodgson resuming a distinguished career as a writer and commentator. The episode showed that challenging conventional television news

was not going to be easy. But this was what Jeremy Isaacs, the first chief executive of Channel 4, demanded from the programme's producers, ITN.

'We did not want stories of individual crime,' Isaacs has written, 'or of minor natural disaster. We did not want coverage of the daily diaries of the Royal Family. *Channel 4 News* would deal with politics and the economy. It would bring coverage of the City, and of industry. It was to report the developments in science and technology, and in the arts. It was to cover the politics of other countries and to supplement that reporting with the output and insights of foreign television news programmes.'[1]

....

***Channel 4 News* integrated reportage of the event with analysis of the issues**

....

To do all this the programme would last an unprecedented one prime-time hour each night. I was the third editor in the first year to be handed the task of implementing that brief. I discovered, after taking the job, that Jeremy had told ITN that if I didn't increase the audience from a quarter of a million to three quarters of a million in a year the channel had the right to shut the programme down. (We made the target with months to spare.)

Some of the short-term difficulties arose from differences about what such an agenda would look like on air. The things we weren't allowed to do were the easy bit. We just didn't do them. The demand for 'no crime and no Royals' was at one level a knee-jerk reaction to the continuing obsessions of the media in post-war Britain. But it was also a reflection of changing priorities. Changes in technology meant more people were paid by electronic bank transfers so less cash was moved around the country for criminals to nab, and changes in social attitudes meant more scepticism about Royal lifestyles.

There were, of course, days when

When *Channel 4 News* made the news

<u>The Exclusive Everyone Wanted</u>, 2005
Jon Snow holding the Attorney General's legal opinion on the legitimacy of the Iraq War.

boycotting crime and the Royals produced running orders vastly different from other media. Royal wedding days, when BBC1 and ITV devoted most of their news airtime and resources to the nuptials, were particularly memorable. Such days gave rise to a guideline not in the Isaacs mission statement, but which summarises it perfectly. As programme editors would try out one idea after another for a lead story on presenter Peter Sissons, he would ask, 'What's the issue in that story?' The *Channel 4 News* team decided it was a programme not about the events of the day but about the issues those events raised. *Channel 4 News* integrated the reportage of the event with analysis of the issues. That way we got the best out of ITN's strong narrative reporting heritage whilst satisfying Jeremy's demand for 'nightly identifiable elements of news analysis'.

Just as one big story, the Falklands War of 1982, had allowed *Newsnight* to demonstrate its *raison d'etre* as a daily news/current affairs programme, so the Miners' Strike of 1984-85 was the making of *Channel 4 News* as a daily news-analysis programme. There were so many events, so many issues and so many new ideas for analysis that night after night most of the programme could be devoted to this one story without repetition.

Arthur Scargill of the Miners' Union and Ian MacGregor of the National Coal Board agreed to make their own video reports on what they thought were the real issues of the dispute. These turned out to be significantly different from what we in the media said they were. It was a turning point. Giving access to non-journalists wasn't just innovative, it produced a different and revealing form of journalism. It was 'user-generated content' decades ahead of its time.

These back-to-back reports from conflicting perspectives had first been

shown on *Channel 4 News* on the day cruise missiles arrived at Greenham Common. The technique was copied widely.

The programme found other ways of getting to the heart of issues. MacGregor and Scargill agreed to debate live on the programme – the only time they ever did it on television, and one of the few times they ever spoke to each other at all in private or public during the whole dispute.

But the programme's most distinctive feature was the time that *Channel 4 News* gave to miners talking, both striking and non-striking miners. Conventionally, such elements were 'packaged' either into a sequence of vox pops or into a reporter's profile of an individual or community. Freed from the convention by its longer running time, *Channel 4 News* gambled successfully that more airtime for comment and opinion might increase viewer appreciation of the issues.

Over the past 25 years, *Channel 4 News* has met its brief – especially in covering British politics, under Political Editor Elinor Goodman, who was there from day one. Analysis has consistently shown that *Channel 4 News* covers more foreign news than most rivals. The programme's budget has always been smaller, so it has never been able to afford its own running daily coverage of a long-term conflict such as the wars in the former Yugoslavia. But by focusing on key moments and fresh ideas it has been able to make a real difference. For instance, the initiative in 1992 to find the camps where Serbian troops were holding detainees produced an exclusive (shared with the *Guardian* and ITN colleagues on ITV) that had an enormous impact on world opinion. And when the validity of the story was later challenged by Serbian supporters, *Channel 4 News*'s journalism emerged intact and even enhanced after a courtroom encounter with those in denial about what happened in those camps.

MacGregor and Scargill agreed to debate live – the only time they ever did on television, and one of the few times they spoke to each other at all in private or public during the whole dispute

© Magnum

In more recent times, *Channel 4 News* has combined on-the-day analysis of major international events with assignments to under-reported parts of the world, producing individual reports or week-long projects such as the Royal Television Society award-winning 'News from Iran', presented live from a different Iranian city for five nights in 2006. Peter Sissons constantly asking 'What's the Issue?' began one *Channel 4 News* revolution, and his successor Jon Snow created another by nagging his editors, 'I should be there'.

A distinguished ITN foreign correspondent when he joined *Channel 4 News*, Jon wasn't a very good newsreader. Coached by colleagues, especially editor Richard Tait, he improved his studio presenting skills without losing any of his personality. The next logical step was for him to go out on the road to combine presenting and reporting.

When New Orleans flooded in 2005, Jon filed reports from his own small boat, searching for survivors amid the poorly organised official rescue

Presenting from location wasn't completely new. In the 1970s, Alastair Burnet presented whole editions of ITV's *News at Ten* from the British political party conferences. What was new about Snow's expeditions was that he was damned if he was going to fly off to somewhere just to say, 'Good Evening', lead into somebody else's report, say 'That's all from here, now back to the studio' and fly home. He wanted to do the journalism as well as the television. So when New Orleans flooded in 2005, Jon presented the programme live from the flooded streets, but also filed brilliant eye-witness reports from his own small boat, searching for survivors amid the poorly organised official rescue operation. As soon as

he was back in London he was off again, to the Pakistan earthquake.

It isn't Snow's hyperactivity but his top-quality journalism, in a creative coupling with current editor Jim Gray, that other on-location presenters struggle to match. By comparison, some of his BBC counterparts in Pakistan were embarrassing to watch.

Channel 4 News will have the last laugh

The foreign TV coverage that Jeremy Isaacs had hoped would provide 'insights' turned out to be the only part of his prescription that didn't work out. In the early days, so much of the world's television news was still in state hands that the most common insight came from what was not reported rather than what was. The rest of the elements Jeremy specified now appear quite regularly – on all five terrestrial channels and on the news channels. We no longer find it odd to see a news report about new technology or the arts. Perhaps the greatest achievement of *Channel 4 News* is that what it made unique has now become mainstream and all television news in Britain is the better for that.

So for me and the other three editors of *Channel 4 News* – Richard Tait, Sarah Nathan and Jim Gray – and the three commissioning editors – Liz Forgan, David Lloyd and Dorothy Byrne – the challenge has been further innovation. The rewards have come not just in multiple industry awards but also an audience that is passionate, younger and with a greater ethnic mix than other TV news services.

And what of the man who thought it all up? In the summer of 1983 when ratings for *Channel 4 News* were officially 'zero', Jeremy Isaacs was asked at the Edinburgh Television Festival if the programme had a future. He answered: '*Channel 4 News* will have the last laugh'.

[1] Jeremy Isaacs, <u>Storm Over 4: A Personal Account</u> (Weidenfeld & Nicholson 1989)

When *Channel 4 News* made the news

<u>Exposing the Serbian Detention Camps</u>, 1992
Ian Williams' report for *Channel 4 News* from the Serbian detention camps changed world opinion about the situation.

Provoking Debate

Channel 4 is unique in British television in provoking debate. As it has no shareholders and a limited level of public support, it is far more independent than its competitors. This independence has been put to good use, interrogating authority, challenging the consensus and airing opinions often too provocative or uncomfortable for other broadcasters to transmit. This editorial policy has also pervaded its drama, entertainment and softer educational programming, from *Brass Eye* to *The Mark of Cain* to *The Big Food Fight*. The aim has not just been controversy – although that has often been the outcome – but to raise public consciousness and broaden debate on key political and social issues.

The political columnist Peter Oborne on
how Channel 4's current affairs agenda
has consistently challenged the status quo

Dispatches: Beneath
the Veil, 2001

Provoking Debate

The Mark of Cain,
2007

Bremner, Bird and
Fortune, 1999

Hamburg Cell, 2004

G.B.H. 1991

The current affairs output of Channel 4 has been driven by a mischievous agenda ever since its inception. The duty of the channel is to produce, night after night, the unofficial history of Britain. That history is conditional, experimental and profoundly disrespectful of all entrenched opinion and the entire governing class. Channel 4 has no interest at all in the preservation of existing reputations and established power structures.

This is because Channel 4 believes in the limitless potential of the human spirit. It is on the side of the dispossessed, the voiceless and the future. Channel 4's over-riding duty is to search out voices that have not been heard and truths that have not yet been articulated. The essence of its job is the enfranchisement of the powerless. It is always on the side of minorities.

Channel 4 is the mirror image of the BBC, the only other British broadcaster with a public service remit. The BBC is modern, Channel 4 postmodern. BBC news coverage seeks to be definitive, while Channel 4 is sceptical of any kind of confident assertion. The BBC is reverential of power elites, while Channel 4 scorns them. The BBC looks to answer questions, Channel 4 poses them. The BBC is conservative but Channel 4 justifies its always-precarious existence by taking spectacular risks. It is restless, moving on, always pushing back the boundaries. It is the public duty of Channel 4 to unravel conventional structures of thought, to open up new areas of understanding, and to devise fresh methods of analysis. Channel 4 understands that it must be an instrument of social change, and a vehicle for uncomfortable truth-telling.

But this state of permanent revolution is perilous. There is always the danger that Channel 4 current affairs will take an outlandish line for no reason except perversity. At its worst, the channel can descend into nihilism – a state of mind that contradicts everything it stands for. This is the central dilemma of Channel 4: its constitutional duty to challenge the boundaries of conventional reporting always carries risk of catastrophe.

This imperative to constantly reinvent itself has been with Channel 4 ever since it was set up 25 years ago. Today, with the benefit of hindsight, it is possible to state categorically that, 'Channel 4 ranks as one of the great legacies of the Thatcher government, alongside privatisation and council house sales.' It was created at the moment of maximum Thatcherite hubris: after the Falklands War, and before the miners' strike, which it covered with a harsh truthfulness that put every other broadcasting outlet to shame. (Channel 4 showed no favour to either camp, so much so that Ian MacGregor and Arthur Scargill, who would not talk to each other face to face, were ready to do so through the medium of the young television channel.)

Channel 4 understands it must be an instrument of social change, and a vehicle for uncomfortable truth-telling

IRAQ: THE BLOODY CIRCUS

A WEEK LONG SEASON EXCLUSIVELY ON MORE4
STARTS WITH 'WHY WE WENT TO WAR' TONIGHT 9.00PM .

Available on Sky Digital 165, ntl 166, Telewest Broadband 142 & Freeview 13

MORE

One should not fall into the error, however, of assuming that Margaret Thatcher liked, admired or understood her creation. Channel 4 receives only the most cursory reference in Baroness Thatcher's autobiography, *The Downing Street Years,* and then only in the context of repeated attempts, thwarted by senior cabinet colleagues, to privatise it. Luckily her Home Secretary, Willie Whitelaw, the cabinet minister who masterminded the creation of the new channel, got the point. 'I suppose there is no decision I made in my political career that had more of an impact on the daily life of families in Britain.' The one time Whitelaw tried to watch Channel 4, however, he fell asleep at once. As Channel 4 Chief Executive Jeremy Isaacs reports in *Storm Over 4* (Weidenfeld and Nicolson, 1989), 'He thought it his duty to go to the other room, switch on the television, and see how his new creation was getting on. There, twenty minutes later, his wife Cecilia found him zizzing, peacefully asleep.'

Margaret Thatcher rightly considered that Channel 4 would provide an alternative to the BBC/ITV duopoly. She envisaged a new television channel that would, like her government, challenge what she saw as a hegemonic liberal establishment. 'You've got it all wrong doing all these programmes for homosexuals and such,' so Norman Tebbit informed Jeremy Isaacs. 'Parliament never meant that sort of thing. The different interests you are supposed to cater for are golf and sailing and fishing. Hobbies. That's what we intended.'

It was one of the glories of the young television channel that at no stage did it consider engaging with the governing vision of the Thatcher years. It is impossible to underestimate the magnitude of Isaacs' achievement. He refused to engage with conventional expectations. In its early years he was driven forward by the doctrine, articulated by the first head of news and current affairs, Liz Forgan, that viewers 'would forgive us anything except wasting this amazing chance to be different.'

The Isaacs doctrine meant never playing safe, always courting disaster, and braving charges – by no means always without foundation – of rank amateurism. Isaacs persisted in interpreting minority interests in a profoundly original way. It failed to engage – at any rate until Channel 4 brilliantly reinvented the concept of horseracing coverage five years on – with the leisure pursuits of the already enfranchised middle classes. Instead it sought to grant a purposeful voice to groups that had never before been welcome in mainstream public culture: ethnic minorities, gays, women, the working class, the very young. It is very easy to forget, only 25 years later, how incredible this was, and what a profound contribution Channel 4 has made to changing Britain.

Channel 4 set out to achieve things in the field of current affairs that had never been done before. The weekly programme *Union World,* presented by the future New Labour minister Gus (now Lord) MacDonald, reported the trade unions as they wished to be seen. No other voices – most conspicuously neither employers nor ministers – were allowed. The concept of balanced and impartial broadcasting was being re-examined by the subversives at Channel 4. They concluded that the time honoured formula for broadcasting impartiality – the award of equal time to all protagonists – was arid. So they entertained a startling current affairs doctrine which sought to understand political and social movements in their own terms.

Channel 4's <u>Lost for Words</u> season highlighted Britain's low primary school literacy rates. As top authors sent over 500 letters to Downing Street, <u>Richard and Judy's Best Kids' Books</u> show led to publishers pledging to adopt 'ability bands' to make the right level of book more readily available for Britain's children.

Lost for Words
The fight to help kids read
Season starts Monday 22nd October

This unilateral structure of *Union World* was duplicated in *Broadside,* a current affairs series concentrating on women's issues. Only women were allowed to edit this series. It concentrated on sexual politics, and gave a reasonably full and sympathetic portrait of the campaign against an American nuclear presence on British soil launched by the Greenham Common women over a number of years. 'We tested the proposition that if you gave women the *World in Action* brief something different would come out. Would it or wouldn't it?' notes Liz Forgan today. 'To the immense satisfaction of all the chauvinist pigs in the world it fell apart with a thunderous internal explosion, but not before making some very good programmes.'

Channel 4's *Opinions* series allowed speakers to address viewers, uninterrupted, for 30 minutes. The most famous of these lectures came from the magnificent radical historian EP Thompson, author of *The Making of the English Working Class,* arguably the greatest work of British history published since World War Two. Thompson had been invited to give the 1981 Dimbleby Lecture (named after the famous broadcaster Richard Dimbleby). Then the BBC board (as terrified then as now of official opinion) changed its mind. Thompson, in a prescient piece of oratory that nicely coincided with the Channel 4 mission, denounced media complicity in existing power structures.

Opinions was by no means all left wing. Edmund Teller defended nuclear deterrence, and the polemicist Paul Johnson – the father of Channel 4's present-day chairman, the entrepreneur Luke Johnson – gave a powerful defence of market economics. The week Johnson gave his lecture he brooded, in his *Spectator* column, on the moral dilemma presented to him

by invitations to appear on TV shows dominated by the 'soft centre radicals who dominate BBC current affairs output' and 'condition the public to regard extreme left-wing views as "normal"'. He went on: 'The same goes for ITV, or Channel 4, as our new sub-Marxist network calls itself. Here again I find myself in a dilemma: people like me are eagerly solicited by Channel 4 as token rightists: it helps them to maintain the pretence of 'impartiality' and 'balance'. Should one tell them to stew in their pseudo-egalitarian juice? Or take the opportunity to breathe a little sanity into what its Controller of Programmes calls 'the *Guardian* of the air.' Channel 4 has proved an even bigger disaster than people like myself predicted. It is pretentious, doctrinaire, humourless, amateurish and, above all, unpopular.' He continued: 'Four-letter words are not a substitute for creative imagination. Black is not necessarily beautiful. Militant homosexuality and shrieking feminism are unlikely to constitute compulsive viewing.' (*Spectator*, 18 December 1982)

Paul Johnson's diatribe came as Channel 4 was under ferocious political attack from the right. The Conservative MP John Carlisle urged that the channel be banned. Carlisle's demand, splashed over the front page of the *Daily Mail*, came after it emerged that Channel 4 proposed to broadcast what the *Mail* called a 'homosexual entertainment programme' on New Year's Day, 1983. Carlisle declared: 'I am horrified by the thought of this programme. This is TV for minorities indeed and I hope the majority will show their contempt for it by switching off in their millions. A large section of the public is already thoroughly disgusted by the low standards on Channel 4, and now I feel it is my duty to protest in the strongest terms at this latest departure. The channel is an offence to public taste and decency and should be drummed off the air forthwith.' (*Daily Mail*, 2 December 1982). At the time he spoke out against Channel 4, John Carlisle enjoyed a reputation as the strongest supporter of South Africa's Apartheid government – he was jokingly known as the MP for Johannesburg North.

Even today Carlisle refuses to recant. 'It *was* the gay channel,' he insists. 'I stand by every word I said. We didn't need a new channel and we still don't need it. It claims to be sexy, edgy and distinctive. That's code for more sex and violence.'

Campaigns like these have left a folk memory that the Tory right, through its *Daily Mail* mouthpiece, ran a permanent vendetta against Channel 4. This is not quite the case. Here is what the Daily Mail television reviewer Herbert Kretzmer said about the new channel in December 1982, just a month after it had started: 'For all its obvious frailties Channel 4 is unique in its readiness to grant great wads of time to the individual voice. In unhurried programmes like *Opinions* and the hour long *Voices* we have seen and heard some extremely bright men and women talking to the ceiling of their intelligence without having to keep one nervous eye on the studio clock. It is a freedom unparalleled elsewhere on the box. I hope that when Channel 4 alters its present doubtful course, as inevitably it must if it is to earn its keep, it will remain no less generous in allowing time and elbow room to discerning and articulate speakers. Ratings aren't everything. It is said that *Voices,* chaired by the able and tactful Al Alvarez, is watched by an audience so small that it cannot be measured. What of that? Barbara Cartland regularly outsells TS Eliot. But does anyone doubt who of the pair is the more worthwhile writer?' (*Daily Mail*, 22 December 1982).

In this thoughtful article Kretzmer gave a powerful definition of the driving force behind the current affairs output of Jeremy Isaacs' Channel 4: a refusal to allow the search for ratings to determine the output; a readiness to allow unpopular voices on air; a connection with the intellectual movements of the age.

This meant that Channel 4 approached everything it did with fresh eyes. ITN – the outside contractor – insisted that 'the news is the news is the news'. Channel 4 considered this proposition hopeless. Unlike its other current affairs strands, *Channel 4 News* did indeed pay homage to traditional notions of impartial and scrupulous reporting. But it was subversive of the methodologies of news production in every other respect. There was no sport and (in an anticipation of *The Independent,* founded some five years later) nothing royal. One third of the programme was dedicated to economic news, and one third to foreign affairs. Above all it brought a new seriousness to news presentation by allocating a full hour to it, rather than the conventional 30 minutes.

At first this formula failed, but it came into its own during the long winter of 1984/5 and the miners' strike. Only Channel 4 could offer the space to fully explore this national tragedy, to look carefully behind the headlines and capture the essential truths. Protagonists from both sides came to trust Channel 4. News crews from rival programmes sometimes resorted to putting C4 News stickers on their cameras in order to avoid harassment on the picket line. (Sue Summers, Good News Man, *Sunday Times,* 28 October 1984). Both sides knew they could set out their positions at respectful length and in their own terms, rather than be hacked into the two or three sentences allowed in a conventional news package. It was for this reason that Scargill

and McGregor, who would never engage personally, were ready to meet across the airwaves through Channel 4. Today, presented by Jon Snow and Krishnan Guru-Murthy, Channel 4 News remains an abiding justification of the broadcaster.

Channel 4's current affairs coverage over the last quarter century can be divided schematically into three parts. There is the early, liberal-Maoist period which started to come to an end when David Lloyd joined Channel 4 in 1988. Lloyd brought with him some of the disciplines and methodologies of the BBC, where he had been trained. Lloyd's influence was felt at a moment that Channel 4 was in any case reinventing itself. It was ceasing to exist only as an alternative channel and starting to enter mainstream broadcasting culture. Money from commercial advertising was starting to pour in, especially after the ending of control by the Independent Broadcasting Authority and the setting up of the Channel 4 Television Corporation in 1993. As ITV began to collapse as a generator of serious current affairs, Channel 4 emerged as the only mainstream competitor to the BBC.

Lloyd was a massive influence, bringing with him a new professionalism while sustaining Channel 4's alternative approach. 'Lloyd was unafraid to fail,' remembers Jan Tomalin, head of the Channel 4 legal department. 'If you are constantly testing the boundaries, sometimes you cross the line.' When the government banned Sinn Fein spokesmen from appearing, Channel 4 solved the problem by using actors' voices, lip synching for the banned speakers. When the Birmingham Six case went to the appeal court, Channel 4 infuriated the legal establishment by filming a nightly re-enactment of the court's proceedings (an idea developed under Forgan), which the outraged court duly banned.

It is very easy to forget, only 25 years later, how incredible this was, and what a profound contribution Channel 4 has made to changing Britain

One of the hallmark films of the Lloyd era was *The Committee,* which presented evidence, via an anonymous source, that there was systematic collusion between loyalist paramilitaries and the security forces to plan the murder of Catholics. History has shown this to be a profoundly flawed programme, though one that was made and broadcast in good faith. But the brutal public controversy that ensued showed Channel 4 at its best. As pressure mounted from the Attorney General – and the programme makers faced death threats – Channel 4 chairman Michael Grade and his board combined to fend off government attack. They defended what they saw as the channel's right to broadcast the allegations, and not to reveal the identity of the anonymous source even in the face of a court order, which caused Channel 4 to be fined £75,000 for contempt.

By the turn of the century, Channel 4 current affairs was facing a different kind of identity crisis. The radicalism of

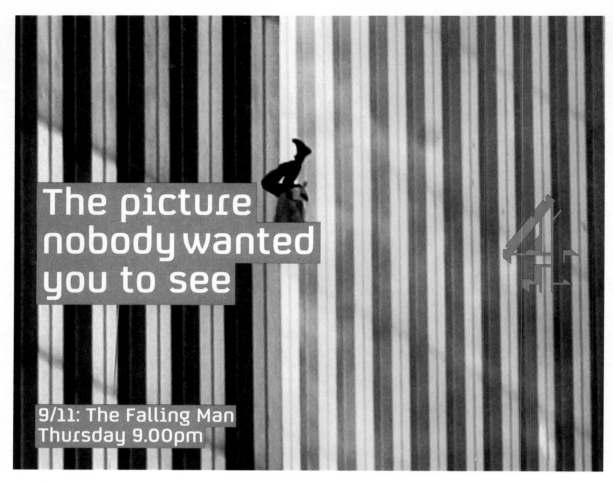

The picture nobody wanted you to see

9/11: The Falling Man
Thursday 9.00pm

the early years was in danger of becoming conventional piety. After a quarter century of social and political change, many of the progressives of the early Channel 4 years had themselves mutated into a complacent ruling elite. Conversely, some of the establishment targets of early Channel 4 had become victims. Perhaps for this reason, Channel 4's current affairs was slower to diagnose the internal contradictions of the Blairite political class than it had been to challenge the Thatcher establishment. In 1997, Paul Watson's *The Dinner Party* satirically recorded the conversation of Conservative Party members in suburban England. 'It was the wrong dinner party,' sighs Tim Gardam, later Channel 4's Director of Programmes. 'The dinner party we should have been attending to was in Islington.'

The task of creating a fresh narrative fell to Dorothy Byrne, who took charge of News and Current Affairs in 2002. For Byrne, allegiance to the Channel 4 tradition meant revisiting with a more sceptical eye the minorities which Channel 4 had celebrated and helped to enfranchise in the 1980s. 'We are there to give you views and perspectives,' states Byrne, 'that you will not get anywhere else in the broadcast media or possibly not anywhere else at all.'

Byrne's extremely brave decision to engage with the problems thrown up by multi-cultural Britain contrasted sharply with the institutional conservatism of the BBC. Documentaries like *Gang Rape* – which revealed that every gang rape in a public place ever reported to the police involved a black or mixed race gang – challenged the liberal dogma that there was no link between ethnicity and crime. Saira Shah's classic documentary, *Beneath the Veil,* used the techniques of secret filming to tell the truth about life in Afghanistan under the Taliban.

Channel 4 started to engage with Muslim extremism with the film *Kill or be Killed* in 1999. The *Dispatches* film *Undercover Mosque*, based on film footage gathered from twelve months of secret investigation throughout Britain, exposed disquieting evidence that a small minority of imams in mainstream mosques and Islamic organisations were preaching extremist and unpalatable views, in particular about women and gay people, and in rare cases an especially noxious form of anti-semitism. The film brought Channel 4 into conflict with the police in a paradoxical way. A quarter of a century ago Channel 4 represented political correctness in opposition to the mainstream and sometimes racist consciousness of the British police. Now it was the West Midlands Police which condemned the *Dispatches* programme, that stood for political correctness. But Channel 4 was not negative about Islam. *The Hajj*, which told the story of the journey made by five pilgrims to Mecca, celebrated Islam in a moving and original way.

Channel 4 engaged profoundly with the Iraq invasion and its dreadful consequences. 'We made the decision early,' says Kevin Sutcliffe, head of *Dispatches*, 'to ask the big, difficult questions.' Deborah Davies's awesome documentary, *The Death Squads*, told for the first time the story of how organised killings are linked to politicians wanting to turn Iraq into a Shia state aligned to Iran. Another film, *Iraq: The Reckoning*, was the first to describe on British television how the US and British armies had been obliged to hand control of Iraq to local militias. Sean Langan's superb *Dispatches* reports from Afghanistan told truths about the conflict unavailable elsewhere.

Dispatches: The Hurricane That Shamed America
Monday 8.00pm

The novel social and economic formation of the first decade of the 21st century threw up the need for different kinds of voices. So Channel 4 reinvented Rod Liddle, once editor of the BBC *Today* programme, as a dazzlingly articulate spokesman for a white working class whose fears, hatreds and enthusiasms had all been contemptuously ignored by the dominant progressive establishment. Peter Hitchens was brought into play as a rare public spokesman for the English lower middle class, a section of society which has been abandoned both by the hegemonic progressive elite and by a Tory opposition which had lost confidence in its own authenticity. Hitchens was unleashed on the idols of the progressive left. His targets ranged from David Cameron to Nelson Mandela. In *Beneath the Halo* Hitchens re-examined the record and legacy of the South African president with the same flair with which his brother Christopher had earlier challenged Mother Teresa, also on Channel 4.

Channel 4 undermined orthodox belief. In *Sex on the Street* Maggie O'Kane argued as a feminist against the law pursuing kerb crawlers. Nick Davies in *Drugs: The Phoney War* made a very powerful and well-informed argument for heroin to be given legally to addicts in order to reduce crime and the effects of contaminated drugs.

By the second half of the first decade of the 21st century, the power and audacity of the Channel 4 *Dispatches* coverage was putting the BBC to shame. No less than 40 agenda-setting documentaries were being produced every year, all given confident public billing and screened in prime time. In current affairs it was Channel 4, not BBC television, which had come to represent the great legacy of public service broadcasting left behind by Lord Reith, the first BBC director general. In due course the strength, liveliness and vigour of Channel 4 coverage shamed ratings-obsessed BBC bosses to drop plans to hide *Panorama* in the obscurity of a dead late night slot on Sunday nights.

The BBC concession came as another reminder that Channel 4's systematic policy of promoting unorthodoxy makes impossible demands. Whenever Channel 4 is successful, its vision is soon embedded in the common consciousness. This means that Channel 4, like King Sisyphus, is doomed always to start again at the beginning. It must perpetually engage in its endless search for fresh injustices to challenge, fresh received wisdoms to annihilate, fresh truths to cherish, fresh voices to articulate. That is the unbearable privilege of the amazing television experience that is Channel 4.

by Tony Harrison
1987

In 1987, Channel 4 caused controversy by
broadcasting V, a haunting meditation on
the provocative use of language in the 1980s
by the English poet, Tony Harrison

The language of this graveyard ranges from
a bit of Latin for a former Mayor
or those who laid their lives down at the Somme,
the hymnal fragments and the gilded prayer,

how people 'fell asleep in the Good Lord',
brief chisellable bits from the good book
and rhymes whatever length they could afford,
to CUNT, PISS, SHIT and (mostly) FUCK!

Or, more expansively, there's LEEDS v.
The opponent of last week, this week, or next,
And a repertoire of blunt four-letters curses
On the team or race that makes the sprayer vexed.

Then, pushed for time, or fleeing some observer,
Dodging between tall family vaults and trees
Like his team's best ever winger, dribbler, swerver,
Fills every space he finds versus Vs.

Vs sprayed on the run at such a lick,
The sprayer master of his flourished tool,
Get short-armed on the left like that red tick
They never marked his work much with at school.

Half this skinhead's age but with approval
I helped whitewash a V on a brick wall.
No one clamoured in the press for its removal
Or thought the sign, in wartime, rude at all.

These Vs are all the versuses of life
From LEEDS v. Derby, Black/White
And (as I've known to my cost) man v.wife,
Communist v. Fascist, Left v. Right,

Class v. class as bitter as before,
The unending violence of US and THEM,
Personified in 1984
By Coal Board MacGregor and the NUM,

Hindu/Sikh, soul/body, heart v. mind,
East/West, male/female, and the ground
these fixtures are fought out on's Man, resigned
to hope from his future what his past has never found.

The prospects for the present aren't too grand
When a swastika with NF (National Front)'s
Sprayed on a grave, to which another hand
Has added, in a reddish colour, CUNTS.

Michael Gallagher, father of an Omagh
victim, recalls his reasons for participating
in a Channel 4 film on the tragedy written
by Paul Greengrass

The Omagh Bomb

Omagh, 2004

Omagh, 2004

My name is Michael Gallagher. I am married with two daughters. Our only son Aidan was killed by the Omagh bomb.

The Omagh bomb was the most devastating terrorist attack in the 35 year history of the Troubles in Northern Ireland. On 15 August 1998 a breakaway Republican group called the Real IRA parked an explosive-laden car outside a school uniform shop in the small market town of Omagh, 75 miles west of Belfast. At 2.30pm that Saturday afternoon the police received a telephone warning saying that a bomb was near the Courthouse. It was a confusing and deceptive warning. While the town was being cleared, the car bomb detonated at 3.10pm with devastating consequences. Thirty-one people died, including a mother with unborn twins. Hundreds were injured, mainly women and children, many losing limbs. One young girl was blinded for life. The injured suffered mainly from burns. Northern Ireland had never experienced death or injury on this scale before.

The people affected came from three nations. Children from the Irish Republic and Spain were on an educational trip to Omagh that day. Five were killed and seventeen injured. Every hospital in the province received the injured, the RAF and Army helicopters transported the seriously injured to Belfast hospitals.

In the weeks after the bomb many of the families formed a support group. I was elected chairperson. The bomb did not discriminate. People from all religious and political opinion died or were injured. So the group's membership reflected this. We soon moved from a support group to a lobby group for justice. This brought us into contention with the police forces on both sides of the border, who were investigating this wicked crime. Our journey was extraordinary – meeting with senior members of both governments, including the Prime Minister and Home Secretary, the Taoiseach and the President of the USA – but having no result at the end of that. We started a civil action against the Real IRA and those individuals we believed were responsible. This was the first time in the world that victims' families had taken such a step.

We were approached by Paul Greengrass, the filmmaker, about making a film of our journey since the bomb. After many meetings, the families agreed to tell their stories so that a true and accurate film could be made. The film was based on my family's experiences. Our only son, Aidan, went into town with his friend on the 15 August 1998 to buy a pair of jeans. He never came home. He was killed and his friend was badly injured.

Our decision to take part in the film was a very difficult one, as it was going to put our lives under a microscope and we would lose our privacy, which at that time we believed was all we had. I felt that it was important because I played a pivotal role in the group as chairman, and continue to hold that position. I remember asking the filmmakers: whatever you do, tell the story how it is, do not over glamorise it or understate the difficult bits.

I believe Omagh was important because it showed that, even in the midst of evil, people can put their difficulties to one side. This must have given hope to a divided society – that is why I wanted *Omagh* to be a film of hope and not despair.

Sadly, car bombs have become the chosen weapons of terrorists. My hope is that all who have watched this film and have had their lives violated by terrorism can take courage from our experiences. And I hope that the people whose lives have been changed for ever will not give up hope.

In 2007, Channel 4 broadcast *The Lie of the Land* by controversial documentary filmmaker Molly Dineen, who talks to Rosie Boycott about her passion for the countryside

Are We Telling a Lie About the Land?

The Lie of the Land, 2007

The Lie of the Land, 2007

The Lie of the Land, 2007

Why did you pick the countryside as a subject?

It was a very good fusion between a commissioning editor and a director. I'd been toying with making a hunting film, but had never gone far enough into it, then the ban happened and Peter Dale phoned and said, 'Shouldn't you get out there now?' He knew it was a big news story. I went to some posh hunt in the Home Counties. I didn't like the culture at all, but I met Glynn Pearman and my antenna immediately went out because to me it is all about casting. If you've got the right character, then whatever they believe becomes the ballast of the film. I knew from the way he leapt off his horse. He was polite and much shorter than me, so easy to talk to. He said, 'What do you want to know? I'll help you.'

At what point did the film change from hunting to a bigger picture of the countryside?

When I went out with Ian [a farmer featured in *Lie of the Land*] on a flesh run and watched him shoot healthy animals. He said, 'Oh, it's just something that goes on in the countryside now, it's just the way things are' and I realised there was a story.

What does your film tell us about the countryside today?

I come from a modern, urban life and I romanticise the countryside. I passionately believe that it has got more ballast, more self-belief, more structure to it, more continuity. When I was shooting, what was heart-breaking about the calves being shot and stripped like that was just how any living thing can be so worthless, so valueless.

I'm not an insane church-goer but on quite a religious level it seemed to me deeply immoral that life should be created just to be destroyed, purely because of money. Where do you draw the line? When do you value a life and when do you not?

When did you see that the farmers' lives and the calves' lives were one and the same?

Immediately. Watching Ian in the shed, knowing that he's living off a couple of pounds and not worth anything at all, the hounds that he was feeding are now doing something illegal and the whole thing was just negative upon negative upon negative. On the other hand, when I had first gone to the hunt, I found a small group of people who came out of the gloom in remote areas to meet up in this portakabin and drink cups of tea and that, to me, is the essence of the hunt, its social infrastructure, the point it gave their lives.

Did you anticipate the reaction to the film?

I have never had a film that had a more passionate response. Different films have different reactions but this one was thrilling to me because it was also the point of making a documentary which is

The British Working Class
Class in Britain series starts tonight 8.00pm

you start to enter into policy. I was on the radio discussing it and someone phoned in and said the Commons select committee, who were discussing the countryside, hadn't the right to sit and discuss the future of the rural economy without seeing Molly Dineen's *The Lie of The Land*. The MP Michael Jack asked to see it, so it entered the political process and that was really exciting. But in the end, it made a big splash in a small bubble and that's all too often the limitation of TV – you raise issues, you light a touch paper and get people talking, but then where does the debate carry on?

I think television has a responsibility to throw its weight and its massive power of communication behind important issues. What right has it got to just sit there in the corner of our rooms, rooms all over the world?

What do you think we lost by losing our local farming culture and our local food culture as well?

I ended up feeling absolutely distressed about the state we are in, in both town and country. Every building that had a function is now a luxury home. *Country Life* is an obituary for the countryside, all those working farm buildings are now studios and swimming pools, but not even for local people to live in, but for rich outsiders to go and play in. But I would argue that a similar thing is happening in the town. I live in a road where nobody lives, the houses are just foreign investments, so I live alone surrounded by bricks and mortar owned by Saudis, and there are all sorts of extremely poverty-stricken Eastern Europeans living behind hoardings in homes staffed by equally poverty-stricken Filipinos, while the government will build 250,000 new homes in London as we apparently don't have enough. I just don't get it.

If you are commuting from Cornwall to Holland Park, as I did while I was filming, you see that both places are dormitories and that's why you can make a film like that with passion and understanding. We are living as machines, becoming so removed from our animal base, whether it's to do with growing, planting, cooking, eating, the way we communicate with family. I think it ends in catastrophe. It creates the sort of casualties that people now talk about, such as obesity, childhood behaviour, I think you can trace a lot of the problems that are written about back to the lack of local food production, farming, growing eating and understanding. I mean, you have to be humble about it; in the end we are animals, and it really is quite simple.

Television has a responsibility to throw its weight and its massive power of communication behind important issues

We Got There First

In his visionary Channel 4 drama, Peter Morgan imagines what really went down at the historic Granita meeting between Tony Blair and Gordon Brown

<u>The Deal</u>, 2003

113

EXT. GRANITA – EVENING (31ST MAY 1994)

A neon sign, 'Granita'. GORDON and ED BALLS arrive outside the restaurant. GORDON takes a deep breath, then opens the door, and walks in. In the far corner, TONY is as we left him – reading the newspaper. His expression changes when he looks up to see GORDON and ED BALLS walking towards him. TONY gets to his feet, there's that disarming smile.

> TONY
> Thanks for coming, Gordon.
> (shaking hands)
> Ed.

The THREE MEN sit down. TONY calls the WAITER.

> TONY
> You sure you won't eat?

> GORDON
> Positive.

> TONY
> OK – then let's get down to it.

TONY clears his throat, then looks meaningfully at ED BALLS, giving him the stare.

> ED
> (taking the hint)
> Er ... I'll go for a walk around the block.

ED gets to his feet and goes. It leaves TONY and GORDON together. An awkward silence. TONY and GORDON stare at one another. Tension you could cut with a knife.
The WAITER arrives.

> WAITER
> Ready to order?

> TONY
> Yes – I'll have the rabbit.

> WAITER
> Tuscan rabbit on a bed of polenta?

> TONY
> And a glass of white.

> GORDON
> Water for me will be fine.

Message received loud and clear. Business, not pleasure.
The WAITER goes. TONY and GORDON are left alone.

> TONY
> I'm sorry it's come to this.

GORDON stares anywhere but at TONY.

> I've hated the last few days.

> GORDON
> Why? In years to come, you may come to see them as your finest hour.

> TONY
> How can you say that?

> GORDON
> It's a stunning coup. You've come from nowhere – and will probably become Prime Minister.

> TONY
> (thrown by this, and smiles nervously)
> Come from nowhere?

TONY is blown away – shakes his head, unable to believe what he has just heard.

> TONY
> I accept I may not have been out there, barefoot on cobbled streets, handing our party leaflets aged 12, but I have hardly <u>come from nowhere</u> either. You and I have been MP's exactly the same amount of time.

> GORDON
> But, I taught you everything. Without me – you'd have been consigned to the dustbin of also – rans in this party.

> TONY
> With respect, Gordon, that's just delusional crap, and an insult to my supporters.

TONY's eyes flash in anger ...

> ... but I don't want to get into a slanging match. All I want – all I have <u>ever</u> wanted, is to get out of opposition and be part of a Labour government. If I thought that having you as leader would give us the best chance of achieving that, believe me, I would step aside in a second.

> GORDON
> Bollocks.

> TONY
> That is the truth.

> GORDON
> A man who does what you have done the last few days – that is not a man who steps aside.

> TONY
> We all come into politics for the big job, Gordon.

> GORDON
> Ah, so you admit it.

> TONY
> And when the opportunity came again – I went for it.

> GORDON
> Despite our understanding?

> TONY
> (holding head in disbelief)
> What understanding?

The WAITER brings their drinks.

>Look – I accept you are the stronger candidate
>in many ways. You are the better thinker – the
>better strategist – and you undoubtedly have the
>better party pedigree. It is a quirk of fate that
>at this moment that might be counting against you,
>and that I emerge as the better candidate to
>lead this party, but that fact remains.

GORDON flinches privately, his eyes are haunted.

>TONY
>
>I also acknowledge that without your support –
>without your influence in the party –
>my leadership might fail.

>GORDON
>
>Would.

>TONY
>
>So, I propose the following.

TONY leans forward.

>That I make you the most powerful
>Chancellor in history.

GORDON flinches, 'Chancellor'; it's a stab in the heart.

>You will have complete control over social and
>economic policy – you can chose your own team.
>I won't interfere.

>GORDON
>
>And if we get re-elected for a second term?

TONY looks at GORDON, checking whether he's joking.

>TONY
>
>Gordon, we haven't been in power for fifteen years.
>You want to discuss a second term?

>GORDON
>
>C'mon ... if the opposition continues to disintegrate
>at the current rate, it's not inconceivable that we
>become the only party in power for a generation.

TONY takes a deep breath, then.

>TONY
>
>Well ...
>
>(giddy at the thought)
>... under those circumstances, I wouldn't make
>the mistake Thatcher made, and go on too long.

GORDON'S expression changes, immediately understanding
the implications.

>GORDON
>
>And after a second term?
>
>(beat)
>Would you stand down after that?

>TONY
>
>C'mon ...
>
>(gestures)
>... this whole conversation is crazy.

>GORDON
>
>Not to me, it isn't.

TONY looks up, can see the intensity in GORDON'S eyes.

>TONY
>
>Well, whatever the circumstances, obviously
>I couldn't go on forever.

>GORDON
>
>In which case, would you support my candidacy?

>TONY
>
>(shrugs, this is madness, a meaningless pledge)

>I suppose so.

>GORDON
>
>Good.

GORDON stares at TONY. An uncomfortable silence. At that
moment, the WAITER swoops, bringing TONY'S food.

>WAITER
>
>One Tuscan rabbit, crushed polenta, sauteed
>pumpkin and raspberry sauce.

GORDON'S eyes widen in horror.

>GORDON
>
>(shudders)
>I 'll leave you to it.

GORDON takes out his wallet, leaves money for his drink.
Over his back, TONY notices a brown-haired WOMAN entering
the restaurant.

>TONY
>
>One last thing, before you go.
>
>(stares at GORDON)
>I think we should do a photo call.

>GORDON
>
>What?

>TONY
>
>People will need reassuring this was done ... amicably.

>GORDON
>
>What?
>
>(can't help smiling)
>You want me to step aside, and look happy
>about it too?

>TONY
>
>I thought outside number 1, Parliament
>St. Or on College Green?

>GORDON
>
>No. The hacks get close enough to ask questions
>there. I might say the wrong thing.

>TONY
>
>All right. I'll give it some thought.

GORDON gets to his feet.

>Say hello to Michelle on the way out.

The Deal, 2003

>GORDON
>
>Who?

>TONY
>
>Michelle, you know. From EastEnders?

TONY indicates the brown-haired WOMAN sitting in the
corner.

>Got pregnant by Dirty Den.

From GORDON'S blank expression.

>(shoots look, 'don't you know <u>anything</u>?')
>Den and Angie?

GORDON stares bewildered and not understanding, then
goes, passing the actress's table. The actress, (SUSAN
TULLY), raises her glass across the room to TONY, who raises
his glass back. Celebrities one and all.

Journalist Lucie Willan discusses the strange goings-on around the death of Dr Kelly and the resulting Channel 4 film *The Government Inspector*

The Government Inspector

The Government
Inspector, 2005

The Government Inspector, 2005

On 18 July 2003, the body of the government weapons inspector, Dr David Kelly, was found in woodland near his Oxfordshire home. Dr Kelly's death brought to a head months of public and media speculation and intrigue over the September Iraq Weapons Dossier. Two days after the apparent suicide, the BBC confirmed that Dr Kelly had been the main source for Andrew Gilligan's incendiary report on the *Today* programme. The report claimed that the government had misled the public over the 45-minute question in the September Dossier, deliberately inserting unreliable intelligence in order to make a more compelling case for the invasion of Iraq.

Lord Falconer immediately called for an investigation into the circumstances surrounding the death of Dr Kelly, and so the Hutton Inquiry was born. It was without doubt one of the most eagerly anticipated reports in recent years – and one of the most disappointing. When the inquiry's findings were published in January 2004, the report and Lord Hutton received widespread criticism for the apparent whitewash of the government. The inquiry failed to answer important questions about the use of intelligence in the run-up to the Iraq War and, while it damned Andrew Gilligan, the BBC and the MOD, the government was exonerated from any wrongdoing. As a result, Lord Hutton's impartiality has been questioned.

In March 2005, Peter Kosminsky's docu-drama, *The Government Inspector*, reignited the public debate surrounding the case. Like the Hutton Inquiry that it dramatises, *The Government Inspector* caused much controversy. Was it too soon after the event? How reliable was the depiction of the characters involved? Was it in bad taste? Etc, etc. These are all valid

questions but they do not change the fact that *The Government Inspector* is a compelling and powerful portrayal of the Kelly affair. It was important that the Kelly case should be re-examined by someone independent, without any affiliation to the government. Kosminsky's film painstakingly re-creates much of the evidence from the Hutton Inquiry, incorporating contemporary news footage and including independent research. In

It was important that the Kelly case should be re-examined by someone independent, without any affiliation to the government

To die for

Have animal rights activists gone too far?
Dispatches: Mad About Animals
Monday 8.00pm

this way the viewer is presented with a rather unsettling but far wider-reaching picture of Kelly. The opening sequence shows Dr Kelly taking a knife and painkillers, and walking towards the woodland where his body was found. This is interspersed with flashbacks of Kelly searching for evidence of Iraq's weapons by torchlight. The flashbacks give context to the story and suggest a reason for his suicide. They present two very different views of the weapons expert: Kelly the vital, energetic figure determined to prove Iraq's chemical and biological weapons capability; and Kelly the vulnerable man torn by guilt and doubt that we see quietly preparing for his death. There is no dialogue in the first few minutes, only Mark Rylance's extraordinary perform-ance as Kelly, underpinned by a haunting soundtrack that veers between Middle Eastern folk song and Christian choral music.

Through the inclusion of fictional details, plus intricately recreated evidence such as the dialogue of the Foreign Affairs Select Committee, Kosminsky tries to present a more human element to the Kelly story. This is best shown in the inclusion of a fictional Iraqi official called Qasim, who is used as a foil to Kelly in the story. Through this device Kosminsky exposes Kelly's conviction that Iraq was concealing its weapons, thus challenging the apocryphal view of Kelly as an anti-war propo-nent. Fictional exchange is used to highlight the government's callousness throughout the whole affair – the guitar scene shows an imagined exchange between Campbell and Blair where they are discussing whether to name Dr Kelly. Blair is only half con-centrating while asking Campbell's opinion of his riffs.

These devices may seem frivolous but they have an impor-tant role in the film, challenging received wisdom about the Kelly affair. In Kosminsky's film, no one is right or wrong. Kelly lies about his exchange with Susan Watts, and the government is shown up for its arrogance and spin. The crassness of the gov-ernment's handling of the case is highlighted at the end of this film by juxtaposing Blair's speech to Congress with Dr Kelly leaving to take his own life. Blair is seen recounting his success in America when he is told about Dr Kelly's suicide. While this was admittedly fictional, in reality the government's wanton lack of sensitivity was demonstrated by auctioning off a copy of the Hutton Inquiry signed by Cherie Blair and Alastair Campbell in order to raise funds for the Labour party in May 2006.

Since *The Government Inspector* was made, in March 2005, another independent look at the Kelly affair has been conduct-ed, this time in the form of a year-long investigation by Lib Dem MP Norman Baker. Baker has published his findings in a book, *The Strange Death of David Kelly*, which claims that the weapons inspector was murdered.

Since Channel 4 made *The Government Inspector* in March 2005, another independent look at the Kelly affair has been conducted

Nick Broomfield, the award-winning documentary filmmaker, discusses whether film can make a difference with Rosie Boycott

Look At It My Way

Do political films make a difference?

I think some have. Oddly, a lot of food films have made a difference.

Like *Supersize Me*?

Yes, or Jamie Oliver. I think the reason is that food films are very specific, you can actually measure the change, can't you? Maybe some other films do influence us a bit, but they are not measurable in an instantaneous way. It is hard to measure perception; it's hard to measure attitude and change.

Do you think any of your films have made a difference?

Yes, I think – certainly I think a lot of people have changed their opinions about people like Aileen (Wuornos, a notorious American serial killer). They have understood her. Just today I was in the shoe shop down below and the shopkeeper said 'I saw your Chinese film'. She kept saying, 'God! It's so horrible! It's so horrible!' So I said, 'What do you think about the Chinese' and she said, 'Oh God! I really got to understand something about the Chinese that I would never have known; I totally saw it from their point of view.' Which I think is always useful.

Did you make *Ghosts* because it was an extraordinary story, a human tragedy, or did you make it thinking maybe I'll make people understand the dark side of the quest for cheap food?

I made it because of the cheap food issue. I made it really because I wanted to do something about the supermarkets, and Morecambe just happened to be a means of highlighting the issues. The original idea was to do something about modern slavery. We researched lots of different subjects, some obvious ones like the sex trade; but I wanted to do something where there was clearly modern slavery exploitation by big corporations, that it was a financial capitalist's issue.

It was really Hsaio-Hung Pai, the Chinese journalist, who said I should really do the story. She lived undercover with the Chinese, and she introduced me to many of them.

I actually thought it was so amazing, to be in all these houses in England, it was a bit like getting to know *The People of the Abyss*.

Did *Ghosts* do okay or do you think we've got a real revulsion to

knowing? Is it the same thing that is happening with anti-war films – we just don't want to go there?

I think politically we are pretty much at the opposite end to the time immediately after Vietnam. What reaction requires is the middle classes and the educated classes being more directly affected: if their kids got drafted, that would get them going again. As it is, it is just the white trash and the Mexicans and the Puerto Ricans and the blacks who are going out to fight these wars, so it doesn't affect people in the same way that Vietnam affected them. That caused a whole political consciousness, didn't it? It was probably the Vietnam War that politicised a whole generation.

Why did you go from *Ghosts* to *Haditha*?

For me what making a film has always been about is partly the subject, and partly telling a story. I obviously learned a lot making *Ghosts*; *Haditha* is a more complicated story told from three different points of view. It is also a story which is centred around a major piece of action. It is like an action story and an action film.

What came first, the idea that you wanted to make a film about Iraq or the discovery of the Haditha story?

I remembered the Haditha story but I think that if I hadn't found the angle of telling it from three different points of view, it would not have told any more than the news told me.

Does this come back to what you did with _Aileen_, which is to make people look at it in different ways?

I think it was more. A lot of people, for example, who have seen the film have said, 'I had no idea what it is like to be an Iraqi now, what they go through, what it's like to have their lives, what their day is like'. And you know likewise with the insurgents. It is difficult just to understand who an insurgent is, how they see their lives, why they are doing what they are doing and that the insurgents are different from each other. They have very different positions and so I tried to make it a compassionate and complicated story.

So did you go for compassion with the marines?

They were in a way the hardest. The ones we met who had been there that day were terrified little boys who joined at seventeen, had seen so much death and carnage, had lost friends and had killed far too many people. They were traumatised beyond words, they were all on medication and they couldn't sit still. They had terrible dreams and nightmares, they were human beings who had been ruined, so it was hard not to feel compassion for them.

They can't relate to their families and they can't relate to their girlfriends.

They can only relate to each other. They are victims too. It's the same old army story: disadvantaged kids, many of whom had been in gangs, join up and they are totally expendable. It has always been the same really.

A film can also be incredibly compassionate

But did you think _Haditha_ would change anything?

Well audiences, people that I have talked to who have seen the film, are more angry and deeply disturbed and they are totally convinced that nothing of any good is going to come of it. I think that there is a lot of uncertainty, even amongst the liberal classes, because there hasn't been that much information. It's a war where there has been very inadequate coverage. There has been a lot of reporting but it has all been very thin; journalists have barely got out of the green zone, and those who have, have been embedded with the troops – which is not a good way to report anything.

We have very thin information but how did you get good information?

Well, we met with the insurgents and we met with the marines.

Are they still in the marines?

They were at the time. We met with one and got his story, and then met another – three of them altogether. We met with other people who had been in Haditha, but specifically it was that particular company we wanted to get to know. So we spent a few days with them, and then we went on Amman and we met with survivors of the massacre – all men, because the women were not allowed to travel. We knew that some of them were insurgents too. We realised that there was a big split between the Sunni insurgency and the Al Qaeda insurgency. You begin to realise that they are not all the same, in fact they kind of semi-hated each other.

So what films do you think have led to political change? Could you apply it to David Attenborough's wildlife programmes in the sense that he made us care about polar bears or gorillas?

Well, I think he makes you intrigued about polar bears and gorillas, but I don't know that you are moved to think that the next time you meet a polar bear or a gorilla that you are going to try to have a relationship with it. So, alright, you don't think that but you do think that our planet is a precious place, you do get a sense of one world.

I think a film can also be incredibly compassionate; in a good film you are emotionally moved, which means that the film can't operate all on one level. It has to operate on many different levels. You can't keep pounding someone with one emotion. You need to take the audience on a journey with you so they respond to the characters, and I think this response stays with you for a long time and you aren't the same when you go into any situation, because you look at people differently.

Ghosts advert, 2007

GHOSTS: THE CHINESE COCKLE PICKERS AT MORECAMBE BAY
A DRAMA ABOUT MODERN SLAVERY BY NICK BROOMFIELD. TUESDAY 17TH APRIL 10PM
Freeview 13 Sky 142 Virgin Media 142

MORE

Our Multi-Culture

Since 1982, Channel 4 has interpreted its role to serve alternative interests by catering for minorities, particularly those from different ethnic backgrounds. From the anchors on the *News* to special interest magazines such as *Eastern Eye* and *Black Bag*, from comedies like *Desmond's* to dramas such as *My Beautiful Laundrette*, people learned about the different cultural backgrounds of their fellow citizens. Today the schedule is equally, if not even more diverse, but then Britain is now home to some of the most ethnically varied and integrated communities in the world and Channel 4 continues to make a difference by interrogating the economic, political and social issues arising from ongoing immigration, and the tensions caused within Britain's Muslim communities by the War on Terror.

Festivals showing
the different faces
of celebration in
multicultural Britain,
Eid

The Nativity

The novelist Hanif Kureishi discusses
multicultural society with Rosie Boycott

A Liberal Society is in an Impossible Position

My Beautiful
Laundrette, 1985

My Beautiful
Laundrette, 1985

My Beautiful
Laundrette, 1985

Rosie Boycott: How did you come to write *My Beautiful Laundrette*?
Hanif Kureishi: When Channel 4 started FilmFour in 1982, David Rhodes was running the department and they didn't have any films. It was a clean slate and you could do whatever you wanted. I was a Paki, the only Asian writer, so I got the ethnic work.

I felt grateful for a job. I had been working at the Royal Court for Max Stafford-Clark, but had not made much money. I was hanging around with a friend of my family whom I called 'Uncle'. He ran laundrettes around Westbourne Grove and he said to me, 'Why don't you run one of these fucking laundrettes with me?' Which I decided not to do: instead I decided to write a film about someone running a laundrette.

I had grown up in the suburbs in the 1960s and 1970s, at the time of the National Front marches. Many of my

mates at schools were skinheads and they would come round to our house wearing the gear. *My Beautiful Laundrette* was my childhood; my youth went into that picture. There was the black movement, feminism and the gay stuff, but there hadn't been any gay stuff on television, no one had ever shown it as explicitly as we did in *Laundrette*.

I went round to see Stephen [Frears] and he said he liked the script and wanted to make it, but for television, not the cinema. He didn't want all the bother of making a film for the cinema and no one going to see it. Channel 4 agreed to do it.

What was the reaction?
We showed it at the Edinburgh Festival and it became a hit.

The gay community seemed rather grateful that we had made a film in which people were just gays without going on about it. The so-called Asians were annoyed about it, because they were never represented in the cinema and when they were represented they were shown as gays or drug dealers or bad landlords or whatever. So an argument began about whether writers like me represented the

community or spoke for the community. There were demonstrations in New York against the film; they would march up and down threatening to bomb the cinema, so it got a bit tricky.

I decided that I wasn't the person who would speak for the community. I just spoke for myself and that was more valuable.

Did the film change the way ethnic communities were portrayed on TV and in films?
EastEnders started a year or so later, and then all the soaps started having Asian characters. *EastEnders* had one Asian family who had a corner shop and an arranged marriage, so Britain became more aware that we were here and we were not going to go away, and that if you wanted to write or make films about Britain you had to show Asian people and black people and all that. By the time Major had gone and we were into the age of Blair, it had almost become compulsory to have Asian or black characters and directors.

That all sounds very innocent: how did we get from there to today's fundamentalism?

I had been in Pakistan in the early Eighties and I was aware that fundamentalism had begun to emerge. I'd go and talk to my uncles who were all Thatcherites and I'd say, 'why are you Thatcherites?' and they would go, 'because we hate Muslim fundamentalists'. I didn't even know what fundamentalism was.

My uncles, who were journalists and part of the so-called liberal intelligentsia, were terrified of these right wing Fascists who were going to take over and kill them. That struggle is still going on in Pakistan.

Throughout the Muslim world at the time the mosques were organising themselves to fight the American-backed right wing corruption of the sort the Shah had practised in Teheran. Muslim fundamentalism began as a liberation movement to get the Americans out and make their own society. But like a lot of revolutions, it turned into a kind of Fascism. None of that really started happening here until much later, in 1989, when we all became aware of the Rushdie fatwa. It was the first time that I became aware of fundamentalism in Britain. Then I started going to colleges and mosques and so on and I saw that these kids had really moved to the right.

What were they so angry about?
It was all to do with the really important identification which springs from racism. If you were a Paki you could then become a Muslim and that meant you could be identified with all other Muslims. You weren't just an Asian kid trying to fit in to a narrow Paki or ethnic Muslim world or the white world, which you considered racist. The fundamentalists were going to start the revolution; they were going to turn Britain into an Islamic state. It was a bit like Trotskyism, like the Trotskyism we grew up with.

Did they want you to be a part of it?
There was never any chance of my becoming a voice for it. I hated the whole thing. By the early 1990s it was really very heavy, you really felt the alienation. You would go into a Muslim flat and they would be married to Yemeni women who would walk in the room and bend over backwards with their backs to you, bringing food. They would say, 'we are not going to live in Britain we are going to live in the Middle East'.

If you were a Muslim kid and you wanted to rebel against your family it was very difficult just to run down the

road and start taking drugs and become a hippy. So one of the ways in which they rebelled was to become more right wing than their parents. Their parents were rather liberal, they wanted to fit in and do well in England, so the kids suddenly became very condemnatory of their own parents. I'd sit around with these kids and they'd go 'my parents don't pray, they are shit parents they are terrible people'. It was just a fantastic ideology to belong to if you were a Muslim kid; it was very powerful because it was inclusive. It was going to make a revolution.

Did British society make a big mistake somewhere?
A liberal society is in an impossible position. If you want to remain liberal then you have to be nice to ethnic minorities, when the ethnic minorities themselves are not liberal. It's taken a long time to play out. It would have been very difficult for the liberals to say in the beginning, these guys are Muslims, these people are Rastafarians, these people

100% English, 2006

are Hindus, and we should strip them of their identity in order that they be white and democratic like us, you couldn't do that, you had to say, 'Well if they want to be Jewish, if they want to be Muslim why should they not be…?' But when they begin to turn on you, or they start to blow you up, you are in a really tricky position. What do you do then?

Where do you see it going?
The faith school issue is very important; nobody has ever had the balls to say 'OK we are not going to have any faith schools'.

The problem with faith schools is that nobody learns anything there, they learn an ideology.

Thatcher probably had the right idea with secular education. If you want a secular state then you must have secular education. But what politician in Britain wants to dump all those schools?

Did art ever do any good here?
Art does good in the sense that if you have culture, you have a place where all these issues are discussed and you do get a sense of the rest of the world. One of the things I felt in the Fifties, Sixties and Seventies was that we didn't have any kind of voice anywhere. We were never on the telly and when we were on the telly we were abused and were talked about as being Pakis and so on. So the arts opened a space, where other people could see us.

Some of these issues were discussed in *My Beautiful Laundrette* and the film I wrote, *My Son the Fanatic*. Blair was pretty good about that in the beginning; he was obviously a liberal, and he wanted Asian people not to be discriminated against and have a voice and so on. I don't think that they were really aware for a long time how powerful, despite the fatwa, the Muslim thing could really be. It took a long time for all that to kick in.

Do you think it took 9/11 for us to take it seriously?
Yes, and after the London bombings people started to ask, 'What do we do with people who live in our society and do not have our values, who want to overthrow us and indeed will blow us up?'

We have to think and talk about these issues, and we can dramatise them. But on the whole film and other forms of media are not really didactic and it's better if they are not didactic; don't make films saying Muslims are bad, make a film to show all the issues.

It seems to me that at the moment we really have to resist Islam and all its forms. The real problem, and they are only beginning to realise this now, always was in the mosques. They have always been places where you organised; mosques are political centres.

When I went down to the Whitechapel mosque in about 1990, 1991, 1992, they were making huge political speeches. It wasn't like going to church. I'd go in there and they would be talking about gays burning in hell, pushing gays off mountains, women, that you must convert, you couldn't be a non-believer and so on. Everyone would go, 'It's free speech, what are they going to do?'. It

Bandung File, 1985

Chinese New Year

didn't become hate crime. You didn't get arrested for saying you could kill gays in a mosque till the other day. All that stuff went on for years.

How did the liberals deal with that?

It was very tricky for the liberals, very tricky. They'd go, 'Poor Muslims they are oppressed people, they suffer from racism, they are having a bad time over here; they are emigrants who have come over here to work and now you are saying their customs and their way of life are shit'.

I'm totally against veils. For me the veil is another curtailment of personal freedom that represents the suppression of women. It is a symbol of oppression just like someone I saw in the bank the other day who was wearing a Nazi badge and I thought, that's your personal freedom to wear a Nazi badge but I'd rather you fucking didn't because it really offends me and a lot of people. So, for me the veil is a symbol of oppression. I don't support it.

Would you ban the veil?

I'd ban it in public places; I mean inside institutions, schools and colleges. It would be very tricky for a politician to ban the veil, even though they have done it in France.

These people are really powerful and they really believe; they believe with much more strength than we believe anything. It's very tricky for the liberals to wake up and make draconian rules. You would have to have a much more structured, organised, law-heavy society than we have now. But the more laws you have, the less liberal you are.

So what do we do?

I think we have to keep fighting Islam, I really do. I wouldn't allow it in schools and I wouldn't allow it in any institution. I think it is very dangerous.

They are a minority but the revolution in Russia was made by a minority. Huge revolutions are made by very small numbers of people all the time. You don't need a lot of people to kill a lot of people. Violence is possible against the state and there will be more I guess. It just means you have to put more people under surveillance. The police and the law are picking Asians off the street. They picked me up and searched me. It makes you furious being picked on.

On the other hand we are all living in a really dangerous time. It is very tricky. What are we going to do? Are we

going to go round to peoples' houses and use surveillance, phone tapping and all that stuff? People like us who grew up in the Sixties and Seventies know it's not the kind of stuff we like, but on the other hand we are fighting against something which is actually really dangerous and it makes it really hard. Nothing like this has really ever happened here before.

Britz, 2007

Is this a result of our increasingly divided society – at least on a material level?

The recent bombers were doctors, some of the others were teachers; I mean they were very educated people. They are the real revolutionaries like Lenin. They are not the disaffected bums on the street who are going to blow things up. These are highly educated, very motivated, very intelligent people. So the social deprivation argument doesn't make sense. They are not deprived, the revolution is important to their identification, it's about deprivation in Chechnya, Palestine, Lebanon, Syria and Pakistan, wherever. These guys are there to contribute to the revolution but they themselves, like Lenin and Trotsky, are not necessarily deprived themselves.

Are we still a racist society?

We are much less racist than we were, and much less racist than the society I grew up in, in which the racism was overt.

England was racist in those days. People took it for granted that if you were

Indian you were inferior, they really did. It's incredible to think about that now.

Today there are other forms of racism, particularly the penchant of the West for only bombing Muslim countries. They don't bomb France or Germany, they bomb Iran or Iraq or Lebanon, so there are real grudges here that are based on real events, and these grudges aren't just total invention, it is absolutely the case that Muslim countries are discriminated against by the West.

My whole family grew up in Bombay, in British India, and they felt that they were treated like shit by them. It wasn't their country and there were soldiers everywhere; soldiers bossed you around, you know.

Fundamentalism is the price you pay for colonialism. If you make people feel that they're the underdog, they're victims, later on this can be carried on, and they'll pay for it. But that does not mean that there is any justification for what is going on now and I don't support that.

When I was in Pakistan, my family and most of the families I met didn't want to be more religious. They wanted more VCRs, more tellies - they wanted materialism too. The idea that Muslims love religion and the West loves shopping is bunk. That division is not true at all. Most people in Muslim countries want what we want. They want clothes, they want shoes, they want good schools for their kids, they want good hospitals, they want exactly the same things, except that Islam became an ideology that they believe might liberate them.

What do the fundamentalists want to achieve in Britain?

They want to make a revolution. They want to start a Muslim state. There are certain parts of the country now where

East is East, 1999

they are trying to get Sharia law imposed. 'This bit of our village is totally Muslim' they say, 'so why can't we have our own law? Why should we live under the white man's law? It's not our law'. To the strictest Muslims, the only people who are fully human are people who are submissive to God, who believe in Islam. They believe that people outside Islam are scum and will burn in hell.

It is a very medieval view of the world and very difficult for us to comprehend at all. These people are very heavy. The penny has now finally dropped after 9/11 and the bombings of 7/7 and so on; these people really are very serious. I think the whole thing has got to be played out over the next five, ten, twenty years and then it may eventually run out of its own steam.

East is East, 1999

How do we move forward?

You have got to get to the younger generation, the kids who are five, six and seven years-old now. That's why you shouldn't have faith schools. Because after school they go to the mosque which is the same or a good substitute for the faith schools. My son's school go to the mosque after school, they go at four or six o'clock to read and to study the Qur'an. I don't send my son there, but how many boys go there, how many boys of the school go off to the mosque?

What I am aware of is that these guys are really fervent and they are much more indefatigable than we are. That's the problem; they will keep on fighting in every area. They will turn up to school meetings. They are like the Trotskyites; the Trotskyites were always the last ones to leave. At four o'clock in the morning they were there with the newspaper outside the factory, the fervent ones… Muslims are like that. The fervent ones really believe they are going to have their revolution. And this is really difficult to fight.

But Trotskyism has failed

Trotskyism didn't have the mass following in the way that the Muslims do. Most of the Muslims would not say to you that they believed in the bombings,

Britz advert, 2007

Whose Side Are You On?
BRITZ – A two-part thriller

but they would have a lot of sympathy for those guys, as we all know. There is a lot of bitterness and resentment about Iraq, huge resentment. 'Why are they bombing Muslims?' they ask. 'How many of us have they killed today?' What do you say, how do you argue?

Bush is trying to impose his form of what he calls democracy on the Middle East. It's actually extreme capitalism and it will never work. You can't go to Baghdad and turn it into Houston by bombing it. It is a ridiculous idea.

It is impossible to turn round to these guys and say, 'Look we are democrats, we are fair'. They say, 'What about Guantanamo Bay?' And there you go. You're fucked. It's really tricky. The idea was that the West would have a moral position but the West no longer has a moral position to support itself by.

We have to really fight to keep our freedoms. We must work out the liberalism we want, and why we believe shopping is important. Why what sexuality you have is important. Why it is important that people take drugs. All the things that the Muslims think are corrupt about our society are also part of our society, part of its pleasures.

So what defence do we have?

That our society is a good one, it allows people to behave how they want, but it is very hard to argue against the backdrop of Guantamano, because they will say, 'You are talking about democracy' and I'll say, 'Yes, I'm talking about democracy.' They will say: 'Actually we live in the West and what we see is racism, drug abuse, addiction, single parent families, poverty.' We try to sell them a democracy but the bum side of democracy are all these other things.

The Muslim structure provides a very strong family. Everyone behaves in a certain way. People love religion, they love being helped, and they love the strength of that. On the other hand it kills you, it stifles you.

They say freedom for what? To take drugs, to go to clubs, to go shopping and vomit on the street. These are your children. Look at our children, they are in the schools and in the mosques, they are very good kids.

That's the argument. It's a tricky one. A very tricky one. You have got to defend these freedoms. They are corrupt in one sense but they are important in another sense. It is really difficult, but it has got to be done. We have to argue about these things all the way through.

What happened to our own religion?

It is very very interesting because until it began to break down in the 1960s we were a religious country. By the 1990s religion returned from the outside. It is an extraordinary sort of Freudian thing. The part that we repressed, that we couldn't bear any more and we got rid of came back in through another door. It came from the outside. It has not brought people back to the Church of England, but the US has become more and more religious apparently and in Africa too there are many more Catholics and Christians now.

The British are so cynical about authority. We have no language to talk about religion any more. It has become the new age, spiritualism, crystal waving. The secular version of it is environmentalism. We can be good by loving the earth. We put our rubbish out in green bags while our soldiers are bombing the shit out of Afghanistan and Iraq every single day and you want to talk about pollution.

I also feel the struggle has not gone far enough. The struggle amongst women and feminism for instance; all those women in the Muslim world need our support. You have got to make those women feel that they are supported. You can't have a revolution which results in freedom in just one country. It has to work all over. It's got to work.

Diwali

Chanukah

Four

Our Multi-Culture

Channel 4's nurturing of cricket turned it into a connoisseurship for novelist Diran Adebayo, author of *Some Kind of Black*

Caribbean Summer, 2000

Urban Cricket

Caribbean Summer, 2000

The 4 logo used as a boundary poster

I had fallen for cricket, in my working-class part of north London, in very different times, the early Seventies, around the same time I fell for Enid Blyton's adventure stories, Anthony Buckeridge's prep school *Jennings* books, tales of Greek and Roman myths, and the elan-laden French rugby team (not, cricket apart, a black one amongst them). The game came courtesy of those two enablers to the thing-in-itself, those dual routes to access: watching and actually playing. My first fully remembered televisual season was 1975, and its standout image will be etched for just as long as Lewis's interview: the inaugural World Cup final, Lord's, a muggy morning, and Roy Fredericks, the West Indies' dashing left-hand blade, clad in a wide-brimmed white sunhat and white shirt open to the torso, hooking Australia's demon bowler Dennis Lillee gloriously for six in an opening over, only to tread on his own stumps in the process. He departed to the roars of a crowd of every hue gathered on the grass beyond the boundary edge. A little later that same summer I remember waking up thrilled in my stomach, the way I always was when it was a cricket day, and turning on the telly to find, to my horror, that a group, protesting over the imprisonment of a man they believed innocent, had vandalised the Headingley test match pitch, and thus there would be no play that day. Ah, televised cricket, the time-honoured companion of the unemployed and of children, those without the means or the permission to pursue other pleasures.

Ours was an uncommon childhood, I grant you. We laboured, in the school holidays, under a strict academic regime supervised by my father. When he was out, at work, we'd convert our maths and latin primers into table tennis bats and a net across the table, or else play cricket in the hallway and outside. Our home backed onto a number of gardens, most of them overgrown, so you couldn't play football in them, but a long stony strip ran alongside, just wide and flat enough to accommodate a bit of turn from the off for this apprentice spinner.

Cricket, then, was part of our route into normality, into mainstream Britishness, into the world outside our strange doors. We'd play it across the road on a neighbouring sidestreet or in the park, along and with other boys, and even at state junior school, with a tennis ball and the white wicket painted on the wall. We'd talk about Muhammad Ali and Bruce Lee, and

Cricket, then, was part of our route into normality, into mainstream Britishness, into the world outside our strange doors

The Summer Sessions
Two Culture Clash
Asian Dub Foundation   Soul II Soul
New Soca MCs   Roots Manuva

A series of live music events across London to celebrate
the West Indian cricket tour summer 2004

Channel 4 advert
celebrating the
cricket season, 2004

know about show jumping and Harvey Smith (big on the box
in those days), and play this game too. The big local park –
Finsbury – always had a big people's game going on in the
summer – these were the days when urbanites, not *so* many,
but some really did play cricket in the summer and football
the rest of the time. Bizarre isn't it, now, to imagine cricket as
a way into the urban mainstream?

It seemed, if anything, more multicultural than British
football then. There were various overseas stars in most of the
county sides, and numerous non-white faces in those crowds
of the Seventies to mid Eighties – especially when the West
Indies were over, especially at the Oval, south London – black
Britain's heartland. Far more than I'd see on my occasional,
somewhat wary trips to Tottenham Hotspur's White Hart Lane.
Those black folk at the cricket were, looking back, of a certain
age – men for the most part, not youngsters, no doubt many
born elsewhere, and this, allied with the serious racial pressure
of those times (the NF, the sus laws, the riots); may have given
them the confidence and the defiant mindset to make those
grounds their own with their klaxons and whistles and curries
and general other-country vibe.

The sport also appeared multicultural to me in another,
non-racial way. I loved the fact that the playing surface was different from venue to venue, as were the weather conditions, that
the pitch changed character over the course of a three or five day
game, and that all this affected the outcome. It seemed a richer
game than football where teams pretty much played the way
they always did across the world and conditions didn't matter,

and more *real*, more in tune with nature and science – just as the
world felt more real to me in summer when you could smell the
cut grass and people. This was a game that incorporated change
over time, that understood dx over dt. This was a sport that more
than any other had narrative, a novel-like relationship with time.

Time, like reading, is not for everyone. Perhaps it is most
of all for Hindus who, if you subscribe to the take recently put
forward by United Nations Under Secretary and cricket nut
Shashi Tharoor on *Test Match Special*, have such an affinity
for the game because their religion is big on eternity – but even
this no longer prevents sparse Test Match crowds in India. It
has become less even for me, I confess, as I've got older, and
least so for young western boys, as the world has got busier,
freer, quicker.

This was a sport that more than any other had narrative, a novel-like relationship with time

----

It strikes me that what Channel 4 was most seriously up
against was widespread changes in our relationship to time, and
hence to many's perception of this thing. Granted, in the black-

Channel 4 cricket advert, 2005

Channel 4 cricket advert, 2002

Brit part of its anticipated multicultural audience at least, there was a class issue too – a political shift amongst British-Caribbeans between a first generation migrant community that was essentially Anglophile, and who saw in cricket an arena to assert pride and dignity, and a second and third UK-born generation that was less Anglophile but properly English working class, 'street', in both environment and ideology, who saw the game through English eyes in a decade when the game had all but slipped from urban vernacular, from its streets and schools. It's almost as if we needed to relearn how to watch and appreciate this game. English cricket, characteristically, did not help itself through the Eighties and early Nineties when the team that, slow overrates aside, best embodied this quicker sense of time, and modernity more widely – the West Indies with their speed merchants and general dynamism, their liberation from the class issues that remained in the English game, a team that like their musical and street-cool counterparts were more popular, more trend-setting amongst white Britons than many realised – faced the repeated sniping that they did. It was no coincidence, perhaps, that the one English player to truly catch the public imagination in those years, the brash Ian Botham, was best mates with the West Indies' star, attitude-stacked Viv Richards. In the end, those stuffier quarters got what they wanted – a ban on musical instruments at grounds that contributed to a diminution in those black throngs by the turn of the Nineties.

When it came, Channel 4, in that English starless, pre-Twenty-Twenty, pre-earstudded Flintoff era, did what it could and what it did did not turn out as crudely as I'd feared. In bouffant-haired former player Mark Nicholas they had a lead presenter – smooth, authoritative, not too Ra-Ra. Crucially, he was an enthusiast for the thing-in-itself – his commentary paid full due to the game's aesthetic appeal while the Saturday roadshows he hosted focused on skills sessions involving local budding youngsters. His colleague Simon Hughes, in his OB spyhole, carried the illumination process further, with his forensic graphics-aided rewinds of passages of play. He'd show you, for example, how a bowler ended a batsman's life by 'working' him over a number of particularly placed balls. The viewer was given a sense of how time and pressure worked in this game – that it might not be thrills-a-minute football, but contained its periods

of situational intensity. Another use of technology, Channel 4's deployment of on-field microphones (initiated by Sky TV, to be fair), drew attention to aspects like the verbal abuse between opponents that the previous broadcaster, for some overly-protective reason, had ignored. In short, stuff for the connoisseurs and the casuals.

Time, like reading, is not for everyone. Perhaps Hindus have such an affinity for the game because their religion is big on eternity

Inclusivity was there, also, but not crowbarred. When the roadshow arrived in a more Asian part of the country, you'd see more Asian youngsters in the roadshows. When the West Indies toured in 2000, it was the cue for a 'Caribbean Summer' and the sounds and smells once again, at grounds (yeah, even at Lord's) of drums and bass and curried foods. And if this was partly Channel 4-induced, and some of the bands quaintly old school, at least this time you felt there was no ambivalence or unwelcome in the air. The change in tone across the media to stadium diversity, to the Brit-Asians who these days throng the grounds in the blue and green of their mother countries is marked, and Channel 4 played its part.

None of this, to be sure, could save cricket in black-Brit land. Channel 4's time at the helm concluded with the epic 2005 series between the Anglo cousins – England and Australia – for the Ashes. Its coverage gave it, on the rubber's climactic final day, a staggering twenty-three per cent audience share, 7.4 million viewers, and beyond that, thousands famously stretched outside an already full Oval, serenading a triumphant England.

Four   Our Multi-Culture

Alkarim Jivani, author of *A History of Lesbian and Gay Britain in the Twentieth Century*, unravels the depictions of ethnic minorities on Channel 4 over the past 25 years

Marginal Figures?

Young Black Farmers, 2005

White Teeth, 2002

Desmond's, 1989

My teenage years were punctuated by my father shouting from the living room whenever an Asian person appeared on television. Invariably, by the time I got there, the object of all the excitement had disappeared because, up until the Eighties, television literally marginalised black and Asian people. They generally appeared on the edge of the screen, lingering on the sidelines, rarely taking centre stage. The arrival of Channel 4 changed that forever – and its impact was so great that all other channels were forced to follow suit.

It is a measure of how successful this initiative was that 25 years later it seems rather quaint that anybody should find the routine appearance of a black or Asian person on television as being anything remarkable. But in order to get to this happy position, broadcasters had first to acknowledge how dire the situation was, which none of the first three channels were ready to do. Channel 4 not only took cognisance of the problem but tackled it head on, which resulted in a wealth of challenging and innovative programmes (and a few disasters – but let's not dwell on those).

The first of such programmes to hit the screens were two magazine shows, *Eastern Eye* and *Black on Black*. They brought a nuanced approach and subtlety of language to the reporting

of black and Asian issues that hadn't been seen before on British television. Their subject matter was eclectic, ranging from politics, social affairs and the arts to nostalgia and humour. This set the tone for Channel 4's multicultural output as a whole; in its opening years, the Channel aired a dizzyingly rich mix of programmes: foreign-affairs series like *Bandung File*, dramas such as *Partition*, and sitcoms like *No Problem* and *Tandoori Nights*. Many of these programmes broke new ground not just in their subject matter but also in terms of how they chose to express themselves, which resulted in some genuine innovation.

My teenage years were punctuated by my father shouting from the living room whenever an Asian person appeared on television

----

The other distinguishing factor about Channel 4's multicultural output was that because the programmes – documentaries in particular – were made by and for members of the same community, there was a fearlessness about exposing issues that outsiders might have hesitated over. It is arguable that series like *Karachi Cops* or Darcus Howe's discussion programme, *Devil's Advocate* – which poked and prodded away at issues that the black community felt most sensitive about – would not have been commissioned outside the multicultural department. Perhaps the most controversial of these programmes was a late-night entertainment show, *Baadass TV*: supporters argued that it was irreverent and iconoclastic, while others, including Trevor Philips, described it as a 'minstrel show' and called for it to be taken off air.

While many of Channel 4's multicultural programmes were radical in their own way, perhaps the most radical thing about them collectively was this: although they were made from a black or Asian stance they weren't intended to be watched only by black and Asian audiences, any more than *Coronation Street* is intended only for white people living in Greater Manchester. Many of the programmes found a wide constituency, most notably dramas and, in particular, comedies like *Desmond's*, which remains one of Channel 4's most successful home-grown sitcoms.

The irony was that while programmes from the multicultural department tried to draw in as many white viewers as possible without compromising or diluting the content, the favour wasn't returned by other departments. By the late 1990s, there was an increasing feeling that the very existence of the multicultural department led to a form of ghettoisation. Britain had changed very rapidly in the previous decade; Marks and Spencer's best-selling sandwich was chicken tikka and rap was the biggest thing to hit the music industry since punk. In other words, what had been considered minority culture was now part of the mainstream. It was time for Channel 4's output to reflect that, so all departments took cognisance of the black and Asian audience: property programmes should routinely have Asian participants (the sector of the population with the highest number of owner-occupiers); current affairs should tackle news from black and Asian communities; observational documentaries should focus their lenses on Brick Lane and Brixton just as readily as they turned to Glasgow or Godalming; comedy and drama should look for stories and plotlines from beyond the pale. As long as there was a commissioning editor for multicultural programmes, it let other departments off the hook in that respect.

Bandung File, 1985

The counter-argument was that axing the multicultural department would mean that no one would take responsibility for ensuring the multicultural audience was properly served, leading to a weakening of the black and Asian presence on the channel. Happily those fears haven't been realised. Since the multicultural department came to an end in 2003, Channel 4's coverage of issues from outside the white mainstream has gone from strength to strength. The list of programmes is endless – much longer than it would have been if one commissioning editor had sole responsibility for green-lighting them –and

Tippoo Sultan's Incredible White-Man-Eating Tiger-Toy Machine*

by Daljit Nagra
2007

Wound

to knock out a poem
you rifle through
your store of white-man
Word, raring
to blood your diction
hoard swotted
since kid at school,
your jaw-is-brain
mechanically charged
(with penned hand)
chewing the fat
of the raw meat minty
tongue that English

is

your wrought-up state
where you won't rest
on each worked poem –
each Tippoo-toy
for the white man's game,
like galloping sahibs
a-tiger hunting
you whip up new lines
to relive the race
-related kick
that sparks you up
so you're pouncing on beats
so your eyes – burning –
are Sher Punjaaab on the

rrrrraaaaaaaaaaaaaaaj!!!

* Tippoo Sultan's Tiger is an automata of a tiger eating a Sahib; it can be seen at the Victoria and Albert Museum

Sher Punjaaab – The Tiger of Punjab: many claim this epithet for themselves such as the mighty Ranjit Singh to present day musical groups and vigilantes, even colonialists such as Brigadier General John Nicholson toyed with this name when he called himself 'the Lion of the Punjab'

includes controversial dramas like *Bradford Riots* and *The Road to Guantanamo* and a whole range of documentaries and arts programmes including *Dubplate Drama, Empire's Children, Women Only Jihad, The Last Slave, 100% English* and *God's Waiting room.*

Channel 4 has on-screen diversity targets across all commissioning genres

Dispatches regularly tackles difficult subjects involving race, most recently a programme on extremist preachers in British mosques. *Channel 4 News* has the most diverse news agenda of any of the news programmes and remains the favoured bulletin for ethnic minorities. If any further proof were needed about Channel 4's commitment to putting challenging programmes about race and cultural identity at the heart of its schedule, one need look no further than the programmes commissioned to celebrate its 25th anniversary. The centrepiece of the season was Peter Kosminsky's two-part drama *Britz*, which explored the reasons why one British Asian was compelled to become a suicide bomber and the factors that led her brother to join MI5 in order to stop people like her. In addition to programmes that deal directly with subjects of interest to a non-white audience, Channel 4 has on-screen diversity targets in place across all commissioning genres so that every programme, be it *Big Brother* or *Deal Or No Deal*, accurately reflects Britain's population.

 Hajj, 2003

Finally, no analysis of Channel 4's record on multicultural programming would be complete without mentioning its efforts to create a pool of new black talent, giving voice to individual writers, producers, directors and presenters, without which many of today's programme-makers and TV personalities wouldn't have got their first break. That commitment continues with a series of scholarships and training programmes aiming to bring new people into television at the bottom. There are now plenty of black and Asian researchers, producers and directors working throughout the industry, but on the executive floor, where the crucial decisions about programme content, style and tone are taken, there are virtually no black faces.

Channel 4 should make this its next challenge. In the last twenty-five years it has transformed black and Asian people's presence on-screen – in the next twenty-five it should work the same magic off-screen.

Laughter

Britain's nascent 'alternative' comedy scene
burst into life with The Comic Strip's *Five Go
Mad In Dorset*, broadcast on launch night in 1982.
Instantly, edge and vibrancy were added to the
spectrum of TV comedy. Comic Strip regulars
such as French and Saunders and Rik Mayall went
on to star on the channel's live comedy showcase,
Saturday Live, which gave airtime to a new generation of comedians – including Harry Enfield,
Ben Elton, Stephen Fry, Hugh Laurie and Jo
Brand. Channel 4 has continued to unearth and
nurture fresh comic voices – Simon Pegg and Jes-
sica Stevenson, Ali G, Ricky Gervais, Peter Kay
– and create fresh formats – *Father Ted, Brass Eye,
Spaced, Smack the Pony, Peep Show, Green Wing*.
It has never lost sight of comedy's power to expose
wider truths, never shying from satire led by Chris
Morris, Rory Bremner and hit shows like *Drop the
Dead Donkey*.

Alan Carr, presenter of Channel 4's *Friday Night Project*, reveals that comedy didn't save him from a footballing life, but it did help save the friendship between him and his father

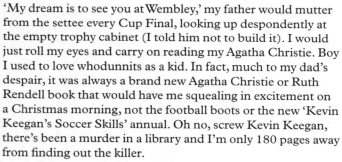

Saved From a Life in Football

Alan Carr

'My dream is to see you at Wembley,' my father would mutter from the settee every Cup Final, looking up despondently at the empty trophy cabinet (I told him not to build it). I would just roll my eyes and carry on reading my Agatha Christie. Boy I used to love whodunnits as a kid. In fact, much to my dad's despair, it was always a brand new Agatha Christie or Ruth Rendell book that would have me squealing in excitement on a Christmas morning, not the football boots or the new 'Kevin Keegan's Soccer Skills' annual. Oh no, screw Kevin Keegan, there's been a murder in a library and I'm only 180 pages away from finding out the killer.

To the few people who don't know, I come from good footballing stock; my footballing pedigree is second to none, I'll have you know. My father was football manager of the town I was growing up in, Northampton Town Football Club. My grandad had played for Newcastle United and West Brom. And there were various uncles and cousins who at some point had played professionally or flirted with the idea. So there was a lot of expectation when I, a new Carr boy, was born.

You could almost sense the disappointment when I didn't drop kick my way out of the womb, do a sliding tackle on the placenta, and start chanting 'Who are ya? Who are ya?' to my parents. Oh dear, how could I tell them there'd been 'an accident'? Basically I couldn't, so I spent my teenage years with everyone assuming I was going to become Georgie Best. Being cross-examined by my Dad's old professional footballer friends was a traumatic experience. I'd be frozen mute because once they heard this voice, or saw me move any part of my body, they would realise how unbelievably camp I was, and the questioning

would stop with an abrupt 'oh' and an anxious look towards my father. The questions would always be the same anyway. 'Does he play, Graham?' 'What position is he going to be?' 'Is he reading an Agatha Christie?'

People mistakenly think that comedy saved me from a life in football, which is slightly misleading as it gives the impression that I was actually good at football. On second thoughts, maybe I should tell people that, yeah, I had trials with Man U but you know what, I was so goddamn funny, they let me go. Alex Ferguson said, 'There is a working men's club stage that needs you boy. Go. Just go'. A tear staining the broken capillaries on his face.

To be honest, a lot of people did laugh when I kicked the ball. Yes, well, I soon wiped the smirk of their faces when they had to go and get the football back off the dual carriageway. How did I know it was going to deflect off that woman walking the dog? The fact that my dad was a football manager strangely didn't help things. He just couldn't switch off. We could never have a normal kick-about down the park like the other kids.

I soon wiped the smile off their faces when they had to get the football off the dual carriageway

Their squeals of laughter being punctuated by 'faster you fat fairy'

<u>Friday Night Project</u>, from 2005

Dad, my brother Gary and I would all go down to the park, he would bring his bollards along and we'd all start to play a 'game' called 'touch the bollards'. This wonderfully exciting game was to run and touch the bollards and run back in the quickest time. I know, whoop-dee-do.

'Football isn't about scoring goals,' he would say to us. 'It's about fitness,' he would reiterate firmly before tapping his stopwatch and barking 'SPRINT! SPRINT! SPRINT!' So there I would be dashing up and down, the velour of the tracksuit rubbing against my large sweaty thighs, looking over enviously at the other families kicking the football to each other playfully and having fun, their squeals of laughter every so often punctuated by: 'Faster you fat fairy'.

I didn't take 'fairy' too badly, I had heard him use it at training with his own players; especially if they had long hair they'd be a fairy; if they had an earring they'd be a fairy, if they could read they'd be a fairy... well, you get the gist. Men were fairies unless they were fucking a woman right there in front of him. Don't get me wrong. I joined my father in his frustration. I wanted to be a footballer too. Nothing would have given me more pleasure than to have become a professional footballer. Well, the ones in the Premiership. The ones who earn £100,000 a week and have four homes and a fancy car. Not the ones in the Vauxhall Conference who have to supplement their wages by driving a forklift in a warehouse. I wanted the whole she-bang. The advertising deals, the bling, the beautiful wife. But I will have to draw the line at those grubby 'roasting gangbangs' that surface in the Sunday papers; I could probably manage one woman but no more, please. My psoriasis flares up if I'm overworked.

The day I left school was like falling off a precipice. What could I possibly do? I was technically useless. And before long I was doing various dead-end jobs in various industrial estates across Northamptonshire. Packing shampoos. Data entry for Cesar, the new name for Mr Dog. De-greasing gearboxes. The jobs the careers advisor at school kept in a 'special box'. These really weren't the kind of jobs where you'd say, 'Don't worry, I'll work through my lunch'. I felt embarrassed for my parents doing these kinds of jobs. Yes, I'd had crappy summer jobs before but at least you had the safety net and relief of going back to school in a few weeks, time. At one point, 'shampoo packer' was my actual job title. It was on my badge for Christ's sake. I packed shampoo for a living and wished I was dead.

It didn't help that my old class freak, Paul Grantham, was my supervisor. 'Who thought I'd be your boss?' he said jovially, before driving his spotty little face off on his truck. Yeah, who'd have thought – dickhead.

My career needed a shot in the arm so I racked my brains for things that I was good at. The only thing I could think of was drama, but then again I was only good at the parts where I was playing camp people with buck teeth and glasses and I know exactly how those Hollywood actresses in their forties feel

– there aren't that many good roles out there. Unless anyone was writing 'Alan Carr – The Musical' I couldn't really see me getting much work on the West End.

Nevertheless, I decided to audition for drama schools and performing arts courses, which as you can imagine was the icing on the cake for my dad. Couldn't I have said no to football and taken up rugby, cricket, welding, something remotely masculine? No, I had to go and do a course where you spend three years trying to find a space, and once you've found that space, you learn to breathe in it. I realised soon enough that I wasn't going to get onto a drama course because I didn't have any range. My acting ability was very limited and it showed. Admittedly, the choice of audition piece wasn't ideal. My *Macbeth* was about as dark and menacing as a tiramisu. But I gave it my best shot. Dejected, I ended up on a theatre studies course being a stage hand, which is basically moving furniture around in a black body stocking when the lights go down and then complaining about why you never get spotted by any talent scouts. It was there that I enrolled on a stand-up comedy module and loved it – although the nerves proved too much for me, so much so that I never performed for another five years.

I wish I'd done it sooner, though, because ironically 'comedy' didn't save me from a footballing life, but it did help save the friendship between me and my father. My dad is so unbelievably proud of me, and for any son or daughter that is an amazing feeling. I think my dad has recognised the similarities between football and comedy. The nerves, the sense of occasion, the social networking that goes on after a gig/match. The bravery of going out there with only your talent to hide behind is very much akin to football and he respects that. Growing up, I think I read him wrong. He's always been proud of me. He didn't give two hoots about my sexuality. Or the fact that I was shit at sport. He just didn't want me to be a loser.

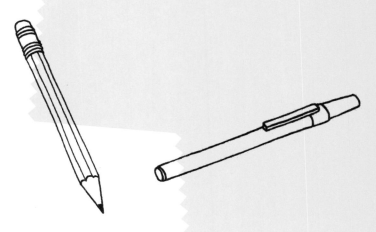

Five   Laughter

Critic Stephen Armstrong looks back on the past great 25 years of alternative comedy and says raising a laugh in the next 25 years will be much harder work as a result

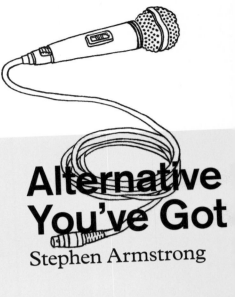

Alternative Comedy: You've Got to Laugh

Stephen Armstrong

Alternative You've Got

Stephen Armstrong

Phoenix Nights, 2001

1982 was a dark year. Unemployment reached three million for the first time, the Falklands War broke out, Israel attacked Lebanon and the Soviet Union invaded Afghanistan. Politics seemed to penetrate every corner of Britain, even reaching the singles charts. When *The Clash* opened their Brixton gig with 'White Riot' – barely six months after the streets outside saw the largest violent protests of the 20th century – the audience exploded in such an orgy of rage that they crushed steel crowd control barriers. The only part of British culture where this global turmoil was roundly ignored was comedy.

Cannon and Ball were touring, selling out the Winter Gardens in Bournemouth. The likes of Bernard Manning and Frank Carson dominated the club circuit. TV sitcoms included *Terry and June*, *Shine On Harvey Moon* and *Never The Twain* – with Donald Sinden and Windsor Davies as rival antiques dealers whose son and daughter marry. Imagine the hilarity when Sinden lit a bonfire to blow smoke over Davies's garden. 'Aren't you being a bit juvenile?' his son asks. 'Certainly not,' Sinden replies. 'It's

a privilege of middle age. Only children aren't allowed to be juvenile.' And this, bear in mind, is the top gag on a *Never the Twain* fan site.

In a sleazy Soho strip bar, however, a team of young stand-ups had started a weekly night called *The Comic Strip*. Their humour was a bizarre mix of abrasive politics, intelligent surrealism and old-school slapstick. They attacked the government and they attacked each other. They swore, they ranted and they referenced French art-house cinema. They made comedy urgent and relevant again, in a way that hadn't been seen since the 1960s satire boom.

The BBC realised something was up, but wasn't sure how to handle such an explosion of energy. People started looking into the idea of a sitcom written by and starring the scene's leading lights, but Auntie's nervousness meant *The Young Ones* would take a year to move from script to screen. By the time it finally hit the airwaves, it already looked as if the Beeb was playing catch-up. Channel 4's opening-night schedule featured as its centerpiece an insane Edith Blyton spoof called *Five Go Mad In Dorset* – written by

and starring most of the people the BBC was talking to.

Five Go Mad wove slyly subversive gags with complex writing and high production values. Comic Strip regulars Adrian Edmonson, Rik Mayall, Dawn French and Jennifer Saunders clearly relished their buddy Peter Richardson's script and direction. The following day, their insolent weirdness was imitated on the playground and talked about around water coolers. Although, this being the early 1980s, there weren't that many water coolers about. Even so, it was clear the broadcaster had staked its claim to cutting-edge comedy and would take an almost unholy relish in zigging when the rest of the industry zagged.

C4 went on, in rapid succession, to screen *No Problem*, the UK's first comedy series from black writers and performers and *Who Dares Wins*, a sketch show which outraged the Christian right and Mary Whitehouse on a weekly basis as well as showing Peter Cook and Dudley Moore's film *Derek and Clive Get the Horn*, despite it having been seized under the obscene publications act when released on home video.

Ali G, 2000

The 11 O'Clock show, 1998

Saturday Live, 1985

Brass Eye, 1997

The Comic Strip Presents, from 1982

Indeed, at the height of the Thatcher revolution, when the likes of Kenny Everett, Jimmy Tarbuck and Jim Davidson lined up to perform at Tory conferences and deliver crude or downright racist sketch shows, C4 nurtured and nourished the comedy opposition. *Fairly Secret Army*, which ran between 1984 and 1986, starred Geoffrey Palmer as a rabid ex-soldier forming an urban army to shoot the loony left. *The National Theatre of Brent* destroyed the militaristic account of British history. *Scully* made a hero out of a working class Liverpool lad at a time when Scousers were thought worse than Communists. *Tandoori Nights* mocked the overblown Raj sentimentality of the *The Far Pavillions* and *The Jewel In The Crown*, with Asian writers and actors taking on the dewy-eyed nostalgia for empire that seemed to dominate the British film industry at the time.

Then, in 1985, it launched the ship that would deliver alternative comedy's Normandy landings. *Saturday Live* (and later *Friday Night Live*) gave us Harry Enfield's Stavros and Loadsamoney and Ben Elton's diatribes, as well as the early talents of (deep breath) Stephen Fry,

Hugh Laurie, Paul Whitehouse, Jeremy Hardy, Andy De La Tour, Angus Deayton, Morwenna Banks, Robbie Coltrane, Josie Lawrence, Jo Brand, Dame Edna Everage, Paul Merton, Nigel Planer, Punt and Dennis, Emo Phillips, Stephen Wright, Lenny Henry, Hale And Pace and Julian Clary – backed by The Comic Strip regulars like Dawn French, Jennifer Saunders, Adrian Edmondson, Rik Mayall and satire legends like Peter Cook, John Wells and John Bird. It even rejuvenated Frankie Howerd's career.

Perhaps the astonishing thing about *Saturday Live* was that it was allowed to go out at all. The majority of the comedy

was overtly political, with Elton's rants against 'Thatch' linking each skit and music from angry young bands. Surprisingly, the regulator only stepped in when *The Pogues* performed a protest song about the Birmingham Six on the show. Otherwise, the revolution continued to be televised.

In a subtler way, however, the fact that C4 comedy refused to play to stereotypes and allowed the creation of savage but inclusive gags contributed to an attitude change across the nation

Of course, jokes – like songs – don't change society. In 1987, *Saturday Live* was joined by a series of comedy polemics attacking 1980s Britain, loosely grouped under the series title *Tickets for the Titanic*. In the same year these comics' most-hated target, Margaret Thatcher, was re-elected. In a subtler way, however, the fact that C4 comedy refused to play to stereotypes and allowed the creation of savage but inclusive gags contributed to an attitude change across the nation.

In the 1970s, sitcoms like *Love Thy Neighbour* and *Mind Your Language* worked on the premise that black people and foreigners were inherently funny. By the 1990s, an Independent Television Commission survey found the racist insults were deemed the most offensive kind of language by a majority of the population. It would be a ludicrous over-simplification to claim Channel 4 comedy made this happen – but there were very few homes for the ideas that alternative comedy espoused during that bridging decade, and few sections of the media did anything other than support the phobias of the right.

Star Stories, 2006

And yet, if comedy could ever claim any higher purpose, it can only be to fulfil the role of the medieval court jester – the one person permitted to mock the king. Smug establishment comedy is tedious and repetitive. It confirms rather than challenges. It comforts rather than annoys. As the new decade dawned, Channel 4 found itself in the awkward position – in comedy terms at least – of inhabiting the establishment, albeit a very different establishment to the one it had helped destroy.

Fortunately, it threw off this ermine as soon as possible. Shows like *Vic Reeves Big Night Out*, *Brass Eye*, *Spaced* and *The 11 O'Clock Show* ignored the rules of so-called alternative comedy. They played with surrealism, emotion and irony whilst retaining – via the likes of Chris Morris and Ali G – the power to slap the pompous across both cheeks and knee them in the groin for good measure. Ricky Gervais spouted unacceptable gags about the disabled to shock mainstream celebrities. Shows like *Desmond's* and

Attacking the weak is no longer funny for a nation that supports the underdog

Meet the Magoons, whilst set in black and Asian communities, paid little attention to the politics of race and more to classic tomfoolery.

Today the brash, ironic and often very camp comedy of Russell Brand, Jimmy Carr and Alan Carr is set against the blokey concerns of Peter Kay and *The IT Crowd.* After years when mentioning a woman's body was deemed automatically misogynistic, the mainly female producers and performers of *Smack the Pony* and its bastard offspring *Green Wing* were happy to get their tits out if it was going to be funny. Sketch shows like *Spoons* played heavily on the battle of the sexes, with both sides looking amusingly pathetic.

So Channel 4 still zigs where others zag. That's not to say it has become the Bernard Manning of terrestrial television, for all the hand-wringing over *Celebrity Big Brother.* Attacking the weak is no longer funny for a nation that supports the underdog. The station's comedy output, however, delights in teasing everyone else, from Outraged of Tunbridge Wells to the earnest lecturer for whom everything is about the struggle. If there isn't something on Channel 4 that annoys you, it's failed to do its job.

And this is both increasingly important and increasingly difficult as time goes on. In the early 1980s, C4 had its pick of the new generation of comics. Today, every major broadcaster and plenty of cable and satellite stations are stalking the clubs and festivals, desperate to haul new talent onto the screen. In comedy more than any other genre, Channel 4 cannot afford to rest on its laurels. If you hear a joke once, it's funny. If you hear it twice, well yeah, it's OK. If you hear it a third time it becomes a little annoying. Comedy relies on surprise, on difference and on the new. Your track record means nothing. In other words, it's been a great twenty-five years but, if anything, that's going to make the next twenty-five years harder work. Still, you've got to laugh, haven't you?

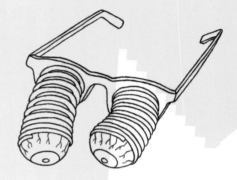

Five   Laughter

Comedy swot Tamsin Greig, the female star of Channel 4's ground-breaking *Green Wing* comedy series and of *Black Books*, salutes great comedy writing, believing it to be a bit like Sudoku, but with more point

The Swot Memoirs

Tamsin Greig

The Swot Memoirs

Tamsin Greig

The Sw Memoir

Tamsin Greig

I was a swot at school. I think it was out of fear. On the level of my fear of spiders, not handing in homework was a nest of spiders at the bottom of my bed ready to spin nocturnal webs across my eyelids. So envision me sitting attentively in a chemistry lab at the age of fifteen where I learn from my less fearful fellow pupils that a new television channel is to begin broadcasting that very evening. The fact that I remember this remarkable event in televisual history at all is in itself remarkable. The family TV set was heavily controlled by my mother and the black and white portable one in my bedroom had an intermittent relationship with BBC2 alone.

Mum rarely watched ITV. It was commercial, so it was common. So a further choice of a side that 'advertised' was met with indifference and contempt. Thank God the BBC showed *Dad's Army*, *Porridge* and *M*A*S*H*. Thank God Mum liked them. Not for us the weekly delights of traumatised soap *Scousers* that Channel 4 had in store for its fledgling viewers. Anything from Liverpool was common. Which is ironic because Mum was from Leeds and secretly loved *Coronation Street*.

Green Wing, 2004

When I was offered an odd little series called *Black Books*, Mum suppressed her channel snobbery and showered me with vague indifference – the perfect parental response to a swot's rebellion. But Channel 4 had its revenge.

Mum became an ardent *BB* devotee.

I'd never heard of Dylan Moran or Bill Bailey when I went for the audition. Good job actually. If I'd known then what I know now I would have been a contemptible, gibbering sycophant. As it was, I went in to read with a dusty Irish awkward and a bloke with hair. I didn't know what style they were after, so I copied what Dylan did. Or Bill. Whoever was there, I just copied them. Directors gave this great piece of direction. They said, 'Don't catch his rhythm'. What that really means is, 'Can you stop copying and come up with your own ideas please.' It was secretly liberating to catch the heady Moran/Bailey rhythms.

So envision me sitting attentively in a chemistry lab at the age of fifteen where I learn from my less fearful fellow pupils that a new television channel is to begin broadcasting that very evening

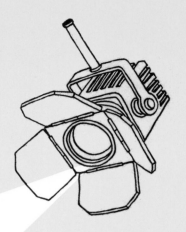

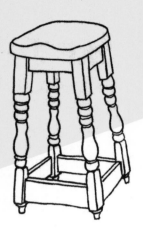

Black Books began as part of the now extinct Riverside Sitcom Festival, where new sitcom ideas were trialled before a live theatre audience. Dylan describes it as a series of rants by two blokes in a shop. But it must have twinkled, because it was the only one that year to be developed as a TV series. A channel's vision is only as good as the eyesight of the commissioning editors. Channel 4 has had a canny ability to attract 20/20 see-ers, especially in comedy. Cheryl Taylor – great eyes and a fantastic laugh – encouraged, wheedled, challenged and changed the nappy of this black bookish baby. The show couldn't have appeared on any other channel. Channel 4, as an alternative to the mainstream, excels in championing the alternative. They're interested in good TV, not just in stars, and were prepared to invest in (then) relative unknowns because the material promised dividends.

The trouble with a commercial channel is the adverts. Alright, they bring in a bit of cash, but it means your half-hour comedy is actually your 24-minute comedy. That's not very long for set-up, theme, character development, comic

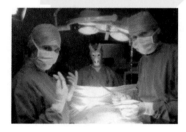

Green Wing, 2004

obstacle, resolution and pay-off. Not that I would know. I haven't an inkling about comic structure. But a look at the furrowed sweating Irish brows of Dylan Moran and Graham Linehan (the co-writers of the first series) after we'd done a read-through and were then sent home because they hated it and wanted to re-write the whole thing, gave a clue. It's really, really hard. I imagine it's a bit like Sudoku, but with more point. We played to a live studio audience on Saturday

night; often the script was incomplete by Friday and even in front of the camera Dylan was coming up with new lines, better jokes, crisper gags. He would say to me, 'That line you say there, it's not funny – what else do you want to say?'

He may as well have said, 'There's a funnel spider making a 40 foot nest in your hair.' This level of artistic immediacy was unheard-of on other channels because it was uncontrollable and dangerous. But Channel 4 trusted Dylan and Graham, believed producer Nira Park when she offered calm reassurance that they would eventually deliver, and gambled on the unknown. It was hair-raising, but fantastically exciting.

The Spider of Fear never really moved out, but was joined by another, more welcome lodger, the Puppy of Gratitude. At some point in every day of the three series we filmed I would think, 'I can't believe I'm here. I can't believe

This level of artistic immediacy was unheard-of on other channels

Green Wing advert, 2006

this is happening.' And I laughed all the time. I mean all the time. A right cackling nuisance. But before I had even left the warm, if rank, bosom of Bernard Black, Channel 4 presented me with another fear-fuelled opportunity.

Victoria Pile, the genius creator/producer/writer/visionary behind *Smack the Pony*, was challenged to come up with a programme that combined sketch-show gags with a character-rooted narrative thrust. She became the genius creator/producer/writer/visionary behind *Green Wing*, nurtured and upheld by another Channel 4 commissioning editor with good eyes, Caroline Leddy. There's a bizarre false economy that most TV production companies adhere to – little or no rehearsal time. Most TV jobs involve actors going to one read-through and then having to turn up on set to deliver a performance. Victoria Pile, via the supportive conduit of Leddy, secured an unprecedented agreement from Channel 4 for a minimum of three months workshop and experimental rehearsal time. They instinctively knew that cooking good pies takes time. And good equipment.

Improvising around semi-developed scripts by the *Smack the Pony* writing team, with the comic talent Victoria Pile, had attracted me and filled me with a mixture of exhilaration and dread. That feeling you get just before you jump out of the plane and pray your parachute will open. It was all very well watching and waiting for Dylan to give birth to each new joke baby. But having to labour through the process myself was the nightmare where you have to play the tuba, nude, in front of your entire school, guaranteed embarrassment but secret pride when you manage to get a note out of the thing.

It was a very clever move by Channel 4. Let actors and writers muck about a lot together, and this imperceptible and tantalising odour develops. The whiff of deeper trust. When an ensemble trusts all

its members, extraordinarily unexpected and delightful things begin to happen. Without the growth of that trust I would never have been able to control myself while Steve Mangan played a Bontempi organ during an operation and improvised ginger sperm-related lyrics for Julian Rhind-Tutt's benefit.

Love it or hate it, *Green Wing*'s distinctive editing style was groundbreaking. When we were making the pilot, Victoria Pile tried to explain how the show would hang together technically. I didn't really get it. I thought she meant that sometimes we would have to do really quick acting and sometimes we would have to do really slow acting. It was only when we saw a screening of the pilot that we got a glimpse into the misty wonders of Pile's vision. We either looked like we were in *Reservoir Dogs*

Channel 4 instinctively knew that cooking good pies takes time. And good equipment

(slow and sexy) or a Benny Hill sketch (fast and stupid). But the whole concept seemed to reflect that bizarre yet universal life experience of certain events taking forever to happen, and others disappearing in a flash. Once again, Channel 4 was the champion of the unconventional, and established technical style as a vital player on the team. Add the audio phonic genius of Jonathan Whitehead, composer of the *Green Wing* soundtrack (and the *Black Books* theme tune), and something beautiful was born.

These two unique shows were not fly-by-night flashes in the proverbial pans, but have shown themselves to have enduring appeal and no sign of a sell-by date. The proof of the pudding is in the royalty cheques. They've kept this erstwhile swot in spiders and puppies for a good few years, and long may it continue.

Improvising around semi-developed scripts filled me with that feeling you get just before you jump out of the plane and pray your parachute will open

Black Books, 2000

Jessica Hynes, actress, comic and writer, created and starred in Channel 4's *Spaced*. Here, she explains how we learned to know and love The Geek through laughter

Geeks are Good – How We Learned to Love The Geek Through Laughter

Jessica Hynes

Geek
We L
Geek

Jessica Hy

The Fifties had The Rocker. The Sixties had The Hippie. The Eighties had The Goth. And the Noughties have The Geek. The download has not been easy though – there were technical difficulties, incompatible files and wrong regions. Now, though, The Geek is permanently on our hard drive – let's face it, we love geeks.

'Loving' geeks is not just about tolerating their diminutive, muscle-free frames and allowing them to hang out with us. Geek love is about wanting to lick their acne-ridden faces and kneel before their joysticks in sexual ecstasy at the prospect of becoming the subject of their undivided attention, even if it is just for the length of the advert break.

Geeks are not just good, geeks are gods. The meek inheriting the earth, the ultimate twist in the sci-fi movie of evolution, the final episode where the speccy guy wins and the chiselled bully repents or dies, all played out on a floating microclimate headed towards a black hole.

What this reflects is a society in which 'skills' are no longer considered to be splitting logs and wrestling bears – unless of course you are playing *Woodland Copse Carnage III*, available

Spaced, 1999

only on Nintendo. We are now entering cyber-space: worlds within worlds within worlds created and mastered by men who couldn't crush a coke can. Bill Gates heralded the dawning of Nerdworld, with him as reigning monarch. Geekland is Nerdworld's Greenwich

Geekland is Nerdworld's Greenwich Village – the arty district

Village – the arty district. In Nerdworld, people know how to build computers. In Geekland you are more likely to have an encyclopaedic knowledge of sci-fi, an unhealthy obsession with pop culture and an obscure back catalogue of horror/cult sex films and comics. One or more of the above makes you a geek – all of them and you are a Geek god, a giant among men, a fountain of knowledge, a purveyor of rabid opinion and, these days, a bit of a hot ticket. But it was not always so, and the story begins long ago in a galaxy far, far away.

In the sci-fi world there is Before *Star Wars* (BSW) and After *Star Wars* (ASW). It was to sci-fi what the New Testament was to Christianity – the dawning of a new era. And with that came a generation of disciples, a generation of boys; encyclopaedias of fantasy knowledge who grew into people who knew Leia's second name and whether it was Yavin's third or fourth moon that the rebel's were based on. Films, television and music were the tools of the cultural revolutionaries and what they produced was grasped upon by the fertile minds of a generation. But like all good counter-cultures there were those that leaped into this new world (Jedi Knights) and those that eyed it with suspicion (evil Storm Troopers). There was no internet to bolster the growing number of geeks back then, they had to make do loitering by the counter in comic shops and attending conventions in disguise. They were laughed at, pushed about, portrayed on television as figures of fun, the butt of everyone's jokes.

Enter Samuel 'Screech' Powers through the cafeteria doors with pin-head, jew-fro and sloping shoulders – a cartoon geek if you will, but as much as we couldn't bear to look, we couldn't look away. And with beautiful irony and poetic justice it was Screech who outstripped his fellow 'students', becoming far more successful than any of them. Perhaps it was because he was the most memorable, perhaps it was because he brought the alleged 'humour' to the show, but either way he was on to something. It was Screech in the end who was *Saved by the Bell*.

Soon, every studio comedy show from America had one. Steve Urkel – the clown-like geek of colour from *Family Matters* still has a fan club on MySpace;

Spaced, 1999

himself plays Bob from the duo Jay and Silent Bob, *Star Wars* obsessives who are like oracles, elusive figures of profound knowledge and insight. The film about a group of shop workers who sit around and chat became a cult hit – the children of the revolution had found a voice – the voice of Silent Bob. He followed up *Klerks* with *Mallrats*, *Chasing Amy* and *Dogma*; films about geeks, for geeks, by geeks.

A couple of years later, in the UK, *Spaced* tuned in to this zeitgeist. I wrote the treatment when I was also 24, on a

incredibly, *Spaced* has become a massive cult, about geeks by geeks for the love of geeks.

These days a 'Vote for Pedro' T-shirt pretty much lets you know if someone is going to be your type or not. In *Napoleon Dynamite* the geek became politicised in an exquisite, effortless metaphor, reminding us that if we geeks stick together, anything is possible. Like a better world or something. Sweet. There are even faux fashion geeks – good looking 'normal' people who try and look like geeks but actually aren't because they think it makes them more attractive to the opposite sex. I sometimes wonder if it is more than a cultural trend. If the biological imperative subconsciously dictates our choices. Could it be that our concept of what it means to be an Alpha male has shifted? If being in expert control of your world makes you Alpha and your world is virtual, then it could be said that the Geek has finally inherited the earth.

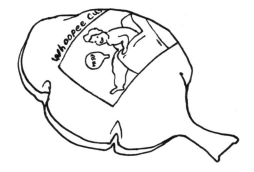

These days a 'Vote for Pedro' T-shirt pretty much lets you know if someone is going to be your type or not

Paul Pfeffer from *The Wonder Years*, the classic geek with black-rimmed specks; and not forgetting Professor Frink from *The Simpsons*, inventor of Hamburger Earmuffs and the House That Runs Away From Thieves. These television caricatures cemented the geek's place in our cultural landscape, but they were unsophisticated parodies compared to what would follow, an attempt by TV execs to portray people they actually did not know or truly understand. *Revenge of the Nerds* was a comedy hit, hinting at an untapped cinema market, but the nerds were still nerds; it was only when geeks started portraying themselves that they became sexy.

Kevin Smith is a Geekland poster boy. He was only 24 when he wrote *Klerks*, a film about his friends and his world. In geek film history it is seminal, the first time geeks are portrayed on film with sensitivity and, ultimately, love. He

cheap electric typewriter on the floor of my sister's living room. Simon [Pegg] already had the US in his sights and was just back from LA when I showed him the first treatment. I wrote Tim for Simon as a comic-book artist, skate-boarding sci-fi geek, because I knew he would bring his world-class knowledge of all things fi to it. He gave me a master class in *The Simpsons* – 'The film parody must be equal to the sum of believability and the story…' – and we were off.

My references ranged from *Pulp Fiction* to *The Preacher*, Simon's followed his various endearing crushes on sci-fi pin-ups; Buffy, Scully, Skywalker. Our interests and film knowledge complemented one another's and we became dedicated to making something unparalleled in ambition and laughs. When Edgar 'Fried Gold' Wright agreed to direct, we knew we had a hit on our hands, and

Ardal O'Hanlon
Photographed by
Martin Parr, 2007

Stephen Mangan,
Julian Rhind-Tutt
and Tamsin Grieg
Photographed by
Martin Parr, 2007

Five   Laughter

Father Seed is a Catholic priest and has published works including *Will I See You in Heaven?* Here and now, he finds that *Father Ted* was closer to the priestly reality than one might think

Father Ted of Craggy Island

Father Seed

Father Ted of Craggy Island

Father Ted of Craggy Island

Father Seed

Fath Cr

Fa Cr

Father Se

Father

A great mystery has been revealed. In the minds of most people, the words 'parochial house' (as in Craggy Island), 'presbytery', 'priest's house' or 'clergy house' conjure up a totally other world. People wonder what goes on inside. Religion at its best is about mystery. My late grandmother would always say, 'You can be so heavenly-minded as to be no earthly use.' We are all asked 'What do you do?' and the reaction to a priest's response can be very amusing, a cross between being a mortician and a psychiatrist – I do apologise to both professions but even they know what I mean.

Father Ted, the parish priest (Dermot Morgan), brought us into a new dimension to say the least, and Channel 4 is to be congratulated for opening up one very important aspect of the mystery of faith: humour and fun. However, for me as a priest, *Father Ted* is perfectly normal. For the most part, priests are like that. It is almost too close to home; it is reality television, complete with redoubtable housekeeper from hell, Mrs Doyle (Pauline McLynn), who keeps the whole household afloat under her watchful eye on tea, biscuits and gossip.

Father Ted, 1995

People love nothing more than seeing the most holy and dignified being portrayed as very human. Pope John Paul II often used humour and joking, particularly when among the young, to express a warm and inviting persona, which of course was absolutely true and sincere. One amusing photograph, now a postcard, shows the late Pope holding his hands to his eyes to pretend that he is

looking at the crowd through binoculars. And of course there is the famous series of photographs of him wearing Bono's sunglasses. When the crowds during his 1982 visit to England chanted out 'JPII, we love you', he responded: 'JPII loves you too'. When a priest cries, it conveys more than any words, for example attending the dying, whether babies or the very elderly. And when a priest is seen laughing, this conveys absolute joy and utter normality.

I remember the story of the late and deeply admired Archbishop of Westminster, Cardinal Hume, when he and his brother bishops could not come to a decision on a particular item. The Cardinal proposed a solution – a frisbee! The sight of a gaggle of bishops throwing the frisbee around caused tremendous alarm among onlookers. This was not 'normal'

Father Ted is perhaps the pinnacle of taking the roof off the mystery of the priesthood

An English priest, with no clothes, in the middle of the night and in the middle of a massive riot, confounded even him and he left me to my own devices

behaviour. Or was it? Why not? *Father Ted* more than exemplifies this behaviour.

Father Ted is perhaps the pinnacle of taking the roof off the mystery of the priesthood. Of course, this follows a long line of distinguished comedy predecessors. As a child I loved Donald Sinden and Derek Nimmo playing in the establishment end of ecclesiastical life. Then there was Dick Emery's vicar with the celebrated dentures and love of crumpet. All a world away from 'Edelweiss' and Julie Andrews, the absent-minded nun who marries a Captain and ends up a Baroness. They are all rather high-brow, educated and 'society'. None has a Father Jack, the retired parish priest (Frank Kelly), slumped in the armchair with his frequent and monosyllabic interjections!

In more recent years, Dawn French's fantastic and immediately loveable *Vicar of Dibley* has trodden the *via media* between the establishment and where *Father Ted* does not fear to go. As much as the Vicar rebels against it – and not least because she is a lady priest – she has to appear in public as very establishment and is still part of the very English system. Dawn French tries to be anti-establishment but is so often confounded in her attempts by the class-bound environment in which she operates.

The down side of these particular portrayals is perhaps the 'cleanliness' of the humour. A Catholic presbytery may appear to those on the outside to be the epitome of establishment, but once the blinds are closed something very different appears. The virtue of *Father Ted* is its normality and freedom of expression. It is much more common for Catholic clergy to live together in one big house, but not necessarily sharing the same bedroom, like Fathers Ted and Dougal, his assistant (Ardal O'Hanlon), with Father Jack in a nearby, coffin-like box! Of its very nature, this scenario creates humour.

You may remember the graphic footage of police officers beating a black man, Rodney King, which led to the Los Angeles riots in the early 1990s. The whole area was a horrific war zone. I was visiting an old classmate, a fellow Franciscan, staying in a friary in the very heart of the rioting a day or so after the assault. I awoke in the middle of the night to answer a call of nature. Unfortunately the door slammed and I was locked out in an office wearing absolutely nothing. I searched and found quite a few keys, but none opened the offending door. I then had what I thought was a bright idea of going outside and seeing if any would open the main door of the friary. Wrapping myself in an enormous map (and thanking God that the US is so big), I ventured out into the dark. Whilst I was trying the front door, a startled policeman approached. An English priest, with no clothes, in the middle of the night and in the middle of a massive riot confounded even him, and he left me to my own devices. So I sat on the step watching various people walk by on their way to a peace vigil in our church and listening to the gunfire. I was finally let in by a shocked friar at 7am.

I am certain that every single priest or bishop, or even Pope, will have a tale of wonderful hilarity. From those that I know, I can testify that this is true – though I haven't known too many Popes. My favourite *Father Ted* scenes include the over-seventy-five five-a-side football match against Rugged Island, with Craggy Island's 'ace' Father Jack sound asleep in a wheelchair having consumed an entire bottle. Father Ted, ably assisted by Father Dougal, operates the wheelchair by secret remote control and victory is assured.

Having lost a bet to another priest, Father Ted has to kick the bishop in the rear. Bishops are not always playful and this is the case with Bishop Brennan, who arrives to view his 'miraculous image' in Father Ted's skirting board. He is accompanied by his overbearing secretary, noted for a sarcastic manner and feline disposition. While the bishop is in the necessary position, Father Ted does the deed, leaving the bishop in shocked amnesia, which totally ruins his audience with the Pope the following day. Father Jack soon gives the secretary short shrift and he is not seen for days.

When Fathers Ted and Dougal go on an adventure to mainland Ireland and visit some caves, they inevitably get lost. They encounter Father Noel (Graham Norton), part of another group, who is annoying in his attempts at keeping spirits up with a rendition of 'Bohemian Rhapsody', complete with all the Freddy Mercury moves. When his shrill tones cause a rock fall, they leave him behind with nothing visible but one hand, which continues to make encouraging gestures.

In conclusion, *Father Ted* has continued in a long line of ecclesiastical comedy and achieved a genuine pathway through religion that is truly funny.

It has used the establishment as a backdrop and yet has been able to challenge its very mystique by being so real.

The Drug Deal

Television is seldom brave enough to offer anything but a heavily sanitised depiction of drugs and drug users. Drug use is commonplace amongst the majority of young people and a continuing lifestyle choice for many others, and yet television barely reflects the thriving drug subculture of middle England or questions why so many choose to consume substances the Government classifies as illegal. Drug users on TV are invariably social losers, about to get their comeuppance under a tidal wave of negative consequences. In contrast, Channel 4 has always prided itself on accurately reflecting the lives of its viewers, including a more rounded picture of the role that drugs play in their lives. The channel has never shied away from telling truths about the disastrous repercussions of misuse for some individuals and the wider impact on society. But in dramas like *Skins* and *Shameless*, it has also realistically depicted the pleasures derived and how so many people manage to accommodate regular social drug use within the normal, everyday processes of living.

Nick Davies, the award-winning journalist, reiterates the case for legalising heroin that he first raised in his Channel 4 one-hour special in 2001

Going Cold Turkey
advert, 2006

Equinox: Rave New World, 1994

Heroin: the Global Lie

Trainspotting, 1996

Trainspotting, 1996

Heroin screws you up. Everybody knows that. At least, everybody who was alive and literate in the mid-1980s should know that, because Mrs Thatcher's government slapped the slogan on posters all over the UK, illustrated with the emaciated figure of an adolescent victim and a list of his heroin-related screw-ups: skin infections, liver complaints, blood diseases, mental problems.

It was all a lie.

It wasn't Mrs Thatcher's own personal lie. The bizarre campaign of official misinformation about heroin goes back to the 1920s, specifically to the congressional committee in Washington DC, which met in April 1924 to consider the facts about heroin. Solemnly, they recorded the views of physicians of the utmost fame that heroin obliterated the herd instinct, strengthened the muscular reflexes of criminals and caused insanity. Emboldened by these exciting fantasies, the committee decided that heroin must be banned not only in the United States but also around the entire planet. Within two months, their proposal had been converted into law, and the War Against Drugs was born.

The truth about heroin is that it is a benign drug. It is addictive – and that is a very good reason not to use it – but the only significant screw-up it inflicts on the physical, mental and moral condition of its users is constipation. Contrary to many decades of official claims, it is rather difficult to kill yourself with heroin: the gap between a therapeutic and a fatal dose is far wider than it is, for example, with paracetamol. The truth, which

for decades has scarcely dared to speak its name, is that all of the illness, misery, death and crime associated with heroin are, in fact, the effect not of the drug itself but of the black market on which it is sold as a result of this war against drugs.

Black market heroin becomes poisonous and dangerous because criminals cut it with pollutants to increase their profit. Black market addicts contract diseases, because they use dirty injecting equipment. Black market users overdose accidentally, because they have no idea of the purity of the batch they are using. Black market addicts are thin, not because the drug makes them thin, but because they have to give all their money to dealers. Black market addicts commit crime and sell themselves for sex, not because the drug makes them immoral, but because they have no other way to fund their habit.

For decades, pharmaceutical heroin was prescribed by doctors to patients who had become addicted after operations, particularly soldiers who had undergone battlefield surgery. They spent years on a legal supply: it didn't screw them up or even faintly obliterate their herd instinct. Enid Bagnold, who wrote *National Velvet*, spent the last twelve years of her life injecting herself with heroin after becoming addicted during a hip operation. It's fair to say she would have been surprised to be told that this was going to induce her to sell her elderly body on street corners.

Until the American prohibitionists closed him down in the 1920s, Dr Willis Butler ran a famous clinic in Shreveport, Louisiana for some of these 'therapeutic addicts'. Among his patients he included four doctors, two church ministers, two retired judges, an attorney, an architect, a newspaper editor, a musician from the symphony orchestra, a printer, two glass blowers and the mother of the commissioner of police. None of them showed any ill effect from the years they spent on Dr Butler's prescriptions. And, as Dr Butler later recalled: 'I never found one we could give an overdose to, even if we had wanted to. I saw one man take twelve grains intravenously at one time. He stood up and said, "There, that's just fine," and went on about his business.'

By the time I came to make a one-hour special about heroin for Channel 4, in the winter of 2000, this screw-up had become a global epidemic of extraordinary viciousness, in which governments around the planet steadfastly created the very problems which they were pretending to solve: causing the sickness and death which they claimed to be preventing; provoking the crime and disorder which they wanted to stop.

The UK had stayed out of the war for longer than most, allowing its doctors to prescribe heroin as they saw fit until the late 1960s, when three doctors in London were caught selling heroin to patients for profit. Never mind that these were the first such cases. Never mind that the system had been working so well that the Home Office tribunals set up to police the prescribing of heroin had been disbanded. There was an outburst of moral panic, much encouraged by the US administration of Nixon, and British doctors were told they could no longer prescribe heroin unless they had a special license from the Home Office.

At that time, the heroin black market in Britain consisted largely of two small pools of addicts – one in Chinatown on the southern side of Shaftesbury Avenue and the other among the old jazz cats on the northern side. But as the Home Office progressively choked off the supply of legal heroin, these users started looking for new sources. In the early days, they broke into chemists and sold what they found on a small black market around Piccadilly Circus. To fund their own habits, they sought out new users to whom they could sell for profit. And as the market started to expand, the first illicit supply lines were opened up across the border, first through American GIs in south-east Asia; then through the Pakistani community which had connections in Afghanistan; and, at the end of the 1970s, through an influx of Iranian exiles who fled the new regime of Ayatollah Khomeini, converting their cash into heroin.

Trainspotting, 1996

With all the skill and understanding of a drunkard in the dark, Mrs Thatcher's Home Office reacted by increasing its attack on the legal supply of heroin, replacing almost all of the restricted prescription of heroin with methadone, a substitute which happens to be clearly more dangerous than heroin and which is also notoriously unpopular with most heroin users. This cunning move succeeded in pushing up the price of black market heroin and thus in attracting all the major London crime families into the procurement and distribution of opiates.

By the time our programme was broadcast in June 2001, the original black market of several hundred registered addicts had been replaced by some 300,000 'chaotic users', many of them suffering from hepatitis, septicaemia, ruptured veins,

Nick Davies, 2001

Officials from the Home Office and the Department of Health managed to screw it up again

dramatic weight loss and, occasionally, overdoses; some of them had become heavily involved in prostitution and crime. A more recent internal Downing Street report credits black market drug users with 85 per cent of shoplifting, between 70 per cent and 80 per cent of burglaries and 54 per cent of robberies. Now, that's a screw-up.

For a long moment, it looked as though the programme might make a difference. One of those who saw it was the Labour MP and former TV researcher Chris Mullin, who by then had become chair of the Home Affairs Select Committee. He set up a formal inquiry; called me among other, better qualified witnesses; publicly berated the Home Office for its failure to come up with answers to justify their policy; and, with the support of all but the most bovine of his colleagues on the select committee, produced a brave report which called for 'a substantial increase' in the prescription of heroin to users. In the background, the new Home Secretary, David Blunkett, was prepared to be bold and made it policy that heroin should be available to all those with a clinical need. At that moment, things looked good.

But officials from the Home Office and the Department of Health managed to screw it up again. They buried the initiative in a working party that then took twenty months to report. When the issue finally surfaced in that report, the officials buried it again by insisting that the whole idea must be diverted into a handful of pilot studies before being rolled out. And in the background, they dreamed up a collection of bureaucratic restrictions that will deter the very users they are supposed to be attracting if they ever do get as far as launching a national campaign to prescribe clean heroin. (For example, they want users to spend the first three months injecting several times a day in a clinic in front of a nurse, which will deter anybody who needs to work or travel any significant distance away from the clinic.)

The Swiss started prescribing clean heroin to their most chaotic users in the mid-1990s. When they published the results for the first three years, they reported a 'drastic improvement' in individual health, both physical and mental, clear improvements in family links, employment and housing, as well as a steep fall in crime. There are equally impressive results from similar projects in Holland, Luxemburg and Naples. And yet still the global screw-up continues.

Drug quotes illustrated by Mario Hugo

HASHISH WILL GIVE HIM THE COURAGE OF A HERO, THE ELOQUENCE OF A POET, AND THE ARDOR OF AN ITALIAN. REMEMBER THAT GENTLEMEN, AND COME TO ME WHEN THE CRISIS APPROACHES.

LOUISA MAY ALCOTT

Prize-winning author Horatio Clare
describes how marketing changed
cannabis into something far more sinister

Skunk: the Dirty Great Profit

Pot Night, 1995

There is a jumpy atmosphere in the
Green Room. One more item, one more
ad break, and then it is our turn. Three
of us have been assembled for the skunk
discussion. There is the anxious woman
who went to prison for supplying heroin,
who now tours schools telling children
to say 'no' to everything, advocating zero
tolerance. I sympathise with her anxiety
and admire her endeavour, but statisti-
cally she is wasting her time. Neither
education nor prohibition has ever been
shown to reduce cannabis use. There
is the smiley TV shrink, disgraced for
allegedly attempting to pass off someone
else's work as his own, still clinging to
his position as this programme's tame
psychiatrist, who has already informed
me, giggling, that he means to be 'controversial'. 'The important thing,' he says, 'is
that we mustn't agree.'

And there is me, promoting a book
about why so many of my generation
smoked dope, hoping to make the case
that honest, informed discussion is the
best way to help young people negotiate
the infamous 'phase'.

I plead with the TV shrink as our
slot approaches. 'We need to help people

distinguish between problematic and rec-
reational drug use: we don't want to panic
them, or sound as though we don't know
what we're talking about, do we?'

'I think that's too complicated,'
he says.

The television in the corner is
tuned to the show. The host addresses us
through it. He looks solemn. 'And coming
up after the break,' he says, 'Skunk. The
terrifying new drug that is driving our
children to madness – and even murder.
Stay with us.'

We take our seats on the sofas as the
ads roll. How many times I have sat on
sofas with dope on the table. If we actually had a little, rather than the idea of lots,
it would be the host's joint. He passes
to the shrink first. The shrink exhales a
cloud of mashed-up anecdote and statistics. Almost half of his tormented patients

Skunk is a sad symbol of the way greed kills joy

are skunk smokers, he says. (The fact is,
around 40 per cent of the population have
smoked dope, so it follows that almost
half of any random group will have tried it.
But listening to this, you would think that
a qualified doctor is telling you that half
of skunk smokers go nuts.) Job done, you
can see the shrink thinking, as he sits back
and the host hands it to me.

Yes, I admit, I had a terrible time on
it, but I am one of the few who do way too
much, and one of the few of them who
lost the plot. 'One per cent of one per
cent,' I say, fighting baloney with, quite
possibly (I do not know the actual stat),
baloney. Dope – yes, including skunk – is
more complicated than…

The host is not having it. Somewhere he has seen something about a high
percentage of crime being committed by
people who have used drugs. Ergo, skunk
causes crime as well as madness. The
hostess has a go. She is worried, paranoid.
She is a mother, her children have friends
– young people – drugs – madness – crime
– what to do?

Anxious drug educator takes her hit.
We pass it around again, then our time is
up. I am still speaking when the credits

roll. From all the bumble, blurb and bluster, only one line of clear, cool comment emerged. I found it the next day, looking for reactions to the item on the internet. On a stoner website, someone wrote, 'I can't believe I woke up to this shit.'

The programme goes out at teatime. Which just goes to show you can sleep all day, drag yourself out of bed, spark up a spliff, and still make more sense than the 'drugs debate'. Skunk is a sad symbol of the way greed kills joy. When you find cannabis in one of its ancestral homes, like Morocco, it is a rather lovely thing; either gold-green kif, dried leaves, lovingly chopped into fine powder and smoked through a wooden pipe, or hashish, an aromatic chocolate solid which smells darkly floral. But nowhere in Morocco, or anywhere else where the weed grows wild, will you find skunk. Skunk is what cunning, mechanised man has done to cannabis. Skunk is what happens when the Western market mentality goes to work on nature. If cannabis is a little natural pleasure, skunk is a dirty great profit.

The leaves are a livid, luminous green. The buds are a sticky bright yellow, with a crystalline sheen. It looks like it has been designed by a teenager to spike the red dunes of a science fiction planet. It smells as though it is already burning, a yellow-white stink, a queasy, smoky, skunky reek. You can sniff it through two plastic bags: there is never any doubt what you are dealing with when skunk is involved.

It reached my university around 1994, where most of us were sucking our way through something called Soap Bar, a reddish mongrel of a hash. 'White Widow, Northern Lights, Super Skunk!' exulted Joe, one of our dealers, just back from Amsterdam and telling stories of new strains, new fashions on the dope frontier. He was one of those who prided themselves on being able to smoke more and stronger stuff than anyone else, who loved to talk about all the different ways he had taken it. Buckets, bongs, chillums, hot

knives, vaporisers: 'You couldn't take one hit / Off my blunt,' as the RZA, a hiphop star put it. That was Joe's line too. To the manufacturers, in their Dutch laboratories, he would have been an early adopter, a key disseminator. Give these people what they want, and they will spread it through the rest. By the turn of the millennium you could barely buy anything else off the street. If you wanted to smoke anything else, you needed a sophisticated and sympathetic dealer. Not many teenagers have one.

We took something that was foolish and frivolous and loquacious, and made it strong and threatening and mute. We made a soft drug harder. If, like Joe, you had graduated through the Nineties, when drug use rocketed, taking more and more of whatever you liked, by the time you came to skunk you were as tough as it was. Joe needed a handful of ecstasy to give him the same kick he once felt from one pill. He needed something twice as strong as the tame old weed our parents smoked to make him feel stoned. Skunk, which bypasses all the giggly-gabbly, sunny-silly, munchy-mumbly fun of dope, just makes you really stoned. At some point in the mid Nineties we were no longer 'getting high': now we were caned, boxed, mothered, hammered, blitzed. When we started smoking dope, the point was the lovely effect it had on thought, which it made stranger, on conversation, which it made funnier, on sex, which it made sexier, and even on sweets, which it made sweeter. But we were greedy. And our dealers were greedy, so we ended up with something that gets you wasted, fast; something which numbs you to pretty well anything. We took the original party drug and made it something people smoke in silence, staring, dazed, at the television. We made the comic tragic.

The links between depression, psychosis and heavy cannabis use are becoming clearer to science all the time. To my generation it is all empirical common sense. Most people use a bit and move on. Some people get stuck into it and it does them no good. And some of those, be they the weak, the greedy, or merely the fragile, get into terrible trouble with it. The younger you are when you start, the more damage it will do. It seems reasonable to suppose that skunk, because it is twice as strong, does twice as much damage twice as quickly as milder weed. If weed can be addictive, skunk can be twice as addictive.

If weed is a risk, skunk is twice as risky. The more you use it the less you should.

You could say the same of alcohol, of course. Lifting the prohibition of dope, legalising, labelling and licensing it, is surely the only way for the state to participate in reducing the harm it does. But it is not a simple case for a government to make: because this stuff is dangerous, we are going to legalise it. Can you imagine the fun the media and the opposition would have with that? What would the Health Minister say?

'If you smoke dope, you may be having a bit of harmless fun, but you are also taking a risk. Nevertheless, you are still a valued member of our society. You are doing what many valued members of our society – including Ministers – do at some stage, and, as your government, we are going to show we understand you, and we are going to try to help you. We are going to put your dealers out of business: their interest is that you should smoke more of it, yours is that you should smoke less. We are going to make you wait until you are 21. We are going to allow it to be sold to you only when it has been tested and taxed and plastered with graphic health warnings. We are going to help you distinguish, as between beer and spirits, between mild and dangerous. We are going to reform social attitudes, so that no one will think you immoral or illegal, so that everyone understands, as they do with booze, that if you must do it, then moderation is the only sensible way. By taking the secrecy out of it, we will give those who care about you more chance of spotting warning signs. By taking the illegality out of it, we are hoping you will speak freely about it, and seek help if you need it. We will help you understand that dope, like cigarettes, is not for rebels, but for fools.'

It is never going to happen. Complexity does not write headlines. Drugs bad, dealers evil, users mad. Madness and even murder. Now you're talking. Now you're selling papers. Christ, it's depressing. Pass the …

COCAINE IS GOD'S WAY OF SAYING YOU'RE MAKING TOO MUCH MONEY

ROBIN WILLIAMS

In 1994, Melvyn Bragg interviewed a dying Dennis Potter as he sipped liquid morphine to combat the pain of pancreatic cancer. This astounding interview on *Without Walls* was his final public appearance

Pottering About

Without Walls: An Interview with Dennis Potter, 1994

Dennis Potter and Melvyn Bragg enter the studio with assistants.

Dennis Potter: I think mine's [my chair's] with the ashtray. Hmmmm, is that too conspicuous there? [moving hip-flask of liquid morphine from the table]… I'll only need it when I need it – if there are any spasms – or… I should put it out of sight, yeah.

Melvyn Bragg: How long have you been working on this new thing?

Since I knew [about his cancer]. February the 14th, since I knew, you know what was happening, but I've just got to hope I've got enough days to finish it, you know, I'm keeping to a… I'm working to a very hard schedule… I'm driving myself, you know even when I walk up and down – with the pain sometimes you've just got to keep moving – I still have a pen in my hand so I can put a sentence down when it… you know it's like

that. It keeps me going really. There'd be no point in being, in remaining if I didn't, because it's just simply blank. There's no treatment possible, it's just simply blanking out pain with morphine, so it's finding the balance between the amount of pain that allows you to work and the amount that you need to blank out – because if you blank it out totally you can't work, but if you don't … The pain and the work: it's one of those ratios that you have to kind of work out daily.

Are you set now, shall we? How did you and when did you first find out you had this, err, cancer?

Well, I knew for sure on St Valentine's Day, it was like a little gift, a little kiss from somebody or something. I had – obviously, I had, suspicions… I had a lot of pain before then and there was a quite accidental sort of misdiagnosis of the condition in London when I was on the wing on something, and an assumption being made initially that it was, I don't know, an ulcer or a spastic colon and all that sort of thing which meant unfortunately, because Margaret my wife was ill and I was unwilling to leave her at that time, so I was not mixing up doctors, that

I had, er, December, and January particularly, when I was trying to control what in effect I now realise was the pain of

cancer with, err, with Panadol, which was ludicrous so in a way it was almost a relief to find out what it was – cancer of the pancreas, with secondary cancers already in the liver and with the knowledge that it can't be treated. You know there's nothing – neither chemotherapy nor surgery are appropriate, it's simply analgesic care 'til you 'goodnight Vienna', as they say in football I believe nowadays. And I've been working since then, flat out, at strange hours because I'm done in the evenings, mostly because of the morphine and also the pain is very energy sapping, but I do find that I can be at my desk at five o'clock in the morning and I'm keeping to a schedule of pages and I *will* and *do* that schedule everyday. I've had to attend to my affairs as well, [laughs] I remember

reading that phrase when I was a kid 'he had time to attend to his affairs' but what it did give me also, I mean I've always... I mean as a child without question I knew for a fact – and there's no argument about this – that I was a coward, a physical coward and often I'm also, I'm a very, I'm a really cripplingly shy person actually. I hate new situations, new people, with almost a dread. Now those two consequences in your adult life can really create serious wrong impressions of yourself to yourself and of yourself to other people because you try to compensate for what you know that a) you're a coward and b) you're shy; so that can lead to aggression and a sort of the reverse, the obverse of shy, the arrogance if you like, because you're wearing it like a cloak in order to get through a particular... but having to let that drop and to find out that in fact, at the last, thank God you're not actually a coward. I haven't shed a tear since I knew. I grieve for my family and friends who know me closely; obviously they're going through it, in a sense more than I am, you know, but I discover also what you always know to be true but you never know it until you know it – sorry but my voice

is echoing in my head for some reason-hmmm that the, I think it was actually to you that I remember Martin Amis saying something about you reach 40 or your middle age and nobody ever tells you, nobody's ever told you, you know, what it's like. Well, it's the same about knowing about death. We're the one animal that knows we're going to die and yet we carry on, you know, paying our mortgages, doing our jobs, moving about, behaving as though there's eternity in a sense and we forget or tend to forget that life can only be defined in the present tense it is, *is*, *is* and it is now *only*. I mean much as we would like to call back yesterday and indeed yearn to, and ache to sometimes, we can't, it's in us but we can't – it's not

there in front of us. And however predictable tomorrow is – and unfortunately for most people, most of the time, it's too predictable: they're locked into whatever situation they're locked into. Even so, no matter how predictable it is there's the element of unpredictable – you don't know – the only thing you know for sure is the present tense and that now-ness becomes so vivid to me now that almost, in a perverse sort of way, I'm almost serene. You know, I can celebrate life... And things are both more trivial than they ever were, and more important than they ever were and the difference between the trivial and the important doesn't seem to matter. But the *now-ness* of everything is absolutely wondrous. If people could see that, there's no way of telling you, you have to experience it, you know. But the glory of it, if you like, the comfort of it, the reassurance – not that I'm interested in reassuring people, you know, bugger that – the, the truth, the fact is that if you *see* the present tense, boy do you see it and boy can you celebrate it, you know.

...

Of course now I'm just practically chain-smoking, because there's no point, there's so many things... I can't keep food down anymore, I can't have a meal, my digestive system's gone, but I can drink things: those prepared, those horrible chemical things with all the vitamins and minerals and stuff in them, but I can add a dash of this and that to it, which I do and er – like cream, like cholesterol, oohh, and you know, I can break any rule now, you know, but the cigarette, well I love stroking this lovely tube of delight. Look at it! [laughing]

...

Do you think the driving themes of your work have come from your childhood or did they come from the break to university and the first few years of university journalism?

I don't know, no. They come as you grow. And your childhood remains, I mean, I forgot, I've forgotten who said it, but I remember reading some essay by some writer saying that for any writer the first fourteen years of his of her life are the crucible, anyway, no matter what you do, you know. But of course you add on and you use your experiences and I've always

deliberately as a device used the equivalent of the novelist's first person narrative. You know, when the novelist says 'I', you know he doesn't mean I and yet you want him to mean I. And I've used, for example in *The Singing Detective*, I used the Forest of Dean, I used the physical circumstance of psoriatic arthropathy, I have still got bloody psoriasis itching away at me, which is a bugger. You'd think that would lay off now wouldn't you? But it won't. But I used that and geographical realities, and it seemed so personal then, you know, that I often do that: I make it up, you know, the story, the wife thing, you know, the whole, er, the whole inner structure of that man is different to me. Now, I have never been like that and the dramatic story was very simple, it was simply seeing a man pick up his bed and walk. It's interesting, I always fall back into biblical language but that again you see is part of my *heritage,* which I, in a sense, am grateful for.

What about bringing in popular songs as you did in, say, Pennies from Heaven?

Well again, I wanted to write about that, in a way it sounds condescending, I don't mean it quite this way, but I wanted to write about the way popular culture is an inheritor of something else. You know that cheap songs, so called, actually do have something of the Psalms of David about them, they do say the world is other than it is, they do *illuminate*. This is why people saying 'this is our song' or whatever, it's not because that particular song actually expressed the depths of the feelings that they felt when they met each other and heard it. It is that somehow it re-evokes and pulls out of them yet again but with a different coating of irony and self knowledge, those feelings come bubbling back. So I wanted to write about popular culture, songs, in a direct way, so

it became just a technical problem. How do I get the music from way down there in the back, or here in the ear, or at the side, how do I get it straight, bang up in front? And then I thought well they lip synch things now and again, you know like sometimes there's a bad performance, and they dub from one language to another that way, why don't I just try making the actor move his lips to the words of the song and see. And then I tried it a little bit with myself in a mirror and [chuckles] that was fun and I mean I was a great singer – in fact it was pre-karaoke- and again you see rather than.... I wasn't breaking a mould as such, I just found the ideal way of making these songs so real.

Just like, and I understand it, the use of this word controversial, but there's many times; let's take a couple of the times when you really seemed to bump into opinion in this country. You're on this most popular, extraordinary medium of television, which is doing things in the Sixties and Seventies, in many areas which people had never dreamt it could do, in terms of original writing in your case. it was reaching out in all directions and taking on the public in a big way. Can we talk about two times you really bumped into them? One was to do with when you brought the notion of the devil, brimstone and treacle. Now somehow it seems that these two things are directly related but let's talk about them one at a time. What do you think was happening in Brimstone and Treacle and then in the business of sex on television?

Brimstone and Treacle was errrrrr. Can I break off for a second? I need a swig of that liquid morphine in that thing, if I can, I'll keep going but I... Can you unscrew that cap [hands the hipflask back to Bragg]. This is not agitation about *Brimstone and Treacle* by the way. [drinks from the hipflask]

Do you want another drink?

I wouldn't mind, yes. [gets up from his chair and leaves the room]

Are you feeling? I mean, how much?

It's ok, it's better to go on.

Right. Why do you think you got so much resistance to Brimstone and Treacle?

It's a very complicated story but if I can put it in the essence, as I saw what I was trying to do. In a way it's a simple flip over of an orthodox, of an ordinary sentimental *religiose* rather than religious parable, in that there is an afflicted house, variously afflicted but in particular with a crippled, seemingly mindless struck young girl and there is a visitor, and the visitor brings her to life and makes her speak. Now, if that visitor were an angel then that's all you would have – sanctimoniousness – you would learn nothing about anything. And I chose in my head, and this is how it began, this is why I'm talking this way. It began in my head as like that. What if it were the devil? Instead of making that easy distinction, which on the whole only the blasphemous make – non-religious people make this distinction very easily between so-called good and so-called evil. When, of course, they are inter-related and one is defined in terms of the other and one cannot exist without the other, which is why Satan was an angel and all art of any kind that has attempted to deal with this has had to deal with the dualism of it. So instead of the angel coming and rescuing the crippled and the dumb and the afflicted, I had the devil do it and an evil act can lead to good consequences a good act can lead to evil consequences. This is often the case and it is incomprehensible; it is as though you know the rain falls upon the just and upon the unjust. It is so. Now, it appeared *disgusting* because it was the devil and it was a rape or the beginning of a rape that made her cry out and interestingly the cry out was an accusation against her past. That complexity is, as I say, simply a reversal of what would have been sanctimonious and sentimental. *That* is what offended and afflicted people. I remember Alistair Milne the Director

of Programmes at the time, sent a letter to me saying something like 'brilliantly made' and so on, so on, 'but nauseating', nauseating, '*diabolical*', exactly the right word, it was diabolical, it was meant to be. Nauseating, not in the sense that he meant, nauseating in the sense of making you think about those forces, those circumstances, those afflictions and the way we manipulate the words good and bad. That to me is what it was about.

Did you think it strange that that should be banned?

No. Mrs Whitehouse wanted me prosecuted for blasphemy after the *Son of Man* about Jesus, because my Jesus was, if you like, a Forest of Dean Jesus. He'd want the wood on the cross before his crucifixion, to know if it was good timber and then the uses cruel man, puts timber – instead of making tables, or chairs, and useful things – they kill other men with it. And because he was that sort of Jesus and there are millions of Jesuses, obviously, and mine was just one of them. And you know there was a row in the Australian Parliament about it, things like that, and I think well if people get so conditioned that they watch these endless pappy series, you know, without any… there's violence every twenty, 30 seconds, whatever the audience rating system demands, there's sex used just like that you know – bang. There are constant sanctimonious references to God or the good. If you question, if you try and make people see the real, real, real use of these words they get hopping mad sometimes, but so be it, but that's what television is for too.

This interview was recorded on 15 March, 1994 and broadcast on 5 April,1994. Dennis Potter died on 7 June, 1994.

Filmmaker Simon Moore discusses the creation of his series *Traffik* and questions the society which creates the demand for such drugs

Traffik, 1989

Traffik

Equinox: Rave New World, 1994

Traffik, 1989

Writing and making *Traffik* was an extraordinary experience, which came about almost on impulse. At lunch with the producer, Brian Eastman, he said that Channel 4 was looking for a contemporary social drama. Did I have any ideas? I said immediately that I'd always wanted to do something big and international about drugs, but without any morality attached. I had nothing more – no story, no characters, and certainly nothing to say about the subject. I talked as though I had been thinking about the idea for years, but in truth it had just surged into my head, in response to his question. It was a good start.

Whenever I begin writing a project I spend a long time thinking about what I do not want it to be. Drugs was one of those subjects that TV had done to death, with endless thrillers and cop shows, but they all tended to have a simple moral battle between the forces of law and order (good) and the criminals (bad). To reassure the audience that the war on drugs was not futile, and to provide a suitably dramatic climax, they invariably ended with 'Mr Big' being captured and an enormous haul of drugs being taken

off the streets, saving our children once again. Not only was this predictable, but it also seemed to me to be dishonest and unhelpful. Supposing our drugs policies were making things worse rather than better? Supposing people took drugs not because they were stupid but because drugs made them feel better, or less terrified of life? Or the people who grew and sold drugs were doing so simply to survive? Supposing the war on drugs was completely unwinnable?

So, instead of ending with a big drugs bust, *Traffik* starts with one, and then shows how the route is put back together over the next six months. It is not the story that audiences are used to, and it is a depressing one, but I wanted to examine the drug business as though it were just like any other industry; how it works, and what kind of people are involved in all stages of production and distribution.

It became obvious to me that if I wanted to cover the subject in depth I had to tell the story from multiple points of view. The three main stories show the struggle of three families involved in growing, distribution and consumption – the farmer in Pakistan, the supplier in Germany and the addict in the UK. Each was going to be a central character in my story, and I wanted to make their objectives contradictory, so that there was no obvious place to point the finger of blame. Did we want the drug dealer's wife, Helen, to outwit the cops and save her husband from going to jail? The opium grower Fazal was a good man, trying to save his family, but could we condone him supplying heroin which might kill one of our other central characters, Caroline? By denying the audience an easy route through the drama, I was hoping to dig a bit deeper into the complexity of the drugs problem. More than anything else,

I was hoping to dig a bit deeper into the complexity of the drugs problem

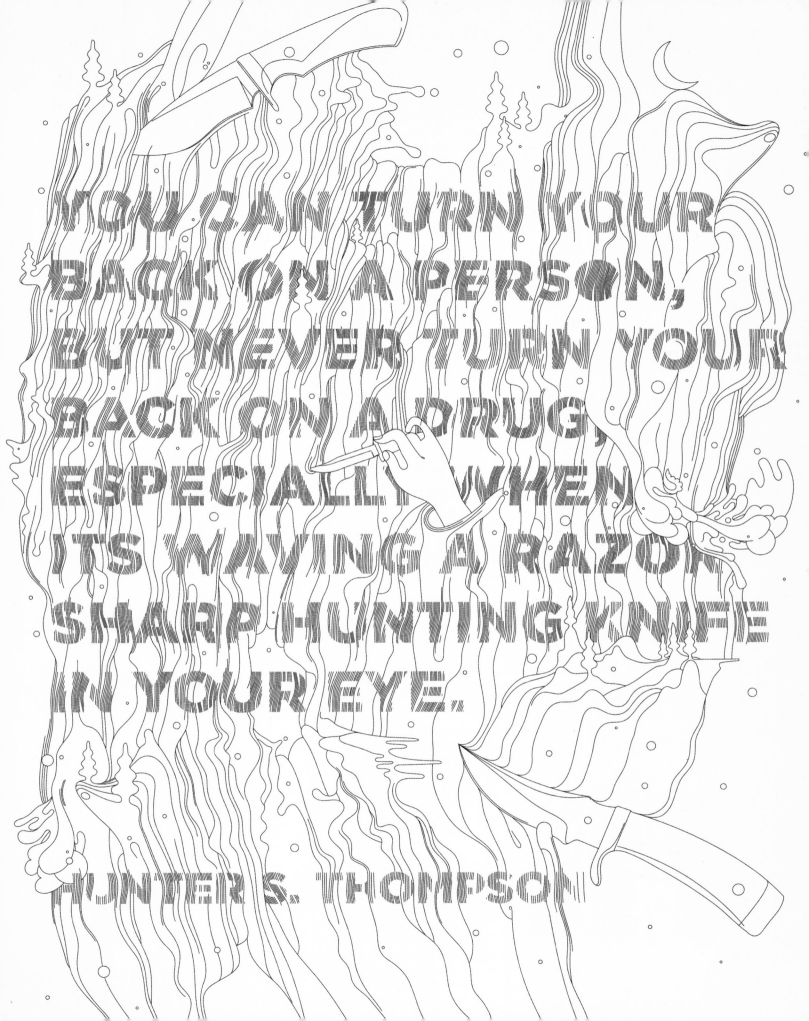

YOU CAN TURN YOUR BACK ON A PERSON, BUT NEVER TURN YOUR BACK ON A DRUG, ESPECIALLY WHEN ITS WAVING A RAZOR SHARP HUNTING KNIFE IN YOUR EYE.

HUNTER S. THOMPSON

I wanted to try and get away from the feeling of 'them and us' that pervades so much international drama, where 'we' are civilized, and 'they' are a more primitive, brutal society.

The real central character of *Traffik* is the drug itself; by following the drug you can move around the world, dipping into different people's lives and actions. Something else happens, too, when you jump frequently between different countries and cultures – the world becomes smaller and more connected. We realise that all our actions have consequences, some of which are the direct opposite of our intentions. As each episode reaches its climax, the inter-cutting between the stories became more and more rapid. We used the same piece of music by Shostakovitch to span all three countries, to show that all the different stories were really just one.

I wanted to shoot in real locations and have characters speak in their own language whenever appropriate. This was a problem for C4, which commissioning editor Peter Ansorge expressed very honestly to me: when you show drama with subtitles, people turn over. So I made an agreement that no subtitled scene would last longer than 60 seconds. I also tried to follow every serious, documentary-style sequence with some red-meat action to keep viewers entertained. There is no point saying something interesting if no one is listening.

To shoot in Britain, Germany and Pakistan for about the same cost as an episode of *Minder* was a truly remarkable achievement by producer Brian Eastman, and involved sacrifices by the cast and crew, including carrying all the camera equipment as personal luggage to Pakistan. Director Alasdair Reid and his cinematographer, Clive Tickner, made Pakistan look hauntingly beautiful instead of the gritty, grainy look that drug

dramas usually have, and the international cast were simply outstanding, including a very young Julia Ormond in her first major TV role, and Jamal Shah, who had never acted before.

The shooting was hard and at times dangerous. When the crew was stoned by a crowd in Pakistan, there was a vote on whether to abandon shooting and come home. Alasdair strove for realism throughout. When you see the opium made into heroin, the process was actually done for real in front of the camera; so simple and primitive it is staggering – no hi-tech chemistry laboratories – just peasants with buckets and simple chemicals.

Interestingly, the critics were not particularly impressed when the series was first broadcast (the *News Of The World* had my favorite, very short review – 'Sprawling drug drama leaves viewers in coma'). But by the time *Traffik* was repeated, the same critics had decided it was a classic. It has since spawned a big-budget feature film, which won four

Although I was not looking for a personal point of view, one did emerge during the writing and filming of *Traffik*. When we were looking for locations in Hamburg, we drove straight into the docks and on to a big boat from Pakistan. I knew in that moment that we could have carried out hundreds of thousands of pounds' worth of drugs in our van and no one would have stopped us. The biggest port in Europe was wide open and the idea of trying to find tiny, smuggled drugs on any of the gigantic boats constantly arriving and departing was immediately and obviously absurd. We cannot police the world. If by any remote chance we could eradicate heroin production in Pakistan and Afghanistan, it would simply move somewhere else. The research I did

I knew that we could have carried out hundreds of thousands of pounds' worth of drugs in our van and no one would have stopped us

Oscars, and which in turn gave birth to an American television drama – the series of the film of the series! It has stood the test of time, I think, because the radical structure of the series leads audiences into unfamiliar, uncertain territory, and gets them arguing about the issues.

Almost every incident in *Traffik* actually happened, and was taken from real news stories. Much of the dialogue was lifted from real interviews. Very little is made up apart from the framing device I chose to tell my story.

When I wrote the series I had no strong personal opinion about drugs. That might sound a strange thing to say, but as a writer I am invariably drawn to subjects because I do not know what I really feel about them, rather than because I have a particular opinion or belief to impart. By not filtering the characters through my own viewpoint, I hope the drama becomes more multi-faceted and provocative.

and the conversations I had with police and customs officers led me in the same direction – we were not winning any war, not by any stretch of the imagination, despite the considerable and heroic efforts of the people involved.

We spend an absolute fortune trying and failing to limit the supply of drugs, because the world is simply too big, and there are too many poor people with nothing to lose. We want to trade and travel freely, which is incompatible with eradicating the drug trade. Drugs will always be around and will always create serious problems for people, but my own personal belief after making *Traffik* (and even more so now, two decades later) is that we should move those massive resources away from fighting the supply of drugs and into trying to reduce the demand for drugs. And we do this by creating a society that people want to live in, rather than escape from.

Adventures in Art

In 1982, who would have believed that a handful of young British artists would gain the status and notoriety of footballers? In 1992 Channel 4 put the Turner Prize on television and so helped start a revolution in public attitudes that has thrust contemporary visual arts into the centre of Britain's cultural life. Programmes like *Operatunity* and *Ballet Changed My Life* have engaged millions of new viewers with the high arts. Channel 4 has been a powerful force as a patron of cutting edge contemporary arts – commissioning some of the world's greatest filmmakers to produce the entire canon of Samuel Beckett's dramatic work on film, commissioning more than a dozen operas, including the only production of John Adams's *The Death of Klinghoffer*, and, most recently, working with communities and artists to commission half a dozen major pieces of public art through *The Big Art Project*.

Sir Christopher Frayling is Rector of the Royal College of Art, Chairman of the Arts Council and a leading cultural writer and critic. In l984, he started a debate about culture and art. Almost 25 years later, he observes that the relationship between artists and audience has been transformed

The New Bauhaus

Christopher Frayling

The New Bauhaus

Christopher Frayling

The New Bauhaus

Christopher Frayling

The New Bauhaus

Christopher Fraylir

The Big Art Project

I made the six-part series *The Art of Persuasion* for Channel 4 in its early days – about the changing relationship between art and advertising, and by extension between 'high' and 'popular' culture – for two main reasons. One was that I'd recently re-read and still been mightily impressed by cultural theorist Walter Benjamin's essay written in the mid-1930s called *The Work of Art in the Age of Mechanical Reproduction*, which argued that our relationship with original works of art changes utterly once we have seen reproductions of them. In Benjamin's case, this meant reproductions by print technologies. So when we go and see the *Mona Lisa* the experience is filtered through the painting's many uses in other contexts – and we tend to concentrate on the close-up zone rather than 'the big picture'. The other reason was that from my experience of teaching in art schools and especially at the Royal College of Art, where I'd been Professor of Cultural History since 1979, it seemed to me that the fixed categories of the post-war period – fine art, applied art, design, communications – were beginning to blur at the edges with interesting results along various two-way streets. Yet these fixed categories remained at the heart of art education, as they had done for as long as anyone could remember.

For example, Daniel Weil – then a postgraduate student designer – exhibited in his final show of 1981 a series of mini radio speakers and a circuit board encased in polythene bags on metal hangers inside a large see-through tent and he called the piece *Homage to Duchamp*. Weil was an industrial designer and at the time no one on the staff knew how to react to his exhibition. Was it design? Was it art? Was it an installation? Did it matter? At the same time, some painters were turning towards installation and video work as well – and, in the post-Pop Art era, had fewer and fewer problems with the imagery and technologies of popular culture.

Was it design? Was it art? Was it an installation? Did it matter?

Meanwhile, out in the high street, the word 'products' seemed to be about to change its meaning: 'sun products' for holidays, 'life products' for insurance, 'parking products' for leaving your car, 'investment products' for a bundle of financial services. The *OED* still defined a 'product' as a 'thing assembled or manufactured', but something was definitely on the move: as Karl Marx had once predicted would happen, 'all that is solid will melt into the air'. Yet art schools created and made *things*. Food for thought.

These were the first stirrings of post-modernism – challenging old boundaries, value systems and hierarchies, which went back at least as far as the modernism of the original Bauhaus, an art and design school which operated in the two German towns of Weimar and Dessau between 1919 and 1932. The Bauhaus had since become by far the most influential school of its kind in post-war Britain.

Its teaching had been based on specialised craft workshops, run by masters and technicians – an updated version of the British arts and crafts model of late Victorian times. The students would make either one-off pieces or prototypes for industry after studying for eight months the basic components of visual language: texture, colour, form, shape and materials. So you began by understanding the individual elements and how they might be conjugated and then you brought them together in the process of making. The great debates at the Bauhaus were about the relative merits of fine art and craft, conceiving and making, about the relationship between craft and industry, and – a particular interest of some of the better known teachers such as Kandinsky and Klee – about the role of spiritual values in a modern, increasingly materialistic and violent world. Some of the students wandered around Weimar in medieval-style tunics looking for shops selling macrobiotic food – which caused something of a sensation in 1920s provincial Germany. But the biggest debate was about how to engage with the outside world while holding on to the modernist values of the school.

One stumbling block was that the right kind of technology could not be accommodated in the workshops, and only a few local factories were prepared to play host to visiting staff and students – who looked and sometimes behaved like medieval mendicants. Another was that nearly all the workshop masters were artists rather than designers, so they were much stronger on writing manifestos about industry and producing wonderful visual aids – especially Paul Klee's – than practical results.

Peter and the Wolf, 2006

By the early 1980s, when I was planning *The Art of Persuasion*, the relatively stable assumptions of the Bauhaus and its legacy seemed to be up for grabs. Almost everything in the cultural sector was in a confusing state of flux. Between the present and the past, as history was reworked to supply a culture of quotations. Between art and design, traditionally at loggerheads but now becoming part of a seamless spectrum. Between the 'new technologies' and the visual disciplines, as digital and electronic developments meant that for the first time in the long history of art and design education the technology available to students was very similar to the technology they would be using in their professional lives. Between 'high art' and 'pop' or 'mass culture'. Between design and packaging, at a time when 'the mechanism' inside a product had become a thin plastic sheet with microchips on it. Between the world inside the academy

Grayson Perry wins the Turner Prize, 2003

and the expanding world of the creative industries, both of them now beginning to be part of knowledge interchange rather than of a supply chain – which was how the Bauhaus people had seen it. The Bauhaus, in short, had maybe had its day.

The series, directed by Jeffrey Milland for HTV West, would explore some of these tendencies – the fleeting quality of much contemporary culture – taking the advertising business as its focus. Naomi Sargent, then commissioning editor for education at Channel 4, proved deeply sympathetic at a personal and political level with what we were trying to do: she particularly warmed to the kinds of art experience where there weren't any expensive seats.

Some of the students wandered around Weimar in medieval-style tunics looking for shops selling macrobiotic food – which caused something of a sensation in 1920s provincial Germany

Programme one looked at the evolution of one particular advertising campaign – for Cinzano, just after the classic Joan Collins and Leonard Rossiter mini-narrative ads – focusing on the role of 'the creatives' in the process. Programme two looked at how much the relationship between art and advertising had changed, since the pre-war days when Shell UK commissioned painters such as Paul Nash and Graham Sutherland to 'bring art to the people' on the sides of lorries delivering cans of petrol. Programme three looked at indirect forms of selling – which some called the distinctively British tradition of TV advertising – with help from David Ogilvy. I remember Ogilvy explaining how 'creative' had become the latest buzzword – applied to just about everything, with sometimes hilarious results: he hadn't, of course, seen anything yet. The series finished with some then-recent examples of advertisers, often art school graduates, using the work of fine artists to short cut their visual problems or to create witty and flattering punch-lines: Shell oil rigs and Turner's seascapes; the Royal Bank of Scotland, Henry Moore and Giacometti; cigarette advertisers being legislated in the direction of first Surrealism, and then Abstraction – and this at a time when the general public, even the exhibition-going public, were thought to have problems with both. Meanwhile, advertisers talked about artists post-Peter Blake and Andy Warhol who had used the images of advertising for their own purposes. A two-way street. The series won a Gold Medal at the New York Film & TV Festival of 1985.

Ballet Changed my Life, 2006

But there were some who worried about the implications. At the big annual design gathering in Aspen, Colorado – shortly after it was first broadcast – the theme of the year was 'British Design Now' and I gave a multi-media presentation on the series, extending it well beyond advertising to rock videos, art school influences on rock'n'roll, early computer graphics and film. In the discussion that followed, several American and British educators in the audience became aerated about the implied challenge to established hierarchies: there was art, there was applied art, there was popular imagery – and ever more shall it be so. It was not a spectrum, it was a series of fixed categories. To suggest otherwise was to let the show down. Popular culture honoured only itself. The barbarians were at the gates. Meanwhile, one art journal asked rather snootily of the series, what do you expect from 'a man who is Professor of the sort of art you lean against?'. *Campaign*, the advertiser's parish magazine, by contrast, thought I was being much too arty.

Another kind of shift – from artists alone to artists and audiences

All this seems a long time ago now. The very word 'culture' has undergone a complete redefinition in the intervening quarter century – from the 'culcha' of connoisseurs to a more broadly based anthropological meaning: culture as everything that nature isn't. We now have assorted 'culture' magazines, the 'cultural' industries and so on. Rock music, fashion, interiors, design, film, video games and even advertisements are now reviewed side-by-side with the traditional arts, and with equal, sometimes equally ponderous, seriousness.

Postmodernism has taken the long journey from philosophy seminar to journalistic cliché. The mid-evening makeover slot on television seems almost entirely devoted to design and visual culture of a sort: improving kitchens, interiors, gardens, homes. Even *Big Brother* in its first series prominently featured

chairs and a couch by Ron Arad – Professor of Product Design at the RCA. Programmes about the more traditional arts, meanwhile, have risen from their knees and developed a community focus – *Ballet Changed my Life, Operatunity,* the visual arts in inner cities, public art – on the assumption that artists aren't special kinds of people, but that people are special kinds of artist. The latest in the line is *Big Art Project*, which explores public engagement in the initiating, commissioning and building of a work of 'public' art in seven major sites. The series involves curators, artists and local communities. It partners Channel 4, the Arts Council, The Art Fund and numerous other creative partnerships and regional arts organisations and it explores, from various points of view, what 'public' means in this context. Another kind of shift – from artists alone to artists and audiences.

In art schools, meanwhile, the New Bauhaus has become a place where young artists and designers directly and unhesitatingly engage with the post-industrial age that surrounds them – just try and stop them – and where they are expected to have their fingers on the pulse of contemporary culture: a culture where we have indeed moved on from net curtains to the internet, from the space of places to the space of flows. A place where architects and installation artists, environmental artists and interior designers, painters and textile designers, sculptors and product designers, communications people and event designers – are all getting closer to one another all the time. A place where art and design students are five times more likely to be self-employed than any other university graduates. And where they have proved to be particularly good at constructing worlds around themselves and their friends in very entrepreneurial and improvisatory ways. Where there's a sense of stimulating industry rather than criticising it or serving it. Because 'the creative industries' – now an official category – want and need above all to be constantly stimulated.

Ballet Boyz, 1999

This hadn't yet happened when we made our series, but the signs were already there. It tried to take stock of something that was in the air, that could be a passing fad or could prove to be more significant. There have been other series about advertising since (the BBC soon bounced back one called *Washes Whiter*), and how broadcasters approach culture has changed beyond all recognition. Jeremy Issacs saw the point in 1984, and thanked us for getting the debate going. Channel 4 proved an excellent place to start.

ANDY WARHOL STREET EXHIBITION

A SELECTION OF 50 ARTWORKS EXHIBITED ON POSTERS AROUND LONDON, BROUGHT TO YOU BY CHANNEL FOUR
16 JANUARY – 4 FEBRUARY 2002

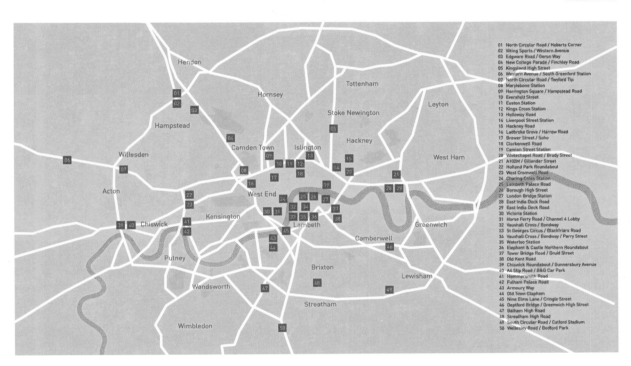

01 North Circular Road / Roberts Corner
02 Viking Sports / Western Avenue
03 Edgware Road / Geron Way
04 New College Parade / Finchley Road
05 Kingsland High Street
06 Western Avenue / South Greenford Station
07 North Circular Road / Twyford Tip
08 Marylebone Station
09 Harrington Square / Hampstead Road
10 Eversholt Street
11 Euston Station
12 Kings Cross Station
13 Holloway Road
14 Liverpool Street Station
15 Hackney Road
16 Ladbroke Grove / Harrow Road
17 Brewer Street / Soho
18 Clerkenwell Road
19 Cannon Street Station
20 Whitechapel Road / Brady Street
21 A102M / Gillender Street
22 Holland Park Roundabout
23 West Cromwell Road
24 Charing Cross Station
25 Lambeth Palace Road
26 Borough High Street
27 London Bridge Station
28 East India Dock Road
29 East India Dock Road
30 Victoria Station
31 Horse Ferry Road / Channel 4 Lobby
32 Vauxhall Cross / Bondway
33 St Georges Circus / Blackfriars Road
34 Vauxhall Cross / Bondway / Parry Street
35 Waterloo Station
36 Elephant & Castle Northern Roundabout
37 Tower Bridge Road / Druid Street
38 Old Kent Road
39 Chiswick Roundabout / Gunnersbury Avenue
40 A4 Slip Road / B&Q Car Park
41 Hammersmith Road
42 Fulham Palace Road
43 Armoury Way
44 Old Town Clapham
45 Nine Elms Lane / Cringle Street
46 Deptford Bridge / Greenwich High Street
47 Balham High Road
48 Streatham High Road
49 South Circular Road / Catford Stadium
50 Wellesley Road / Bedford Park

In January 2002, Channel 4 put art on to the streets turning the great city of London into a vast art gallery. Optimising the advantage of the opportunity presented by their four-part series on the artist Andy Warhol, Channel 4 was allowed to display some of Warhol's iconic images on billboards around London, offering a unique exhibiton of 50 artworks literally hung in the cityscape of the capital. As Martin Cribb from the Warhol Foundation said: 'This poster campaign seems particularly apt because Warhol always observed that Pop was all around on billboards and hoardings.'

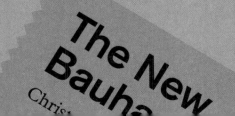

Howard Goodall, the British composer, is also a great musical educationalist, having presented six award-winning Channel 4 series on musical history. Here, he reflects on how music works

Tune In

Howard Goodall

How Music Works, 2006

How Music Works, 2006

There are many mysteries surrounding the writing, performing and enjoying of music. How do chains and sequences of seemingly random notes penetrate our emotional defences with such speed and power, even if we don't consider ourselves 'musical'? How is it that some composers' work captures the imaginations of people living two, three, four hundred years later in societies that are radically different from those that gave birth to it? How is it that a child growing up in a small village in rural China, who struggles for years to wrap his or her tongue around the foreignness, the weirdness, the stubborn illogicality of a European language, can master totally, in just a few months, the apparent complexities of the sound and patterns of European music? How is it that some music is immensely, persistently popular in its own time and yet utterly abandoned half a century later, never to be loved again? All these questions are difficult to answer.

But the very nature of how western music works – its notation, its pitches, its structures, its moving parts, its habits, tricks and techniques – these are not mysteries. Nor should they be to any rea-sonably literate, interested human being. It has been my mission over the past decade to make music documentaries on Channel 4 that take this straightforward premise as their starting point.

People who have not been musically trained at school have an unreasonable and totally unmerited fear of their lack of knowledge of music, even when they have strong opinions and feelings about a great deal of music. I believe I have a duty to confront this fear and help remove it, so that music lovers can be musically adept and observant, listen with informa-tion, and enjoy something with a new sense of context and perspective. It is my experience that it comes as a great relief to many lovers of music that a piece they particularly relish turns out to deserve being relished. They knew they liked a composer's work but they love being told *why* what they like seems so powerful, or moving, or heart-lifting, or stirring, or ingenious. And there usually are reasons – demonstrable techniques and creative decisions that have lead to the richness or the durability of the music. To some

They knew they liked a composer's work but they love being told *why* what they like seems so powerful, or moving, or heart-lifting, or stirring, or ingenious

extent it is as if I am revealing the magi-cian's cherished tricks against his or her will, but there is an important difference. When you know how the pack of cards got on the ceiling or how the elephant dis-appeared, the magic trick loses its appeal for the viewer. It is hard to wonder in amazement at the trick ever again. When you know more about the music you love, though, it only ever enhances and enriches its appeal. No one minds being told why Bach's *Air On a G String* sounds so satisfying, so perfect, or so pleasing.

We divided *How Music Works* into four parts – melody, harmony, rhythm and bass – and looked at the rudiments of musical theory across the stylistic piste. One moment we might be analysing a technique as applied in a Henry Purcell lament, then we would see the same technique at work in a Stevie Wonder song. There was nothing artificial or politically correct about this approach. Its intention was to make listeners, all listeners, hear things afresh, to challenge what they thought they knew about music and to nudge them towards an understanding of music as a transferable *skill*, not a mystical wand that only the worthy are qualified to wave. Contemporary popular music has derived many of its shapes and sounds from the older 'classical' tradition, so it is hardly surprising that the two worlds have much in common under the surface. I have found, in the past, that lovers of classical music are often lamentably ignorant about popular music and vice versa. Since gifted young musicians of all backgrounds increasingly treat the distinction between classical and popular as a meaningless one, I was adamant that *How Music Works* would too (in fact the blurring of these boundaries had begun in earnest in my previous series, *Howard Goodall's Twentieth Century Greats*).

One of the conclusions I was forced to draw when writing the script for *How Music Works* was that the terminology of music, that we have inherited from the thousand year old back catalogue, is misleading and unhelpful. I dearly wish we could start again from scratch, but we cannot and for many people the language of music is a huge, antiquated obstacle. A tone is not one step on the musical ladder, it is two. A semitone is actually one perfectly acceptable step on the western musical scale – there is nothing semi about it. An octave, derived from the Latin word 'eight' is not eight notes up the ladder, but twelve. A breve, derived from the Latin word meaning 'short', is, in classical music's theory, a long note. Even a semi breve is a long note. A key is both the wooden tab you press to make a sound on a piano and a family of several virtual notes at your disposal. An interval does not describe a period of time, an interruption or a space, as it should: it

describes a vertical distance between two sounds. A major key isn't any bigger than a minor key. And so on. Almost all of the basic music theory I learnt slavishly as a boy (and which still torments young people whose only desire is to play the sax like Courtney Pine or the violin like Nicola Benedetti) turns out to be perverse and confusing when you are trying to explain to non-musicians how the whole thing fits together. I was determined therefore to avoid jargon for the sake of it.

Music's architecture, though, notwithstanding the archaic terminology, is in fact not very complicated, nor in the end very frightening. Most of the tricky stuff can be heard clearly at work, so long as we know what it is we are listening out for. An 'inversion' might sound like something dry and technical but the opening phrases of Elton John's *Goodbye Yellow Brick Road* are not at all scary or dry. And they are full of inversions.

One of the issues the director, producer and I grappled with when constructing the series was how to portray something visually which mostly existed as a concept. Rhythm is a case in point. A rhythmic pattern moves along in time, but it follows an invisible, aural route. Not only that, a rhythmic pattern's journey through time travels according to a time-measuring system entirely independent of seconds, minutes and hours. A bar (another misleading term, by the way: portion, sector or package would all be better) of four beats uses up conventional time units of seconds but its clock is quite separate from that which regulates the seconds, and, unlike 'real' time, its velocity is flexible. Most listeners are aware that as they listen to longer pieces of music – a movement of a symphony, a section of film score, a sacred choral work, an act of an opera or musical – their perception of normal time (i.e. the seconds and minutes ticking by on their watches) is all but suspended while they are inside the alternative time system of the music. Speed in music also obeys its own rules that do not

conform to our other ways of measuring velocity. It is quite possible, for example, for a piece of music to be labelled 'fast' by a composer and yet for it to sound slow because its note values – the durations of the notes as opposed to the fundamental pulse or beat beneath them – are long and drawn-out. These concepts would need to be explained in the documentary script, of course, perhaps with an analogy or an example or both, but they would also need to be visualised on screen. Graphics are all well and good (and expensive) but a little of them goes a long way – we are hoping to make entertaining programmes, after all, not prepare PowerPoint presentations.

Reducing the theory of music to four programmes of less than an hour each inevitably means making hard choices about what one leaves in and what one discards. At one stage in the development of the script, we had a whole section devoted to the fascinating – but now largely ignored – musical technique of isorhythm. Isorhythm is a way of organising your musical patterns which reached its high water mark in the mid 14th century with a Burgundian composer called Guillaume de Machaut. It seems probable that isorhythmic techniques were learnt from Islamic musicians long before Machaut's time, a historical debt that has never been owned up to by classical musicologists. On the other hand, the Muslim colonists who spread through parts of Europe in the middle ages probably didn't know that their musicians had got isorhythm from India in the first place, via Persia. Isorhythm still underpins most Indian classical music though it is not known there by that name. This kind of unexpected historical nugget is what makes researching my programmes so much fun. That it didn't make it into the final cut of the programme is a shame, though I must confess that for the general viewer it might have turned a relatively easy-to-follow journey through music theory into a boffin's common room. That's why I have a producer.

Music's architecture, though, notwithstanding the archaic terminology, is in fact not very complicated, nor in the end very frightening

Six   Adventures in Art

What happened to modern art when Channel 4 married the Turner Prize? Waldemar Januszczak, art critic and maker of art documentaries, comes up with the answers

Tate & Style

Waldemar Januszczak

Damien Hirst,
Turner Prize Winner 1995

Do you remember how people used to hate modern art? I do. Because it wasn't very long ago. Actually, I can be more precise than that. People hated modern art until about 1991. Which was also the year that Channel 4 began broadcasting the Turner Prize. I know. I was there.

This is my thirtieth year as an art critic. My first review appeared in *The Guardian* on 1 April 1977. April Fool's Day. I mention it here not because I too want to have my back slapped – parties cloud your judgment – but because those 30 years of incessant art criticism qualify me perfectly to write about the impact of Channel 4 and the Turner Prize. I was around before either of them. I know what effect both of them have had. I remember vividly the situation before the two of them got together.

These days, of course, it's all so different. Not only do we take modern art in our stride, we appear to have developed an unquenchable appetite for it. Queues of excited kidults wind their way around Tate Modern waiting for a go on the slides. Newspaper headlines blare out on a daily basis how much this hedge-fundist has paid for that Damien Hirst.

It's a favourite national topic. Yes, the odd grumplestiltskin from Somerset can still be heard at Turner Prize time posing that tedious annual question: is it art? But no one takes that kind of complaint too seriously anymore. It's part of the theatre of the Turner Prize. It's not serious. It's not vicious. It's not like it used to be.

In the old days, I kept a box in which I collected all the rude letters I received referring me to the story of *The Emperor's New Clothes*. I called it my Emperor Box.

in the land. Everyone except for a little boy, who comes along to the procession, sees immediately that the king is bollock naked, and begins shouting it out.

So many readers of my articles in support of modern art felt the need to remind me of this story that my Emperor Box quickly overflowed, and I ended up chucking it away in about 1985. Had I kept up the collection there would now be no room in my house for me. What amused me most about this correspond-

Not only do we take modern art in our stride, we appear to have developed an unquenchable appetite for it

It's one of Hans Christian Andersen's most quoted offerings. A king gets conned into believing that he's wearing a beautiful suit of clothing, when, actually, there's nothing there. He's naked. But the king believes the conmen because he doesn't want to appear a fool. The same goes for his queen, his court, and everyone else

ence was the way that everyone who wrote seemed to believe that only they were clever or truthful enough to make the comparison between Andersen's story and the modern art con. Their hero was the little boy, with whom they identified fiercely. And whenever they encountered modern art that they did not like, or did not understand, they began frantically casting themselves in his role, and insisting that all the other inhabitants of the land were being fooled.

When the rude letters first started arriving, I used to write back dutifully to their senders, pointing out a crucial flaw in their thinking. In Andersen's fairy tale, the people who believed that the king was clothed made up the majority, and the little boy was the exception. In the case of modern art, it was the other way around. In England, in 1985, the vast majority of people seemed convinced that modern art was a con. The newspapers agreed, and kept up an incessant attack on all and any new art. Remember the Tate gallery bricks? Critics like me, who were trying to write supportively about it, and who didn't believe that anyone was trying to con anyone else, were branded fools and charlatans too, and subjected to a nasty barrage of mockery.

Looking back now on those days, it's hard to believe how much has changed. Today, Tate Modern is nothing less than the most visited museum in the world. People love going there. And the Turner Prize exhibition is usually the best-attended show of the year at Tate Britain. What's been forgotten is how much smaller and more local an event it used to be before Channel 4 took it on.

Frankly, the early history of the Turner Prize is embarrassing. In the first few years after its inception in 1984, even I could have won because it was open to anyone involved in art – critics, curators, museum directors, the lot. You didn't even need to be an artist. No one was sure what the rules were. Or who was eligible. And although a few pictures were sometimes displayed in the rotunda in Tate, there was no proper exhibition of shortlisted artists for visitors to see or judge. The winners just seemed to emerge in that mysterious British way that you also find with knighthoods, or membership applications to the Garrick.

All this changed when Channel 4 got involved. I was at Channel 4 at the time, and vividly remember the debate with Tate over what the prize should be. Clearly it had to be a prize for artists, but what sort of artist, and how many of them? In previous years, there had been short-lists of five, six, seven and even eight. It was Channel 4 that insisted that the shortlist be kept at the manageable number of four. And set a younger age

limit so that the prize could become an encouragement for artists in the first half of their career rather than a good-service gong slipped to them just before the end.

The other big change was the exhibition. Tate, which had struggled hopelessly for so many years to attract audiences to its displays of modern art, was reluctant to give over any space to an annual display of shortlisted artists. They were afraid no one would come and that the galleries would remain empty. That was what they were used to. These days, the Turner Prize show can be relied upon to pull in hundreds of thousands of punters. Back in 1990, when Channel 4 got involved, if you put up a sign outside a gallery saying Modern Art Inside, everyone would have gone the other way.

As it happens, the first year of Channel 4's involvement was worryingly quiet. Having been re-invented from scratch, the prize was finding its way. So

The Samuel Beckett Film Project, *Breath*, 2001

of course, that it wasn't the Turner Prize alone, or Channel 4's coverage of it, that was responsible. Various forces were at work here. A rare generation of talented artists, the YBAs, had emerged in unison, producing work that appeared to capture a new national optimism. And the revamped Turner Prize, with its younger

....

A rare generation of talented artists, the YBAs, had emerged in unison, producing work that appeared to capture a new national optimism

....

quiet was the reaction that I remember getting called into a meeting with the Director of Programmes at C4, John Willis, and being told that C4 should drop it and sponsor something at the British Film Institute instead. I disagreed, and was granted another go. Then came 1992. Everything changed.

Damien Hirst was invited onto the short-list for the first time, and through some potent chemical reaction caused by the fusion of his pushy personality with the rightness of the moment, everyone suddenly noticed what was going on at Tate. From a story that was buried somewhere after the obituaries in the newspapers, the Turner Prize turned abruptly into a front-pager.

The following year, when Rachel Whiteread's sad and iconic plaster cast of a Victorian house in the East End was included, and won, was even crazier. One moment no one was interested. The next moment the whole world seemed to be. Looking back now on this extraordinary sea-change in mood and pace, I can see,

rules, became a brilliant shop window for them. After all those years of Margaret Thatcher and the regressive Britishness she embodied, the country was sick of grumplestiltskin-thinking. A change in aesthetics was as desirable as a new Prime Minister. All those designer lofts that began springing up in the Docklands didn't need frilly paintings in frilly gold frames to decorate them either. They needed art that was fresh, modern and of its time. Basically, Britain had finally learned to accept modernity. It had taken a century, but, finally, it had happened.

Without a pixel of doubt, it was the biggest cultural turnaround of my critical life. And although you can argue for ever about the exact ratio of responsibility for this change that should be allotted to the Turner Prize and to Channel 4, what is unarguable is that both of them were involved in it, up to their necks.

Rupert Christiansen, critic for *The Daily Telegraph,* finds out that what might have been a false Channel 4 start is now an achievement to sing about

Record Breakers:
Opera on Channel 4
Rupert Christiansen

Record Breakers: Opera on Channel 4
Rupert Christiansen

The Death of Klinghoffer, 2003

Can opera on television ever succeed without one medium compromising the other? How do you scale down an art form as outsized as opera to fit a small flat screen? Perhaps one has to start from the premise that television can open opera up in new dimensions, letting the eye of the camera see it from unexpected and intimate perspectives, editing out the melodramatic excess that opera is prone to and reinventing the convention of people singing what they would normally speak. But isn't there a danger that such a reduction desiccates opera of its theatrical lifeblood?

These are issues that make the history of opera on television a saga dotted by false starts and fruitless experiments. The problems can never be altogether solved: in the end, opera will always be a gallon's worth and television a pint-pot. But the creativity that has gone into

squeezing one into the other has produced programming of extraordinary quality and ambition.

Not surprisingly, Channel 4, with its brief to extend the boundaries, has a particularly distinguished record in this field – a kick-start being provided by the network's first Chief Executive Jeremy Isaacs, an opera buff who went on to run the Royal Opera House. Under commissioning editors Michael Kustow and Gillian Widdicombe coverage began with a brave refusal to resort to the easy option of using fixed cameras to relay performances from opera houses. Peter Brook's reinvention of Bizet's *Carmen*, Birtwistle's acerbically modernist *Punch and Judy*, Michael Nyman's delightful whimsy *The Man who Mistook his Wife for a Hat* (which Channel 4 co-commissioned with the ICA) – all these were designed for television, filmed rather than merely recorded.

In 1988 Avril McRory took over. Her output over the next five years was phenomenal, capitalising on the opera boom that came with the huge popularity of Pavarotti and the arrival of the CD. Perhaps her biggest coup – via a tip-off from a viewer who had heard about the

event from her travel agent before it was officially announced – was winning the rights to the first Three Tenors concert which brought the 1990 World Cup to a climax and made Pavarotti's singing of *Nessun dorma* the best-known operatic aria since Caruso's *Vesti la giubba*. The audience for the relay came close to seven million – one of the highest figures ever recorded by Channel 4.

How do you scale down an art form as outsized as opera to fit a small flat screen?

McRory broke several other boundaries. An *Orfeo ed Euridice* from the Royal Opera House in 1989 was the first relay to use high-definition technology. *Tosca*, co-produced by Channel 4 in 1992 with a cast led by Plácido Domingo, was an even more extraordinary venture, filming Puccini's opera live in the real locations in Rome. In six half-hour programmes broadcast in 1993, *Harry Enfield's Guide to Opera* brought a welcome touch of comedy to the difficult business of introducing an art form to the unconverted.

McRory also commissioned more new operas conceived for television. As she freely admits, some of the six new 50-minute pieces seen in 1993 and 1994 'worked much better than others. That's what happens if you take risks'. Highlights of the series included Orlando Gough's *The Empress of Newfoundland*, with brilliant designs by Bruce McLean, and Gerald Barry's flamboyantly camp *The Triumph of Beauty and Deceit*. By common consent *Horse Opera*, a cowboy-orientated frolic by Stewart Copeland (of Police fame) featuring a rapping Rik Mayall didn't score – 'the atmosphere is of lads having a whale of a time at Channel 4's expense' commented one reviewer drily.

McRory is also enormously proud of a version of Stravinsky's *Oedipus Rex*, which introduced the genius of Julie Taymor – latterly of *Lion King* fame – to British audiences; as well as a complete *Ring* cycle from New York's Metropolitan Opera, broadcast in 1990 during primetime over two weekends. 'May Wagner forgive me for scheduling commercial breaks,' McRory jokes, but Gunther Schneider-Siemssen's gorgeously atmospheric settings and a superb cast made it 'worth every penny'.

The Death of Klinghoffer, 2003

McRory was succeeded by Helen Sprott. In her five years at Channel 4, Sprott consolidated a relationship with the newly rebuilt Glyndebourne, broadcasting two of its productions every year in transmissions that were both popular and admired (many were subsequently released on DVD). To balance this relatively conservative enterprise, Sprott also commissioned some remarkable documentaries which, as she puts it, 'posed awkward questions and weren't afraid to be maverick and unpredictable.' Pro-

grammes on Wagner's Nazi heritage, the Soviet musical archives, the controversial tenor Roberto Alagna, and a speculative fictionalised account of the origins of the libretto for *Don Giovanni* all caused a stir. A more straightforward charmer was *My Night with Handel,* an enchanting fantasy following the composer's progress through London, interspersed with arias sung by leading young singers and shot in evocative modern locations.

The contract with Glyndebourne terminated in 2000, freeing up the opera slots for commissioning editor Jan Younghusband. An instant hit was *Operatunity*, a hugely jolly and likeable reality show, broadcast in 2003, which pitched aspiring amateur singers against the professionals at the English National Opera. Younghusband's regime has seen several such surprises, with fewer straightforward transmissions of staged

The Death of Klinghoffer, 2003

the Apollo missions – Jonathan Dove's *Man on the Moon*, directed by Rupert Edwards. Dove and Edwards also collaborated with the librettist David Harsent on *When She Died*, a touching and faintly chilling examination of the effect that the death of the Princess of Wales had on a variety of ordinary people. The audience topped a million.

It helps that singers have got so much better at pitching their performances to the camera rather than the back of the stalls

performances and a rigorous insistence that 'only opera which appears at its best on television' is worth broadcasting. 'It helps that singers have got so much better at pitching their performances to the camera rather than the back of the stalls,' she says, and 'it's now easy to record singing voices live on location, which makes a degree of realism possible.' Margaret Williams's version of Britten's pacifist parable *Owen Wingrave* (written for BBC television in 1971) and Thomas Adès' tragi-comic portrait of Margaret Duchess of Argyll, *Powder Her Face* (boldly broadcast by Channel 4 in a primetime slot on Christmas Day) are cases in point – they convince so fluently as films that you almost forget that they're opera.

Younghusband has co-commissioned several live filmed performances of 19th-century classics, including *La Traviata*, but she is more concerned to show that opera can engage with contemporary issues, whether it's the dilemmas of war reporting, as in Judith Weir's *Armida*, directed by Margaret Williams, or the disillusion which followed

But the supreme achievement of Younghusband's regime to date is undoubtedly Penny Woolcock's stunning film of *The Death of Klinghoffer*, John Adams and Alice Goodman's problematic opera about the terrorist kidnapping of an elderly American tourist on board a Mediterranean cruise ship. By dint of brilliant camerawork and sharp cutting of the unwieldy score, Woolcock created a thrilling drama with an intense inner life which made the tragedy unbearably moving. Having justly won the Prix Italia and a cinema release, *The Death of Klinghoffer* is now recognized as one of the classics of opera on film and Younghusband has now commissioned an original television opera from Adams, which Woolcock will also direct.

Opera will always struggle on television – it is expensive to produce and only appeals to a minority audience. But Channel 4 has proved that it can form a vital element in a rich mix of programming, as well as suggesting future creative directions for an art form threatened elsewhere with museum status.

Building the Big 4 to celebrate
the launch of The Big Art Project.
The 4 will be outside Channel 4's
Horseferry Road headquarters for
a year. During that period four major
artists are staging an intervention
with the 4 to bring art into the
public space.
Photographs by Michelle Sadgrove,
Mike Smith Studio

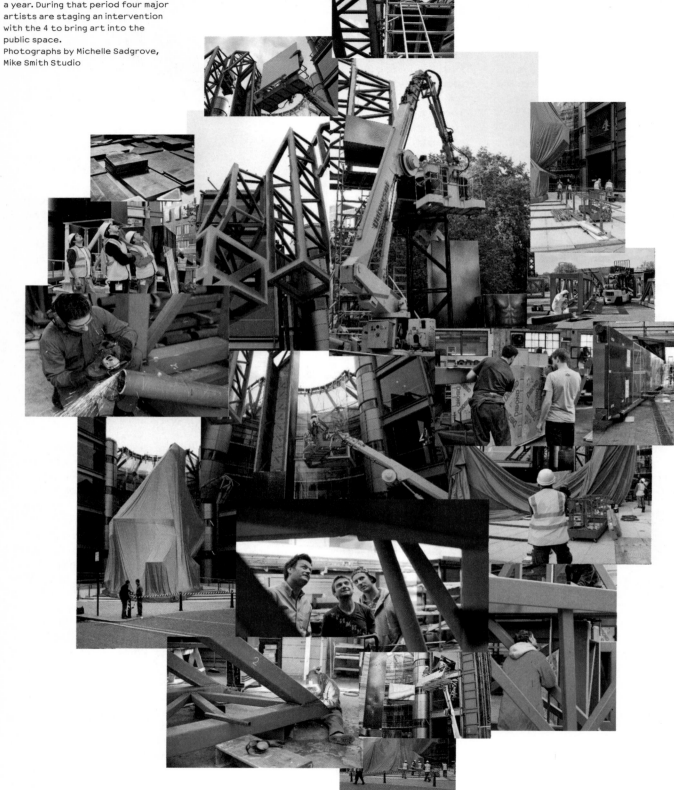

Paul Daniel, formerly Director of Music at The English National Opera, looks back over the amazing risks and the resulting achievements of Channel 4's *Operatunity*

Operatunity, 2003

Serious

Serious Operation

Paul Daniel

Operatunity, 2003

Expectations and ambitions were heavily loaded. Channel 4 and ENO were ideal partners in the search for ways to break down prejudices against opera, but Jan Younghusband had patiently watched Nicholas Payne and me turn down one programme idea after another, determined to reel us in. We all knew that Boxing Day televised productions were sending the nation to sleep, but for an opera company renowned for challenging perceptions and opening doors to new audiences, we were wary. In those days, we were well known and acclaimed for our work beyond the main repertory, using every part of the company in education projects, new writing and commissions, working up the first young singers programme in the UK, bringing 350 young people at a time to the Coliseum's stage to sing and act with our orchestra. The Baylis programme, which directed much of this work, was driven by the inspiring and visionary Steve Moffitt. Mary King's *The Knack* was ENO's ground-breaking annual training programme for amateur performers and singers. We made projects that felt like *Operatunity* every week. Just without the cameras.

But not quite like the *Operatunity* that Michael Waldman and Diverse introduced to us. Their blueprint already contained much of the shape and flavour of the series: the nationwide search for singers who had lost, or never found the opportunity to sing for their lives, finally given the chance to compete for a role in a live ENO performance, and the subsequent CD recording, produced by John Fraser, one of classical music's foremost recording producers. It would tell the story of each of these (hopefully) talented participants as they encountered the

skills and talents of the professionals who would guide them.

Tremendously worthy and box-ticking, it was nevertheless a competition, to be played out in the distorting world of television. It contained small seeds that could poison the whole project. We all knew that the competition format would distort the real work of training sing-

....

Everyone agreed that humiliation was a cheap trick. If this was an opportunity to enlighten, encourage and explore, then humiliation was the last thing you wanted

....

ers and perfecting performances, that it implied as much failure as success, and that television could be cruel in its pursuit of both. Tony Legge, my Head of Music at the time, whose formidable talent as a coach has brought out the best from the greatest singers in the greatest opera houses in the world, was clear about the dangers. 'We did not want to reject anybody. We did not want to stop anybody singing'. Mary King, devoted to training and inspiring amateurs and professionals alike to find their voices and the music in their souls, was adamant: 'Everyone agreed that humiliation was a cheap trick. If this was an opportunity to enlighten, encourage and explore, then humiliation was the last thing you wanted'.

on yet another period of role coaching followed by six weeks of production rehearsal with Alan Opie and the rest of the cast of ENO's *Rigoletto*, before the televised final night. Trying to make an operatic *Pop Idol* was clearly going to have to be left to another channel. *Operatunity* was going to take its participants a long way away from the exploitation of competition, and cost rather more in time and money. Channel 4 invested.

people to go to live opera? Maybe - just under two million people watched the programmes each week, and 75 per cent of the capacity *Rigoletto* audience at the Coliseum had never been to an opera before. Diverse Ltd added a significant and rightly acclaimed series to its portfolio of over 2000 broadcast programmes, and the awards flowed in.

Beyond all this, what we did get was unexpected. Beyond the intentions and ambitions, the plans and policies, *Operatunity* blazed with a heart-warming flame, lit by the huge talents of the participants and brilliance of the help they got from their mentors. No one, participants, ENO with its orchestra and chorus and cast who supported the project so finely, Channel 4 or Diverse Ltd quite expected the flood of good will.

Operatunity blazed with a heart-warming flame, lit by the huge talents of the participants and brilliance of the help they got from their mentors

We set about making wholesale transformations to the blueprint. Finding well over 2000 singers who could record themselves singing on video (singing in the shower was a popular location for the men) was one thing, but accelerating them up a very long ladder which properly took years of training to climb was dangerous to their health, and our artistic integrity. We had started the first UK young singers' academy some years before, and we knew the perils of launching newly trained voices onto the main stage only too well. We needed vastly more time: Michael and Jan stretched the project (and the budget!) to eighteen months, the minimum time we knew it would take to bring our singers through. We knew that we had to run workshop sessions, not shoot-and-scream auditions, to delve into the talents of the first hundred singers. At the regional auditions, they gave us the time and the money for Mary, Tony and Steve Moffitt to dig deeper into each and every auditionee's talent. We knew that we needed to give at least twenty singers lengthy music coaching and production rehearsals in London to discover more of their potential, even though this work would only be shown for minutes in the televised version. We knew that the final six participants would need intensive summer school weeks in London, learning how to rehearse together and apart, to act in ensembles as much as to perfect arias. We would have then to conceal the winner from the press while we insisted

Competition? Yes: 2253 people lost, and only two won. Rather like the course to the top of many professions. At the end of the day, we expected at best to put one singer into a few modest minutes of our 2003 *Rigoletto* production. In the event, we had to take ourselves on a crash course, honing our skills to deal with and learn from the passion of all the chosen 105 singers. Every one of them contributed towards the opportunity we all gained, and to the final success of Denise Leigh and Jane Gilchrist, the two wonderfully feisty and proud sopranos who had shown us that they were ready to sing far more than a mere walk-on role.

Could we make a series like *Operatunity* now? Could we put furiously talented teachers, artists and coaches on television to encourage and nourish exciting but vulnerable, little-trained singers to join a cast at the top of the professional ladder? It all seems far too cumbersome and unsensational for today's idea of reality television – where contestants are selected and groomed to look either sensational or stupid, to laugh or weep, long before they reach the first camera session. Even a second bite at *Operatunity* would be laced through with the vanity of experience – with singers intently aware of a success that our series didn't even dare to dream of. *Operatunity* would also have looked and felt very different without the sensitivity of Michael Waldman's cameras.

Did we get what we wanted? Did ENO and Channel 4 succeed in shifting perceptions, or encouraging more

We have seen our winners go on to make much of their success. Inevitably, the harsh light of television exposure was always going to be the brightest part of their experience, and it challenged as much as fulfilled expectations. One of ENO's more audacious demands on the time and purse strings of Channel 4 during programme development was that we should provide help and back-up for all of the final participants, continuing well after the cameras had gone. That support, coaching and advice has created perhaps even more remarkable stories. As a direct result of this hidden part of the programme, one of the other finalist singers left her prosperous career in merchant banking behind, worked with us, and won a place on a postgraduate performing course, from where she went on to sing abroad. Another transformed her life, leaving behind her work as a social worker for the elderly to train her voice intensively. She has now gone on to sing with the choruses of the UK's other national opera companies in Scotland and Wales, and recently found her way back to the stage where she discovered her potential five years ago, to join the extra chorus of ENO. Without the company, without its Mary King, its Tony Legge, its Steve Moffitt and all the other incredible individuals across the company who gave so much to the series, and without the driving investment of Channel 4 and Diverse, those stories would only be ideas for another series. They came true thanks to a crazy idea called *Operatunity*.

The Food Fight

If we are what we eat, then what we eat tells a story. In 1982 every high street in the land boasted a Wimpy burger bar. A quarter of a century on, the Wimpy is replaced by a Fair Trade coffee shop, and a Saturday farmers' market. Britain's gastronomic revolution has been profound and Jamie, Gordon, Hugh have become household names. Food programmes have become much more than cooking demonstrations – our eating habits top political agendas: *Jamie's School Dinners* and *Hugh's Chicken Run* effect positive change. But the revolution is not yet complete and Channel 4 continues to raise consciousness about how and where our food comes from and how it is produced, knowing this affects not only our health but the environment, local producers and communities.

Rose Prince, food columnist, local produce campaigner, author and cook, explains how educational food TV morphed into entertainment, spearheaded by Channel 4

The Big Food Fight: Season starts 7 Jan
channel4.com/food

Here's One I Made Earlier

If there is a food photograph that encompasses television's impact on the way we eat, it is that one showing mothers passing bags of chips over a school fence; 'sustenance' for their kids, who were experiencing the Jamie Oliver effect. The snap, which was plastered across the national press, portrays a trinity of victims: the children, unlucky recipients of their parents' bad feeding habits; the parents, who themselves suffered a poor quality food education; and the school itself, whose now unenviable task was to fill in those nurturing, cultural and educational gaps and deal both with the rebels in the playground and the guerrilla tactics of the mothers.

The greatest achievement of *Jamie's School Dinners,* and its exposure of the true wrong misdoings of school kitchens nationwide, was that it brought the issue to the attention of millions and created a national debate that lasted weeks. But the series also confirmed how television has become the surrogate for basic needs; the ability to cook and understand nutrition being one of them. Where once there would have been a public sector department debating on and acting upon the

gastronomic requirements of families (the Ministry of Food was abolished after the war), a television entertainer faces the job alone, hoping for a government reaction. On the subject of food, the media has become the sole educator, with food broadcasting the most potent form of all.

Cookery television had more than one parent, but the more remarkable of them – perhaps oddly – was feminism. The paradox of the newly emancipated woman with equal career opportunities would be her realisation, decades on, that the overfed yet undernourished kids in Jamie's target schools may be her responsibility. Yet the female academics wanted girls' cookery off the syllabus, the pigeon hole plugged. Meanwhile that other party responsible for passing down any remotely responsible information vis-à-vis nutrition was heading out the front door every morning to the job that had replaced her role as housewife.

By the time Channel 4 launched, food programmes were being regularly commissioned under education by the main broadcasters, yet featured – with one or two exceptions – a gallery of

eccentrics using a studio kitchen to tell the middle classes (now bereft of kitchen staff) how to pull off a dinner party. The C2s were not taking any notice, prompting the editors to beg for more entertainment from production companies. Presenters presiding over a 'kitchen' worktop dotted with previously weighed out ingredients, and '*one I made earlier*' in the oven, were heading out. Characters were back, only this time looking for a mass audience. The genre morphed into entertainment, with romantic travels with coastal fishermen (Stein), character double acts (Dickson Wright and Patterson) and boy about town (Oliver).

In the end it was the audience that mattered when Channel 4 set its agenda for food in the late Eighties. A young channel could 'do food' for young viewers with alternative concerns and aspirations.

It was the moment to not just say eat your greens but *Grow Your Greens*, too (Wall to Wall, 1993). Sophie Grigson was accessible, practical and curious about the peculiar. She looked like a punk housewife – jagged haircut, funny earrings and square, dirndl skirts. In one memorable episode we were introduced to an edible thistle. Grigson met the then unknown Clarissa Dickson Wright, number one exponent of this particular lost vegetable. There was some wrangling over the future Fat Lady's presentation on the day of filming. Clarissa did not want to wear a bra, but producer Pat Llewellyn insisted. In the end Dixon Wright stomped to the loo with a carrier bag containing the garment, minutes before the camera rolled. Llewellyn had made her discovery, but you saw her on Channel 4 first.

Entering the era of Hugh Fearnley-Whittingstall, it wasn't enough to grow your own. Meet the new hunter gatherer with a caveman hairstyle to match. Every-

not expect to find a new mother seasoning and potting the placenta she delivered along with her new baby, then serving it up at a party that was a thinly disguised pagan ritual.

Here – for once – was a programme that was not hectoring you to reach for a pan but which allowed viewers to peep into the wonderfully dysfunctional UK kitchen. Here was the damage done by 30 years without formal food education. There was something terrifying about the warped ideas, the Bacchanalian feasts, the clever fools – the cooks who *thought* they knew what they were doing at the stove. Is this really how Britain cooked? Well, probably not every night, but it is interesting to note that the unorthodox smorgasbord of food media had sent out some very mixed messages. Were you a Delia person: methodical, afraid of failure, faithfully shopping at Sainsbury's? Or were you the type to seek out a plate of snake?

was of course highly suitable for Channel 4's documentary makers.

Dispatches tackled genetic modification, the food industry's latest innovation, in a film that proved devastating to the biotech firms. On 12 February 1999 Dr Arpad Pusztai, a scientist employed by the Rowett Research Institute in Aberdeen, blew the whistle on air. He said that his experiments showed that eating genetically modified potatoes may damage human immunity to disease. He had found, when studying rats, that their internal organs and immune systems were altered by the presence of an additional, artificially inserted gene in the potatoes. The impact of this documentary was electrifying. We were accustomed to green activists voicing their concerns but here was a scientist, working *within* the biotech industry – their expert attacking their product. Dr Pusztai did not have his contract renewed by the Rowett Research Institute and, putting the affair in context, it was a defining moment for consumers who had up to that point accepted that genetic modification was an inevitable element in the future of food. It created a consumer-led revolution that convinced the big four supermarkets to insist farmers supply them with meat that was not fed GM material, and for the retailers to make further statements declaring unwillingness to stock GM foods – no matter any given go-ahead from the government or the EU for its sale in the UK. This stance remains in place.

Where once there would have been a public sector department debating the gastronomic requirements of families, a television entertainer faces the job alone

thing about the channel's new find was fresh. He came from nowhere, the kind of young guy you might meet in any English town or city but who, untypical of his gender at that time, knew how to cook a Sunday lunch. A pure enthusiast who was neither a chef nor a member of cookery royalty, he took the professional naturalist out of foraging and discovery. The response to *A Cook On The Wild Side* was noticeable. Walking the dog on the playing fields became a hunt for a puffball; no razor clam was safe. But in 1996 the airspace cadet turned from unearthing unfamiliar flora and fauna to foraging for food stories behind the closed doors of British households. What do we imagine happens in most kitchens? We picture mum, at most making sausage and mash for tea, at least bunging dinner in the microwave. But we do not expect to find families who feast on snails, cooked outdoors, at weekends. And we certainly do

But there was a dark side to this 'eating disorder'. Until the early 1990s TV broadcasting had largely ignored the fact that having shifted responsibility for feeding the nation to the market and away from the authorities, there was some very sinister practice in food production. And, with food inflation (prices) low, questions had not been asked. The authorities were happy with the status quo (abundant cheap food makes any party very re-electable) and British consumers were contentedly paying rock-bottom prices for previously expensive items like salmon, beef and tiger prawns. No-one stopped to wonder if the situation was sustainable. When the BSE crisis hit in 1996 and government scientists linked the human form of the disease to that in cattle, everything changed. There was genuine horror at the discovery that cattle had been fed their own species and the questioning began in earnest. The subject

Dispatches: Hot Potato, 1999

I had my own experience of Channel 4 taking on unconventional material. In 1999 they commissioned Diverse Productions (I was co-producer with Mark Halliley) to make a biographical film about Britain's most admired food writer, Elizabeth David. The channel had (exactly ten years previously) secured a scoop in the first and only filmed interview with the media shy doyenne, but it had made uncomfortable viewing. A young Jancis Robinson faced the irascible

Mrs David across a restaurant table. The author refused to play ball. No anecdotes, not one snippet of the zeal so apparent in her books. Answers to questions were awkward and monosyllabic and she even seemed to delight in the pain she was causing her interviewer.

Walking the dog on the playing fields became a hunt for a puffball; no razor clam was safe

The press hinted that David was drunk. In other words, like all grumpy writers, she was perfect stuff for biography. Her secrets had been well-guarded but the material – once it had come to light – was outstanding. Channel 4 agreed that the life of a writer whose books had brought awareness of Mediterranean food to the UK (no Elizabeth David, no Jamie Oliver) should be presented not by a celebrity chef but a politician. The former governor of Hong Kong and lifelong David follower, Chris Patten, presented *In the Footsteps of Elizabeth David*. His skill in analysis, knowledge of food and its history and clear enjoyment of the job (he had to eat his way around four European countries) earned high praise. At the end of the film, David's nephew admitted on camera that she was 'not nice', prompting a complaint from the family. But 'nice' is conventional. Nice is an epithet neither the writer or the broadcaster would want.

There was, anyway, a certain amount of expectation that cooks, and chefs, were fiends. Hot tempered, highly strung brigadiers who did not suffer fools. A year earlier Gordon Ramsay had appeared in *Boiling Point,* a fly-on-the-wall documentary about the tensions and temperaments of the restaurant business.

Ramsay was already showing promise as a personality who could and would repeatedly lose it on camera. But his frustrations with the dysfunctional cooks of Britain, both amateur and professional, were nothing compared with what was about to happen.

Jamie Oliver had an idea. He had been commissioned by the BBC to make a film about how he put his own reputation, and fortune, on the line to train fifteen out of work, no-hope kids to become chefs. But, since signing up with the supermarket chain Sainsbury's to front their TV commercials, the BBC had had to let their most talented TV presenter move on. As it was, Oliver wanted to be seen in a new light. Three series of *The Naked Chef*, Pat Llewellyn's lad-with-a-pan concept, had raised the bar for presenters. Oliver's unscripted naturalness shaded every food presenter to date. By series three, however, he knew his cheeky chappie image was losing its impact on a formerly adulatory audience, and that his Sainsbury's earnings were provoking envy. In *Jamie's Kitchen* (2002) he risked both image and money, personally financing the scheme to start a restaurant with unskilled amateurs. Oliver proved he was smart, as well as gifted in front of the camera. Depending on taste, the regular wrath and fulminations, tears and tantrums in reality shows can seem the best or worst of television – but Oliver's bollockings were delivered with unarguable logic, a skill he took to *Jamie's School Dinners*.

In the same way that *Dispatches* delivered a coup to the food industry and the authorities, *Jamie's School Dinners* changed something. It is not known yet whether the campaign to improve school food is working, but that surely is the point. Television does not run the country – it can only influence and hope, in the case of kids' food, that someone seizes the idea and runs with it. In the absence of a basic, home-grown training in domestic skills, food television has become adopted teacher and mother (though it should be pointed out that, with the exception of Nigella Lawson, there are shockingly few women fronting shows). And to a good degree TV succeeds in its role. The world of food, thanks to the media, has been opened to proper scrutiny; the dilemma of food safety is addressed and the obesity problem has been given the exposure it

desperately needs. We know more about world cuisine, can forage for fungi, catch and cook a sea bass or stuff a sausage. Ironically we are at the stage where young men see cooking as a cool pursuit. Think back 25 years, an era when the educators were driving girls to be equal to the kitchen-shy boys in their class – TV has changed that. All that is needed is one last series: *Jamie Does the Dishes*.

Daily Telegraph, March 2005

Eight   The Food Fight

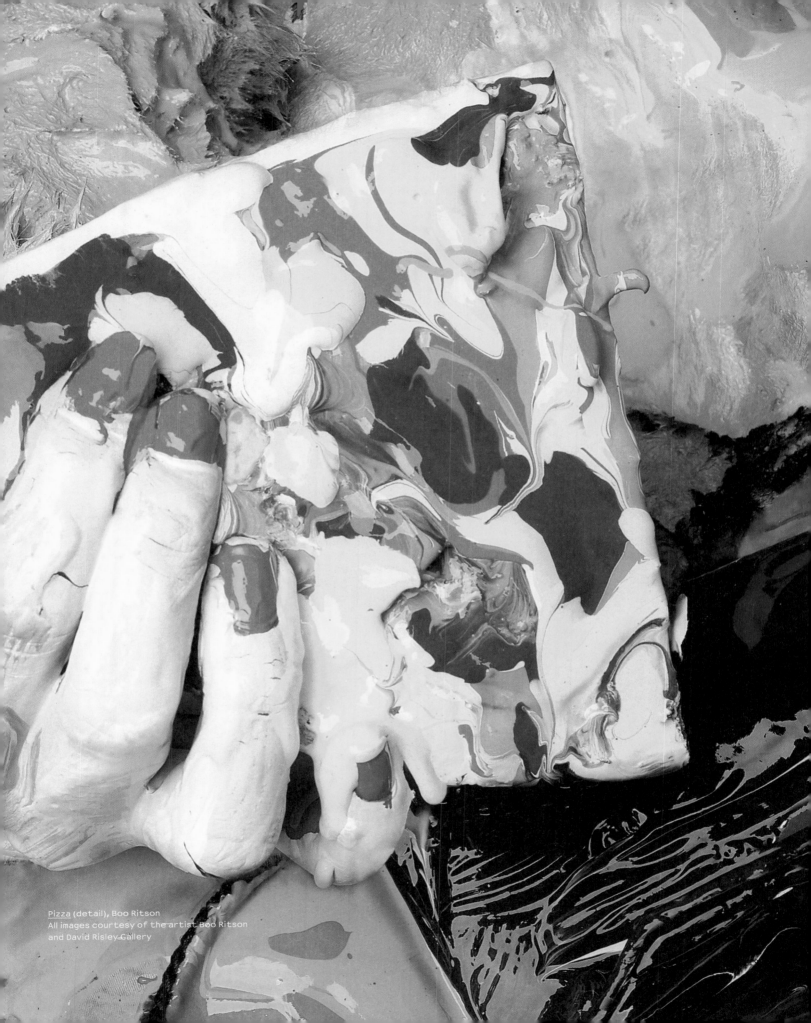

Pizza (detail), Boo Ritson
All images courtesy of the artist Boo Ritson
and David Risley Gallery

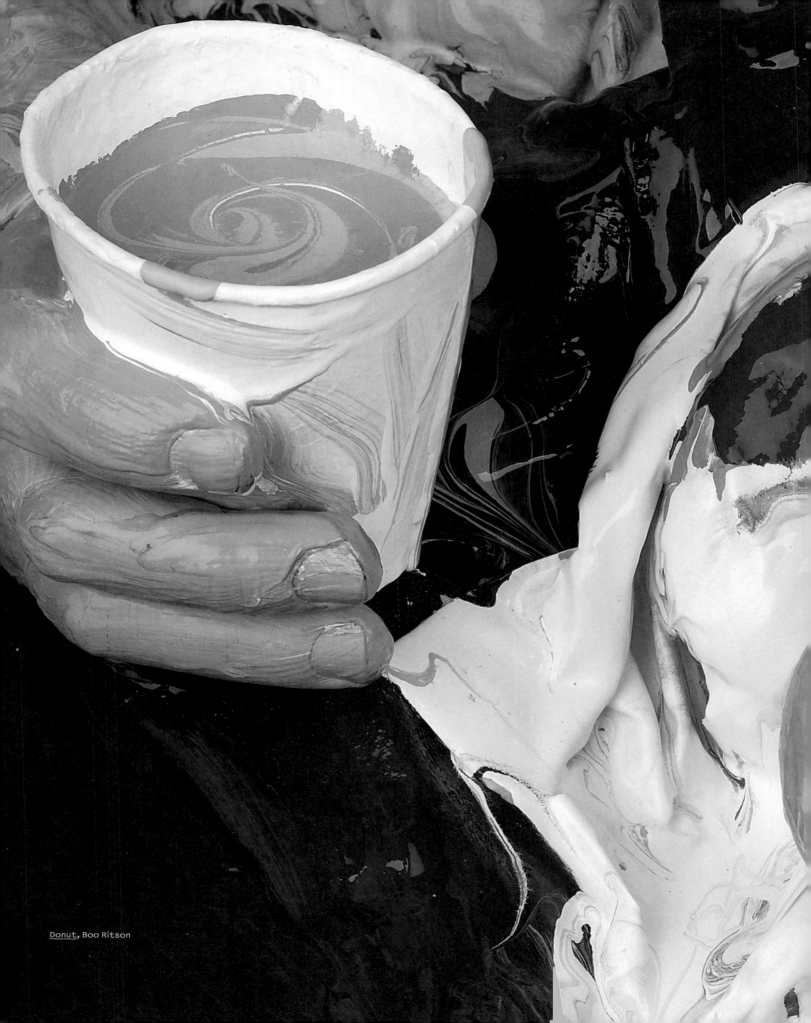

Donut, Boo Ritson

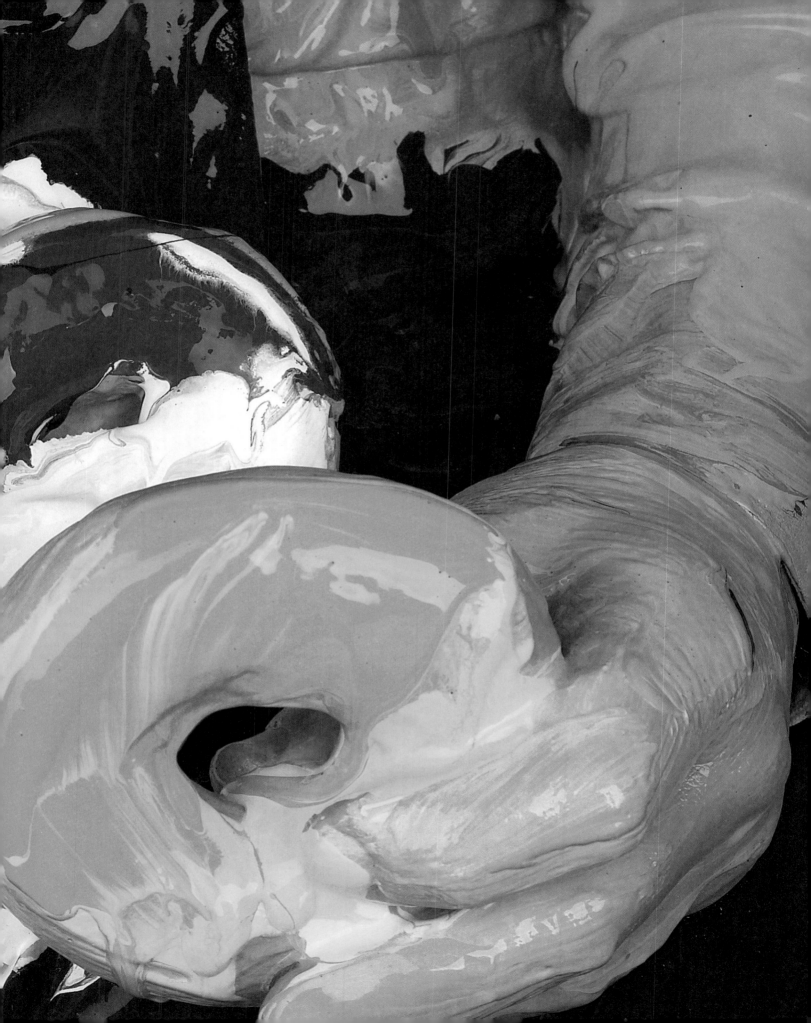

To eat properly we need to take food seriously argues Tamasin Day-Lewis, the food writer and author

Changing Tastes?

Jamie's School Dinners advert, 2005

There's as much comfort in the turning of leftovers into the best home-made dishes, as there is in the eating

Has anything changed? Just that thinking about food, talking about food and watching food as a television spectator sport have all become national obsessions.

There's one change we are convinced we've made as a nation, but I'm not so sure. Everyone seems to think we've left behind the Dark Ages of industrial food and crappy cooking, and are now the most diversely educated and dazzlingly ethnic of cooks and eaters. That England and the new English melting-pot cuisine is where it's at; the French are over, their regional food losing its edge, its defining qualities, its boundaries blurred into homogeneity. As for the Italians, we've absorbed their cucina like stock into a risotto; we almost believe their classic dishes are our own, the spag bols, lasagnes, pestos. But we've become watchers not doers. And we've lost a lot of our traditional British food along the way. In our eagerness to embrace a new world of cuisines and ingredients we've lost our identity.

We don't home-cook an 'Indian'; we go *out* to eat it or get a take-away. And that's how most of us shop for food, not to cook it but to eat it. We are all too

oven-ready and taste-the-difference lazy to disbelieve the supermarkets' 'wholefood', 'home-cooked' labels. They try to make us believe in a new food world where the spuds are washed and prepped, carrots come ready-battoned. Their ads soothe, cajole and comfort us but their food doesn't. What we choose to ignore is that the pictures are only pictures, the words are only words, and the food

itself is primped and groomed to stand out like a girl in a cocktail dress at a football match.

A simple shepherd's or cottage pie has achieved a sort of lapsed, iconic status, something you buy ready-made or eat in a pub. Too much trouble to take the meat off the bone from the Sunday roast (what Sunday roast?), chop it fine, add onions, celery, tinned tomatoes, a good squirt of tomato paste and the darkly gelled remains of yesterday's home-made gravy; shake in a few drops of Worcester and Tabasco; simmer; cover with a mantle of buttery mash; crisp to bubbling, the meat juices seeping up into the browned spud. There's as much comfort in the preparation, the turning of leftovers into the best home-made dishes, as there is in the eating. What comfort the 'comfort food' zapped in the ready-meal tray?

The rich now choose to eat the 'peasant' diet they would have once despised

They're all in it together, the food conglomerates, the agri-businesses, the supermarkets, conspiring to de-skill us and make us cook what they want to sell us. And in a couple of decades they've scrambled the seasons and we've got what we deserve. We are subtly prevented from the pleasures of cooking and baking for our families, our friends. We don't cook, we 'cater', we cheat, we are driven by novelty and immediacy and food fashion. Twenty-five years ago it was all about cooking, now it's all about looking. And restaurants. It's the democratisation of food. The croissants and pasta everyone first ate on holiday have gone baking-counter and chill-cabinet mainstream. The class structure of Britain has been levelled more by food than by anything else. Nowadays nearly everyone can afford to eat more or less the same food. There used to be no real restaurant culture in Britain, but in the short skip of a couple of decades, the luxury of dining out has become a national pastime, alongside 'retail therapy', EasyJetting and going to the gym.

So has the democratisation and better knowledge of food made us all take more pleasure in what we eat? And has it made us healthier? This is something we began to concern ourselves with in the Sixties, when we started to question industrial food processes, but the word 'organic' hadn't been invented. Well, it certainly hasn't made us healthier.

These days, mostly, the rich get thin and the poor get fat. I know there are plenty of affluent people who indulge and are overweight, but they are more likely to indulge in things less likely to be bad for them and to have a well-balanced diet in the main. They eat too much of a good thing rather than too much of a bad. And look how the wheel turns full circle. The rich now choose to eat the 'peasant' diet they would once have despised. They glug olive oil and chomp roast vegetables, cook with less meat, eat butter not hydrogenated fats. But here's the rub – we have more malnourishment and morbid obesity than probably ever before. Malnourishment used to be a Third World disease, but now it's a First World one. There's something obscene about that. How could these polar opposites co-exist? How could we worship the cult of thin and starve ourselves at one end of the scale, while at the other, ignorance, poverty, bloody-mindedness, junk-food, fast food and ready-made dinners have turned a huge section of the population into fat people? Fat, malnourished people. There is a very real danger of our children being the first generation to die younger than us as a result. I find that shocking and saddening and crazy.

Jamie's Return To School Dinners advert, 2006

Our relationship to food has changed as much as the food we eat. What was fuel – what we struggled to catch and kill or grow and harvest, the bare necessities of life with all its seasonal gluts and deficits, the enforced periods of austerity, preserving, storing, brining, pickling – has been succeeded by waste, the lack of a balanced diet, by stomach stapling and tummy tucks, super-sizing, snacking and all-you-can-eat buffets. What was about survival is now about conspicuous, wanton consumption, about capitalism gone mad. Even those aware of the fragility of the planet, the collapse of our eco-systems, the impact that the weather and oil have on agriculture in ways we are only just beginning to discover, believe

they can still reap and indulge and enjoy as much food as they wish as long as they have bought into green hedonism. They talk about composting and carbon footprints, food-miles and sustainability as though the discussion of food politics will somehow prevent what could possibly face us, a future where stir-crazy weather systems have more power and influence than anything else on the planet.

Without the ability to grow good food and move it from A to B, we are back in the Dark Ages but with fewer tools than we had before. We have lost land, the farmers and their skills and our cooking skills. If we are no longer able to produce what we need when the climate is so changed and uncertain around the world and prices fluctuate beyond our control, it will take more than a little government intervention of the sort we had in the Jarrow March Thirties, when there was a very real problem of nutrition and the poor really weren't getting enough calcium, vitamins and minerals simply because they couldn't afford them.

We may be the last generation to be able to indulge in novelty food fashion, the latest dish or ingredient, but perhaps it would not be a bad thing if we were thrown back on our own resources. Just getting the next generation to cook and understand where food comes from has to be an integral part of our children's education. Given the recent statistics that show how many children don't even recognise that milk comes from cows, it is obvious where we should start.

If the rural economy is compromised and government doesn't look after its greatest assets, the farmers and their land, our national obsession with celebrity chefs and food as TV entertainment will appear as no more than a transitory historical oddity reflecting a generation hungry to show it had succeeded. That they could indulge, treat famine as though it were a far-away problem which they could ignore so long as they could buy the farmed salmon and Californian strawberries that showed they had food-cred.

We should really begin to take food seriously again – and that means on television too.

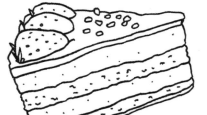

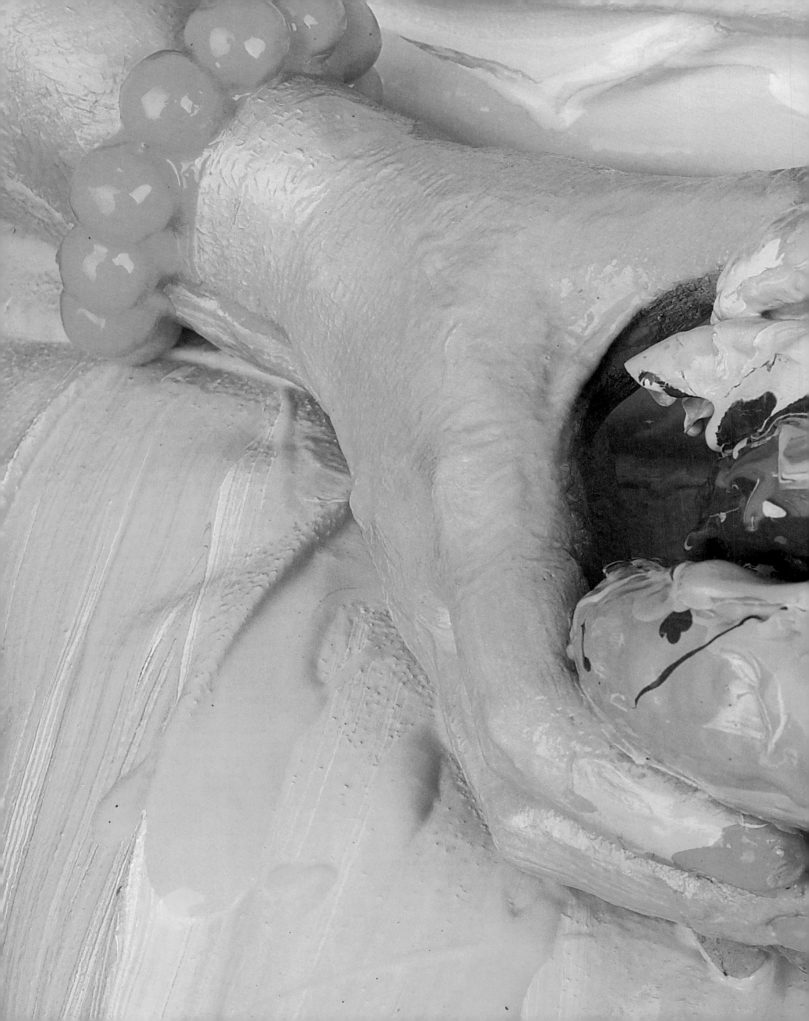

Cheeseburger, Boo Ritson

Chocolate Mousse

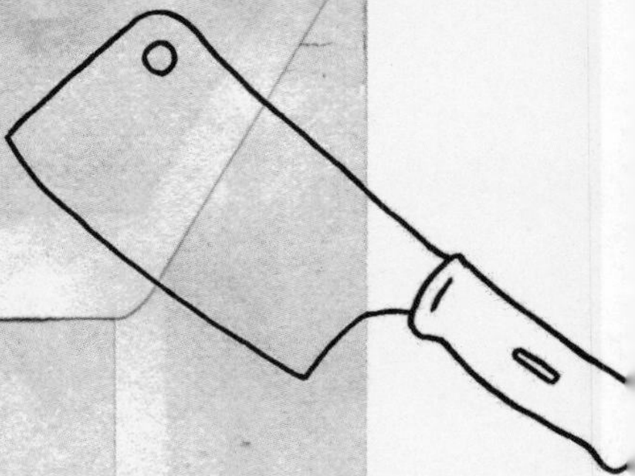

½ Pt — Double Cream

200 ml — Creme fraiche

150 g — Dark Chocolate 70% Coco

1 — Crunchie Bar

2 — tbspn. Tia Maria.

Melt the chocolate over a bain marie and remove from heat. Whisk in the creme fraiche until smooth. Whip the double cream and fold into the chocolate. Break up the crunchie bar and fold into the chocolate mousse. Divide between four cups or glasses and chill for 10 mins. Serve.

Gordon

Gordon Ramsay teaches DJ Chris Moyles all about home-made chicken curry on Channel 4's *The F Word*

Currying Up a Storm

Constructive criticism
Ramsay's F Word returns
Tonight 8.30pm

GORDON RAMSAY
How often do you have takeaways?
CHRIS MOYLES
Couple of times a week. I would say four, four to five times a week.
GORDON
Four times a week.
CHRIS
I got a Christmas card from my local Indian restaurant.
GORDON
Jesus Christ almighty. First name terms. I'm going to set a surprise for you. I'm going to phone them.
CHRIS
Please don't upset them.
GORDON
I won't upset them.
Telephone call to the Indian restaurant.
GORDON
Hi, it's Gordon Ramsay. I'm calling on behalf of one of your regular customers, Mr Chris Moyles. Do you know him?
MAHABUB
Yes I do, he's a regular customer of ours.
Background laughs.

GORDON
What does he normally take away? What is it?
MAHABUB
I think it's the chicken curries with no onions.
GORDON
The chicken curries with no onions, is that right?
MAHABUB
Yeah.
GORDON
Right, now, I'd like to place the exact same order delivered to *The F Word* restaurant. Listen, I'll give you a £20 tip if you get here within 20 minutes, OK?
MAHABUB
Yep, sure no problems. OK, we'll see you shortly.
GORDON
Thank you.
MAHABUB
Bye.
GORDON
Right, just as a challenge. No, no. I'm serious. I'm gonna show you before he gets here that we'll cook together.

CHRIS
When?
GORDON
Now.
CHRIS
I'm not going to cook.
GORDON
Something fresh, delicious, fast food curry. Let's go. Right. Ginger, chillies, garlic, lemon grass. Right, all into there. Just pour it all in OK, ease in, lemon grass. We're going to make, like, a lemon grass paste. OK, bit of oil, shake, shake, shake. That's it, good. OK... good. Right into the pan... good... nice.
Chris pours the lemon paste off and tips in the blending blade by mistake.
CHRIS
Oh no, no, the thing fell off.
GORDON
Not the fucking blade. Chicken in.
CHRIS
OK, you didn't tell me.
GORDON
Right, I'm doing the same. Lime leaves in, soy sauce in.
Gesturing to the soy sauce
All the way around.

127

CHRIS

How much?

GORDON

About 100ml. We've got to move our arse now otherwise fucking Mahabub will get here soon.

CHRIS

Trust me.

GORDON

In relation to what Chris is doing with the food

That's good.

CHRIS

Trust me.

GORDON

That's nice.

CHRIS

It will never be here in 20 minutes.

GORDON

(Holding out a stick of cinnamon) What's that? Seriously, come on, what is that? Come on.

CHRIS

I really don't know. I don't know. What is it?

GORDON

Come on.

CHRIS

I don't know! I don't know.

GORDON

It's a cinnamon stick.

CHRIS

Right, OK, is that what cinnamon is?

GORDON

OK. Chicken seared off. Yes.

CHRIS

Wow.

GORDON

Come on.

CHRIS

It's set on fire.

GORDON

What's the matter with you for God's sake?

CHRIS

Because it set fire.

GORDON

OK, and again.

CHRIS

Right.

GORDON

Smell that.

Holding out coconut milk

What does it smell of?

CHRIS

Cream.

GORDON

Oh fuck off. It's coconut milk. Right. OK. In the sauce. Now aren't you happy with that?

CHRIS

What, um, well, yeah. What do we do with these?

GORDON

Right, these are green beans, yes.

CHRIS

Right.

GORDON

That just gives it a little bit of body. Don't put them all in if you don't want them in.

CHRIS

No, I'm not putting them all in.

Chris now begins to chop up the coriander.

GORDON

Don't cut your fingers off. Right, now,

CHRIS

Yeah. What do I do with it? Just throw it in?

GORDON

Just now you've got to chop it. Do not cut your fingers, please!

CHRIS

(mock scream) Ahhhh. Laughter

GORDON

You fucking… Coriander in.

CHRIS

Out the way.

GORDON

The curry is nearly here. OK, now off, just all in there nicely, OK. OK. Good.

CHRIS

Howls

I've never made that noise before ever in my life.

GORDON

Course you have. Come on, come on.

CHRIS

I have. I'm coming, I'm coming. Bloody hell – fire.

GORDON

Right that's it. Let's go. Bring the apron. Come on quick.

CHRIS

Do I bring the food? What, what?

GORDON

That's part of the challenge. Bring the plate man. You forgot the plate. Go.

CHRIS

You didn't tell me to bring it.

GORDON

That's the challenge, with the plate it's there. Ah, shit. Oh God. OK, OK. Dear oh dear oh dear. Well done. Yeah fucking hell and look who's here – Mahabub.

Applause

GORDON

How are you, big boy?

MAHABUB

Not bad. How are you?

CHRIS

Nice to see you.

GORDON

Let's see what's in there.

MAHABUB

Chicken curry, no onions

CHRIS

You should also get a free poppadom.

GORDON

Free poppadom – is it in?

MAHABUB

Yeah, there is.

GORDON

Now, we should have a taste side by side. Yes

CHRIS

I just cooked this.

GORDON

Right, Soph, have a taste. And you as well.

CHRIS

I cooked this by the way.

GORDON

How is that?

CHRIS

I'm gonna wait for Gordon's reaction before I eat.

GORDON

That's nice.

CHRIS

Really? Seriously?

GORDON

It's seriously nice.

CHRIS

That's very nice.

Gordon then moves on to try Mahabub's curry

CHRIS

Don't get me banned?

GORDON

It's nice but very greasy. But Mr Moyles likes it, doesn't he? I have to say, I prefer the one you made. Let's be honest, it's a lot quicker. And just think good food can be made faster and better than a takeaway.

CHRIS

Yes.

CHRIS

I did a good job.

GORDON

You did.

CHRIS

I know, yeah.

Club Sandwich (detail), Boo Ritson

All-Day Breakfast, Boo Ritson

Hugh Fearnley-Whittingstall leaves *The River Cottage* for the aisles of our supermarkets

Supersize Supermarkets

The other day, I caught the middle of an interview with a man from one of the larger supermarkets on the radio. He was lamenting the fact that, at the moment, *only* 35 per cent of the urban population and *only* 25 per cent of the rural population have access to all four of the big supermarkets.

Only? I thought. Isn't that enough? Not for him it wasn't. What he wants, or what he says he wants, is everyone in Britain to have the choice of shopping at all four major supermarkets.

And I wondered: does anyone listening think this guy is really speaking for them, as a shopper? Was anyone thinking, yeah! That's what I want – four different supermarkets within easy driving distance. Why not build them right outside my door? I can't imagine why anyone would want that. But if you think you do, you should be careful what you wish for… because if the big four ever achieve that level of saturation, 'choice' is the last thing you'll have. Supermarket shopping will be all you're allowed for the rest of your days – you're not going to have any-where else to buy your daily bread.

But then I realised that everyone having access to four supermarkets isn't really what he wants, either. What he really wants is everyone having access to one of his stores. Of course, he put it slightly differently. He put it in a way that allowed him to express his ideal as if it's some kind of gift to the consumer.

And this is what really got my goat. This is the big lie ped-dled every day by the supermarkets. They are constantly telling us that all they ever do is give the consumer what they want. But time and time again they have been guilty of putting their stores where they are emphatically not wanted, and of rail-roading or simply buying out local planning policy to do so.

In the end this man, with his happy, smiley but curiously soulless voice, left me in no doubt about one thing – what they all want is total domination of the British retail sector. And they want it not for the benefit of local communities or for their staff, not for their suppliers, nor even for their loyal customers: they want it for their balance sheets, and their shareholders, and themselves.

In the end this man, with his happy, smiley but curiously soulless voice, left me in no doubt about one thing – what they all want is total domination of the British retail sector

All this, of course, is a massive threat to local food com-munities, by which I mean small town high streets, local markets and farm shops. And I know this from personal experience. Even in the relatively affluent West Country where I live, the market towns and high streets are not what they were before the big fat supermarkets – one, two, sometimes three of them – came and sat on the edge of town and sucked the lifeblood out. In fact, they're often a shadow of their former selves.

How can local businesses, independent grocers and small artisan food stores survive this onslaught of land acquisition and intensive grasping for market share? Often they can't, and the increasing prevalence of what have been dubbed ghost towns, or clone towns, is proof of that.

What we are witnessing is an ugly, brutish fight to win the lion's share of a massive global business selling something that we all need, every single day: food

What scares me the most, however, is not that supermarkets are ignoring the issue of sourcing local food – it's that they're finally acknowledging it. And it scares me because they are beginning to tell us that we needn't worry about local markets, looking after small producers and reducing food miles, because they will do it all for us. They'll dress up a little corner of their store to look like a French market stall and pull in a few local cheeses and a couple of cauliflowers. There you go, they'll say, there's your local food.

This is not a commitment to local food. It is cynical window-dressing. In fact, it's worse than window-dressing: it's deceit, a bare-faced lie about what their business is really up to. It's like a crack dealer deciding that it would be good for public relations if he sold fudge, or flowers, as well as drugs. He'll happily sell you the flowers, he might even give them away, because he knows he'll get you further down the aisle with his main line of business: selling drugs. Buy one gram, get one free. And a free assemble-it-yourself crack pipe with every £100 you spend.

What we are witnessing is an ugly, brutish fight to win the lion's share of a massive global business selling something that we all need, every single day: food. We are innocent bystanders, caught in the cross-fire, and we are finding it very difficult to influence the outcome.

The supermarkets will argue that we benefit hugely from this fight as the cost of food comes down, and down, and down. Many of us may agree – and if you are genuinely struggling to meet the weekly food bill, then that's understandable. But many more of us go along with this as if it's somehow unchangeable and inevitable – it's just the way things are. Either we lack the energy or the focus to fight for something better, or we are cursed with a mentality that can't resist a bargain, even if we can well afford something better.

Well, let's try and banish that bargain mentality, find a bit of focus, and consider the true cost of that price war. I believe it's destroying our farmers, and the land they work on. In particular, it's putting huge stress on the livestock we raise and kill for meat. The constant pressure to cut prices has a direct effect on animal welfare. I've visited intensive poultry units and pig farms – and I've always said that anyone who witnessed how these so-called farms are run would not want anything to do with their products. Pain and suffering are built into these systems. And when you see how an intensively farmed chicken or sow lives, the extra pound or two for a free-range alternative suddenly seems worth paying. And that's something I was finally able to prove in the television programmes I made last year – by taking people who loved cheap chicken, and had never questioned where it came from, to see for themselves how it's produced. Not one of them eats it now.

But it's not just animal welfare we should be worrying about. This kind of factory farming potentially has a devastating human cost: BSE, Foot and Mouth, and Bird Flu are all products of human greed, or perhaps human desperation, in the bid to deliver endless mountains of cheap meat. Taken as a whole, industrial farming across the globe is a bubbling pressure cooker of unsustainable and dangerous practice. And the heat under that pressure cooker, constant and unrelenting, is coming from the supermarkets. When the top blows off, we're all going to be in an awful mess.

Finally, the real reason why this issue means so much to me personally is that I feel the supermarkets are systematically destroying our food culture. They are reducing our national diet to bland and repetitive sludge. They are denying the seasonality of our food-producing landscape. They are promoting sameness and mediocrity.

Those who put quality before profit do not thrive in this culture – they are marginalised. If you would rather grow a tomato that tastes great than one that is perfectly shaped and lasts a month in the fridge, then the supermarket doesn't want to know you. If your bread is made by hand, in small batches, and raised by natural yeast, then you can forget it. If it's made by computerised machines and raised by chemicals, well done, you're in.

The River Cottage, from 1999

The fact is, the supermarkets now control the means of production. You have to do it their way, or go to the wall. This is a totalitarian food state, from farm to plate, from earth to mouth. Consequently, Britain is in danger of becoming a duller place to eat, and a sadder place to live.

But it doesn't have to be like that. If we're going to find the solution to this, it's going to come in part from consumers and the choices they make. But we're now also looking to the government to help protect suppliers and communities from the blight of these all-consuming beasts. Hopefully, its response will take us a lot further down the road to true consumer choice, as opposed to supermarket hegemony.

Courgette Souffle

Slice about a kilo of Courgettes and cook gently with olive oil, garlic and a shake of salt.

When soft, pulpy + reduced, add ¼ litre thick bechemel and a handful of grated cheese. Mix well.

Seperate 5 eggs. Mix yolks in with Courgettes and whisk egg whites until stiff. Fold together.

Pile into ramekins, or a large souffle dish love Hugh

10-15 minutes at 200°C X

Earthly Powers

As environmental issues rise to the top of the political agenda, Channel 4 will continue to raise awareness about the science, economics and politics of climate change. In 2005, Marcel Theroux weighed up all the arguments about man-made climate change starting from a neutral point of view. He heard all sides of the argument from James Lovelock to oil executives in Shell. Six years later, *The Great Global Warming Swindle* raised hackles among some environmentalists as it gave voice to those sceptical about mankind's role in climate change. Phil Agland's powerful documentaries, such as *Baka: People of the Rainforest* and *Fragile Earth*, were visionary in their time, exploring man's relationship to his environment. *Channel 4 News* keeps the environment at the top of the agenda, allowing time for spirited debates on this crucial issue.

<u>Yellow leaves</u>
<u>wrapped around the split end of a fallen bough</u>

Cornell, New York
3 November 2004
Andy Goldsworthy

Phil Agland is the award-winning director of Channel 4 documentaries including *Beyond the Clouds*, *Baka* and *Shanghai Vice*. Here, he unearths another point of view

Ali, a member of the Baka tribe, from <u>Baka: People of the Rainforest</u>, 1987

Human Survival

<u>Beyond the Clouds</u>, 1994

<u>Fragile Earth</u>, from 1982

<u>Baka: People of the Rainforest</u>, 1987

Chimpanzee! The hoots and calls I knew so well were echoing through the rainforest. I could hardly believe my luck. I had been here in this remote corner of south-east Cameroon for almost two years and it had proved so difficult to track these magnificent animals in the dense forest.

Heart in mouth, I crawled slowly through the under-growth. Ahead, I could see movement. But it wasn't a chimpanzee. It was better. There in the clearing, imitating a mother chimpanzee was my friend, Likano. Slung under his belly was his four-year-old son, Ali. Surely they were just playing games. But no, something else was happening – something that was to stand my own sense of education on its head.

Likano was one of the elders of a Baka Pygmy village I had been living in for two years making a documentary for Channel 4, back in 1985. As I watched them, Likano carefully broke off a twig and started to prod the holes of a terrestrial termite. Within seconds, a large fat juicy termite was clinging to the stick. Was this tonight's supper? No, far from it. Likano was explaining to his son that this was a 'worker' termite, not a queen or a soldier and that this was how a chimpanzee mother would 'fish' for termites. So what, you might ask, is so interesting about that?

Well, when Jane Goodall made a similar observation during her groundbreaking study of chimpanzees, her conclusions rocked modern behavioural science. For she deduced that this was clear evidence of a non-human fashioning and using a 'tool' to gain an advantage. Up until the 1960s science had deemed this to be what made us, homo sapiens, unique in the animal kingdom – the ability to fashion tools, to make technology and shape our destiny.

It just so happens that the Baka made this observation many hundreds, if not thousands, of years before. Not only that, but they deemed it important enough to hand down the knowledge from father to son – in just the way that was happening before my very eyes. Likano was passing on to little Ali not only knowledge but also respect for the chimpanzee and the forest world she lived in.

During our time with the Baka we grew to love and respect our new-found friends as the people they really were – not as anthropological curiosities, nor victims of a cultural 'dead end' but as sophisticated people living a dynamic, interactive life with the forest around them.

These two years took me into a world both physically and emotionally far removed from the one I grew up in. Likano had no concept of a world beyond this forest. The 'ocean', for example, was unimaginable, as were deserts, or even the concept of 'countries'. Planes flying at 35,000 feet over the forest were exactly the size they appeared in the sky – tiny. The fact that they held several hundred people seemed just plain silly. It was as if we had been transported back 10,000 years to a life before the 'modern' world. This 'suspension' from my own world made me really think about where both worlds were heading.

Likano would often talk about the sort of life he wanted for Ali. He talked vaguely of education, of learning to read and write. Perhaps Ali should leave the forest and become part of this 'country' called Cameroon, a 'country' he had no real concept of, but it was something he felt might be good for his children's future because people talked about it being 'modern' – and he had seen motor cars and trucks.

Environmentalist Mark Lynas sifts through the climatic changes of the last 25 years

Curved sticks
laid around
river boulder
took longer to collect materials
than to make the work

Woody Creek, Aspen
September 2006
Andy Goldsworthy

Food

About 815 million people in developing countries do not have enough food in today's world, a figure that has dropped only slightly from 1982, when about 900 million went hungry. Because of population growth in this period, the proportion of the overall population lacking sufficient nutrition dropped much more – thanks almost entirely to economic development in Asia. In sub-Saharan Africa, however, things largely got worse over the last 25 years in terms of food resources.

Acid Rain

Although acid rain is still a major problem in eastern Europe and China, the UK has seen a substantial improvement since the 1980s. Between 1987 and 2004 sulphur dioxide emissions fell by 82 per cent, and resulting acid rain by half. This is largely due to new regulations forcing power stations to scrub sulphur pollution from smokestacks, and the switch away from coal to gas.

Birds

In the last 25 years, many UK bird species which were once thought of as common or even as pests, have seen their populations decline dramatically. These include starlings, house sparrows and herring gulls, which join cuckoos, willow tits, yellowhammers and several others on the 2007 'Biodiversity Action Plan' list of birds that have seen their populations fall by half in the last quarter of a century. Woodland and farmland species are worst-hit due to development and intensive agriculture, but some garden species are doing well. Blue tits, great tits and collared doves all increased their populations in recent years.

So, would that be a good thing? Should Ali leave the forest and be 'educated'? What, indeed, is the future for all 'primitive' cultures like the Baka? Should they be encouraged to modernise or should we, the 'modern' world, learn from them?

With the twin challenges of global warming and global terrorism, we live in uncertain times. More than ever, it is a time to take stock of who we are and what kind of world we want to bequeath to our children. In the natural world, Charles Darwin taught us that (biological) diversity is the key to stability. The more species there are, the more stable the environment. Perhaps we could extend this concept to cultural diversity. Perhaps this huge reservoir of human knowledge and experience is our greatest asset in the troubled times ahead. Perhaps the Baka can help sort *us* out.

This was clear evidence of a non-human fashioning and using a 'tool' to gain an advantage

----

So what do we mean by 'cultural richness' and hasn't it all been safely disseminated into computers by now anyway? Which of the myriad 'building blocks' of cultural and social stability can we throw away in reinventing our frantic modern world?

Back in the 1960s, the great French botanist Letouzy made a groundbreaking study of the Pygmy language. Among his many surprising discoveries was that 95 per cent of the current Baka language has been borrowed from the outside world. The remaining five per cent has survived only because it describes the world of the interior of the rainforest where no one else treads, save with chainsaw and bulldozer. This part of their language is home to a knowledge of which we still know so little.

It seems clear that the potential loss of human knowledge stored unknown in cultural minorities around the world might be just as catastrophic as the loss of biodiversity itself. Cultural diversity and its store of knowledge is the 'ballast' of humanity. Contained within it is our cultural memory. It offers knowledge of ourselves and of our environment. It also offers us real help in understanding who we are, where we've come from and what sort of stable society we should seek in order to deal with the radical challenges ahead.

After I came home from Africa, I decided to switch to China for what was to become another television series for Channel 4, *Beyond the Clouds*. Back in 1989, it was already clear that China would dominate the century ahead, but who were they, these Chinese? We really had no idea, beyond a billion people all looking the same.

'You will never find traditional China, it has already gone,' I was told time and time again. Well, my experience with the Baka helped me. There are over one billion Han Chinese but there are also 56 'minority' cultures. What if I looked among them? Could they be hiding some of the secrets of China's past?

After three months of looking, I stumbled across the Nashi people of Lijiang in the south-west of China. Most Chinese will tell you that the Nashi are a minority people with a quaint matrilineal past, something that should be preserved, perhaps, for tourists. But when I dug deeper into the lives of the people of Lijiang, I found that they were living a Chinese Han culture dating back almost a thousand years. Chinese music, architecture, moon festivals, medicines and rituals all rewrapped in Nashi costume. They had adopted these Chinese customs in the aftermath of Kubla Khan's conquest in 1253 and have kept them 'in aspic' ever since. What I was seeing in 1989, amongst the Nashi people of Lijiang, was a vibrant, living 'old' China – a way of life consigned to history books elsewhere.

I was to spend the next ten years filming the rich seam of stories thrown up by the colliding forces of China's past and future. So much has been lost in that time, as old communities have been shunted aside in the race to modernise. There is little doubt that this wholesale dumping of the past threatens China's long-term social stability.

Both on a local and a global scale, we cut our cultural roots at our peril. But sometimes what appears to be an irretrievable loss is not so. Sometimes, a 'lone ranger' comes riding to the rescue of us all. One such man is from Micronesia. Polynesians suffered a catastrophic loss of identity after Captain Cook discovered the islands of the Pacific in the 18th century. A proud and technologically innovative society collapsed within a few decades. For 200 years, Polynesians became second-class citizens in their own islands.

It was believed that the Pacific islands must have been colonised from South America. In 1976 a small group of Hawaiians set out to disprove this by doing the seemingly impossible. They wanted to sail a twin-hulled canoe four thousand kilometres from Hawaii to Tahiti in order to prove that Polynesians settled the Pacific from Asia, two thousand years before Captain Cook and at a time when Europeans still thought the world was square.

The Hawaiians built their canoe but had no one was able to navigate in the fashion of their ancestors – over vast distances, without modern technology. They searched the length and breadth of the Pacific until they finally found one man, Mau Piailug, living two thousand miles away on the tiny island of Satawal. He, it seemed, was the last man alive who was able to navigate the ocean by the stars. And it was he who subsequently sailed the Hawaiian canoe all the way to Tahiti.

In so doing, he and his canoe became a symbol of Polynesian pride, acting as a catalyst for cultural renewal throughout the Pacific. His skills have now been passed on to a new generation of sailors. The direct result of this is that today Polynesians see themselves not as a disparate bunch of scattered islands, but as a proud nation occupying ten million square miles of ocean, arguably the largest nation on Earth.

But for the gossamer thread of one man linking Polynesia with her past, this resurgence of Polynesian self-esteem would have been impossible. Not only that, but in passing on the skills of his ancestors, he has equipped Polynesians with the ancient skills to survive an environmental holocaust. As Mau Piailug says, 'What happens to my kids when the oil runs out or the satellite-navigation systems fail?'

History tells us that great civilisations can collapse spectacularly. If the plug is ever pulled on our increasingly technological world, we may have to turn to our fellow human beings who live in the rainforests, deserts and oceans of the world for clues about our own survival.

Curved branches
worked around tree

San Anselmo, California
27 July 2006
Andy Goldsworthy

Coral reefs

Over the last 30 years, reefs in the Caribbean have lost 80 per cent of their living coral cover; globally, a half of all coral reefs are under threat of collapse, whilst a fifth have already been destroyed. Since the 1980s, coral bleaching caused by climate change has become a major issue – in 1998 a sixth of the world's coral reefs were damaged by a major bleaching event. Some have begun to recover, but more bleaching took place in warm waters in 2002 (especially on the Great Barrier Reef in Australia) and in 2005 in the Caribbean.

Ecological footprint

According to WWF's Living Planet Index, humanity first went into 'ecological overshoot' in the late 1980s. That was the first time that the human economy began to use the planet's natural resources faster than the biosphere was able to regenerate them. To use a banking metaphor, this is like living off the capital of the Earth, rather than the interest. This overshoot is now increasing every year, and reached about 25 per cent in 2003. The majority of this increasing resource consumption took place in rich countries, particularly the United States and in Western Europe.

Population

In 1982 the world population stood at 4.6 billion. Now there are 6.7 billion of us – nearly a third more human beings in the space of only a quarter of a century. Despite these spectacular figures, the growth in population is actually slower now than then. For example, between 1980 and 1985, another 403 million people joined the overall population. Between 2000 and 2005, that figure dropped to 390 million. That still adds up to about 80 million new people a year, or 9,200 each hour – a population about the size of Germany is being added annually, the majority in developing countries.

The Aral Sea

The Aral Sea, once the world's fourth-largest lake, was already in decline by the early 1980s after Soviet engineers dammed the rivers which feed it. The fishing industry had also disappeared by that time. By the beginning of the 1990s, the lake area had declined by half, exposing 28,000 square kilometres of dried-out lakebed. This became a source of dust, with salt-laden winds carrying chemical residues, travelling as far afield as the Arctic and Pakistan. By 1999 it had split into two and continued to reduce in area. Since 2005, the northern half has recovered somewhat, thanks to the construction of a dam between the north and the south – some fishing has even resumed. But the southern part of the former Aral Sea has been left to its fate, and may even disappear altogether.

Amazonia

Since 1970 Brazil has destroyed over 600,000 square kilometres of rainforest. Between 2000 and 2006, 150,000 km² were lost, an area larger than Greece. Two-thirds of this was converted to cattle ranching, and the rate of destruction strongly shadows Brazil's overall economic growth. High growth equals high rates of forest clearance. Amazonian deforestation fell by 60 per cent between 2004 and 2007, according to the Brazilian government due to low prices for crops and tougher law enforcement.

The Ozone Layer

In the early 1980s there was a huge public outcry at the discovery of an ozone 'hole' and the resistance by the chemicals industry to demands that ozone-depleting substances like CFCs be phased out. This was perhaps the first major 'global' environmental issue, and is something of a success story: in 1987 the Montreal Protocol agreed the eventual phase-out of CFCs, first in the rich world and then, later, in developing countries. Ozone-depleting chemicals are now declining in the atmosphere, and although 2006 saw the largest ever Antarctic ozone hole, the ozone layer is expected to recover by mid-century.

Sheet of ice
lifted from nearby pond
wedged in the cleft
between two trees
that had once been a single tree
until split by lightening
covered in wet leaves
torn, crack, line

Tatton, Cheshire
23 November 2005
Andy Goldsworthy

Marcel Theroux reflects on his
Channel 4 documentary, *The End
of the World As We Know It*

The End of the World As We Know It

This past summer, I took my one-year-old daughter to visit her 96-year-old great grandmother at her home in Massachusetts. It was during that week in August when climate activists threatened to disrupt flights out of Heathrow Airport. I thought they were pushing their luck, pinning the blame for global warming on a bunch of harassed holiday makers who fly occasionally, probably reluctantly, and in great discomfort. I remembered meeting an American lawyer a year before who had flown to London from California for the weekend simply because he wanted to maintain his frequent flyer status. Couldn't they have bum-rushed *his* plane? I felt indignant: I'd made a flipping 90 minute documentary on climate change. I knew what my carbon footprint was when these so-called climate activists were still in short trousers.

I reflected on what a quick journey it had been – from disbelief about climate change, to a dawning realisation that it was real and a sense of hostility towards the sceptics, to the inevitable backlash; pure annoyance with the self-righteous climate zealots and a wish to prove them wrong. And that was just me.

When we started making our film about climate change, I had a vague sense that there was a likelihood that human activity had contributed to the phenomenon of global warming. By the time we finished, I was in no doubt that the evidence pointed to a real and probably disastrous man-made heating of the planet.

I came to this conclusion over the course of the film after talking to scientists and insurers, and to Inuit hunters in northern Alaska who admitted that their winters were warming but simultaneously wanted oil production to expand in the far north because they stood to profit from it. Yes, the hockey stick graph was persuasive, the one that shows the extraordinary and unprecedented increase of carbon dioxide in the planet's atmosphere since about the time of the industrial revolution. And so was talking to scientists at Britain's Hadley Centre. And so was meeting James Lovelock, the originator of the Gaia hypothesis, which holds that the Earth behaves like a single, self-regulating organism. Lovelock took a twinkly delight in offering the direst predictions of what was about to happen to our planet – and the dwindling likelihood that we would be able to effect any meaningful change for the better. Even the head of Shell told us that climate change was happening.

I suggested in the film that nuclear power was the least bad of all the possible solutions. To support this – admittedly provocative – argument, I went to Chernobyl to compare the aftermath of the disaster there with the some of the bleak scenarios presented by the scientists we had talked to.

Walking around the abandoned ruins of the Soviet city Pripyat – evacuated after the Chernobyl nuclear disaster – I had a sense, which has never quite left me, of having been given a glimpse of the end of the world. So while the title of our film sounded like a typical piece of television hyperbole, I felt that the journey I had undergone justified it.

Now, as I'm a non-scientist, I never expected people to regard mine as the final word on climate change.

When our programme was aired, we took some criticism for what some people perceived as a lack of balance. It's axiomatic that in making a TV programme of this kind you show balance, but in discussing climate change, the term balance is very misleading.

I think that the debate on climate change has been retarded by the instinct that we have, when covering an issue, to present it as a debate between two equally plausible scenarios. The merits of this approach are obvious, but they're not universal. Does a balanced discussion of evolution mean that every mention of Darwin be countered with an acknowledgement that some people are entitled to the view that the world was made in seven days? How accurate a reflection is it of the state of research about Shakespeare to balance every mainstream academic with one who finds Baconian acrostics in the plays?

Similarly, where climate change is concerned, constantly giving airtime to its opposing viewpoints actually understates the degree of consensus that's emerged in the science, and leaves people with the sense that the case for man-made global warming is largely unproven – which is inaccurate.

And yet, it's also clear that scepticism and doubt are positive attributes. Climate change sceptics would surely point out that many principles we now hold to be fundamental – universal suffrage, freedom of religion, that our earth revolves around the sun – originated from a marginalised and often persecuted set of freethinkers. Those who voice doubts about climate change obviously do so for a variety of reasons, but I'd put them in three broad groups. Firstly, there are some scientists – a smaller number than you might think – and their supporters who have an intellectual objection to some or all of the parts of the following proposition: the earth is heating up because of human activity and we ought to do something about it.

Virtually no one now disputes that the earth has been getting hotter, but there are those who claim that it's not caused by us, and/or that it's not sufficiently serious for us to worry about stopping it. It's entirely right that people should be able to advance these views and have the chance to produce evidence to support them. On the whole, however, they have failed to do so.

Having said that, I fully expect to be buttonholed when I'm in the pub by the second kind of climate sceptic and told that I'm wrong. This man will subject me to a tirade about sunspots, volcanic dust and the errors in the hockey stick graph while his jabbing finger and spit-flecked lips give him away to be a monomaniac. I'll share with him what I have learned of the science, but it will make no difference. He's made his mind up and that's final. There will also always be people who maintain that HIV doesn't cause Aids, that the attack on 9/11 was a CIA conspiracy and that Marxism-Leninism, properly applied, will cure the ailments of human society. What unifies the adherents of these arguments is that there is no evidence that will satisfy them. Their arguments are zombie ones, undead beliefs, stumbling around with heads and arms missing, and absolutely impervious to the missiles of logic.

I must admit that I'm baffled by the degree of certainty that these opponents of the conventional view of climate change seem to be able to muster. It seems to me that our understanding of the way the world works is always probabilistic and tentative. And in a probabilistic and tentative way, the mass of our scientists has been giving us the bad news.

It's the very badness of the news, I think, that creates resistance in the wavering sceptic. This is the third and broadest category of sceptic, ranging from those who dismiss climate change as a media scare story, to those who may feel that there is something to it but resent being told to forego an annual holiday, or use the car less.

And who could fail to have sympathy with the contrarian instinct that hates the sight of a juggernaut in full flow? Isn't it strange how many millionaires and pop stars are now concerned about climate change – and want *me* to alter *my* lifestyle? There was something particularly awful about Live Earth and the spectacle of being preached to about carbon footprints by a lot of people with private jets. Conversely, the not-very-well concealed anti-capitalist agenda of some in the environmental movement has tainted the issue by association, making global warming seem chiefly to be the concern of those who think modern life is rubbish.

The End of the World As We Know it, 2005

Our media too has something to answer for here. There's a sense of the boy who cried wolf. We've lectured people about meteorites, obesity, eating eggs, mobile phone masts, MMR and leukaemia clusters with the same doomy music and grim prognoses. The wavering sceptic has learned to tune out the ambient level of hysteria associated with nearly everything we hear on news and current affairs programmes, and assumes that the media will soon contradict it themselves on this issue as well. As it happened, two years after airing my programme, Channel 4 aired *The Great Global Warming Swindle*, which assembled a gallery of climate change sceptics to assert that everything we'd said in the previous documentary was wrong.

And where does that leave the rest of us? I wish I could tell you. Climate change seems to demand the sort of practical response to crisis that we humans are good at – fire in chip pan, get tea towel, put out fire – but at times the debate around it resembles one of those wars over religious doctrine that start out seemingly trivial and then go on to disfigure human history. And I'm not very sanguine when I think how long it's taken for people to accept and then act on the link between smoking and cancer.

Since finishing the film, I've wrestled with my feelings about it, tried to keep up with the science, and wondered how best to act responsibly. That's all I can recommend to anyone.

But I want to add that thinking about climate change affected me profoundly. Researching the subject awoke in me a vertiginous sense of existing in geological time. It struck me forcibly that we as a race weren't always here and won't necessarily be here for ever, and that the cumulative impact of our behaviour is altering the planet on which we live on and making it less habitable. This is an extraordinary and indigestible set of thoughts to carry on the tube and around the supermarket each Saturday. But I also find it a useful memento mori, like the skull in Holbein's *Ambassadors*, which challenges its subjects to reflect on their own mortality and the shape of the world without them.

Sheet of ice
lifted from nearby river pool
wedged between rocks
over the river
covered with wet elm leaves
torn, crack, line

Scaur Water, Dumfriesshire
December 2005
Andy Goldsworthy

The Rainforests

'Save the Rainforests' first became a popular rallying cry in the 1980s, and interest peaked with high-profile campaigns to reduce deforestation in the Amazon by celebrities like Sting. So what has actually happened since then? In 1982, the rate of tropical deforestation was calculated at 11.3 million hectares each year. But between 1990 and 2000 the situation actually deteriorated, with average annual losses increasing to 15.2 million hectares. Since 2000, tropical deforestation has continued at about 16 million hectares a year – hardly a success for the 'Save the Rainforest' campaign. However, total global forest loss is actually slowing down, however – thanks partly to a small expansion of tree cover in Europe which has already lost almost all its natural old-growth forest, but more importantly to the expansion of artificial forests: plantations.

Mangrove Forests

Coastal mangrove forests – which are vitally important as nurseries for fish, as well as providing protection from storms (and even tsunamis) – have been badly affected by the rise in shrimp production in places like Bangladesh. In the last 20 years, more than a third of mangrove forest area has been cleared, half of that for aquaculture. Currently, 2,800 square kilometres of mangrove forest is destroyed each year.

Fisheries

Harvests of wild fish in the seas peaked in the late 1980s, and have declined ever since – due almost entirely to overfishing, which has left too many boats chasing too few fish. By 2003 the oceanic fish catch had fallen back to levels last seen in 1982, about 70 million tonnes. Overfishing has left three quarters of the world's fish stocks either fished to the limit or over-exploited. Only ten per cent of stocks of big fish species like tuna still remain, and shark populations have crashed too due to fishing for their fins. Many fishermen have shifted to exploiting deeper ocean species, which – because of the long lifetimes and slow reproduction rates of species like Patagonian toothfish and orange roughy – are even more vulnerable.

Eleven arches
Scottish sandstone

The Farm, New Zealand
2005
Andy Goldsworthy

Climate Change

Over the past 30 years, global temperatures have risen by 0.6°C – a much faster rate of change than earlier in the century. 2005 was the hottest year globally according to NASA, whilst the five warmest years on record have all occurred since 1998. Global carbon emissions were 5.1 billion tonnes in 1982 – by 2004 this had risen to 7.6 billion, driving atmospheric concentrations of CO_2 from 341 parts per million in 1982 to 382 today.

The Poles

The poles have seen some of the most dramatic changes. In the Arctic, a fifth of the sea ice has melted in the past 30 years, with the highest melt ever recorded – in 2005 – quickly gazumped by an even more catastrophic ice loss in 2007. In the Antarctic, sea ice has been more stable, but ice shelves fringing the Antarctic Peninsula have gradually collapsed. The Larsen A ice shelf collapsed in 1995, the Wilkins ice shelf in 1998 and Larsen B – in a spectacular month-long disintegration – in 2002. In 2005 the first ever incidence of widespread inland melting on Antarctica was detected by satellites; at its height, an area the size of California had begun to thaw, with melting reaching to within 500 kilometres of the pole itself.

Greenland Ice

The area of the Greenland ice sheet subject to summer melting has increased by 54 per cent between 1979 and 2005, with an extra 137 cubic kilometres of water hitting the North Atlantic. This is now causing a sea level rise of 0.3 millimetres per year as the melt rate continues to accelerate.

Glaciers

Mountain glaciers have seen an accelerated decline in the last 25 years. A global tally kept by the World Glacier Monitoring Service shows that this retreat has accelerated since 1990 – since 1980 the world's highland glaciers have lost, on average, ten metres of thickness in total. Tropical glaciers have been worst-hit – in Peru, the Andean Cordilleras have lost a third of their ice, with some glaciers vanishing altogether. In the Russian Caucasus 94 per cent of glaciers – which are a main source of water for the Caspian Sea – retreated between 1985 and 2000, by 200 metres in length on average. Whilst Scandinavian glaciers bucked the trend for a while thanks to increased snowfall, even they have begun to show strong losses in the last five years.

The Weather

The number of people affected and the direct economic losses vary hugely from year to year due to the random variability of the weather. But superimposed on this is a long-term upward trend, with losses of about 40 billion in 1982 compared to one billion in 2004 and 200 billion in 2005 (thanks in particular, to Hurricane Katrina's devastating impact on New Orleans). The number of people affected by weather-related disasters rose from an average of 97 million a year in the early 1980s to 260 million a year since 2001. Most people die from weather-related extremes in developing countries – an exception was the 2003 European heatwave, which killed upwards of 30 thousand people across the continent, including two thousand in the UK.

Hurricanes

The number of tropical cyclones formed each year varies hugely, and there is no evidence to show that, globally, storms have become any more frequent over the last quarter of a century. However, one scientific study suggests that hurricanes have become markedly more powerful since the mid-1970s, as would be expected from increasing sea temperatures resulting from global warming. In the Atlantic basin, the year 2005 broke records, with the strongest storm ever measured in the region (Hurricane Wilma) hitting the Caribbean. Overall, the number of the strongest storms – Categories 4 and 5 – also seems to have increased over the last 35 years.

<u>Poppy petals</u>
<u>wrapped around</u>
<u>splintered wood</u>
<u>held with water</u>

Woodperry, Oxfordshire
5 July 2004
Andy Goldsworthy

Richard Mabey, the naturalist and author of *Country Matters*, separates the woods from the trees

Sermon in Wood

In 1787, John Wesley, founder of Methodism and charismatic outdoor preacher, decided to create a sermon in wood. He bound two beech saplings together in an Irish garden, hoping that as they matured they would grow closer together and become a model of the unity of nonconformism and orthodox Christianity of which he dreamed. The pleaching took, and for a while there was an ecumenical intertwining. But the trees had agendas of their own. Breakaway branches began to shoot off in all directions. The point where the trees had been joined became a mass of argumentative wood, distorted by scars and bosses and rot-holes. And above them rose two quite new trunks, off on their own unruly business, their own counter-sermon about independence.

The story of Wesley's beeches is a comic allegory of our ancient and contrary relationships with trees. The shepherd of men sought to manipulate their longevity and grandeur for his own ends, to be reverent and masterly at the same time. Trees have been cast in these ambivalent roles since the beginnings of civilisation. They're essential to human culture as raw materials and regulators

of the climate, yet are physical impediments to human 'progress'. Collectively, they've been used as metaphors for the family, for the body politic, for life itself, but also as symbols of chaos. There has been a mythical (and forbidden) Tree of Knowledge and a real tree of knowledge, which dropped its revelatory apple onto Newton's head. In Norse mythology the 'world tree', Yggdrasil, was the ash, whose branches spread over and unified the whole globe. In England, in a more secular vein, it's the oak which has been the symbol of the strength of the nation and the resilient 'heart' of its people.

Yet simultaneously, forests of ash and oak have been hacked down to make way for cities. They've been regarded as refuges for the lawless (Robin Hood now replaced by the hoodie), as wastes of space, as land not yet in a state of grace. In 1712 the writer John Morton summed up the prevailing attitude when he pronounced, 'In a country full of civilised inhabitants, timber could not be suffered to grow. It must give way to fields and pastures, which are of more immediate use and concern to life.' The field versus the forest. Civilisation versus the

wilderness. But also, in our own time, the timber tree versus the ornamental, utility set against beauty – or ecological value.

What is it about these obstinate and immobile beings that has such an indiscriminate hold on us? I think it has something to do with the way they make us recalibrate time. It isn't simply that trees outlive us in life span. They seem immortal, sprouting again like Sir Gawain's Green Knight when they're beheaded. Above all, their presence is inescapable. They tower into the sky, blot out the light, stay put, insinuate themselves into every kind of environment. They are the third dimension into which all the living surfaces of the land aspire to spread. They are a challenge to us.

But trees are individuals. Our ambiguous feelings about them haven't been ones of simple love and hate. We've responded to their nuances of shape and habit, to their different potentials for use and symbolism. The native deciduous trees of Britain have all had muddled cultural roles as workhorses and ornaments, icons of heritage and status, definers of natural beauty and the nature of degeneration, vehicles of national myths and mystical beliefs.

The English elm, which we loved and lost, wasn't English at all. It seems to have been a prehistoric introduction, maybe from Spain. But other elms were here before the English Channel opened, the wych and the small-leaved, the latter reproducing both by seed and sucker, and generating an immense range of genetic varieties. Perhaps that is why they were not entirely wiped out by the first wave of what came to be called Dutch elm disease. We imagine this to be an affliction of modern times, but half the elms of England were wiped out by it in around 3000 BC. Other outbreaks followed, and in the 18th century it was possible to insure the elm trees on one's land against death.

This dark history has been an undercurrent in the cultural image of the tree, a sombre counterpoint to the comforting images of elm trees billowing in the hedgerows; reflections, it sometimes seemed, of the piled cumulus clouds of late summer. 'Elm hateth Man and waiteth', goes an old saying, reminding us that elm is the chosen wood for coffins. John Betjeman's poignant poems – mostly written before the current virulent strain of the disease took hold in the 1970s – caught the elm's double entendre. In *Dear Old Village*, 'The elm leaves patter in a summer shower/ As *lin-lan-lon* pours through them from the tower'. His elm epithets sound the complex depths of the trees' presence. They are 'guardian', 'waiting', 'shadowy' and 'whelming', that perfect adjective from the funeral poem *In Memory of Basil*.

Now they are mostly gone – but not entirely. English elms suffered most because they were genetically identical. The small-leaved strains weren't, and individual 'village clones' have survived all over East Anglia. Even those in which the disease is endemic survive as bushes as the tree is cut back and regrows during successive fungal infections – a reminder that trees are not defenceless against disease and may not always grow in our image of what they should look like.

If the elm represents mortality, the yew has been a symbol of immortality. More than 500 churches have evergreen – everlasting – yews in their yards, which are reckoned to be more than one thousand years old, and most of them are on the side of the church which has the funeral gateway. Evidently, most writers thought, they'd been planted there as reminders of the immemorial, or as

shelters from the wind, or as a sanctified source of wood for English long-bows (they weren't: English bow-wood came from less brittle trees in Italy and Spain). Then the true age of the trees began to be unravelled, and orthodox wisdom was shocked by the discovery that most were vastly older than the churches themselves. Many yews are two to three thousand years old and one, in Fortingall in Scotland, in excess of five thousand years. Their presence suggested that the Christian churches had been built on pagan sacred sites, and that these in turn had been created close to these seemingly immortal evergreen trees.

But belief in tree-planting – the wielding of a human wand into the earth – has been a stubborn and distorting influence on our understanding of trees. In 1664, John Evelyn published his famous treatise *Sylva, or A Discourse of Forest Trees*, prompted by the seeming timber crisis (in fact a politically manipulated shortage) consequent on the naval wars. He advocated something that was quite new, the deliberate planting of whole 'artificial' woods, instead of reliance on those that had grown perfectly well of their own accord since the last ice age. Oak was the tree of choice to rebuild the nation's 'Wooden Walls'. In the expansive mood of the Enlightenment, the idea of planting found nourishing soil. It established human mastery over nature. It brilliantly combined investment in an ancient English denizen with a ritual display of power and status. The gentry – echoing the ancient vernacular practice of using wild trees as boundary markers – prolonged their lives by proxy in their plantings. Oak trees became symbolic as well as literal pieces of real estate – properties in the earth.

The invention of the tree plantation made a dramatic change in the very grammar of our relationship with nature, which persists into the present day. Pre-plantation, the verb 'to grow' was intransitive with respect to trees. Trees grew, and we took what we could from them. Post-plantation, it became transitive. We were the subject and trees the object. *We* grew *them*. We were the cause of their existence on the earth.

This cultural shift has had a profoundly damaging influence on our perception of nature as a whole, and on our practical relationships with trees, best illustrated by the changing fortunes of

another of our great broadleafed species, the beech. Beech, useless as timber for ships or houses because of its lack of durability, spent the first five and a half thousand years of its presence here as a lowly fuelwood. It was part of the North Sea gas of medieval England. Then the 18th century discovered natural beauty. Beeches became the epitome of graciousness and elegance. But again, contrary archetypes flourished. Aspirational landowners favoured the tall, uncluttered beech, the Palladian column in wood, uncorrupted by peasants' hands. Aesthetes of the Picturesque movement leant towards the knobbly, elfin pollards, which they regarded as more truly 'natural' – though they owed their rugged profiles to having been hacked about for centuries.

Today, the beech may be in trouble from climate change. Its shallow root system makes it vulnerable to drought, and it may need to move west, away from the south of England. But its apparent vulnerability may be, in part, our making. Our taken-for-granted 'dominion' over nature has made us plant and nurture beeches that conform to our favoured images – the tall timber beech, the furniture beech. This isn't necessarily a genetic type well adapted to rapid environmental change. Wild beeches – like the wild oaks whose quirky shapes made them the best source of the bent timber needed for ship-building, and the elm types that have survived disease – exist in a huge range of varieties, some of them of proven resistance to increasing temperatures. Maybe it is time for wild trees – the "trees themselves", if such a thing is philosophically possible – to be given a chance alongside the rich, but contradictory and confining, stereotypes we have made of them.

Yellow Elm leaves
laid on a rock
held with water
behind a small waterfall
sun

Scaur Water, Dumfriesshire
18 October 2007
Andy Goldsworthy

Harvests

With such rapid population growth, why didn't food supplies run out as some were warning back in the 1970s? Because global harvests have also risen, though at a slower rate than population. In 1982 the world grew 1.5 billion tonnes of grain (corn, wheat and rice), a total that rose to over 2 billion tonnes in 2005. Recently, however, harvests have begun to flatten out, and the huge amount of grain used by the animal feeds and biofuels industry has meant that world stocks are at unusually low levels – enough to last for only about 70 days of consumption. Rising harvests have also been unsustainable for other reasons: chemical pesticides and fertilisers are destroying biodiversity and soils, for example.

Biodiversity

Over the last twenty years, 27 documented species, around the world have become extinct. The true figure is thought to be much higher because so many species are still unrecorded. The current rate of extinction is at least 1,000 times higher than natural levels, and the groups threatened with extinction currently include a quarter of all mammals, a third of all amphibians and one in eight birds worldwide.

Mesopotamian Marshlands

The destruction by Saddam Hussein of the Mesopotamian Marshlands in the 1990s ranks as one of the world's worst ecological catastrophes – comparable with the drying of the Aral Sea and the deforestation of the Amazon. In 1976 the marshlands were still largely intact. By 2000, 90 per cent of the marshlands area was destroyed by drainage schemes, and half a million Marsh Arabs displaced as a result. One of the few positive effects of the 2003 Iraq invasion by the US-led coalition was the re-flooding of the marshes as local people took direct action and destroyed Saddam's dams. Over 40 per cent of the marshes have been re-flooded, and thousands of birds and fish have returned.

The Average Vital Statistics
from *Genius: The Human Footprint*

The programme took the average life,
all 78.5 years – or 2,475,576,000 seconds
of it – and exposed our voracious habits

1,700
friendships made

7,163
baths taken

10,351
pints of beer drunk

30,301
pounds spent on
clothing

35,815
litres of wind
passed

4.5
cows consumed

1,201
chickens
consumed

254
litres of
urine produced

854
tins of baked
beans

8.49
tons of food
packaging

533
books read

4,239
rolls of
toilet paper

9.14
beard length
in metres if it
is not cut

1,694
bottles of wine
drunk

4,239
times having sex

149
litres of vomit
produced

59
foreign holidays
taken

74,802
cups of
tea drunk

5,272
apples
eaten

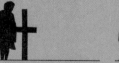

305
friends who will
die from strokes

77,000
cigarettes
smoked

3.5
washing
machines owned

21
sheep consumed

15,464
miles walked

8
cars owned

452,663
miles driven

120,000
litres of fuel used
in our cars

286,311
pounds spent on
taxes

15
pigs consumed

4.8
televisions owned

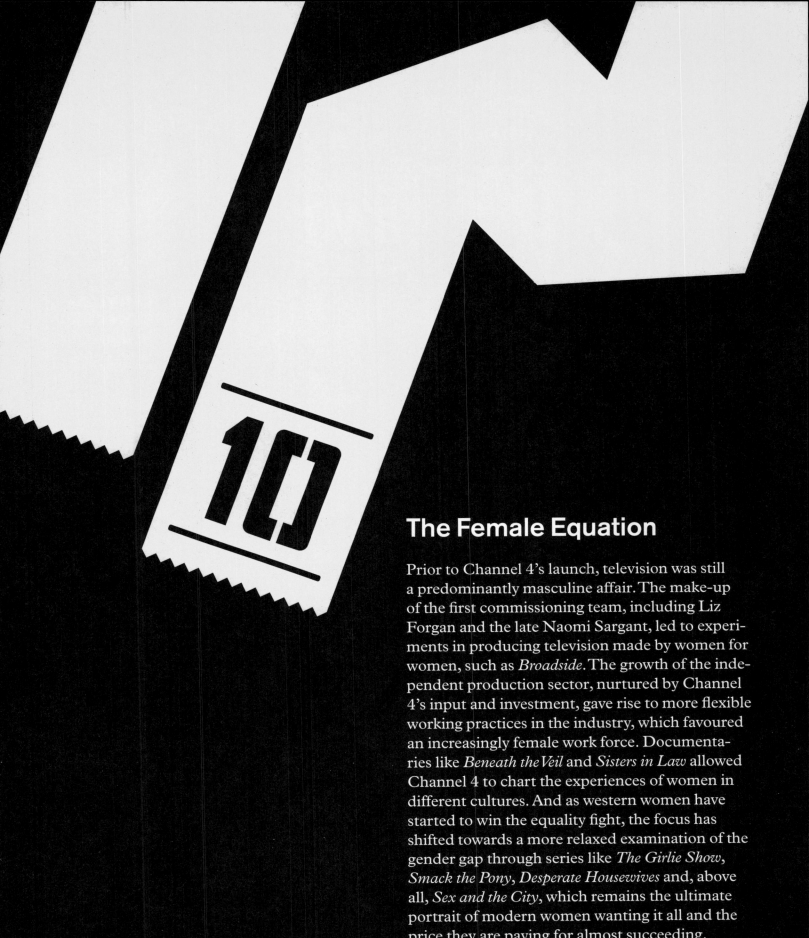

The Female Equation

Prior to Channel 4's launch, television was still
a predominantly masculine affair. The make-up
of the first commissioning team, including Liz
Forgan and the late Naomi Sargant, led to experiments in producing television made by women for
women, such as *Broadside*. The growth of the independent production sector, nurtured by Channel
4's input and investment, gave rise to more flexible
working practices in the industry, which favoured
an increasingly female work force. Documentaries like *Beneath the Veil* and *Sisters in Law* allowed
Channel 4 to chart the experiences of women in
different cultures. And as western women have
started to win the equality fight, the focus has
shifted towards a more relaxed examination of the
gender gap through series like *The Girlie Show*,
Smack the Pony, *Desperate Housewives* and, above
all, *Sex and the City*, which remains the ultimate
portrait of modern women wanting it all and the
price they are paying for almost succeeding.

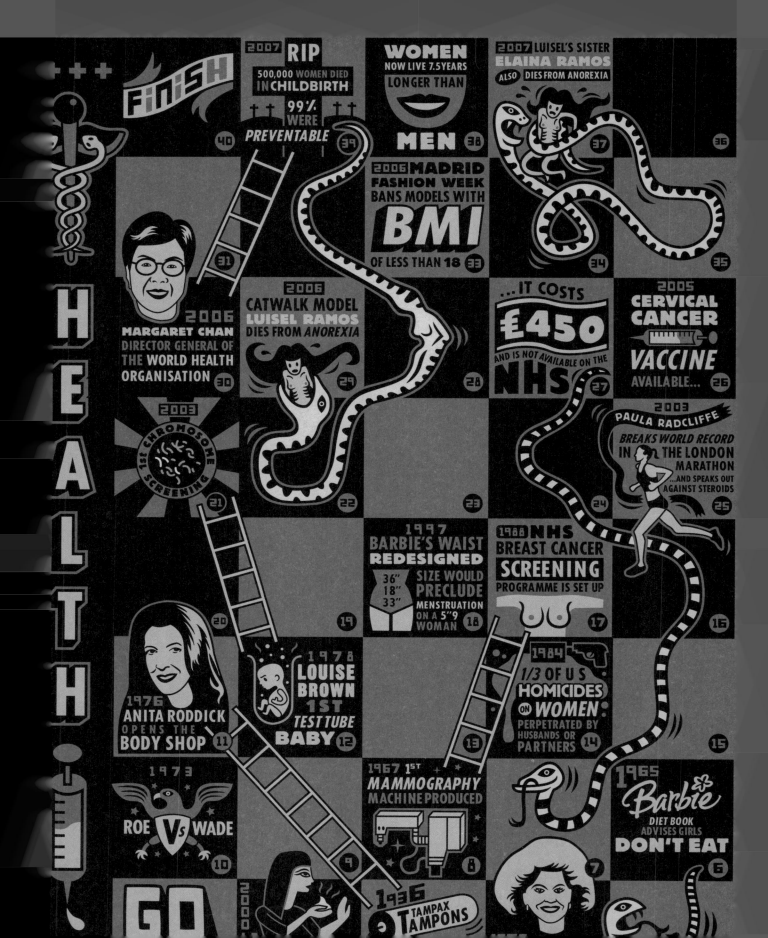

Guardian columnist Zoe Williams sets the scene for the third wave of feminism
Board Game created by Cordelia Jenkins and illustrated by Serge Seidlitz

From *A Woman of Substance* to Beyond *Sex and the City*

Sex and the City, from 1999

If you were watching *A Woman of Substance* right now and you'd gotten over Jenny Seagrove's accent and where, precisely, of the North she was affecting to come from, you could direct your attentions to its gender politics. I'd say the first key question it throws up, not for the prototype feminist in the plot, but for modern feminism in general, is this: how do you resolve the work versus children problem? Our heroine's final scene as matriarch shows her – now morphed into Deborah Kerr, and not affecting any accent at all – presiding over a table full of adult children who all hate her.

The explanation is totally black and white: she wasn't interested in them while they were growing up, she was only interested in her business. This depiction would never happen today, not because it has been subjected to close rational interrogation, I don't think, but just because it lacks the sophistication to reflect anyone's real experience of the work versus motherhood conundrum. That straightforward 'your money or your kids?' question was only compelling when the idea of the working mother was completely theoretical. Now that millions of women do it all the time, we all know that it's not a

choice between the wallet and the heart – there's never that much money kicking about anyway, and your kids can hate you for reasons that are limitless and totally random.

Never mind not withering them, age just bounces off them like the death ray of an arcade game

In the shoulder-pad decade, however, precisely because only women on the telly *had* shoulder-pads, never mind boardroom jobs, these were the topics that culture was grappling with, and it was about more than a conflict of priorities and time-management. Motherhood was just a signal, if you like, of essential femininity. The question was: does the pursuit of money automatically

neuter a woman, thereby making her an unfit mother?

Besides, the Eighties were still wrestling with questions that sound very dated now. Will men and women ever want sex in the same way? Are men naturally predatory? Are women hard-wired to fend them off? Do women even have a sex drive? Are all men either, well, jessies or rapists? Are all women either victims or denatured by their rejection of victim status?

Smack the Pony, 1999

Naturally, this mini-series wasn't based in the era it was made. It starts at the beginning of the 20th century and the engine of its heroine's behaviour is her outrageous treatment at the hands (well, kinda…) of her randy, gutless employer. He makes her pregnant, won't do the decent thing, she has to move to a big town to escape her disgrace, and here

Sex and the City, from 1999

begins her feverish interest in commerce. It was very definitely 'historical' drama – there was no suggestion that these social mores still had a foothold in 1984. And yet, if not the events, then the atmosphere was very Eighties. Men were total bastards. They would do anything to get their ends away. They were spineless and gutless. And if they did happen to be solid, to have integrity, then that somehow scrambled the message of their sex appeal and it was impossible to fancy them. No woman could get any kind of justice until she had cut herself completely free of reliance on these weak, incomplete characters. And this, in all its glory – never mind Jenny in her funny 1910 maid's uniform – is that moment of the Eighties when the Feminist met the Thatcherite: feminism was not about fighting in unison with other women, it was about vigorously putting yourself outside the financial dominance of men. Other women be damned, except for the odd sewing evening, maybe a chat and a giggle. The road to freedom was paved with the flinty cobbles of possessive individualism, the relentless pursuit of one's own interests. The agenda was not justice but self-sufficiency, and you know what, it makes a curious kind of sense, since once you're self-sufficient, you can pursue your own kind of justice. There is no such thing as sisterhood, in other words – you further the cause best by being out for everything you can get.

And now, aw, go on, it's only 27 minutes, watch a quick episode of *Sex and the City*. In theory, it is as far from the rather dated, anti-men tub-thumping of *A Woman of Substance* as it could possibly be. But a lot of the ways in which it

addresses the state of being female (a lot of the disappointments and fumblings and ideological misfires and 'oh my god, I thought we could have it all!'; a lot of what we could umbrella-ly term the gender crises of today) have sprung from that one false turn of the 1980s, when feminism became me-me-me instead of us-us-us.

New femininity is all about shoes and accessories and appearance

Man, they are a foxy foursome when they first appear: Samantha, Miranda, Charlotte and Carrie. If that sounds like a random remark, it is and it isn't – if there's one constant in all six series of the show, it's that they always look frankly wondrous. Never mind not withering them, age just bounces off them like the death ray of an arcade game. To begin with it appears that, in the fullness of the new century, we have resolved the work versus children conundrum by just cutting out the children. Who'd have seen that coming? It's like winning the Olympics by cutting off your arm and inventing the Paralympics. Without children, the idea of being defeminised in that ancient, unknowable way, where your womb is the mainspring of your sexuality, is completely dated. New femininity is all about shoes and accessories and appearance, and new heroines are *intensely* feminine. *SATC* really embodies that culture which you can see all over the mainstream, in which women can say, 'Isn't it weird, how I'm very intelligent and independent, and yet I fixate over silly, teeny things like gaining a few pounds here and there, and oops, I just spunked away my hard-fought financial independence on a pair of shoes because they matched my puppy.'

Where children do intercede, amaz-

ingly, the new conundrum is not 'will I have time for a job?' but 'will I get my figure back?' The vanity of the modern heroine is breathtaking compared to the Eighties version. A female protagonist who thought about her weight and her gym schedule and her highlights to a *SATC* degree would have been laughed off the screen 30 years ago. Such a creation would have been seen as not just demeaningly but, more to the point, *unrealistically* frivolous.

However, there is a reason for all this, and it's not as simple as 'we have all just got a lot more shallow', nor is it as random and disconnected as 'we are all just very different to the way we once were'. You can trace a clear ideological line from Barbara Taylor Bradford's plucky, sincere Emma Harte through to Darren Star's knowingly callow Carrie Bradshaw, but while it's clear, it isn't exactly direct.

First, let's leave money for a second and address ourselves to actual sex. The old preconceptions – where women were de facto exploited by the very business of sex, where men always emerged the winner or at least the exploiter, where women never took any joy from it, only political advantage – have all been trounced by *actual nature*. It's a beautiful thing to behold, in a way: animal urges soaring above the rhetoric of old-school feminism, so that in one generation, women sloughed off the assumption of their prudishness and became meaningfully sexualised.

That's why I don't see the vanity as such a bad thing: superficially, it is immature. Well, hell, it *is* immature. But the idea of going softly into that good night, quietly seceding from the sexual marketplace, is predicated on the idea that women hate sex. When they don't! For Emma Harte, anything that frees her from the attentions of men, whether it be hard work or old age, is a relief. This is the reality of beauty – just being endlessly badgered for sex when you'd rather be getting on with making chutneys and then selling them – and the aspiring independent heroine, therefore, wants nothing more than to be liberated from all these randy goats. As a portrait of womanhood, this had no authenticity, and it didn't even last out the century.

Carrie Bradshaw would be appalled by the idea of beauty as finite; Samantha would laugh in the face of anyone who

The question was: does the pursuit of money automatically neuter a woman, thereby making her an unfit mother?

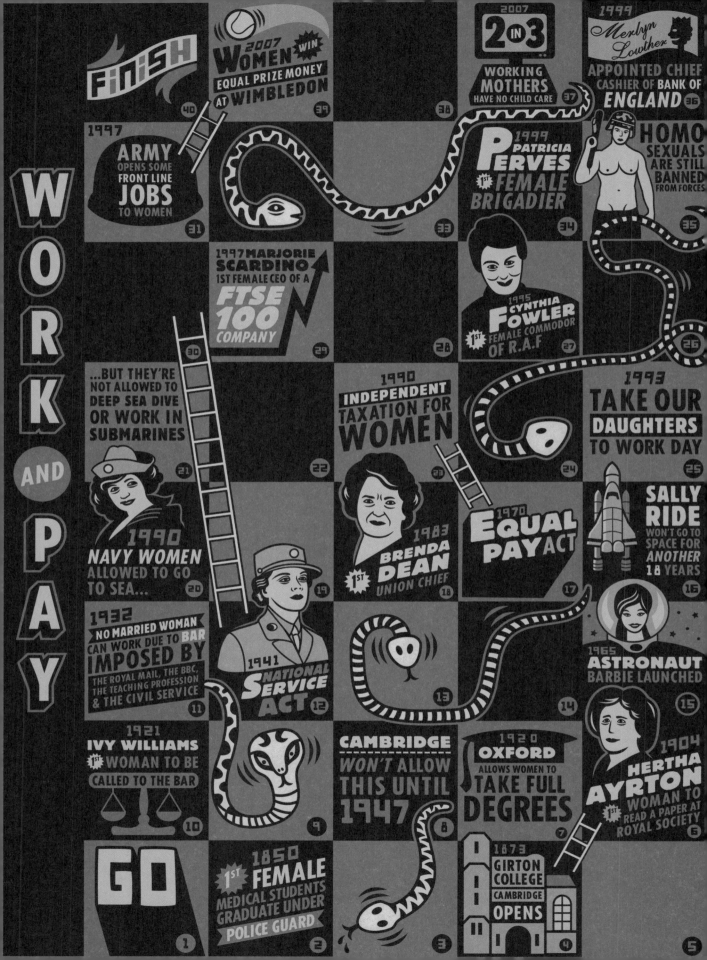

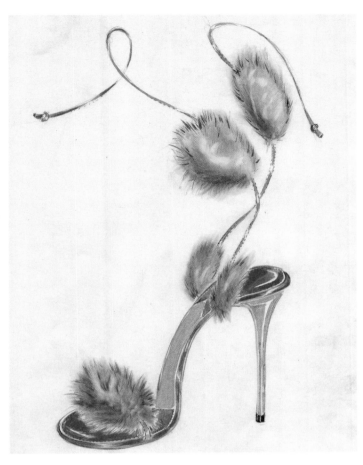

Sex and the City shoe
by Manolo Blahnik

Smack the Pony, 1999

told her that her fertility window determined her net worth in the sexual market. So even though there's an element of this which is ridiculous – ageing is inevitable, all vanity, male and female, will in the end be thwarted – it nevertheless changes the dynamic. Financial independence is still devoutly to be sought and all that, but women and men are not, and more importantly are no longer seen as, pulling in implacably different directions. We are not all out to screw and then desert each other. If it turns out that we all want sex, is it not possible that we all want the same thing more broadly – that really, male-female differences are subtle, and minor, and often more about timing and misunderstanding that chasm and exploitation?

So the savage, pitched battles between the sexes, culturally, last century, have given way to a new state of civilisation. This makes that atavistic greed, embodied by the incongruously angelic Seagrove, look out of place amongst the much more communal, bonded heroines of *Sex and the City*. The Thatcherite position made a lot of sense, pragmatically, in the era *A Woman of Substance* was made, as well as the one in which it was set. It

was empowering – simply the act of seeing any woman succeed was so good for other women that it made any act of selfishness a feminist act. *SATC* caught the tail end of the acceptability of this grabbiness, but it was already getting a bit stale, and by the third season things are growing darker for the new heroines. They all want something *more*, beyond the pursuit of their own interests; this mysterious 'more' is not children, and it isn't a man. Despite the fact that the series ended on a high created by the Big/SJP pairing, the only meaningful and sustaining relationships are between each other (a very Spice Girls *Wannabe* message). Whole episodes were spun out of realisations that, in the description, sound tiny and almost adolescent – I am reminded most forcefully of Samantha, failing to take Miranda's new motherhood seriously. She gets told off; she examines her behaviour; she tips up at Miranda's house and surrenders her hair appointment, plus offering to babysit so that her good good friend may never again be seen around town with crappy hair. Almost every element of that story is so teeny it is almost Enid Blyton in intellectual reach, and yet

that is the energy of the show: that this is a sisterhood, that the resources of one are the resources of all.

SATC shows traditional avenues of fulfillment exhausted: families are a reward, but not the only reward; men can be fun but they are not sustaining; friendships sustain, but if you take those simply at face value, they are just large Mormon marriages without the sex. These friendships were not written for face value, but as a metaphor for acting and living collectively. I'm not kidding, they must be meant metaphorically when you consider how allegorical the characters are, how they are each intended to distill a separate, intensely recognisable, model of womanhood. Refracted through this prism, and however frivolous the characters are on occasion, you have the seed for a new kind of sisterhood, a communality that was impossible in the Eighties while people were still thrashing out the finer details of how individual women could be dragged out of servitude. *A Woman of Substance* was just that – she did have substance, and she used her considerable substance to her own ends, at the expense of her 'femininity'. The *Sex and the City* women, who would object, no doubt, even to being called 'women' (preferring the infantile 'girls' or 'chicks'), nevertheless represent a truer, more nourishing feminism that is no longer based on war with men, that privileges above all else ideas of fellowship and co-operation. This trajectory is entirely understandable – you couldn't have reached the second point without going through the first. And now, ladies – only now – we're ready for our third wave!

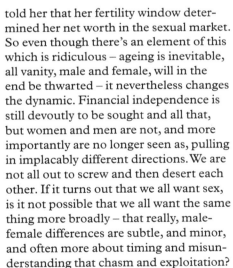

Michelle Hanson, whose column *The Age of Dissent* is published in *The Guardian*, points out that sex has caused problems for girls for centuries

Sex & the Modern Girl

Shere Hite on <u>Channel 4 News</u>, 1998

Shere Hite, author of <u>The Hite Report on Female Sexuality</u>, interviewd by Jon Snow on <u>Channel 4 News</u>, 1998

In the early Eighties my neighbour heard her two daughters, aged ten and twelve, talking about sex. 'Well, if that's what you've got to do,' said the youngest girl, 'I'm never having a baby, ever. I don't care. I'm never, ever doing that.' Now they're both married with children, so they must have managed to do it somehow or other, but it could have been a difficult transition. Sex is an odd thing to imagine, looked at cold, from a position of inexperience. And opinions have, for a long time, contrasted wildly on whether it's a good thing or not, and how much, what sort, with whom it is permissible or advisable, and how, when, under what circumstances, or if at all, a girl should do it. Nowadays the messages seem even more contradictory, intense, relentless and extreme. They come from everywhere: parents, peers, friends, teachers, politicians, religions, films, television, music, literature, and they all clash.

On a more basic level, we're dealing with bottoms here, where excrement and ecstasy are close neighbours. It's an intimate part of your body that tends to get dirty, a source of germs, and needs to be kept scrupulously clean at all times. And it can be the gateway to paradise. It's rude and dirty, so we are often told when young; it's also a thing of beauty, so we're told later on. It's private, but it seems to be everybody's business. No wonder the young are confused. I was, perhaps more than most. So I turned to religion, because God seemed to have a fairly clear line on all this. Perhaps that's why teenage girls often have a bit of a religious crisis while trying to make up their minds which

way to go. Religion at least tells you plainly what not to do. You have some straightforward instructions to follow and some guidance through the morass. And as the worldly messages become more confusing, girls seem to be turning to God in a more extreme and ostentatious way.

I ask a man what boys feel about sex and he tells me that he's still shocked at how powerful the sex drive is, and that boys will fuck a plank

A couple of years ago, Shabina Begum lost her court battle to wear her intensely modest, cover-all jilbab to school. Last summer we had Lydia Playfoot taking her school to court for the right to wear a silver ring. She was a member of the Silver Ring Thing – an evangelical Christian movement that promotes sexual abstinence – and the ring signified that she was still a virgin and intended to remain so until marriage. Eleven more girls in her school began to wear a silver ring, perhaps because teenage girls tend to whip themselves up into a *Crucible*-type frenzy and join in with the latest madness, which may perhaps be down to swirling hormones and sex being repressed like mad and longing for an outlet. Fifty years ago, we used to brazenly

The Big Breakfast, from 1992

throw tennis balls over the school walls at passing builders and milkmen, but nowadays, rebellion has rather hotted up.

Sometimes, behind these religious, 21st century girls are their families and fearsome, fundamentalist movements with thousands or millions of adherents, egging them on to abjure sex and insisting that it is a frightful thing to do before marriage. How terrifying and wicked must sex seem to these girls, with such forces against it? I was scared stiff of it even with my liberal background and fairly robust and vulgar (I thought) parents. I prayed, I attended synagogue, I learned Hebrew, I observed strict dietary rules, I almost starved myself, I longed for purity of mind and body and chose to holiday at a Jewish youth camp, but what did I find? Many of the other campers were at it like knives, while the orthodox boys wore their jackets at all times and insisted that girls should not wear short sleeves.

In my youth in the Fifties, a blow job was a taboo filth-fantasy from another planet. Today, it is as ordinary as adjusting a chap's tie

What confusion. And it still goes on. On the one side we have the Shabinas and Lydias and their hugely powerful religious backing groups. On the other side we have liberal, pragmatic and secular society, trying to present sex as normal and potentially heavenly, and boys, who will always nag girls to do it, and peers, who may also egg them on, and the hugely powerful media, and sex, sex, sex everywhere: on bill-boards, on film and telly, on explicit, unsolicited nasty pop-ups on your computer, on YouTube, on every shelf, not just at the top; sexualised clothes and toys for pre-teens, pole-dancing as an acceptable hobby, Ann Summers an acceptable shop.

This is all a far cry from the romantic poets or novelists, all sighs, longing and summer evenings; or the stuff of fairy tales, promising love and sensitivity and nothing much to do with the body. It is more a barrage of overheated, more or less anything goes, get-in-there sort of carry-on. Today's sex seems to be a commonplace, not a secret and nothing to be ashamed of. Which is fine and liberating in one way, but also increases the pressure to do anything and everything, whether you fancy it or not. In my youth in the Fifties, a blow job was a taboo filth-fantasy from another planet. Today, it is as ordinary as adjusting a chap's tie. Nothing special and so probably more difficult to refuse.

And of course on the 'do it' side is your own body, all ready to go and likely to override all warnings and caution. I heard one teenage girl saying that the only thing nobody had ever told her about sex was that it felt nice. She was probably expecting to have to fight boys off, but she wasn't expecting to have to fight with herself. But what do I know? I'm 65, so I ask my daughter what teenagers do now. They all drink cider and have sex, says she. Most girls try it before they're sixteen, most boys when they are over sixteen. Which is bizarre, she feels, but true according to her research. And boys masturbate five times a day. At least. So she heard. Imagine if a girl said she masturbated five times a day. People would be horrified because, depressingly, and despite all this frankness, openness and equality, the double standards are still flying high. A girl who puts herself about is still a slapper, a boy who does so is just being a boy. Just like Elizabeth Taylor and Errol Flynn. If a girl becomes pregnant it is still her fault. She usually takes the blame and the responsibility.

But who ever heard of a 'fallen' man? A girl ensnares a boy into having a child. A boy does not ensnare, he just can't be fagged to be careful. And a boy does not always think or feel like a girl. I ask a man what boys feel about sex and he tells me that he's still shocked at how powerful the sex drive is, and that boys will fuck a plank. To many of them a girl is more or less a piece of meat who makes irritating phone calls afterwards. How is a teenage girl to understand or imagine that? She probably assumes that a boy, like everyone else, thinks of her as a person.

These are all sweeping statements, but that is the trouble with sex. You can never get at the truth of what anyone is up to. People have tried and thought themselves successful – Shere Hite, Kinsey – but this is the one subject about which nearly everyone fibs, whatever age they are. How can you not? Say that it's fabulous for you and you're at it all the time and people will think you a show-off; say that you hardly bother and you don't know what the fuss is about, or you'd like to, but can't or don't, then you're a weedy failure with hang-ups, or a reject. The older you get, with any luck, the less the opinion of others matters, but to a teenager it matters tremendously. It often matters more than anything else. But how do you work out what you believe when you don't yet know what you want, what you're meant to want, or even whether it's you who wants it?

Divorce Iranian Style, 1999

Many of us never quite work it out. Sex will never be all lovely, thrilling, clean and healthy. It will usually be complicated, muddled up with love, sometimes dull and disappointing, sometimes dangerous – emotionally and physically – sometimes life-enhancing, sometimes destructive, blinding, and a sort of madness. You grow up, you have teenage daughters, you know exactly what they're going through, and you can't warn them or help them or stop them. They think you know nothing about how they feel, but it's almost exactly the same turmoil for them as it was for you. Sex has caused problems for girls for centuries. It probably always will.

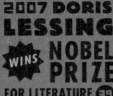
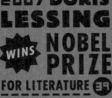

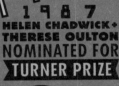

CULTURE AND ARTS

40 FiNiSH

39 2007 DORIS LESSING WINS NOBEL PRIZE FOR LITERATURE

38 2003 GRAYSON PERRY ACCEPTS TURNER PRIZE AS CLAIRE

37 THERE HAS NEVER BEEN A FEMALE POET LAUREATE

36 2005 GWYNETH LEWIS MADE NATIONAL POET OF WALES

31 / **30** 2001 THEA SHARROCK BECOMES BRITAIN'S YOUNGEST ARTISTIC DIRECTOR

33 2000 MARGARET ATWOOD WINS BOOKER PRIZE

34 ONLY 3 WOMEN HAVE WON THE TURNER PRIZE

21 1993 TRACEY EMIN & SARAH LUCAS OPEN 'THE SHOP'

23 1992 INGRID DAUBECHIES WINS MACARTHUR MATH FELLOWSHIP AKA GENIUS GRANT

24 1992 TEEN TALK Barbie SAYS 2+2 = 5 "MATH IS TOUGH"

20 JK ROWLING IS ADVISED TO USE INITIALS TO DISGUISE GENDER 1997

19 1997 J K ROWLING PUBLISHES 1ST POTTER BOOK

11 1973 VIRAGO PRESS LAUNCHED

10 1972 spare Rib MAGAZINE LAUNCHED

12 / **13** 1976 LEINA WESTMILLER 1ST WOMAN NOMINATED FOR BEST DIRECTOR OSCAR

14 ....IN 80 YEARS NO WOMAN HAS EVER WON

15 1987 HELEN CHADWICK + THERESE OULTON NOMINATED FOR TURNER PRIZE

6 1940 SILVIA PLATH PUBLISHES 1ST POEM (AGED 8)

GO

1 1859 GEORGE ELIOT PUBLISHES ADAM BEDE UNDER MALE PSEUDONYM

8 1959 Barbie LAUNCHED

3 1896 ALICE GUY BLACHET DIRECTS LA FÉE AUX CHOUX

4 1909 SELMA LAGERLÖF WINS NOBEL PRIZE FOR LITERATURE

The fantasy of domestic bliss exists because of the sexual revolution, rather than in spite of it, believes Rita Konig, author of *Domestic Bliss: Simple Ways to Add Style to Your Life*

The New Domesticity

<u>Desperate Housewives</u>, from 2005

The rise in domesticity doesn't, in my view, have anything to do with anti-feminism, it is simply to do with femininity. If men liked spritzing linen, baking cakes and getting excited about their dinner party for eight and what china they were using, would it be considered a perfectly ordinary feminist activity? It is such a shame when equality gets confused. It is totally bewildering this idea that being feminine should have anything to do with how seriously a woman is taken at work. I never want to sit through a football match or discuss the power of one car engine over another and I will not expect a heterosexual man to get into a deep and meaningful discussion about 500-count bed linen or lipstick. Equally, I have never thought that I should be treated any differently from a man at work. Just because men aren't into domesticity, it doesn't mean it is putting women back 40 years if they are.

There is another minor detail here. The popular domesticity that everyone is so amazed by today is not exactly what women struggled and fought against 30 years ago. Girls aren't tossing aside their power suits in favour of house coats and heated rollers so that they can run home and look after their husbands. The new domesticity is about looking after themselves: lighting a couple of scented candles, using some expensively efficient cleaning products and having a dinner party.

And before there is a great collective feminist heave and more uproar from the working mothers at the back, this might not be how real life is lived, but this particular 'domesticity' is gaining popularity. It is not the actual hoovering women are dancing about the place over, it's about the end result, using a few nice products.

Shopping opportunities are 'of course' the other great female activity. Previously, domesticity was about everyone else – bringing up children and looking after husbands under the judgmental eye of one's neighbours. Today, it is about us. Who doesn't want to come home from work to a place that looks good, smells delicious and is comfortable to be in? It is in our nature, it is just this time it is on our terms, thanks entirely to the feminist fight.

No one is getting excited about actually scrubbing floors; the new domesticity is entirely about a beautiful brush and an

There is no escaping the laundry, so one might as well make it a somewhat pleasant experience

Desperate Housewives, from 2005

It's about lighting a couple of scented candles, using some expensively efficient cleaning products and having a dinner party

old fashioned bucket from Labour and Wait, the chic retro store, and a tiny canister of Lavandula brought home from Provence. Just like all those cooking books being sold by the gazillion are more about the fantasy of cooking, like that man that swears a lot, than actually doing it. Nigella Lawson made it OK for women to be sexy in their kitchens and she is a very successful business woman; there is nothing down-trodden about her and she is who women are looking to. There is no chance of us becoming a generation of Mrs Minivers or Hilda Ogdens; we are too busy working to pay our mortgages for that. All that is happening is that we are reclaiming our rights to be feminine: the icing on the top of the feminist fight.

On a practical level, this is a generation who were never really cooked for by their mothers. You don't hear the expression 'just like mother used to make' bandied about that often; it is certainly not a phrase I have ever used. Because our mothers worked and weren't in the kitchen cooking our tea when we got home from school, most of us have little idea about how to cook. Maybe that's why we are grappling around trying to find a book that will tell us how on earth to get dinner on the table – or that we see cooking as a pleasure rather than a drudge. I know many more men than women who cook really well, usually in an effort not to starve, since there is no one to cook for them any more.

Isn't this how it all started anyway? Women in the cave making it look nice and men out getting dinner?! This is the new domestic harmony between men and women: he cooks dinner, she lays the table. I am so much more interested in what china,

Ugly Betty, 2007

Beauty and… the PA?

Stories of inner beauty abound in fairy tales – perennially popular plots of hidden beauty winning out are a joy of our narrative tradition. Thank goodness, this rich strand of fables came back into popular consciousness, launched by the effervescent *Ugly Betty*. It swept the world off its feet, sometimes merely being dubbed for different countries but in other instances being re-created and transformed for a new telly-watching nation; it even found its way into Flemish in *Sara*. The PA in Russia played by Nelly Uvarova went from ugly to beautiful when she was cast in Cheek by Jowl's *Three Sisters* to play Chekhov's most beautiful part, Irina. Somehow in Germany the relationship between art and life was even stronger; the lead part was played by Alexandra Neldel who aptly started life as a dental assistant, while Mona Singh in India has moved from the role to present *Extreme Makeover*. Beauty, it seems, is for everyone.

glass and linens to use than burning myself on the stove.

Now let's take the laundry room. Who would have thought that girls could get excited about that, but they are! I think it is more about order and cleanliness – think stacks of fluffy white towels, rows of baskets, large glass jars with washing powders decanted into them and a vintage tea cup floating around in it as a scoop – than a happy morning spent washing someone else's football kit. The whole thing is about marketing; Martha Stewart is almost entirely responsible, but it is girl heaven – and it is all about the 'Look'. We are so skin deep! When I wrote about domesticity, the drive behind the beautifying chat was always about making your place much prettier; there is no escaping the laundry, whether it's your own or your family's, so one might as well make it a somewhat pleasant experience.

The response that amazed me the most when I wrote *Domestic Bliss: How to Live* were the letters from mothers who seemed to be furious that I didn't have children. I wrote the book when I was 27 and was struck by this arrogance: if you didn't have a husband and children then you weren't qualified to run a house. Totally bizarre. I mean, where do they think we live before marriage? Surely that is more sexist than anything, but usually it was a thin veil of fury due to that fact that, I think, they were losing the battle in the feminist ideal. They were working really hard all day and still had to come home and be a housewife – the serious downside of 'winning' the fight for sexual equality is that it isn't really that equal. That's why I think that the domestic revival is most popular amongst the late twenties and early thirties group who do not have children; it is only while you have the time and spare cash that it is fun to put your attentions towards your house, your linen cupboard and ultimately your own comfort.

Isn't this how this all started? Women in the cave making it look nice and men out getting dinner?

'I think domesticity is going to be big!' were the parting words of Alexandra Shulman editor of *Vogue*, as she gave me my domestic tips column, 'Rita Says' in January 2000. I have to admit that while I thought everything to do with pressed linens, lavender and sparkling glasses was completely enticing, I didn't particularly expect anyone else to. I wrote the column dedicated to keeping your toes well pedicured to protect your antique linen sheets, how to archive your books in colour order and dry glass with old, soft linen cloths to get the best shine. It was tongue in cheek, light and very *Vogue*. Since then domesticity, or at least this new, more frivolous version of it, has grown and grown as a highly marketable subject, much to the chagrin of the feminist hardcore, who in my opinion need to lighten up.

So where does that leave us? The fantasy domestic bliss craze exists because of the sexual revolution rather than despite it. The reality for the working mother is that she has it harder than ever before, although she has her own money and therefore freedom, which is invaluable.

Sisters in Law, 2005

Sisters in Law

Documentary maker Kim Longinotto's unerring eye has never flinched from portraying oppressed and victimised women from around the world. She has made films about women in the divorce courts of Iran (*Divorce Iranian Style*, 1998) and Kenyan women challenging the tradition of female circumcision in *The Day I Will Never Forget*, 2003. *Sisters in Law* is her most recent film, the latest in a long line of collaborations with Channel 4. It follows Judge Beatrice in the Court of First Instance in Kumbaand, Cameroon, and a registrar, Juliana, who is trying to become a judge. These women are challenging the status quo in Cameroon and both are courageously attempting to change the rules of the world in which they live and overcome the hostility of a male-dominated environment. Longinotto's film is an all-too-rare example of filmmaking which chronicles women's role in society and, in the chronicling, confronts these very roles.

11

Oh My God

The religious fault-lines running through the foundations of modern Britain have rarely been so complex or so sensitive, making it a subject matter ripe for exploration. Channel 4 has taken an unorthodox and questioning approach, providing a regular platform for the defenders of many faiths and a window for the faithless majority to get a better view and a broader understanding of what they have chosen to reject. Building on the role of long running strands like *Witness*, more recent series such as *Children of Abraham*, *The Root of all Evil?* and *The Cult of the Suicide Bomber* have sought to examine, through the prism of religion, the geopolitical realities of the modern world, a task close to the heart of modern public service broadcasting.

Kevin Toolis, filmmaker and
acknowledged expert on terrorism,
unravels the complexities of suicide
bombing

From Gaza to London

It is 9.07am on a grey July morning in London; a bewildered
young man wanders the streets of the capital. Something has
gone wrong. Again and again, he calls his friends for advice
but they have already left without him. Around him, the city is
descending into chaos. Ambulances are screaming down streets,
train stations are being closed, and thousands of commuters
are trapped. Scotland Yard and Downing Street are on alert
as report after report of explosions fills all of the police radio
channels.

But still this eighteen-year old soldier, this perfect killing
machine, presses on with his mission. Checking and re-check-
ing the electrical connections of his device, Leeds-born Hasib
Hussain finally presses the detonator to reach paradise, and
murders thirteen of his fellow passengers on the number 30 bus
in Tavistock Square.

The 7/7 suicide bomb attacks in London were the most
significant act of premeditated mass murder in British history.
And they remain a baffling crime.

How could four very ordinary British citizens blow themselves up on the London tube and deliberately murder innocent
commuters? And then claim their actions were a justifiable act
of war? How could anyone in our secular world kill themselves
for a cause?

What has this act of terrorism got to do with religious
broadcasting, traditionally seen as the preserve of stories about
leaky church roofs, controversial gay Church of England vicars
and the 'crisis of faith' in the inner city?

In August 2005, just one month after the July 7 attacks,
Channel 4 broadcast the two-part *The Cult of the Suicide Bomber*

We interrogated failed suicide bombers about why and how they were going to blow themselves up

series. For the first time, an audience had a chance to see and
analyse the complex interplay of religion and nationalism that
has given rise to the cult of suicide bombing.

The Cult of the Suicide Bomber was not 'turnaround' television. Channel 4 religious commissioning editor Aaqil Ahmed
had commissioned the programmes in January 2005 and our
company, Many Rivers Films, had been in production since
February. Travelling with our Arabic-speaking, ex-CIA presenter Robert Baer, myself, and fellow director-producer David
Batty, we had already filmed in Iran, Lebanon and Israel. We
had attended prayers at Tehran University, interviewed the head
of the Iranian armed forces, had an exclusive interview with the
family of the world's first suicide bomber, visited the Holy city
of Qom, interviewed members of Hizbollah in Lebanon, and
spoken to the family of the world's first suicide car bomber. We
followed this deadly trail on into Gaza and Israel and finally
deep into the Israeli prison system, where we interrogated failed
suicide bombers about why and how they were going to blow
themselves up.

In 2003, two young Britons had gone to Israel, and blown themselves up in a Tel Aviv bar. Even in early 2005, suicide bombing was, potentially, a 'British story'.

As a writer and producer-director I had wanted to make a film about suicide bombing for five years. My interest had been sparked by an assignment for a national newspaper in Gaza in 2000, where I interviewed the family of a Palestinian suicide bomber who had blown himself up in a Jewish settlement. The Masawabi family showed me a video of their son Ismail, filmed moments before he drove to his death.

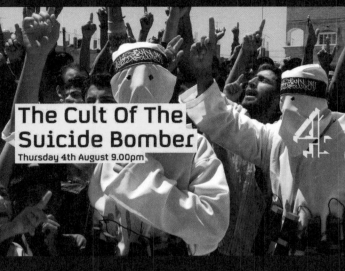

The Cult of the Suicide Bomber advert, 2005

In this film, Ismail plays with the detonation switch inside the car and sheepishly grins like a young man on his first date. The interview continued on after the video and then the parent's four-year-old grandson, Ahmed, entered the room and said something in Arabic. All the adults burst out laughing. But they were also proud. Ahmed beamed with pleasure at the adults' approval. The angelic-looking little boy had said: 'When I grow up I want to be a shahid (a martyr) just like uncle Ismail.'

When Ahmed's comments were translated, I knew then that suicide bombing was more than just a tactic. It was a cult, a virus that grew and mutated. It was bigger than any one conflict, and could seed itself beyond the confines of the Israeli-Palestinian contest. I vowed to myself that I would spend the next few years trying to find out where suicide bombing had arisen and how an ordinary Palestinian family like the Masawabis could celebrate the death of their own son.

Suicide bombing is ultimately an ideological weapon. It utilises interpretations of the Qur'an and fuses them to a nationalist or internationalist cause. Caught up in its ideology, its followers willingly turn away from the living and seek martyrdom and paradise via mass murder. Unlike guns and explosives, it can be shipped across the internet or passed hand to hand via cassette or DVD. And as we discovered on 7 July, suicide bomber cells can spring from within our own society as if from nowhere.

For the next five years after that Gaza interview, I knocked on every door I could think of in British broadcasting to gain a commission. The answer was always resolutely no. Suicide bombing was just too 'current affairs'/ 'too boring'/ 'too foreign'/ 'too Middle East'/ 'not relevant'/ 'not what our audience wants'.

Both I and the commissioners were caught in a narrow matrix that saw religion and current affairs as separate spheres. Finally, Channel 4 broke that log jam by seeing that a religious commission could be both a work of history and a work of investigative journalism.

Every secret thing has an origin, a beginning, somewhere down in the murk of history. Suicide bombing is no different. There were many gaps in our understanding and many puzzles. Why did the Palestinian hijackers of the 1970s never use suicide bombing, even when the grounds of their conflict with Israel remained essentially the same?

The journey in the making of *The Cult of the Suicide Bomber* was one of the richest experiences of my life. We had a complex 28-day continuous shoot that ended in Tehran and included difficulties with visas, access, politics and language and, on one occasion, emergency dentistry.

The Cult of the Suicide Bomber is public service broadcasting at its strongest. And yet it had been commissioned in the so-called backwater of Religious Commissioning. In the real world, and certainly in the world of the suicide bomber, there is no division between religion and politics and their perceived crusade against the West. Drawn into the cult down at his local Leeds gym, eighteen-year-old Hasib Hussain came to see the country in which he had been born as a cruel oppressor. His world view was distorted by the cult's propaganda until he saw his own death, and the murder of others, as an act of martyrdom. A moral good. When he finally pressed the detonator on the top of that No. 30 bus, the innocent passengers around him had lost moral status. His own action, mass murder, was invisible to him.

The Cult of the Suicide Bomber II advert, 2006

The Cult of the Suicide Bomber set out to answer that question – how could anyone in a secular world blow themselves up for a cause? The answer, as we and the viewer found out, is complex, but it is also the most politically relevant 'current affairs' television you could ever watch.

Cavendish Anglican Community Church
Felixstowe, 2007
Photograph: Lee Mawdsley

Eleven   Oh My God

After being introduced to Islam by Channel 4, Karen Armstrong, the former nun turned author whose books include *The Battle for God*, challenges preconceptions surrounding Islamophobia

Islam Today

Had it not been for Channel 4, I might never have become interested in Islam. In 1982, in the very earliest days of the channel, I was commissioned to write and present a documentary series on St Paul, working with an Israeli film company. In Jerusalem, I encountered Islam for the first time: there is, perhaps, no better place to discover its profound connections with both Judaism and Christianity. From that point, I began in my work to develop what I called 'triple vision,' the depiction of the Abrahamic religions as a single tradition that had taken three different but related directions. Later I was commissioned by the channel to do a series with the same Israeli company on the Crusades. Sadly, it was never screened, for somewhat nefarious reasons that had nothing to do with Islam. But during the three years of my work on this project, I had to study the Muslim riposte to these Christian holy wars, and discovered the real meaning of *jihad*.

Somewhat to my surprise, I found that Islam was not a militant faith that had imposed itself on a reluctant world by force of arms, and that until the 20th century it had been a far more peace-able and tolerant religion than western Christianity. The word *jihad* did not mean 'holy war' but 'struggle, endeavour'. Muslims are exhorted to make a concerted effort – intellectually, spiritually, socially, politically and morally – to build a just society where poor and vulnerable people are treated with respect. For five years, Muhammad was forced to fight the city of Mecca, which had persecuted the Muslims, driven them from their homes, and vowed to exterminate the entire Muslim community in Medina. In these terrify-ing circumstances, the Qur'an decided that sometimes it was necessary to fight to preserve decent values, such as religious freedom,[1] but it only permits war in self-defence.[2] Muslims must always make strenuous diplomatic efforts to avoid armed conflict, and are constantly reminded that it is far better to discuss differences respectfully[3] and to forgive an injury.[4] There must be no vengeful retaliation.[5] Once hostilities have begun, however, they must fight energetically to bring the campaign to a speedy end and restore normal relations. The moment the enemy asks for peace, they must lay down their arms and accept even the most dis-advantageous terms and conditions.[6]

Warfare was never the central pillar of Islam and the Qur'an makes it clear that fighting was abhorrent to the first Muslims.[7] There is an important, oft-quoted tradition that on his way home

The word *jihad* did not mean 'holy war' but 'struggle, endeavour'

after a battle, Muhammad once remarked to his companions: 'We are leaving the lesser *jihad* [the battle] and returning to the greater *jihad*,' the far more important and difficult struggle to reform one's own society and one's own heart. It was fascinating to me to see how these principles guided the strategy of Nur ad-Din and Saladin in their war of self-defence

Jesus had, after all, told his followers to love their enemies, not to exterminate them

against the Crusaders, who recognised, somewhat uneasily, that the conduct of these Muslim generals on the battlefield was far more 'Christian' than their own.

I was also interested to learn that the idea of Islam as an inherently violent religion became one of the received ideas of Europe during the Crusades, when it was the Christians of the West who were fighting brutal and gratuitous holy wars against Muslims. The monks who propagated this view were clearly projecting their buried anxieties about current Christian behaviour onto the enemy. Jesus had, after all, told his followers to love their enemies, not to exterminate them. At this formative period, when Europe was emerging from the Dark Ages and creating a new, distinctively Western culture, Muslims – like Jews (the other victims of the Crusaders) – were cast as the shadow-self of Europe, the opposite of 'us'. Our Islamophobia is nearly a millennium old, is entwined with our chronic anti-semitism, and deeply rooted in the Western identity.

There is, therefore, often an entrenched resistance to hearing anything positive about Islam. There was – and

is – an eagerness to believe the worst, because our distorted image of Islam is, at some obscure but powerful level, part of our own self-image. It offends me intellectually because even though Muslims, like everybody else, have often failed to live up to their ideals, it is simply not correct. Not surprisingly, the atrocities of 9/11 reinforced the old stereotype. But while it is important to know who our enemies *are*, it is equally crucial to know who they are *not*.

Gallup has recently conducted a poll in ten Muslim countries, including Saudi Arabia, Pakistan and Afghanistan. They found that only eight per cent of their Muslim respondents approved of 9/11. The remaining 92 per cent may not have liked American policy in their region, but condemned the attacks, which contravened Islamic law. Muslims are not allowed to attack a country where they are permitted to practise their faith freely; they are forbidden to kill non-combatants, destroy buildings or use fire in warfare. When asked what they found most difficult about the West, the overwhelming number of Gallup's respondents replied that it was our disrespect for Islam – this

came way ahead of their second objection: Western interference in their internal affairs. Casual Islamophobia is therefore a gift to extremists and, if it continues unabated, could swell the ranks of organizations such as al-Qaeda.

The criminal violence that we rightly deplore is committed by a tiny minority and motivated by politics rather than religion. It is vital to make this distinction. Most of the so-called 'fundamentalisms' – be they Christian, Jewish, Muslim, Sikh or Hindu – are often religiously articulated nationalisms. Hamas and Hizbollah, for example, are primarily resistance movements. Fundamentalists are usually at odds with their more traditional co-religionists and cannot, therefore, be seen as representatives of the faith. Far from being militantly conservative ideologies, fundamentalisms are highly innovative and self-consciously unorthodox – even anti-orthodox. Al-Qaeda's insistence that Islam should rule the world, for example, is (to use a Christian term) a Muslim 'heresy'. The Qur'an is a pluralistic scripture and explicitly opposes the idea that the world should form a single faith community. For the first 100 years after

Children of Abraham, 2004

Children of Abraham, 2004

Muhammad's death, conversion to Islam was actually discouraged in the Muslim empire, because the Qur'an clearly stated that the 'People of the Book' had received perfectly valid revelations of their own. Islam was seen as a revelation for the Arabs, the sons of Ishmael, as Judaism belonged to the descendents of Isaac and Jacob, and Christianity to the followers of the gospel.

There is no clash of civilisations. At the beginning of the twentieth century, almost every single Muslim intellectual was in love with the West. After a visit to Paris, Muhammad Abdu (1849-1905), Grand Mufti of Egypt, remarked provocatively: 'In France I saw Islam but no Muslims; in Cairo I see Muslims but no Islam.' What he meant was that the modern economies of Europe had inaugurated an egalitarian, just society that approximated more closely to the Qur'anic ideal than the partially modernised Muslim nations. In Iran, leading mullahs campaigned alongside secular intellectuals in 1906 for representational government, Western-style. When their revolution was successful, the Grand Ayatollah of Najaf said that the new constitu-

tion was the next best thing to the coming of the Shiite Messiah, because it would limit the tyranny of the Shah and should, therefore, be dear to every Muslim.

Unfortunately, some two years later, the British discovered oil in Iran and never permitted the new parliament to function freely lest it scupper their plans to fuel the navy. If we have lost their initial good will and admiration, which it is now poignant to recall, it is not because Muslims have been alienated by 'Islam' but because our policies have sometimes made some of our vaunted ideals, such as democracy, seem like a bad joke.

In the present crisis, the media has a vital role to play. Channel 4 gives excellent coverage of the politics of the Middle East, but it is now essential to educate the public about the religion of Islam. We can no longer afford to indulge our Islamophobia. It can, surely, never be right to defend a liberal principle by reviving a medieval bigotry. Muslims, like most religious people, are finding it difficult to adapt their traditions to the post-modern world, but it is difficult to be creative when you feel under attack. Instead of a knee-jerk reaction on such

emotive issues as free speech or the position of women, we need a more informed approach which sees current Muslim attitudes in historical perspective. All too often, insensitive or self-interested Western behaviour has prompted Muslims to adopt a hard-line, fundamentalist view that conflicts with centuries of tradition. This is especially evident in the case of the veil, for example.[8] The disciplined search for a more balanced appraisal of Islam need not be a politically correct chore. Muslim civilisation has been rich and varied and I am grateful to Channel 4 who, however inadvertently, first led me to study it.

1 Qur'an 22:36–40
2 Qur'an 2:190
3 Qur'an 8:62–63
4 Qur'an 3:147–48; 8:16–17; 61:5
5 Qur'an 43:47–43
6 Qur'an 2: 193–94
7 Qur'an 2:216
8 See Leila Ahmed, Women and Gender in Islam: Historical Roots of a Modern Debate (New Haven and London), 144–56

Poplar Central Mosque
2007
Photograph: Lee Mawdsley

The Magpie and the Bull

by Michael Morpurgo,
Children's Laureate,
2003-2005

This short story celebrates the life of Shambo the sacred bull, put down in 2007 following a diagnosis of tuberculosis.

There once lived a bull, a beautiful black bull. He lived on a wonderful farm where every creature was treated with dignity, where kindness ruled.

The bull was much loved and admired by the farmer, and by all the animals too. Indeed he was so adored that every morning the farmer would hang a glorious garland of flowers around his neck. All day long the bull would stand at the door of his pen gazing longingly out over the fields. The farmer cared for him well, tending to his every need, but for weeks and months now the door of his pen had stayed shut.

One evening late a magpie flew down into the farmyard. 'Is something the matter?' he asked the bull. 'You are looking a bit sad? I just thought you might like some company.'

'How very kind of you,' said the bull. 'It's true that tonight I should love to have someone to pass the time with, for I know tonight will be the longest of my life. And to be quite honest with you I don't think I'm going to sleep much. So you can stay and keep me company for as long as you like.'

'I envy you your beautiful garland,' said the magpie.

'That's strange,' replied the bull. 'Because I envy you too. If there's one thing I've always wanted to do, it's to fly. I promise you there's nothing I'd like more than to fly out of here right now, and never come back.'

'But why?' said the magpie, 'This is the most peaceful farm I've ever known. Everyone is kind. I think this must be the best place in the world to live.'

'It was, it was. I used to be able to roam my fields, wander wherever I wanted. Not anymore. But tell me how it is to be up there in the sky,' said the bull, 'to fly wherever you want. What's it like?'

All night long the magpie told him how it was to be a bird, to soar and swoop, to lift off and land, to float on the warm air, to be buffeted by the wind, how it was to fly free. And as she talked, the bull closed his great eyes and dreamed he could fly. All night long he flew free, and was happy.

As the first rays of the morning sun touched the bull's forehead he opened his eyes. It was the dawn he had so much dreaded. The magpie was still there, perched on the door of his pen.

'You have stayed all night with me like a true friend,' said the bull. 'I should like you to have my garland, it is all I have to give.'

Soon after, the magpie flew off, the bull's glorious garland streaming out behind him like a kite. 'I am flying your garland high in the sky, my friend,' he cried. 'You're up here with me. You're flying with me.'

But when the magpie returned later that day, the garland still around her neck, the bull's pen was empty. The farmer was sitting under a tree nearby, his head in his hands.

'Where's the bull gone?' the magpie asked.

'They took him away. They've killed him,' said the farmer.

'But why?'

'Why indeed?' the farmer replied. 'Why indeed?'

The next day they found the garland draped over the door of the pen, and the magpie lying dead on the straw inside, her heart broken.

And the moral of the story is: Kindness is as precious as life itself.

Sri Guru Tegh Bahadur Gurdwara
2007
Photograph: Lee Mawdsley

Gwyneth Lewis, first National
Poet of Wales, on religious wars
in contemporary Britain

Don't Do As I Do, Do What I Say

If anybody had predicted 30 years ago that religion would become one of the most explosive areas of early 20th century life, they would have been regarded as deluded. While institutional Christianity in Britain is on the wane, fundamentalism seems to have mass appeal and atheists have recently found a voice condemning the felt tyranny of the Church over the enlightenment project. The Anglican Church is about to tear itself apart over its attitude to homosexuality and, perhaps the greatest symbol of impotence, crucifixes are worn more often as fashion accessories than as statements of faith.

These are confusing times. Wearing a cross to your job at British Airways causes huge controversy but Christian students are not allowed to wear purity rings to school. Muslim women are permitted certain kinds of headscarves but not the full veil in the classroom.

This is where I declare my hand. I'm no missionary but my Christian faith has been at the centre of my life for nearly twenty years. I don't play guitar in church, I'm married to a rabid atheist. When Richard Dawkins attacks some of the

most blatant abuses of religious power, I have to agree with him, although I find Christopher Hitchens's vein of mockery simply immature. I know that I could

Priest Idol, 2005

not have survived as a person had I not started living my life differently – in reference to God rather than myself – when I was going through a period of utter bankruptcy. I can remember the very moment this decision was made and it changed everything. I've been going along quietly, following my own spiritual path, which has included a twelve-step programme, a period studying Zen meditation and now membership of the Church in Wales,

not bothering anybody and suddenly, I find my kind of faith being attacked from several sides. To the secular mainstream, who think of Christmas as a shopping opportunity, I'm a wet irrelevance. To the fundamentalist Christian, I'm a doctrinal wimp because I don't believe in the literal truth of hell fire. To the Islamic fundamentalist I'm *kafir* and need to be converted to Islam or killed.

I don't recognise what I understand to be the religious life in the recent descriptions in the press. I've become increasingly concerned by the effect of this debate on our religious and political language. I'd like to examine this crisis of language and see if I can offer some principles of discernment which can cut through the emotive name-calling that has taken the place of serious discussion. It matters to me that we should find a way of distinguishing between good religious practice and an abuse of that emotive nexus, be that Christian, Muslim, Hindu or Buddhist. Embarrassment about religious belief has made many liberals reluctant even to approach the subject of religious behaviour. Indeed, I suspect that nervousness about spiritual matters is at the root of the most virulent derision from the atheist left. This squeamishness is a serious liability if we, as a society, are to find a way of talking fairly about the threats posed to us all by religious bigotry when coupled with force. A refusal to do this will, I fear, paralyse our political debate when we need it most.

In my experience, if someone claims to know the will of God for you, you can be almost 100 per cent sure that they don't. The institutional Church is, in some ways, its own worst enemy. I became an Anglican when I decided that I was fed up of hearing middle aged (I'm being kind) nonconformist ministers preaching in ways which made no sense to me and had nothing to do with my problems. At least, in Church, the liturgy minimises the proportion of freelance bullshit in every service. At its worst, church language simply makes the meta-statement: 'I'm a member of a select club. I'm in and you're out.' I've been fortunate to have conversations with theologians who have been able to convey to me what the Trinity might feel like and to suggest that the Holy Ghost might be that part of God which is communicable, say, in med-itation. Forgiveness isn't a matter of fak-ing a benign feeling towards those who've harmed you. It's a strenuous activity which requires you to change your way of being so that you're not defined by the very idea of being wronged.

Because the Church has been bad at talking to its lay members, many of its functions have been taken up by other areas of modern culture and, therefore, their origins as spiritual disciplines have become disguised. Take, for example, the commitment to truth required by psychoanalysis or recovery in Alcohol-ics Anonymous, Narcotics Anonymous and other self-help groups. These actu-ally show you how to act according to spiritual principles but outside a church; these aren't explicitly religious activities but they are the core of the religious life: subordinating the demands of the ego for a greater value.

As the anti-Christians have recently shown, it's easy to point out instances of ecclesiastical hypocrisy. There's little more difficult to cope with than the total-ly unchristian behaviour of those who set themselves up as religious leaders. Sexual abuse, emotional manipulation and bla-tantly dysfunctional behaviour have been sheltered by the power structure of many

religions. While Dawkins and Hitchens hit the mark here, they never ask why institutional religion can bring out the worst in even genuinely well-meaning people. I suspect that it's something to do with being lulled into a false sense of security about one's self when one's try-ing to 'be good'. The fact that our worst blunders happen at such times doesn't mean that the whole endeavour of liv-ing in a religious community should be abandoned. Indeed, it's more of a reason for pursuing the project with even greater urgency and, hopefully, wisdom.

Kumbh Mela, 2001

Like fundamentalists, the biologist Richard Dawkins is a literalist and refuses the strange chemistry of metaphor. This isn't because he's a scientist, but because of his particular discipline. The whole project of physics is predicated on the effort to find what can be said to be true about reality. This requires the use of

witches, shamans, channellers and all kinds of eccentric people, I noticed that it was the irreligious who became most frightened about the occult. Because I'd had experience of therapy, medita-tion and a collective religious life, I felt confident that I had a support network that would protect me. I did, however, take the precaution of formulating some criteria for selection of those taking part in the programme. Here are the questions that I asked myself about each potential contributor:

Does this person's religious activi-ties feed his or her ego or deflate it? For me, the most basic definition of religion is that it should attack the human tendency to serve the ego. There are just as many meglomaniacs in religious communities as there are in the City, and they're more difficult to spot. Does a person turn to God to confirm his or her impulses, or to learn what they never wanted to know about themselves?

Does this person try to keep other people in their power and rob them of their freedom? Cults are adept at sepa-rating people from their identities. The desire to see another person be as well, live as richly as possible, independent of one's own will, is a clue that something genuinely religious is taking place.

When this person or movement uses condemnation, is that language kind, necessary and, most importantly, is it true? Only when all three criteria are fulfilled should harsh words be used.

The most basic definition of religion is that it should attack the human tendency to serve the ego

metaphor and physicists are entirely com-fortable with the knowledge that an atom isn't a billiard ball, but more like a prob-ability smudge. The dominant discourse in Dawkins's *The God Delusion* is attack, rather than any sustained exploration of language which might involve an imagina-tive investigation of what, say, forgiveness of sins might do to you personally.

Some years ago I was working as a documentary programme maker for BBC Wales and decided to make a 50-minute programme about the New Age in Wales. When I told people that I was visiting

The language of damnation is like a toddler's painting: colourful but short on detail. What's this movement's attitude towards money? Are services given for free or is the acquisition of wealth an end in itself, religious teaching a form of con artistry?

Does a spiritual leader have people to whom he or she turns to check his own grandiosity? Does this person live in a community, or is the brand of spirituality just the enactment of a fantasy, fine when you're on your own, but easily punctured when confronted by other people's needs?

God is Black, 2004

Does this person examine their own behaviour before pointing the finger at others? Does this person claim privileges which aren't allowed to the rest of the community? If so, why?

What does this person's speech cost them? If talk is fast and loose, it's less valuable than well-considered, temperate consideration. By this token, the language of good science is privileged because of the rigour of experimental proof as, in a different way, is the multi-dimensional allusiveness and complexity of poetry.

How does this person behave, as opposed to how do they talk? The infamous Jade Goody/ Shilpa Shetty argument in Channel 4's 2006 series of *Big Brother* was, for me, the most important piece of religious broadcasting in recent years. The situation was highly artificial and histrionic on both sides but it did show two opposing models of self in action. Jade Goody showed how a very ill-at-ease person tried to make herself feel better by projecting her distress. Shilpa Shetty, with her experience of Hindu self-restraint, refused to retaliate in kind and

it every day. It's like making your life a work of art that's a partnership between you and something bigger than yourself. If you're practising this art properly, it turns out to be better than what you'd have done on your own and tends to have the element of inspiration and surprise. If you're practising properly, what faith gives you is the opposite of feeling invulnerable and saved. It makes you realise how compromised, corrupt and potentially destructive – but also joyful and loving – a human being can be.

For all our sakes, let's not succumb to the horrible embarrassment that political correctness has shed over religious matters. I don't mind my faith being attacked by Dawkins, but I do mind if the fact that him attacking the easy targets of fundamentalism and foolishness distracts us from real dangers which hide as religious questions, and which may confront us politically when we least expect it. We need to start exercising a serious discussion of religion and politics together and not this mockery of the least dangerous part.

For all our sakes, let's not succumb to the horrible embarrassment that political correctness has shed over religious matters

so won a huge PR victory. The massive response to this drama showed how viewers understood the difference between the two models of self and strongly preferred Shetty's behaviour.

The religious life can't be talked about not because it relies on mystification, but because it has to be lived. It's as senseless as asking an actor who's just performed *Hamlet* to write a critical book on the play - because they're two different and opposed sorts of action. A religious life takes years to develop because it means trying to exist outside the ego at as many levels of your life as possible. It's no good being pious if you're laundering money for the mafia. The infuriating thing about faith, like physical fitness, is that it's a commodity that can't be accumulated in credit. You're as well, in both senses, as your recent practice allows. You can't live spiritually if you don't attempt to do

Science has shown that when making decisions human beings don't, as you might expect, act according to the most rational choice. A cerebral attack on religion as a whole is, therefore, the job only half done. The spiritual life, which necessarily involves the whole of a person, needs a wider scrutiny which takes into account all areas of our lives, as John Gray does in his writing on the religious impulses behind the idea of utopia. I, therefore, find myself in the strange position of decrying Dawkins for not making a serious enough interrogation of religion. He won't have been expecting that.

The Polish Catholic Church of the Holy Trinity
Wolverhampton, 2007
Photograph: Lee Mawdsley

Quaker Meeting House
Wigan, 2007
Photograph: Lee Mawdsley

Eleven   Oh My God

A transcript from Richard Dawkins's *The Root of All Evil?* 2006 documentary for Channel 4

The Root of All Evil?

want to examine that dangerous thing common to Judaism and Christianity as well as the process of non-thinking called 'faith'.

I'm a scientist and I believe there is a profound contradiction between science and religious belief. There is no well demonstrated reason to believe in God, and I think the idea of a divine creator belittles the elegant reality of the universe. The 21st century should be an age of reason, yet irrational militant faith is back on the march. Religious extremism is implicated in the world's most bitter and unending conflicts. In Britain, even as we live in the shadow of holy terror, our government wants to restrict our freedom to criticise religion. Science we are told should not tread on the toes of theology. But why should scientists tiptoe respectfully away? The time has come for people of reason to say, enough is enough. Religious faith discourages independent thought: it's divisive and it's dangerous. Isn't this the beginning of that slippery slope that leads to young men with rucksack bombs on the tube?

If you want to experience the medieval rituals of faith nobody does it better than the Catholics. At Lourdes in southern France the assault on the senses appeals to us not to think, not to doubt, not to probe. And if we can retain our faith against the evidence in the teeth of reality, the more virtuous we are.

People like to say that faith and science can live together side by side but I don't think they can. Science is a discipline of investigation and constructive doubt, questing with logic, evidence and reason to draw conclusions. Faith by stark contrast demands a positive suspension of critical faculties. Science proceeds by setting up hypothesises, ideas, or models and then attempts to disprove them. Religion is about turning untested belief into unshakeable truth through the power of institutions and the passage of time.

Let me give you an example of this with the story of the assumption of Mary. Catholics believe that Jesus's mother, Mary, was so important she didn't physically die. Instead her body shot off into heaven when her life came to a natural end. Of course there is no evidence for this, even the bible says nothing about how Mary died. The belief that her body was lifted into heaven emerged about six centuries after Jesus's time. But it became established tradition. It was handed down over centuries and the odd thing about tradition is that the longer it's been going the more people seem to take it seriously. By 1950 the tradition was so strongly established that it became official truth: it became authority. The Vatican decreed that Roman Catholics must now believe in the doctrine of the assumption of the Virgin. Now if you had asked Pope Pius XII how he knew it was truth, he would have said you had to take his word for it because it had been revealed to him by God. He just thought private thoughts inside his own head, and convinced himself, no doubt on tortuous theological grounds, that it just had to be so.

None of this is particularly harmful when it is limited to the Virgin Mary, but what about the Pope's personal convictions when it comes to, say, discouraging the use of condoms in Aids ridden Africa? Then the power of the church through tradition, authority and revelation comes with an appalling human cost. It would be unfair to pick on the Catholics. All religions are up to the same tricks; it could be Muslim Imams issuing fatwas. It's the same principal. It's issued by the authority. It then passes down through the ranks and all without a shred of evidence.

185

Hindu Temple,
Cardiff, 2007
Photograph: Lee Mawdsley

Eleven

Oh My God

The ongoing paranoia of Britain's Catholic community is explored by novelist and Catholic Ivo Stourton

The Spanish Sent an Armada

A couple of months ago I was at a party in the country, staying in the room next door to a Catholic friend. As I was getting changed for dinner, I heard her through the door asking directory enquiries for the number of the local priest. Slightly alarmed, I knocked on the door to find her putting on mascara. I asked her why she felt she needed to speak with one of God's anointed. 'I'm booking confession for tomorrow,' she replied, without looking away from the compact. Firstly, I was impressed that priests now took bookings. I had always thought of the sacrament as more of an open-surgery thing. When I asked her why she needed urgent shriving, she looked at me as if I were an idiot, and said, 'I intend to have some real fun tonight. And in the morning, I intend to absolve myself.' That response seemed to me to unite many essential Catholic characteristics – a taste for decadence, a fine moral sensibility and an extraordinary capacity to suspend rationality without ever losing sight of logic.

When I told my father and sister that I had been asked to write about my experiences as an English Catholic, they were outraged. They pointed out that I

had stopped going to Church (I gave it up along with confession at eighteen), and that I claimed I didn't believe in God (I do sometimes, but I can't resist winding them up). My father retrieved a copy of the Catechism from his library, and we set about trying to prove who was the best English Catholic by seeing who had memorised more of the Credo, and who could do the requiem mass in

'I intend to have some real fun tonight. And in the morning, I intend to absolve myself'

Latin. I can get up to the bit where the sacred judgment arrives, but then things become a bit sketchy. Beneath all the familial bluster I think they were worried, quite legitimately, that I was going to say something on their behalf with no real right or understanding of what it meant to still practise my faith. In fact, I do lay claim to a certain universality when describing my experiences as an English

Catholic, but it doesn't have much to do with faith. I think everyone experiences their faith privately, in a dialogue between themselves and God, and whether I went to Church or not I still wouldn't want to speak for the man kneeling beside me. I think the thing that I share with my father and sister, my odd lapses into belief aside, is the cultural experience of English Catholicism.

To understand what it means to be a left-footer, you must first recognise that Catholicism has traditionally been the religion of our foreign enemies, people actively trying to invade us, murder us or just tick us off. The Spanish sent an armada. The French gave succour to our Catholic king in exile at great personal expense, just to annoy Parliament. The Irish tried to blow us up, though as a

The Week They Elected the Pope, 2005

Londoner the rise of Islamic terrorism almost makes me nostalgic for the days of the coded warning. The closest thing we have to an Independence Day involves the symbolic burning of a Catholic freedom fighter/anarchistic traitor (delete as applicable) to celebrate the foiling of his Spanish-backed coup. I remember cheerfully warming my hands in front of the bonfire at my Catholic prep school on Guy Fawkes night, blissfully unaware that one of my own forebears had been

In a London increasingly characterised by isolation and the breakdown of community, the Catholics still stick together

incarcerated in the Tower for alleged knowledge of the plot. He had failed to turn up to Westminster on the day the gunpowder was to have been ignited, and his excuse when he was brought before the Star Chamber was that he had stayed in the country to spend more time with his wife. Official records are sketchy, but according to family lore this prompted one of his judges to condemn him on the grounds that he had met his wife, and no one in their right mind could possibly want to spend more time with her than necessity demanded. So, since the days of the Reformation, Catholics have been the natural enemy of English sovereignty. By extension, English recusants were always viewed as a dodgy bunch. Historically,

no one seemed quite sure which way the domestic Catholics would go when the chips were down.

If you want a good litmus test for this attitude, just have a look at the presentation of English Catholics in literature. From the overt threat to English virtue presented by Duessa in Spenser's *Faerie Queene*, right down through the ages to the anti-heroic saints and crazies in Graham Greene and Evelyn Waugh, they seem to occupy in the collective psyche of the British writer the position of the unknowable other. If you ever encounter a Catholic figure in the work of a 20th-century UK novelist, they'll be physically beautiful and faintly otherworldly, and I'll give you good odds on them going mad, or dying tragically, or going mad before dying tragically.

For a Catholic living in the 21st century, this means two things. Firstly, the siege mentality inured in my family by four centuries of punitive taxes, exclusion and wildly romantic literary archetypes has long outlived the conditions that created it. I don't think the Protestants really mistrust Catholics anymore, but Catholics remember being mistrusted. This is what I mean by cultural Catholicism; English Catholics, like Jews, have historically been exiles in their own homes. When we had finished reciting prayers at each other, my father asked me to go to church again at least once before I wrote this piece. Whilst I felt nothing stir at the repetition of the familiar old words, I was struck by the handshaking and casual hellos after the service. It reminded me that in a London increasingly characterised by isolation and the breakdown of community, the Catholics still stick together. The same is true when it comes to marriage and education, creating a common bond that has very little to do with a belief in God, and everything to do with a faint, healthy sense of paranoia.

Secondly, I think we are much more ready to accept the fact that, against all the odds and several decades after the end of history, the looming conflicts of the 21st century appear to be religious. There is a recurrent sense of surprise in the English press that we are currently under threat, real or imagined, from a domestic minority whose monotheistic religion has its spiritual home in a foreign country with whom we do not enjoy particularly good relations. I never sense that surprise when I open a copy of *The Tablet*

(the foremost Catholic rag). I think that in some small way, having been raised in the English Catholic tradition, I'm a little more prepared for the weird way the world appears to be going than my liberal, largely atheistic Protestant friends, who have trouble understanding why anyone would care enough about religion to kill for it. The proof of this theory for me lies with Tony Blair – he more than anyone else in the Labour government seemed to

Since the days of the Reformation Catholics have been the natural enemy of English sovereignty

embrace the concept of religious conflict with shiny-eyed enthusiasm. Though not technically a Catholic himself at the time, something of the ethos must have rubbed off on him through endless hours of mass with Cherie and photo ops with John Paul II. If English voters were ready for the shadow of a Papist behind the dispatch box he might even have converted, and the fact that he didn't speaks volumes for the vague traces of suspicion the Anglican electorate might still feel for such a figure... Or that could just be my recusant paranoia playing tricks on me again.

Reality Check

Few people dispute that *Big Brother* is among the most influential TV programmes of recent times: it gave rise to the phenomenon of 'reality' TV, capturing the minutiae of real lives on screen in a way that documentaries seldom can. *BB* has become a national forum for the voices, prejudices, passions and affections of ordinary people, though its voluble critics believe it shapes rather than reflects the rise of a new form of celebrity culture that puts a premium on exposure over talent. What is not in dispute is that the programme's enduring appeal has raised it above the level of mere entertainment – it has been instrumental in the development of the internet as an audiovisual medium. More importantly, it has had an impact on the perceptions of class, race and sexuality of an entire viewing generation. It continues to demonstrate the extraordinary open-mindedness of today's TV audience, who have voted for winners of every possible racial and sexual hue.

Craig Phillips
Winner Season One: 2000

'I left school in Liverpool with no exam results because I was dyslexic, so I started work hod-carrying on a building site. Since winning *Big Brother*, I set up my own TV production company and I have appeared in over 700 DIY TV shows. I have also set up a construction training academy which teaches kids in Liverpool carpentry, plastering and brick laying. We started with 152 students and this year we will be training 500 students on the course, which goes up to NVQ level two. I also set up my own building company in the Shropshire area, starting by buying and renovating a very small cottage, which I now live in, and moving up from there. I have bought and restored or completely re-built old, ruined houses and my current ambition is to restore a castle – you don't know of one that needs help, do you?'

The Big Brother Confessional

For all its screeching abuse and blow jobs under the blanket, *Big Brother* really represents a return to early Christianity. In the early days of the Church, confession was a public affair. Rather than whisper sheepishly through a grille to a priest who was probably asleep, or engaged in some secret sinful practice himself, people used to proclaim their sins in public. There was a period in the 1960s when this practice was briefly revived. I remember attending a trendy mass at the time, in the course of which people rose from their pews and accused themselves of various offences, most of them disappointingly vague. Then a young woman stood up and declared loudly, 'I have committed adultery'. The rest of us were still recovering from the shock when she pointed dramatically across the church and announced, 'With that man over there'. She was indicating a young father with a baby on his knee, who was turning a slow purple. Then she added, 'in thought,' and sat down again. It struck me later that this might have been an unusually ingenious sort of come-on.

The diary room of *Big Brother* is a kind of equivalent of the confessional, with Big Brother himself acting as a cross between confessor, therapist, superego and troubleshooter, but it is a confessional open to public view. This simply pushes to a logical conclusion the fact that everything on television is public anyway. Privacy on TV is a pretence. We know that the amorous young couple are not actually rolling in a remote haystack, because the haystack is being photographed. Voyeurism, of which the *Big Brother* audience has been accused, usually means spying on a private scene; but the ocular pleasures of the programme involve snooping on public events as though they were private. And if the public are cast in the role of voyeurs, there is a good case that the occupants of the house are professional exhibitionists. Yet in a society in which the private is being taken into public ownership, who isn't?

What is most striking, however, is that the scenes on which we are prying aren't for the most part steamy at all, or even mildly sensational. Nothing is as fascinating as banality, as Samuel Beckett discovered long before Jade Goody was invented. In one sense, this is appalling news for television producers. They have been wasting their time on all those artfully wrought narratives, gorgeous costumes, scintillating snatches of dialogue and ruinously expensive outdoor shots. In a postmodern age, plot, storyline, action and language have all become redundant. Only one thing remains of the whole traditional literary ragbag, and that is character. Character is eternally compelling.

Not character, to be sure, in the sense of rich, complex, in-depth, fully rounded personalities. In another devastating blow to creatively minded TV types, *Big Brother* – like *The Archers* – reveals the dreadful secret that people do not have to be interesting to be fascinating. Once upon a time, people were fascinating for their actions and qualities. Macbeth, for example, or Eric Morecambe. But Shakespeare, it now appears, was wasting his time as well. What is truly irresistible is not seeing people parleying with witches or killing their king, but simply watching them being themselves. Whether those selves are elegant, meditative and subtly ironic, or thick, prejudiced and pig-ignorant, is beside the point. What nobody else can replicate is the fact that I am me. I may be boorish, domineering and mildly repulsive, but the mind-warping fact that only I am me gives me a clear edge over everyone else. This, at least, can compensate for the fact that I cannot speak Slovenian or play the flute. The ultimate democracy is to be supremely important simply for being yourself. Not even Thomas Jefferson could have anticipated that.

It is true that even the apparently raw reality of *Big Brother* has to be subjected to editing, along with a voice-over by an adenoidal Geordie. (More precisely, a Geordie playing a Geordie.) But the programme has nevertheless proved the point that people will cancel holidays to Portugal in order to watch someone watching someone lying on a sofa watching the ceiling. It is an instance of what the French philosopher Jean-François Lyotard once described as our 'pornographic appetite for the real'. The bad news for the creative imagination is that nothing succeeds like good, old-fashioned, humdrum reality. Just by being real, reality, however dilapidated, has the edge over the most elaborately persuasive of fictions. Milton's Satan may be magnificent, but Shilpa Shetty actually exists, and in doing so beats him hands down every time. Realist art narrowed the gap between fiction and reality. Reality TV takes that process a logical step further and closes it until one cannot even spot the join. Just as a pile of bricks becomes art when it is placed in the Tate, so a bunch of not-overwhelmingly-fascinating young people become fascinating by being framed by a TV screen. It is not that they are thereby transformed into magical figures. On the contrary, the whole point of the show is that they continue to be themselves. It is that TV is magical *in*

Milton's Satan may be magnificent, but Shilpa Shetty actually exists, and in doing so beats him hands down every time

itself, just as power and money are. There is no need for tinsel, stardust and Standard English. Everyone is equal in the diary room, just as they are in the polling booth. There is likely to be a rough sort of equality between the members of the house in any case, since only the kind of people who are interested in ending up on the programme will do so, and that excludes whole swathes of the population.

In the end, then, we are not really looking at 'real people'. We are looking at the kind of people who like to share their lives with millions of others which, along with basket weaving and coprophilia, is still a minority taste. It may not be so soon.

The commonplace is infinitely seductive. It confirms what we secretly yearn to know – that other people's lives are just as dingy, makeshift and eventless

as our own. The audience of *Big Brother* is a narcissist peering in a mirror, delighting in the consolation of seeing its own features reflected there. It's a familiar point about realist art that we tend to enjoy it, however unsavoury or even repulsive the things it represents. There is something about the act of representing reality itself that grips us, however tedious or offensive the material we are shown. We are creatures who for some doubtless evolutionary reason take pleasure in doubling, mimesis, reflection, simulacrum; and though some *Big Brother* contestants might not have been able to pronounce some of those words – and a few of them might jump on any contestant rash enough to use them – this, in effect,

The Guardian, 2000

The Guardian, 2000

is what endows these ordinary men and women with their transient moment of glory. The glory is then reflected on to the audience, not least because they have an active role in deciding who stays and who goes. To this extent, *Big Brother* is a skewed version of those weekend house parties organised by MI6 for Oxbridge graduates, in which, under the ever-watchful eye of senior spooks, a few fortunate souls will end up learning how to kill Muslims with a matchbox, while the rest will become stockbrokers.

In the end, it is the puritanism of the programme that is most eye-catching. For the Puritan tradition, nothing can be real unless it is externalised. The original Big Brother society in George Orwell's *1984* drew the grim political conclusions of this belief. Everyone is publicly at stake all the time. Privacy is a crime. Subjectivity itself, since it seems to involve an interior world closed off from others, is a kind of treason. There is, however, a stage beyond even this totalitarian nightmare. It is when there is nothing important enough to keep secret in the first place. The ultimate collapse of privacy does not come about when everything must be compulsively publicised. It comes about when there is nothing of much value to be publicised in the first place, because everything is already on the surface. It's OK to parade your private life in public when everyone can predict its contents already. At this point, the terms 'private'

and 'public' both lose their meaning. When everything is public, the idea of privacy withers away. But so does the idea of the public, since there is now nothing to contrast it with.

Seventeenth-century Puritans endured spiritual torment in getting their chequered souls out in the open. For their postmodern progeny, there is less and less 'in here' to be externalised in the first place. Or rather, what's in here is often enough, just a reflection of what's out there: money, power, celebrity, status. Is what we are witnessing with *Big Brother*, then, the death of the subject? And, if so, does the death presage some wondrous new creation, or some monstrous birth?

The rise of celebrity in Britain is actually the rise of a populist ethos. Andrew O'Hagan explains

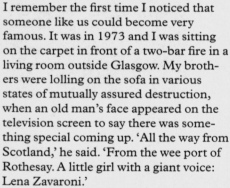

The Ghosts In Our Machines

I remember the first time I noticed that someone like us could become very famous. It was in 1973 and I was sitting on the carpet in front of a two-bar fire in a living room outside Glasgow. My brothers were lolling on the sofa in various states of mutually assured destruction, when an old man's face appeared on the television screen to say there was something special coming up. 'All the way from Scotland,' he said. 'From the wee port of Rothesay. A little girl with a giant voice: Lena Zavaroni.'

There had, of course, been famous people before. In our house we knew all about Muhammad Ali and David Bowie. My brothers could name a hundred football players who used to kick about in playgrounds and now earned £100 a week. But this little girl was from a family just like ours: descendants of immigrants who had come to Scotland a few generations back, who lived around housing estates and chip shops and pubs. When Lena Zavaroni sang my brothers started laughing and I believe they were laughing with recognition. This thirteen-year-old girl was like one of our Glasgow aunties or grannies: she had a whole working-

class culture in her presentation, and right away we could see beneath the show's veneer and glitter and recognise a girl from one of our towns who just wanted to be famous. And she was famous: she won the show five weeks in a row and was in every newspaper. We couldn't have known then – and neither could she, poor love – that within ten years she'd be writing private letters saying, 'I have lost myself', 'I am in a black hole', and that she would be dead by the age of 34, killed by complications and annihilations associated with anorexia nervosa. Her hunger for fame went physical, and over the years I came to see her as a patron saint of British celebrity.

....

The British public now finds it much more satisfying to be reassured than to be astonished

....

When I watch TV now I often think of her, and others pretty much like her – they are the ghosts in the machine. Light entertainment, when it comes to talent, is a modern form of gladiatorial combat, a form that would come to build its Coliseum in the shape of *Big Brother*, a talent show in which your character is your talent and where bad traits are identified by the public and punished with eviction and humiliation. We seem to have travelled quite a long way from the little girl with the big voice, but not really: the real centre of the story of British celebrity is never actually the star, it is the public. The rise of celebrity in Britain is actually the rise of a populist ethos.

As we clapped in our Scottish living room for Lena Zavaroni, I was convinced – being the youngest and the most starry-eyed – that the 'clapometer' in London would pick up the noise and help Lena to win. *Opportunity Knocks* made the public the star: we made her success possible. And that is still the signature of phone-and-text competitions today. 'If I am a star,' Marilyn Monroe once said, 'then it is the public who made me a star.' And it is that power which became a kind of

Brian Dowling

Winner Season Two: 2001

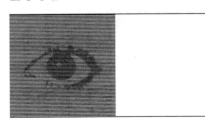

'It's very bizarre. I'd always planned to go back to flying. I was due to go back to my job as a steward on 1 September, and I did all the personal appearances, but was still planning to go back to work. But in fact I came out of that house with an entirely new career. First, I got offered a job presenting an amazing kid's show *SMTV Live* when Ant and Dec left, along with Cat Deeley and Tess Daly. I told them I wasn't a television presenter, I had only been in *Big Brother* – but I got the job. It's now been seven years since I won and I'm still working – I've just landed a new show called *Cirque de Celebrité* where celebrities train to be in the circus. I do the spin-off show every Thursday. It's fabulous, because they want me to be myself, so I have lots of input into the script. I think where I score is that I'm very optimistic. It takes a lot to upset me or bog me down, but I've been very lucky. Really, really lucky.'

contagion in Britain at the end of the 20th century. Margaret Thatcher may have wrecked our former sense of community, but she created a temperament for other forms of mass communion based on spite, many of which seek to mobilise collective feeling at 54 pence a minute.

Celebrity Big Brother, 2006

This is the theatre of the new celebrity and its front-of-house staff are the tabloids. It is sometimes hard to be sure, when reading those papers with their trigger-happy eruptions of populist zeal, whether one is experiencing, say, a common apprehension of some reality TV personality's fatness and horribleness, or whether one is being asked to help kill an alleged paedophile; whether one is being invited to win £1 million, or being told about the terror in Darfur, or encouraged to gape at a woman's breasts, or laugh at a person's downfall. It all comes at you with the same tone of aggressive common sense and unassailable male joy. The whiles of celebrity make the public feel powerful and imperial. We can decide on the fame of ordinary people, which makes us feel very real. It also does what politics cannot do: it makes us feel together.

Celebrity Big Brother, 2005

Togetherness. Now there's a 1960s concept. Just as the counterculture gave way to that over-the-counter-culture of Britain in the 1980s, so did the old Reithian idea of public service broadcasting give way to the new tyranny of choice. The requirement for talent and for cheapness in the digital age has led at last to a denigration of the idea of specialness. Even the *Opportunity Knocks*

format depended on the notion that the participants would be special in some way – big voice, dancing stomach muscles, clever acrobatics, fascinating tricks – but being special is no longer a requirement for British celebrityhood. It may, in fact, be a handicap in one's bid for the public's affection. What we want most of all is ordinariness – we want Jade Goody. The British public now finds it much more satisfying to be reassured than to be astonished, and that alone might begin to explain the trajectory of famousness in our time. We are capable of feeling together in one great respect: we all want to feel that the people entertaining us could just as easily be us.

....

'Famous' was no longer an adjective; it was a job and a condition of being

....

That's how I felt in front of the two-bar fire. The girl on the television could just as easily be me. And as the years passed and the culture changed and that little girl became a suffering woman and a celebrity ghost, I continued to feel she spoke to everyone who cares about who we are. I remember walking through those flowers along The Mall after Diana died, thinking this is the revolution we've been waiting for: the country and the press got the god-like victim it wanted, and now comes the observance and the prayers and the flowers. We wanted a celebrity to die in the cause of our need to feel that normality is everything. People were overwhelmed by the local power of that sentiment and they gathered together and bawled in the street.

A few years after that I was working on a novel and one day I visited a classroom of 30 girls. I gave out pieces of paper and asked them to write down what they wanted to be. It was the question we were always asked at school, and we would write 'astronaut' or 'hairdresser'. Seventy per cent of the paper I'd given out to the girls contained a single word: 'Famous'. I left the school in Hornsey realising that the world was a new place in

respect of celebrity (the summit of human wishes) and that television had perhaps played the major part in that transformation. 'Famous' was no longer an adjective; it was a job and a condition of being.

You used to have to be chosen. You used to have to be chosen over others, lifted up, made special. That is what being famous was all about: the glow of her chosenness, the heat of his recognisability. Producers and directors and editors and talent scouts chose you – they married you to the means of production – and then the public chose you in their turn. But the means of production have altered for ever, and now people can broadcast themselves in ways that make the old entertainment models seem as antique and ghostly as music hall. Young kids make a record in their bedroom and they play it on MySpace. Girls create an audience and a network of contacts on Facebook, letting the world assess them and join them and make them famous. Everyone can make a spectacle of himself nowadays: home computers are increasingly built for that, for iLife, which isn't the same as any life that went on in this country before. Every bedroom is a potential studio and every person with WiFi is a potential star. They are already the stars of their own lives. And perhaps that is where television has ceded most to the new technologies: the fate of togetherness will not, in the future, be served by a diet of programmes served for our collective experience, but by each of us acting as producer and crew and star of our own show, which we then share with selected others. We have gone well past Andy Warhol. In the future everyone will be famous for as long as they like, but only to one person at a time. And in the end we might just arrive at the perfect last stop in our transit to Narcissus, where each screen becomes a mirror: one celebrity, one fan, the same person, one's self.

Celebrity Big Brother, 2005

Kate Lawler

Winner Season Three: 2002

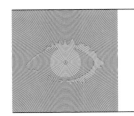

'I was doing well. I had a talented boyfriend, and we went off to Japan to work. I was earning good money. I'd just bought myself a car. But we split up, and I came home to my family. I wanted to move out, but I knew how long it would take me to get a deposit on a flat. So I thought, if I won *Big Brother* I'd be able to do it. When I won, and came out of the house, I didn't realise how much people recognise you and now I find it quite difficult. It's weird; I hate the red carpet, I hate being photographed by the paparazzi, but I don't mind being in front of the camera or a microphone, because that's what I do. I love being on the radio doing my daily show because I'm there in the studio with my friend, having a laugh. I love being a DJ, but a lot of people have said, "She's only doing it because she's been on the telly and she can't possibly be any good at it." It's difficult being taken seriously as a DJ, which is why I am really excited about going to Brazil, because people will be there to listen to my music and I'll be able to play whatever I want.'

Cameron Stout

Winner Season Four: 2003

'I come from the Orkney Islands, on the same latitude as Alaska. I studied International Trade and Languages at Edinburgh, then did my study year in France, then worked in Seville for a year, but I always wanted to go back to the Orkneys. So I did, and applied for a school leaver job as a salesman in a fish company. But when I sent in my CV, they decided to give me a chance as Export Manager. My brother, who makes commercials, made a video of me in the Orkneys, standing on a cliff with the sun behind my head, to enter me for *Big Brother*. Now I'm back in the Orkneys but do quite a lot of writing. I have a column in the *Aberdeen Express* and I do a lot with BBC Scotland. I'm also a veteran on the panto circuit. I've played Prince Charming, Peter Pan, and Hook's assistant. The best thing that happened after *Big Brother* was going to Zambia where the girl who had won *Big Brother Zambia* asked me to cut a ribbon in a park that had been created by raising money from charity, and I met Dr Kenneth Kaunda.'

Gautam Malkani on the day *Big Brother* started asking interesting questions about race

Transcending Entertainment

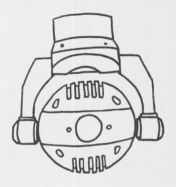

In 1963, a quarter of a million Americans voted with their feet by attending a rally at the Lincoln Memorial and helped beget the 1964 US Civil Rights Act. In 1994, South Africans used their first democratic elections to empower the ANC and abolished apartheid. And in 2007, Britons got their very own referendum on racism – albeit in the more frivolous form of television viewers voting against a reality TV star for bullying a rival contestant.

It might seem ridiculous to compare landmarks in mankind's struggle for racial equality with the infamous racial bullying incident on Channel 4's *Celebrity Big Brother*. But blanket media coverage, and the kind of mass public hysteria not seen since the death of Princess Diana, lent the affair a significance even the holier-than-highbrow cannot deny.

Reality TV contestants are expected to have bust-ups. That's kind of the point. And bullying and bickering among *Big Brother* housemates is *de rigueur*. But when the squabbling took on racist tones, this decade's social angsts came crashing together in one stroke: race relations and the challenges of multiculturalism; the obsession with celebrity; new media and entertainment formats that have made ordinary people instantly famous; the continued descent of the British press into witch-hunts and scorn orgies; and the triumph of entertainment over enlightenment. The *Celebrity Big Brother* affair even threw the social issues that dominated the 20th century into the mix: good old class conflict and the scars of imperialism.

With each day that the contestants spent inside *Big Brother's* hidden-camera-ridden house, the on-screen bullying of Bollywood actress Shilpa Shetty by a trio of D-list British celebrities slowly spiralled into an international incident. A high-profile trade visit to India by Gordon Brown was overshadowed as protestors there burnt effigies of the programme's producers. The show's corporate backer suspended its £3 million sponsorship. And the UK media regulator received around 45,000 complaints from viewers incensed over the abuse to which Shetty was subjected.

The outrage of both white and ethnic minority viewers seemed an encouraging symbol of social progress in Britain. Racism has long been unacceptable in polite society, but now it was equally unacceptable in impolite society. Sure, Shetty's pomposity was so irritating she may as well have sat there scratching a blackboard with her carefully manicured nails. But certain housemates were so vile to her, it was a credit to Shetty's decorum that she didn't scratch their eyes out.

Viewers were treated to the mimicking of her accent and the repeated mispronunciation of her name – she was memorably dubbed 'Shilpa poppadom' by arch-antagonist Jade Goody, herself catapulted to fame on an earlier, non-celebrity series of *Big Brother.* Plus, there were disparaging remarks about cooking in India from Jo O'Meara, one-time pop star with S Club 7; and the suggestion from Danielle Lloyd, former Miss Britain and footballer's girlfriend, that her Indian housemate should 'fuck off home'.

But while the public outcry was justified, the substance of many protests was not. Shrill calls for the series to be pulled off air and the vilification of Dutch production company Endemol, and Channel 4, for broadcasting such unpleasant scenes, were a bit like switching channels to avoid news reports about starving

The Times, 2000

children. This preference for airbrushing out of consciousness scenes that were challenging, uncomfortable and ugly meant the mass of viewer complaints became a measure of how far we have regressed into feelgood evenings on cosy US sitcom-style couches. For all their faults, *Big Brother*-style surveillance cameras at least expose what goes on outside our own homes.

As any British Asian will tell you, the kind of ambiguous barbs directed at Shetty can really smart. If you don't know whether someone's being racist or just plain nasty, you don't know where you stand. Moreover, it is exactly this sort of subtle prejudice and wilful failure to appreciate cultural differences that are the most difficult aspect of racism to capture in drama and documentaries – or even literature. And yet there it was, magically appearing on TV for all to see and comprehend.

I know both Asian and white viewers alike who shared a twinge of empathy when Shetty was mocked for placing an extra bedcover over an older contestant. Respect for elders or sucking up? Ignorance or intolerance? Questions like these extended beyond the pages of newspapers to dominate banter from bus stops to office canteens and from pubs to discussion forums on the internet, radio and TV. It was a national debate.

Hitherto, bigotry then stifling political correctness had prevented people from asking interesting questions about what does or doesn't constitute racism. But the fact was, nobody could possibly watch the antics inside the *Big Brother* house without wondering whether the racial and cultural divisions between the warring contestants were as relevant as their differing levels of education. And in today's relative meritocracy, for education read 'class'.

This element of class conflict also resonated powerfully with viewers. From this perspective, the tables were dramatically turned: suddenly Goody, O'Meara and Lloyd were the underdogs. Screenwriters would kill for such ironies.

Reality TV has been a seductive social leveller, best epitomised by Andy Abraham, the *X Factor* dustman-turned-charttopper. And you don't even need talent to make it on *Big Brother*. If society's obsession with celebrity relates to the immortality it confers, then the mountain of D-list celebrities churned out by reality TV has made that immortality appear more attainable. A product of non-celebrity *Big Brother* now re-appearing on the celebrity version, Goody was a classic case in point.

The trouble was, Goody's fall from grace in front of millions of viewers confirmed what many people were beginning to suspect: so-called D-list celebrities did not exist on a level of moral parity with the so-called A-listers. While an A-lister could come out of jail, morality apparently in tact, Jade has slipped out of the public view. Today's celebrity class system is thus a bit like that in *Titanic* (the celebrity-filled film version if not the real thing): passengers on the lower deck don't have the same access to lifeboats.

So the affair forced fame-seekers nationwide to wake up to the fact that the miraculously democratic fame-making machine that is reality TV doesn't actually work very well. Unlike Shetty's Bollywood, which has done a decent job of containing the proliferation of celebrity so that those who achieve it enjoy it for ever – like 1940s Hollywood.

Whether the bullying was better viewed as a race row, a class conflict, or karma for the celebrity-obsessed, the remarks

Nadia Almada
Winner Season Five: 2004

'Why did I go in for *Big Brother*? I did it to tell my story and the story of people like me who have had a sex change. As it turned out, a lot of people were genuinely interested, and I think it made a big impact on people's attitude towards sex change. And there are a lot of vulnerable people out there who needed the medical, rather than social, message that it was OK to have a sex change. Since winning, I've done some acting, including *Hollyoaks*. I've written fashion columns and done a bit of presenting, but now I'm think-ing of going back to Madeira, where my family lives, to set up a fashion business with a friend of mine. There are a lot of marvellous embroiderers there – my mum makes beautiful drawn threadwork tablecloths, for instance. My whole family has always been extraordinarily support-ive of what I have done and what I have achieved so far.'

Anthony Hutton
Winner Season Six: 2005

'Why do I think I won *Big Brother*? I think I was honest, I did the tasks as best as I could, I didn't act arrogant and I tried to keep pretty much below radar when I was in there, not getting into rows. My boyhood dream, growing up with my grandmother and mother in Newcastle, was to be a footballer. I never made it, but after I won *Big Brother* we put on 'The Match', a charity game at St. James's Park and 52,000 people watched me. That was really, really amazing and Graham Taylor, the coach of Newcastle United, is one of the best blokes I've ever met. When I went in for *Big Brother*, which I got the second time I tried, I was already heavily involved in show business with a Seventies disco revival group I formed with my mates. It was called *Anthony's Boogie Nights*, and we still tour the clubs with it. And last Christmas I was in panto, playing Prince Charming in *Snow White*. And thanks to *Big Brother*, I now own three houses in Newcastle; my gran lives in one of them.'

made by Shetty's tormentors were so embarrassingly dumb, most people concluded that racial intolerance is a subset of stupidity that brings its own penance. School teachers and youth workers may have preached this before, but now everyone could witness its incontrovertible truth.

So, given all of this good that the whole affair was doing Britain, why on earth were people calling for the plug to be pulled? A lot of white people I know simply felt ashamed by Goody, Lloyd and O'Meara. A lot of brown and black people claimed it brought back painful memories of racism that they themselves had experienced. Clearly, neither discomfort outweighs the benefits of broadcasting it – to prevent the exposure of social ills just because it might remind people of social ills is absurd.

The reason *Big Brother* remains the granddaddy of the reality TV genre is that it often demonstrates a potential to transcend entertainment

However, the UK's broadcasting codes stipulate that the airing of offensive material must be justified by 'context' – a deliberately and necessarily loose term. For example, content appropriate in a documentary about racism may not be appropriate in a children's cartoon. So when investigating the complaints, the UK media regulator faced the question: did the *context* justify the discomfort? For viewers who tune into *Big Brother* for light entertainment, the evident answer was no. The regulator's report into the affair and remarks made by government ministers at the time of the uproar left no doubt that as far as the British establishment is concerned, *Big Brother* is merely an entertainment programme.

But the reason *Big Brother* remains the granddaddy of the reality TV genre is that it often demonstrates a potential to transcend entertainment. It began as an interesting social experiment far removed from the kind of glorified game shows and talent contests that make up most of the genre. Accordingly, early series employed behaviourists to comment on the stresses contestants faced in the house. Furthermore, the very fact of 24-hour surveillance means that, when it works well, *Big Brother* allows viewers to experience a special kind of empathy with those on screen – a confluence of intellectual and emotional engagement built from breakfast, through boredom, to bed.

Sadly, the lure of audience ratings meant the show has also often descended into farcical inanity. Instead of exploring how and why sane people crack up under pressure in social situations, producers deliberately selected contestants who were outlandish to start with. Thus, viewing sometimes became a voyeuristic job of seeing who would fornicate on air first.

Nonetheless, surely such things cannot be set in stone.

You need only watch a soap opera to realise any attempt to show 'reality' on television will necessarily oscillate between entertaining frivolity and more edifying drama. The sheer complexity of the *Celebrity Big Brother* affair meant that this particular series patently reclaimed the programme's loftier potential – albeit unintentionally.

Perhaps one difficulty highlighted by the controversy is that, as one person's entertainment might be another's education, the establishment too readily fears that viewers will take away the wrong lesson. Thousands still voted against Shetty, implying support for Goody. And even in an educated democracy, some people still prove dumb enough to vote for the far right or join a terrorist group. The establishment's fear therefore resembles that of the stereotypical Hollywood filmmaker who assumes all audiences are stupid and incapable of sensibly interpreting moral ambiguities for themselves.

In the end, the UK media regulator chastised Channel 4 for its handling of the affair – specifically its failure to act on more overtly racist footage from the house that wasn't actually broadcast but which offered an earlier opportunity to reprimand the contestants in time to prevent the race row from escalating.

Of course, given the subsequent windfall for healthy national debate, this failing was just as well.

Amid the public hullabaloo, the media's role was debated as fiercely as the alleged racism. One reason why the disgraced D-listers fell so hard was because they were deemed fair game by a British press that smelt blood. In the short-term at least, snapping and sniping still helps sell newspapers and Goody's camp duly became prey as soon as they turned predators.

Meanwhile, others attributed Channel 4's dithering to a cynical attempt to nurture the controversy for maximum advertising revenues. This view might overlook the withdrawal of the programme's main sponsor but nevertheless, any gains for the broadcaster in terms of audience ratings clearly came at the expense of Shetty's wellbeing and her tormentors' careers.

But so what? As a former contestant, Goody knew more than anyone about the consequences of her behaviour inside the house and the behaviour of the press outside it. Every contestant knows the place is rigged with cameras and microphones. They should watch what they say. Likewise, Shetty was not the show's first ever contestant to break down in tears under the stress of it all. And her tears had long dried up when she emerged from the house as the series' victor, fireworks overhead and legions of new fans underfoot.

Blissfully ignorant of how her experience had mushroomed into an international race relations incident, Shetty's march along the catwalk-style walkway leading out of the *Big Brother* house was hardly Nelson Mandela's Long Walk to Freedom. But neither was it as simple as a short, stage-managed strut to superstardom.

Twelve Reality Check

Pete Bennett

Winner Season Seven: 2006

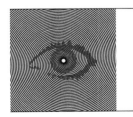

'Why did I go in for *Big Brother*? It was weird really. I am very clairvoyant and I had a dream in which a very close friend who had died in an accident told me to go in for it, and that I would win it. So I did and I'm proud I raised £400,000 with the phone-ins for the Tourette Association. Yes, of course it was difficult for me trying out for *Big Brother* and going on the show, but I wanted to raise people's awareness of Tourette Syndrome, to let them know they didn't have to be scared of us, that they can have a laugh with us. And I also wanted to sort out my mum's £70,000 mortgage and promote my band, which is called Pete Bennett and the Love Dogs. My first single, *Cosmonaut,* is about to appear on an independent label and I'm going on tour with the new band, which we launched at the O2 Dome. Of course, my ambition is to be a rock star.'

Brian Belo

Winner Season Eight: 2007

'I only had a job as a data input technician for two months before I was chosen for *Big Brother*. I'd never spent more than four days away from home before, so to be in the house with so many people was difficult and it's even more difficult now, because having lived for fifteen weeks without newspapers, TV and radio, and with only a few people in the house, I find life on the outside really crowded. It's like a dream really. It's difficult to realise that it's happening to me. It's a problem going out for dinner with my best friend – we have known each other since we were six. Now, people come up to me all the time because they know me, or they think they do, and it's tough on him. I suppose it will wear off, and I do realise the fame thing is only going to last for a little while, and then I'll go back to my normal life and get another job, or go to uni. It's like Andy Warhol, I tell myself, it's only for fifteen minutes, and I have to keep my feet on the ground.'

13

Home Sweet Home

A consequence of the cult of individualism that has grown alongside Channel 4 over the last 25 years is the growing importance of style and design. Channel 4 has captured this in programmes like *Grand Designs*, a property show that's also a paean to aspiration and self-expression (as well as a study in occasional self-delusion). Channel 4 has not just charted how the homes and possessions of a generation have exploded the one-size-fits-all philosophy of the past, but has recognised the wider social impact of the built environment. Architecture has been given shelf space alongside the visual arts through annual coverage of the RIBA Stirling Prize, and documentary series such as *The Perfect Home* have examined the contribution that good design makes to human happiness.

Alain de Botton, presenter of Channel 4's *The Perfect Home*, investigates the emotional values at the heart of design

The Meaning of Design

The Perfect Home, 2006

Is it serious to worry about design and architecture? To think hard about the shape of the bathroom taps, the colour of the bedspread and the dimensions of the window frames?

A long intellectual tradition suggests it isn't quite. A whiff of trivia and self-indulgence floats over the topic. It seems like something best handled by the flamboyant presenters of early evening TV shows (not, of course, anything offered up by C4…). A thought-provoking number of the world's most intelligent people have always disdained any interest in the appearance of buildings, equating contentment with discarnate and invisible matters instead. The ancient Greek Stoic philosopher Epictetus is said to

Location, Location, Location from 2000

have demanded of a heart-broken friend whose house had burnt to the ground, 'If you really understand what governs the universe, how can you yearn for bits of stone and pretty rock?' (It is unclear how much longer the friendship lasted.)

And yet determined efforts to scorn design have also long been matched by equally persistent attempts to mould the material world to graceful ends. People have strained their backs carving flowers into their roof beams and their eyesight embroidering animals onto their tablecloths. They have given up weekends to hide unsightly cables behind ledges. They have thought carefully about appropriate kitchen work surfaces. They have imagined living in unattainably expensive houses pictured in magazines and then felt sad, as one does on passing an attractive stranger in a crowded street.

We seem divided between an urge to override our senses and numb ourselves to the appearance of houses and a contradictory impulse to acknowledge the extent to which our identities are indelibly connected to, and will shift along with, our locations. I personally side with the view that it does (unfortunately, as it's

expensive) matter what things look like: an ugly room can coagulate any loose suspicions as to the incompleteness of life, while a sun-lit one set with honey-coloured limestone tiles can lend support to whatever is most hopeful within us. Belief in the significance of architecture is premised on the notion that we are, for better and for worse, different people in different places – and on the conviction that it is architecture's task to render vivid to us who we might ideally be.

Our sensitivity to our surroundings can be traced back to a troubling feature of human psychology: to the way we harbour within us many different selves, not all of which feel equally like 'us', so much so that in certain moods, we can complain of having come adrift from what we judge to be our true selves.

Unfortunately, the self we miss at such moments, the elusively authentic, creative and spontaneous side of our character, is not ours to summon at will. Our access to it is, to a humbling extent, determined by the places we happen to be in, by the colour of the bricks, the height of the ceilings and the layout of the streets. In a house strangled by three motorways, or in a wasteland of run-down tower blocks, our optimism and sense of purpose are liable to drain away, like water from a punctured container. We may start to forget that we ever had ambitions or reasons to feel spirited and hopeful.

We depend on our surroundings obliquely to embody the moods and ideas we respect and then to remind us of them. We look to our buildings to hold us, like a kind of psychological mould, to a helpful vision of ourselves. We arrange around us material forms which communicate to us what we need – but are at constant risk of forgetting we need – within. We turn to wallpaper, benches, paintings and streets to staunch the disappearance of our true selves.

In turn, those places whose outlook matches and legitimises our own, we tend to honour with the term 'home'. Our homes do not have to offer us permanent occupancy or store our clothes to merit the name. To speak of home in relation to a building is simply to recognise its harmony with our own prized internal song. As the French writer Stendhal put it, 'What we find beautiful is the promise of happiness.'

origins in the notion that where we are critically determines what we are able to believe in. To defenders of religious architecture, however convinced we are at an intellectual level of our commitments to a creed, we will only remain reliably devoted to it when it is continually affirmed by our buildings. We may be nearer or further away from God on account of whether we're in a church, a mosque – or a supermarket. We can't be good, faithful people anywhere.

Ordinary domestic architecture can be said to have just as much of an influence on our characters as religious buildings. What we call a beautiful house is one that rebalances our misshapen natures and encourages emotions that we are in danger of losing sight of. For example, an anxious person may be deeply moved by a white empty minimalist house. Or a business executive who spends her life shuttling between airports and steel and glass conference centres may feel an intense attraction to a simple rustic cottage – which can put her in touch with sides of her personality that are denied to her in the ordinary press of her days. We call something beautiful whenever we detect that it contains in a concentrated

Location, Location, Location from 2000

example, feel two distinct conceptions of fulfilment emanating from a plain crockery set on the one hand and an ornate flower-encrusted one on the other: an invitation to a democratic graceful sensibility in the former case, to a more nostalgic, country-bound disposition in the latter.

In essence, what works of design and architecture talk to us about is the kind of life that would most appropriately unfold within and around them. They tell us of certain moods that they seek to encourage and sustain in their inhabitants. While keeping us warm and helping us in mechanical ways, they simultaneously hold out an invitation for us to be specific sorts of people. They speak of particular visions of happiness.

To describe a building as beautiful therefore suggests more than a mere aesthetic fondness; it implies an attraction to the particular way of life this structure is promoting through its roof, door handles, window frames, staircase and furnishings. A feeling of beauty is a sign that we have come upon a material articulation of certain of our ideas of a good life. Similarly, buildings will strike us as offensive not because they violate a private and mysterious visual preference but because they conflict with our understanding of the rightful sense of existence.

No wonder, then, that our discussions of architecture and design have a tendency to be so heated. Arguments about what is beautiful are at heart arguments about the values we want to live by – rather than merely struggles about how we want things to look.

We depend on our surroundings obliquely to embody the moods and ideas we respect and then to remind us of them

Location, Location, Location from 2000

It is the world's great religions that have perhaps given most thought to the role played by our environment in determining our identity and so – while seldom constructing places where we might fall asleep – have shown the greatest sympathy for our need for a home. The very principle of religious architecture has its

form those qualities in which we personally, or our societies more generally, are deficient. We respect a style that can move us away from what we fear and towards what we crave: a style which carries the correct dosage of our missing virtues.

It is sometimes thought exaggerated to judge people on their tastes in design. It can hardly seem appropriate to pass judgment on the basis of a choice of wallpaper. But the more seriously we take architecture, the more we can come to argue that it is in fact logical to base a sympathy for someone on their visual tastes. For visual taste is never just simply a visual matter. It's indicative of a view of life. Any object of design will give off an impression of the psychological and moral attitudes it supports. We can, for

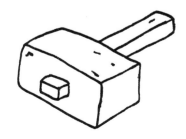

Kevin McCloud picks his favourite
Channel 4 *Grand Designs*

Grandest
Designs

Francis and Karen Shaw – Skipton

Most television series are completed in weeks.
We take months and our coverage of the
restoration of the Peel near Skipton by Francis
and Karen Shaw took over three years. The
result is a 90-minute story which resonates
with veracity, capturing the spirit of such a
large project and demonstrating just how much
stubborn will and stamina were required. What
started for me as an enjoyable exploration of
the different approaches of conservation,
repair work and restoration turned into a
documentary record of how English Heritage
underwent a sea-change in its approach to the
historic environment during those three years.

Ben Law – Sussex

The film we made of Ben Law was remarkable for several reasons. It followed a project that resulted from an extraordinary planning decision to allow a building in open countryside that was uniquely attached to the occupation of its owner (Ben is an underwoodsman), a building which in the event of his selling his business or retiring would have to be demolished. It was also a building constructed entirely from raw materials found and grown on the site. The film and the project grew into an eloquent essay on the fundamentals of sustainability. And the house grew into something absolutely beautiful.

Sarah Wigglesworth & Jeremy Till – north London

Invention is the mother of our series. Without it,
Grand Designs would be just another predictable
format show. But thanks to human ingenuity,
every hour of television we make is different
and sometimes shockingly so. Jeremy Till is
professor of architecture at Sheffield Hallam
University and his wife, Sarah Wigglesworth, has
her own avant-garde international practice.
It was a great pleasure to watch them design
and build their own home and studio next to the
Great Northern railway line in north London,
partly because the film was able to demystify
the more rarified moments of the architectural
process and partly because it captured them so
obviously enjoying the physical action of building
something. We recorded that and if there was
ever a film that stripped Architecture of its
capital A, this was it.

<u>Theo and Elaine Leijser – Stirling</u>

There is a common perception that a sustainable house has to somehow look hairy. It has to be made from edible materials held together with dog-lick. Theo and Elaine Leijser commissioned KAP architects in Glasgow to produce a modest, modernist but highly ecological house, which emerged, despite its crinkly wooden skin, to be one of the most satisfying, crisp and pleasurable homes I've ever visited. In the way views are orientated and managed, to the relationship between both horizontal and vertical open-plan sections, to the sense of compression and release that the building generates, this place is a miniature masterpiece.

Sarah Jordon & Coneyl Jay – London

One of the occasional and private pleasures of making <u>Grand Designs</u> has been getting to know some of the great architectural minds of our time. Some are listed here, and to their ranks I have to add Mike Tonkin and his wife Anna Liu of Tonkin Liu. We filmed a house of theirs in east Hampstead that was constructed for a photographer and jeweller. For once, the owners were not the means to understanding the building. Instead, the character of the building grew out of the rigour of the design narrative and the process of making such an unusual and perfect place. It showed us that there is more than one way to tell a story.

Avant-garde architect and designer
Nigel Coates watches new self-architects

I'll Huff and I'll Puff

When, in 2006, Peter York's book on dictators' homes appeared, he probably knew his readers would use it to justify their own domestic style. Saddam Hussein deserved all he got for such ostentation. And who would want to live like Nicolae Ceausescu and his wife Elena? The no taste of the rich and powerful would make one's modest efforts seem better, more acceptable.

Powerful homes are news to nobody, but we can thank the life-long learning powers of television for everyone muscling in on this. Year on year, week on week, the number of makeover programmes never abates. The top-ranking ones command primetime viewing slots, while others occupy entire channels, or back-to-back daytime viewing. In part, these programmes are a follow on from the mid-Eighties obsession with fashion. Then it was antiques, then the boom in cooking with the *Two Fat Ladies* and Jamie Oliver, and into the Noughties it was the home. So TV is not just entertainment. It's consumer democracy at work.

Since the miserable years of the early Eighties, as we've become richer, more opinionated and freer with money, nowhere shows more change than the average home. Now, the home is a barometer of aspiration, stylistic allegiances and lifestyle choices. It's the very altar of family happiness. But to improve on it we won't call in the experts – the architects and designers. Most likely we'll do it ourselves. We'll do it as they do on the TV. We've learnt how to pump up our homes, second or otherwise, as an expression of autonomy and difference, as well as turning our effort into profit.

When it comes to the sorts of gains to be made with property, everybody wants to learn the insider tricks; how to Italian-ise your kitchen, how to 'get the look', as the magazines say, and get the maximum impact for as little money and effort as possible.

The range of makeover programmes is impressive. There are programmes in the morning like *Trade Secrets*, where the home owner is sent to the spa for the day while the designer runs around with a staple gun and sticky-backed plastic and turns their living room into a temporary stage set, which will of course fall apart the minute it's cleaned. There's the avarice trigger *A Place in the Sun*, which shows us what you could get for your money, but with the attendant consequences of not speaking the language. Then there's every bastard son of *Changing Rooms*, in which the presenter unleashes a tsunami of MDF and laminate flooring. Somehow you're meant to make a Bauhaus loft out of a council flat. Then there's Channel 4's *Grand Designs*, the top of the range, where relatively wealthy people employ aspiring architects to realise their dreams. What all the programmes have in common is a narrator/expert who shares the risk with the audience, both knowing that it could all go horribly wrong.

There's always a certain ghoulish fascination when the subject realises that her comfy, familiar dining room has been turned into a baronial hall. We love the tears, the shrieks, the muffled surprise. This is a branch of reality television, as though we the audience are in the role of *Big Brother*. Then again, the victims in these programmes could be the characters in the nursery rhyme *The Three Little Pigs*, with the presenter fulfilling the role of the Big Bad Designer Wolf.

As an architect myself, these programmes hold my attention less than they might – coals to Newcastle shall we say. But the fact that architecture and the design that goes with it have become so popular means there's been a seismic shift. In the old days, even the smartest homeowners didn't go much further than Peter Jones for their ideas; lots of greige, sofas with fringes to the floor and the odd repro-antique. When, in the mid-Seventies, I emerged fresh faced and idealistic from architecture school, young architects were regularly blamed for the miserable domestic nightmares engendered by the average council tower block. At a chic dinner party near Regent's Park, I remember Bob Geldof trying to pin the blame on me. The only job of architecture I'd done at the time was the refurb of the house we were being entertained in.

It's funny. When it's your house, even if you are an architect, you want to play both designer and client. When I bought my proverbial pile of stones in Italy, it was 1987. I had neither the money, nor the nerve, to submit it to some grand design. I wanted the house to evolve, to stay close to its peasant origins, and of course to be beautiful. I'd do it bit by bit, as I had the ideas and could afford it. The house progressed little by little just when I was doing my most iconoclastic buildings in the UK. It was an escape from being a professional architect, and gave me the dubious pleasure of being my own client.

Now, twenty years later, I guess it's finished. Or is it? I'm describing the antithesis of the architect at work, when he spends other people's money. The trick is for the house to be a good but not a perfect fit, a seduction and a provocation. Your house should be like your partner – on the same wavelength but slightly unpredictable. Too many homes try to be a carbon copy of someone else's.

The new interest in the architecture of the home corresponds to the branded end of architectural taste. Most people don't buy Gucci; they buy the H&M version. They're interested in architecture, but still don't trust architects with their money. It makes much better use of your limited resources to play the architect yourself, and to be your own client too.

I won't go on about architects knowing best and having the capacity to come up with the unexpected solution. It is true that architects aren't really interested in your rear extension or loft conversion. But to the householder, these giant strides into the garden are a chance to dabble in styling space, an opportunity to add something the builder couldn't. And since we're sold so many ways of taking control of our homes through magazines, the aforementioned TV programmes and estate agents', websites, there's no stopping most people from having a go.

The edition of *Grand Designs* I remember in particular told the tale of a lady who was building a spiral house on a piece of land she'd bought in Cornwall. The dynamic form was clearly something of an obsession for both owner and architect and, by default, proof that the most logical shape for building a house

The home is a barometer of aspiration, stylistic allegiances and lifestyle choice, the very altar of family happiness

is a rectangle. Something heroic had been achieved, combining the satisfaction of Ayn Rand's Howard Roark with knowing that she'd move up a notch. Rand had said, 'Man's ego is the fountainhead of human progress.' The Cornish pioneer was now part of that elite few who have built their own house, just how they want it.

Apart from the country mansion, we've never had much of a tradition of architect-designed houses for rich clients in Britain. House builders like Barratt play on the fact that we like to start off on the traditional side and bend our homes towards our personal fantasies. Sameness provides the blank canvas for DIY. We Brits tend to have more of a garden shed mentality when it comes to building our own.

The sort of 'philanthropy' that generated vast suburbs of identical terraced houses had an ideological dimension that even the poor would buy into. There would be equality amongst the working classes; sameness was good. By the mid-wars period of the 20th century, this way of thinking had consolidated into an ethical principle. Through the eyes of the state, sameness equalled no special chances and raising the hygiene threshold. Only far away from the towns and cities, in seaside places like Camber Sands, was freedom of expression held up as a value. On the dunes you were free to be fanciful and build the palace of your dreams out of clapboard.

Indoors you'd be free to combine all kinds of seaside detritus – shells and driftwood – into furniture with mirrors, with nets and glass buoys hanging from the ceiling. These encrustations may be miles from any pedigree design languages you'd see on television, but even these are never that pure. People may think they're being seduced into minimalism, but TV producers know that most people like a bit of flounce built into the clean lines.

Emphasis on property investment has meant a proliferation of second homes and a ready interest in 'desirability'. Estate agents have been slow to realise that people are much more flexible in their thinking about value. In cooler, more loft orientated parts of town they've been selling properties according to area rather than the number of bedrooms. Many of the people I know choose to live on their own and have huge apartments. Bedrooms turn into games rooms, libraries, cinemas and dedicated pet rooms. One friend in particular counted 44 bedrooms between his four properties.

Most people, on the other hand, think themselves lucky to have one home and enough bedrooms to house the family. So it's important to make the most of it. But as the property market continues to climb, money really does start to contaminate the imagination. 'If the neighbours can get that amount for their house, of course we can get more. We've got an extra room in the roof.' Often there's a nagging wrangle between 'how I want my home to look' and 'how much money we can make'. Jocasta Innes starts to give way to the chorus of John Pawson: 'Will I be able to get the price I want, and with the extra money, move up a notch?'

Knowing the potential profit from houses can put other investments in the shade. Most people sink more into their home than anything else, which is great news for the likes of B&Q. But the sub-prime crisis has emphasised how fragile prosperity can be. As people over-borrow, the home has to perform even better. It has to be more comfortable, more efficient, and say more about you.

Daisy Leitch discovers property really
is about Location, Location, Location

The fashionable Trellick Tower
in west London, 2007.
Photographs by Angela Moore

Goldfinger's Lair

Trellick Tower, London W10.
1 bedroom flat £250,000.
A wonderful opportunity to acquire a well
presented one bedroom flat in this iconic
grade II listed building located on the 15th
floor. The property offers a spacious reception
room with a balcony leading off, a good sized
kitchen and a modern bathroom.

Balfron Tower, London E14.
3 bedroom flat £200,000.
Amazing, stunning, spectacular views in this
grade II listed block, moments from Canary
Wharf, with three double bedrooms, makes
this a spectacular first time purchase or for
investment. A must view!

A one bedroom flat on the fifteenth floor
of the Trellick Tower in north Kensington costs 50 grand more than a three-
bedroom flat on the 24th floor of Balfron
Tower in the Poplar area of Tower Hamlets. At first sight, this massive discrepan-
cy is shocking, for these towers are strikingly similar architectural icons. While
they may not be identical twins, they are
certainly very close siblings. Both built by
Erno Goldfinger and completed within
five years of each other, both now grade II

listed buildings. The flats and maisonettes
within the towers are broadly the same,
being functional and designed with large
windows and balconies to offer access to
the fantastic views of their respective ends
of London; Balfron's being the City and
the Thames, and Trellick's west London
and beyond.

However, the difference in price
between the two is not surprising after a
closer inspection. Approaching Trellick is
quite a different experience to approaching Balfron. Trellick's immediate vicinity
is bustling with life – shops catering to a
wide range of tastes and budgets. Choose
from the Trellick Tea rooms (sticky bun,
40p) or Rellik, the vintage designer store
(sunglasses, £300). There's a brand new
playground directly in front of the Tower,
a community garden behind and a school
to the side. It's life, and it's thriving.

Balfron's environs are more deso-
late than lively, the haunt of groups of
teenagers riding bikes, chasing sea gulls
and winding up the neighbours, if not
the police. There are a couple of shops on
the estate, run-down newsagents offering nothing more than the staples. Six
decrepit tennis courts with the remains of

one tattered net between them languish
nearby. The garages under the tower are
now permanently locked, abandoned
after a spate of car burnings. The gardens in front of the ground-floor flats are
entirely unkempt – dead shopping trol-
leys and a partly unhinged door swinging
against the fence.

Trellick has a 24-hour concierge;
Balfron has a security guard barricaded
inside a small office, monitoring a wall of
screens from the comprehensive CCTV
system, facilitated at night by powerful
flood lights. One gives the impression of
good and personable management, the
other of a battle for survival in a decidedly hostile environment. Both towers
started out as social visions, built in two
of the most deprived areas of London.
Slum housing deemed no longer fit for
human habitation was torn down and
replaced by these two uncompromising
modernist beacons.

The Goldborne Road area of north
Kensington was certainly no more salu-
brious than Poplar in Tower Hamlets in
the Fifties and Sixties. Colin McInnes
called it Napoli in *Absolute Beginners,*
referring to its lawlessness in the

Scenes at Balfron, 2007

Trellick Tower, 2007

By the Seventies, Trellick had fallen into dark disrepute, so much so that it became known as the 'Tower of Terror'

Fifties. This was an area of high racial tensions. Indeed, the infamous and still-unsolved racist murder of Antiguan Kelso Cochrane occurred directly outside where Trellick stands today. Roger Mayne's photographs of Southam Street, mostly demolished to make way for Trellick, document the extreme and shocking poverty of local children.

Thus, while Goldfinger's architecture is sublime – brutal and imposing – this was also, crucially, about social engineering and regeneration. Goldfinger, with an eye to the creation of community spirit, designed his towers around internal 'streets' every three floors. Balfron was built first and Goldfinger and his wife Ursula moved in for two months in 1968 to get a feel for the strengths and weaknesses of the building. Both to gain information from the residents

about the building, and to foster integration between them, Goldfinger hosted a series of champagne soirées inviting each 'street' in turn. When Trellick went up in 1972, she was ostensibly very similar to her older sibling but perhaps with a slight upper hand, being more slim-lined, having four extra floors, the service tower harbouring an extra lift and an improved heating system.

However, by the Seventies, Trellick had fallen into dark disrepute, so much so that it became known as the 'Tower of Terror'. The realisation of Goldfinger's vision of community regeneration resembled the social disintegration and chaos of JG Ballard's dystopian novel *High Rise*. For Ballard, the tower block pitted man against man in a violent struggle for survival; high-rise living was built for warfare, not society. As one of the original

residents, Leona Boland, told me, Trellick in the Seventies, 'had violence, vandals and rape'.

Trellick may resemble Balfron closely but today their fortunes couldn't be more different, as the property adverts indicate. The rehabilitation of Trellick began in the Eighties. Thatcher's right-to-buy legislation enabled residents to own their flats for the first time and, as these got sold on, prices began to take off. Although the building still predominantly remains overwhelmingly in the hands of the local authority, a three-bedroom maisonette on an upper floor now costs half a million pounds. Trellick has certainly benefited from improved management, and the residents consistently cite the 24-hour concierge service as pivotal in creating a safe and secure place for all. But the main change is in the neighbourhood. Once a slum, this is now the bohemian hang out of the rich and famous. As W10 flourished, Trellick became a symbol of modern urban living, referred to in songs by Blur.

At the end of the day it's all about location, location, location.

Peter York, who mapped the *Sloane Ranger* 30 years ago, now explores the expansion of the style-conscious since Channel 4 launched

The Style Junkies

When Channel 4 started, the first thing to hit design junkies was that the station ident – those primary-coloured blocks coming together in deep space in a clever modern way – looked more than a bit Memphis. The Italian designer Ettore Sotsass's colourful Memphis furniture was much on the mood boards, if not the shopping lists, of the early Eighties designer classes.

But more important by a mile as an influence on real BHS – British Home Style – was the happy coincidence of *The World of Interiors* magazine (launched 1981), the television adaptation of *Brideshead Revisited* (1981), the 'fairytale' royal wedding (1981), the Falklands victory celebration (1982) and even *The Official Sloane Ranger Handbook,* co-written by Anne Barr and me (1982).

Taken together, they helped create the mainstream interiors trend that current *World of Interiors* editor Rupert Thomas describes as, 'Intensely nostalgic and backward-looking, insistently English, rather show-off, packed with antiques, loaded with knick-knacks… country-house on a budget.' At the richer end, that meant the Country House

Hotel look: yellow-walled drawing rooms with elaborate pink-on-white floral chintz curtains ('swags and tails'), important-looking marble chimneypieces and old rugs – especially Aubussons – on neutral carpeted or wooden floors. These rooms were full of impressive-looking late 18th century furniture – real or fake – made of conker-shiny mahogany. Big bookcases had pediments; big dining tables had three pedestals. Add elaborate pairs of sofas with gimps and braids and tassels, heaped with fancy cushions in tapestry and beadwork and you Get The Look.

At an evolved, self-conscious level, the look came out as Shabby Chic, equally grandiose but everything worn, faded and distressed to high heaven to avoid the shoulder-padded stigma of new money throwing its weight around. And at a more mainstream middle-class level, this mood simply meant Laura Ashley.

The point about these dominant interior styles was that they looked Rich and Reassuring. We wanted that because the Seventies, from the three-day week to the Winter of Discontent, had been neither. The economy, we knew, was catastrophic and we were painfully conscious

of being way behind the Europeans and Americans on practically every standard-of-living index. And, as for mainstream real-world design, there was a particularly British talent for making things that combined cheap and tacky construction (as in British Leyland cars and aluminium replacement patio doors) with a completely joyless Wet-Wednesday-in-Widnes drabness, the very opposite of Gucci-Pucci-Fiorucci Ghetto Fabulousness.

Thirty years on, when we're cherry-picking the best of inventive Seventies British design (and it was – from Centre Pompidou architecture to Zandra Rhodes prints to *Never Mind the Bollocks* graphics), it's easy to forget just how low general standards were then, and just how poor people felt. How exciting a flat like Bryan Ferry's, in that first edition of *Interiors*, must have seemed. Ferry was famous for being stylish in an exaggerated, art-school, ironic way, but his flat, fixed up by the society decorator Nicky Haslam, was classically posh with an Eighties twist. Masses of chintz, a Turkey-carpet pouffe, 18th century architectural prints massed over console tables and a late-Victorian-ish John Singer Sargent-style painting of a pretty girl over the chimneypiece. It looked gloriously, shockingly rich and reactionary and it was endlessly influential.

Translated into the DIY mainstream, this hunger for Rich and Reassuring meant 'swags and drags'. Full-on Fulham-isation. Small houses of all periods were loaded down and larded up with 'period features'. Everything the modernising Sixties and Seventies improvers had removed – cornices, fireplaces, dado rails, panelled doors – were either restored from booming architectural salvage yards, or installed as, often wildly anachronistic, fakes. The revived art of fancy paint finishes, popularised by Jocasta Innes and her Channel 4 *Paintability* series, got millions of suburban mums dragging and rag-rolling, while Lynn Le Grice, with her stencil kits by post, got them stippling like mad.

Over the course of the Eighties, the DIY and furnishings markets grew at every level as more people got access to money, houses and design ideas. In 1980, for instance, 54 per cent of UK households were owner-occupied; by the end of the decade, this had risen to 67 per cent. Deregulation from 1979 made the mortgage market competitive and dynamic where it had been slow and practically Soviet. And the sale of council houses, starting in 1980, brought a large new grouping into the aspirational improver fold. I remember filming in a deconsecrated council house to which absolutely everything had been done. It had grown sideways and to the back. Its plain front had sprouted a pillared, pedimented porch, new 'Georgian' windows and front door, plus new rendering to jazz up the municipal brick. Inside, there was everything B&Q offered: dark brown polystyrene 'oak' ceiling beams, dados, cornices and picture rails, six-panel doors in pressed fibreboard. The lot. Every proud council-house owner did *something* to show he'd joined the property-owning classes. The first move was usually to replace those maroon or turquoise council-painted front doors with mock-Georgian ones with built-in fanlights.

And then there were the Design Ideas. By the end of the decade, WHSmith had had to build new shelves for all the new 'shelter' titles. Television was limbering up for Nineties lifestyle programming and a new breed of Big Book, full of knock 'em dead double-page spreads,

showed the houses of the rich. There was a booming global trade in those pictures (Tom Wolfe called it 'plutography, the pornography of wealth'). Architects (most of them) and the professionally-trained design classes (most of them) hated this wave of Little England retro-design, even while they were (some of them) obliged to help produce it commercially as graphics or shop interiors or pastiche-Georgian extensions. But there *was* a market for new architecture, in the huge City office blocks being constructed after the Big Bang deregulation of 1987, and in the new flats (increasingly, estate agents called them 'apartments') being built or converted for the people who worked in Money World, or in the burgeoning media and marketing businesses. The architecture of the City looked to America for its models; those giant atria, curious post-modern classical pediments and arched windows, the Rotten Gotham

worked and expressed their exciting new status. The papers called them Yuppies, and conflated them with Sloanes and spivs of various kinds. But the real test was whether they understood the idea of living in, say, a 'loft' (essentially a New York Seventies precedent), or a new-built riverside flat with urban buzz, rather than an Edwardian semi done up as a Georgian rectory, and whether they understood the one-upmanship of sleek architectural luxury and 'designer' furniture.

A growing minority did. Yuppie style was the new Urban Alternative look. The emphasis was on expensive hard surfaces, high-design furniture, masses of light and amazing Master of the Universe views. Plus tremendously smart kitchens and bathrooms and as much New Tech as you could muster. These were people with mobile phones, faxes, filofaxes and early PCs at home and on display. And the

Shabby Chic was faded and distressed to high heaven to avoid the shoulder-padded stigma of new money throwing its weight around

vaguely Thirties look of much of Broadgate and Canary Wharf, very different from the European modernist tradition.

But those late Eighties New People doing new jobs with what sounded like astonishing new rewards, many of them Americans and other ex-pats and globalists, wanted new places that actually

Property Ladder, from 2001

biggest tellies with the new flatter screens. The architectural precedents were American, the furniture mostly European – the clever 'Tizio' lamp by Richard Sapper was ubiquitous. These apartments, with their emphasis on boys' toys and the black-leather-and-chrome combo, tended to look rather like advertising agency meeting rooms.

By the late Eighties, we were a nation obsessed with houses' potential and value. The end of the housing boom and the miserable collapse into negative equity and repossession marked the end of the decade. Interior design in the early Nineties was deeply unconfident. The key Eighties looks, the nostalgic one and the brash Yuppie style, were both starting to look embarrassing, overblown and crassly Loadsamoney, but there was no new packageable vernacular to replace them.

But as the London economy picked up from 1993 onwards, so new clubs and hotels and restaurants were being done out in influential new ways. Crisper, cleaner, lighter, simpler, were

These apartments, with their emphasis on boys' toys and the black-leather-and-chrome combo, look like advertising agency meeting rooms

the key words, and amazingly, modernist. Britain had never really got the European modernist idea between the wars, in architecture or design; then those grim low-budget Sixties council blocks and the Brutalist, shuttered-concrete Sixties public buildings seemed to put us off for good. It certainly made us a ready market for the American post-modernist show-off look.

Restaurants of the period, like *The Avenue* in St James's (1995), looked so crisp, smart and simple with their scale, their double-height ceilings, white walls, wood and glass everywhere, that diners went home resolved on living like that.

The key words for the rash of middle-brow interior design books that appeared from the mid-Nineties on were 'simple' and 'contemporary'. This new knocked-back style was a bit architectural and very understated. These books banished curtains, carpets, bright colour, most antiques – certainly the 'brown furniture' kind – patterns, close hung pictures and paint finishes at a stroke. Instead, there was Mid-Century Modern, the more comfortable – and, for Boomers, oddly nostalgic – post-war American and Scandinavian design (as Rupert Thomas has pointed out, 'the new mainstream look is actually as retro as Country House'). And a reduced palette of white

and neutrals, interesting materials and textures – zinc and stainless steel instead of chrome and black leather. And masses of wood, usually as pale wood strip floors and cladding, along with every other kind of expensive plain natural hard surface possible. Limestone, as flooring slabs, and even carved into expensive baths and basins. Marble (but honed matt), plain frosted glass, or that modernist favourite, glass bricks.

This expensive kind of simplicity seemed to put the Eighties behind us for good – just like New Labour – while at the same time being rather sleek, safe and obviously tasteful.

It was all hugely influential in creating the 21st century mainstream consensus – the look you get in the high street shops and mid-market catalogues and newer 'shelter' magazines like *Living etc.* These typically feature architects' light-filled white houses with their white Eames chairs banked around plain Conran tables of matt solid oak planking. Or the whimsical houses of lady stylists who paint up old furniture and jazz up their pale, curtainless houses with sparkly bits of pink. But while this pale and simple, less-is-more tastefulness (knock-offs of all the great 20th century pioneers from Eileen Gray to Eero Saarinen are really big business now) is the dominant style, the design classes themselves are bored rigid with it now. Their new watchword is ecletic. They want more colour and curly-wurly patterns, more borderline-naff Seventies, and even Eighties things. Some of them are even edging towards strong colours on walls, carpeting, curtains... and even antiques.

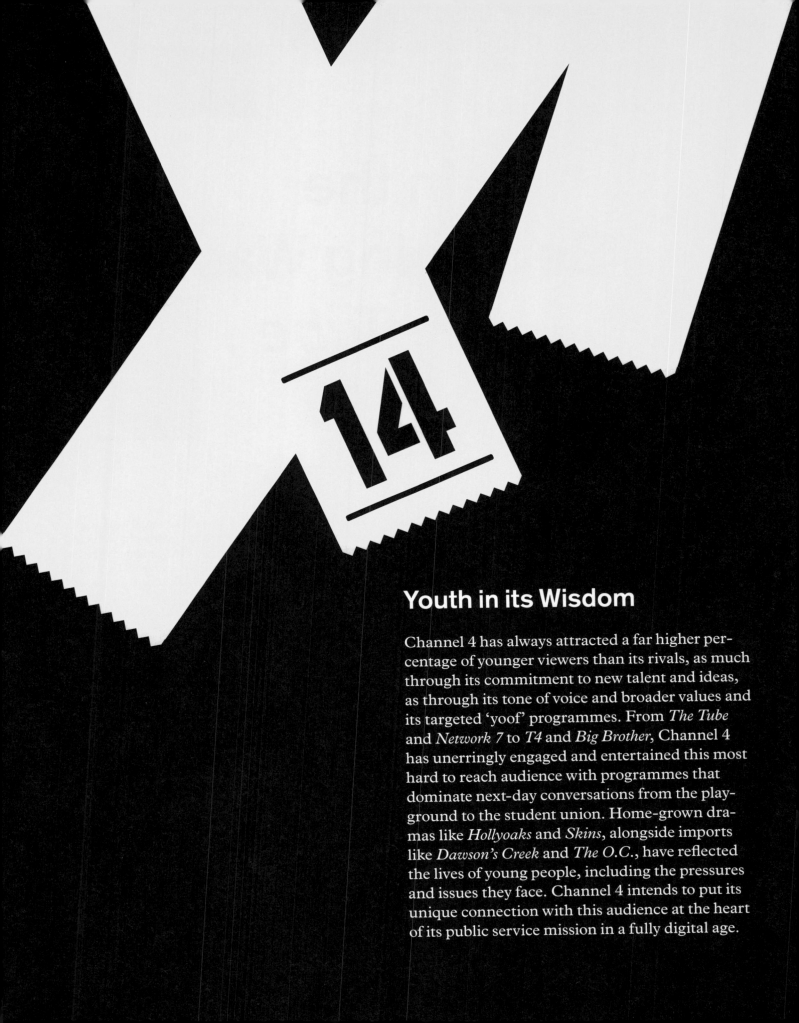

Youth in its Wisdom

Channel 4 has always attracted a far higher percentage of younger viewers than its rivals, as much through its commitment to new talent and ideas, as through its tone of voice and broader values and its targeted 'yoof' programmes. From *The Tube* and *Network 7* to *T4* and *Big Brother*, Channel 4 has unerringly engaged and entertained this most hard to reach audience with programmes that dominate next-day conversations from the playground to the student union. Home-grown dramas like *Hollyoaks* and *Skins*, alongside imports like *Dawson's Creek* and *The O.C.*, have reflected the lives of young people, including the pressures and issues they face. Channel 4 intends to put its unique connection with this audience at the heart of its public service mission in a fully digital age.

The Word, 1990

In the Beginning Was... *The Tube*

Max Headroom, 1985

The Word, 1990

In the beginning was *The Word*. Except, of course, it was *The Tube* that came first, in 1982, a stroppy, silly-trousered teenager of a pop show in a children's tea-time slot. (As I recall, you flipped over straight after *Crackerjack* on a Friday, though that might be my memory playing Sky Plus.) *The Tube*, to a suburban fifteen-year-old like me, was fascinatingly outrageous: saucy, hectic and all-over-the-shop, with real live bands playing real live music and presenters that were DIY rather than DLT. Jools Holland was deadpan and disrespectful; Paula Yates flirted so hard you thought the TV might explode (which it did, in the titles). They both kept messing things up. I thought they, and *The Tube*, were brilliant. I couldn't quite believe that any of it was allowed.

The Tube's anarchic air was part of the DNA of the new Channel 4. Of course, no primetime telly show is ever commissioned without a grown-up saying yes, but in its early years Channel 4 seemed to be sneaking an entire new generation in the back door whilst the adults tapped their watches at the front. And, for teenage viewers brought up on the sedate thrills of *Morecambe and Wise*, that was truly exciting. Drunkenness, swearing, innuendo, actual filth; Channel 4 brought them all to a nation's spotty youth. We were very grateful, even if sometimes we had to sit through a two-hour art movie to find the naughty bits we were promised.

Still, *The Tube*. The first pop show that felt alive. Because it went out live, and from Newcastle. Away from London's easy cab-ride home, bands would act as though they were on tour. They got drunk, they got bored, they talked to/rowed with/took the mickey out of each other. Several interviews took place in their dressing rooms, including a notoriously stiff chat between

Muriel Gray and Paul Weller around the time The Jam split up. When I watch that clip now, I cringe in sympathy with Gray: it reminds me of umpteen interviews I've conducted myself with tricky musicians. When I saw it then, I was agog. Up until *The Tube*, I'd never realised that pop stars and presenters were real people, with personalities that might clash.

Actually, up until *The Tube*, I'd never realised, properly, that bands could sound different to the way they did on record. Duran Duran were ropey, to say the least. Terence Trent D'Arby was stunning. Madonna performing *Holiday* at The Hacienda (just up the road!) was ace, though the reaction of the Mancunian crowd was typically snotty. Still, if I was honest, it was the interviews I looked forward to. Jools Holland and Paula Yates were gifted presenters, in an unselfconscious way you rarely see any more. They weren't styled (Holland always looked terrible), they weren't clever-clever, they were themselves. Jittery and caustic in the case of Holland, intelligent and disarming from Yates. With them at the helm *The Tube* couldn't fail, no matter how hard some bands tried.

The other big show from the early Channel 4, for me, was *Brookside*. I've never got involved in another soap, before or since, but *Brookside* was different. For one major reason: it had the Grants. Bobby and Sheila, plus children scally Barry, stroppy Karen and kid Damon. I liked Karen the best: a Scouse version of Trisha from *Grange Hill*, big hair, big eyes (narrowed), big attitude. But they were all brilliant, the Grants, every one of them a flawed but likeable character, people who weren't so far from yourself and dealt with similar problems. Though *Brookside*, these days, is mostly recalled for the high drama of the body

226

under the patio, the lesbian kiss, the siege, it was all about the Grants for me. I even watched *Damon and Debbie*, the spin-off series where Damon eloped with his posh diabetic girlfriend to wind up stabbed in a hotel room in York. Moral? When working class and middle class meet, it's not the bourgeois that end up suffering. *Common People* before Pulp.

Anyway, with *The Tube, Brookside, The Comic Strip Presents* and Max Headroom's pop-video show, Channel 4 was my channel, in a way that none of the other three were. I wasn't particularly aware of the media furore around its output – 'Channel Swore' passed me by – but I could sense C4's underlying ethos of mischief, snippiness and enthusiasm that chimed so well with my own teenage sensibility. In fact, I identified with Channel 4 so strongly that, up until writing this article, I was convinced that it was Channel 4, rather than ITV, that first broadcast throughout the night; and C4, rather than ITV, that gave us 24-hour telly people the joy of *Night Network* and the madness that was *American Gladiators*. (Grown men fighting with giant cotton buds! Alright!)

But then, ITV would never have ventured into late-night broadcasting if it wasn't for Channel 4. Part of the greatness of Channel 4's early years was that its attitude was catching. It wasn't long before it warped the broadcasting landscape. Look at *Network 7*, broadcast in 1987. (Not for too long now: it'll make you feel sick.) By that point, I was a twenty-year-old student, and thus, *Network 7*'s target market. It went out for two hours from midday on a Sunday, to catch you just waking up, and like most of my friends, I both loved and hated the show. The camera angles made my hangover worse, but I liked Oliver James's celebrity interview slot and the way the show used graphics to give you a quick burst of information. Useful if you were over-opinionated, but under-informed (ah, the makings of a journalist even then). I couldn't get on with Magenta De Vine's sunglasses, however. Far too poncey London.

The Word, 1990

Anyway, underneath all the flash, the big thing about *Network 7* was its refusal to slot news items into their long-established hierarchy. A hierarchy which went something like: Royals, Politics, Money, Foreign and Just Time For A Heartwarming Kitty-cat On A Skateboard at the end. Instead, pieces about death row prisoners and ATM fraud cuddled up to stories on celebrity premieres. This approach is now so prevalent that Radio 4's *Today Programme* can blithely broadcast an inane chat with Naomi Campbell straight after a forensic piece of business analysis. Back in 1987, though, this was revolutionary. *Network 7* was the future of British news, though no one knew it then. Its successor, the eye-wateringly terrible *Club X*, was the future of

The Tube, 1982

nothing, however. I rarely watched it, as it went out when I did, but I sometimes caught the Sunday omnibus. It was sod-awful. It took all the worst elements of *The Tube* and *Network 7* and shoved them into the Hippodrome with presenters who didn't appear to know where, or indeed who, they were.

Paula Yates flirted so hard you thought the TV might explode

Club X was a shame because, once again, Channel 4 was affecting the other terrestrial channels for the better. From *Network 7*, Janet Street-Porter hopped over to BBC 2, to start the *DEF II* brand, which included *The Rough Guide*, an excellent show still imitated by most mainstream travel programmes. In years to come, some of *Network 7*'s team would go on to create *The Late Show*, and, from there, today's none-more-BBC stalwarts, *Newsnight Review* and *Later with Jools Holland*. Charlie Parsons, responsible for *Club X*, formed a company, Planet 24, which created *The Big Breakfast* and *The Word*.

By the time of those programmes, I was working in the media and so my relationship with Channel 4 had changed. I wrote about its programmes in pop papers, I met the presenters at parties. Somehow, I'd managed to get close to the world that had fascinated me just a few years earlier. But if Channel 4 hadn't existed, I'd never have thought I could get anywhere. Like *Smash Hits*, which gave me my first job, Channel 4 somehow articulated my hidden beliefs: that pop was important, that being young was great, that the mainstream was there to be subverted, that questions didn't have to be perfectly constructed to get to the truth.

And there are many out there who still hate the channel for this, who blame Channel 4 for the tsunami of celebrity drivel that exists today. I think that's unfair. Sure, it invented *Big Brother*, but it didn't invent Simon Cowell, and, anyway, the first two series of *BB* were genuinely riveting. Yes, there's an equality of agenda now that sees Britney Spears discussed in the same breath as Somalia. But for me the spirit of early Channel 4 is elsewhere. I see it in Keith Allen's confrontational documentaries, in Charlie Brooker dissecting TV, Simon Amstell's scissor-sharp presenting, *Dubplate Drama*'s you-choose episode endings, Lauren Laverne's arch questions, Jonathan Ross's wit, the blanket BBC coverage of every music festival still twitching. You might not like these things, but I do, and that's why the legacy of Channel 4 is still important, to this suburban teenager at least.

fourteen   youth

Skin Deep

Dawson's Creek, 1998

There was clearly a moment, however brief, in the Nineties when teenage dreams stretched as far as small-town, coastal America. In fact they aimed, not just for the town, but for a single creek, *Dawson's Creek*. And that creek saw emotional melodrama and swathes of verbiage as deep and as thrilling as the creek was narrow. It was thrilling because this was the apotheosis of adolescent angst reassuringly set against the comfortable,

viewer. It was not, however, England. The lesser-spotted English teenager had to wait for *Skins* before they became identifiable on TV. If *Dawson's Creek* showed teenagers how to talk with the fluency of a badly translated Freud case study, *Skins* shows them the world. And you know what? It's way more fun than in the movies, but it isn't all that comfortable or small-town homely. A visit to the writers' room certainly explains part of this.

way down to an inferiority-inducing teenage.

This tribe of writers gather together for their weekly writing meetings on two sofas and as many chairs as they can find. Two Ikea coffee tables sag under the weight of cartons of fruit juice (apple and orange), biscuits (custard creams and jammy dodgers) and a bowl of fruit (grapes and apples). You might hope that, despite the smallness of this room, everyone is at least offered a lavishly padded chair. For now they must make do with a couple of sofas, not large, and some rackety, hard chairs. In the summer heat, a fan with a suspicious safety record whirs by a window, occasionally sucking the odd lock of hair into its tenacious grip. The whir of the fan blades against the stale air offers a rather charming rhythm against which the discussions, of plot, character development, jokes and general fun, take place.

These discussions are probably not what you might think. They are certainly less pretentious than half the chats between Joey Potter and Dawson Leary. Josie Long, mid-twenties, Eddie Award-winning comic (the new Perrier Awards),

The world being created here is new, not neophile, not in love with its own novelty, but young, fresh

homely vision of Capeside; the feelings were risky but the territory was safe. With its inescapable and perpetual movie referencing and its casual forays into adult problems, *Dawson's Creek* was also a new chapter in teenage TV, allowing (apparent) adolescents acres of screen time, hectares of lines and hedgerows of intricately plotted stories to stop the heart of any

In a room, barely large enough for a pygmies' drinks party, about twelve people cram together to put together the scripts for the show under the watchful presence of Brian Elsley, the creator of *Skins*. It isn't all the writers for the series but it's still quite a spread. The age range in the room is quite daunting. Elsley tops it in his mid-forties and they wind their

with her knitted iPod cover and charming humour, gently injects a modern wryness to proceedings, a humour which chimes well with the near double-act of Jack Thorne (27) and Ben Schiffer (24) who have a camaraderie which fills the room, momentarily, until their rumbling excitement is picked up by one of the others. They also had a fine line in gently jesting as Lucy Kirkwood's (23) hair came closer and closer to that fan. It's bursts of energy from these sorts of relationships that seem to drive everything on. The careful revelation from Jamie Brittain (23) that he has introduced an overarching scheme of the Orpheus myth into the episode he has been working on suddenly gets everyone's attention. The exact intricacies of this are tested and proved until everyone is content that it works. It is persistently examined by Daniel Kaluuya (flush with post A-level success), one of the series writers and also – rather delightfully – the actor responsible for Posh Kenneth within the series, until he is finally sure of its merit and rests back into the sofa where he can comfortably consult with Daisy Swain-Wright. Daisy, in her final A-level year at school, interjects with a studiously casual cool which, in a sense, feels imparted to the entire show. It's this authentic attitude which is everywhere in the *Skins* DNA.

There is a very matter-of-fact attitude in the room. Everyone is here to discuss their scripts and the characters; it's not an issue, it's just the way things are and if you are not comfortable with that then perhaps this isn't the place to be. There is certainly a feeling of group understanding and badinage about the place. Someone can crack a gag and it flies round the room being polished until it is transformed into a new species of observation. Then someone mentions they like the idea of a harmonium in one of the character's rooms. A chatter breaks out, questions fly:

'What's a harmonium?' – 'You know one of those instruments.'

'How big is one?'
(a worried producer)
'What, exactly, do they look like?'
'They're quite big.'
'They used to travel with them.'
'You know in the 1850s, there are, like, travelling ones.'
'So can we fit it in the bedroom?'
(the producer again)
'Well they come in all sizes, don't they?'

The definitive answer, that settles it then: harmonium in, worries out. On to the next plot twist. Each member of the team seems to have their own episode, their own baby. They work on it in the privacy of their own time and then show and tell, as it were. The others say what they like about it and what they don't. Questions arise, questions are answered. There is no competition because it is the same for everyone. Everyone is playing on the same field. Tripping someone up with a sneering comment doesn't happen because it is self-defeating. Cutting someone with a joke really is like cutting off your own nose to spite your face. There is a deft trick going on in this room. Anywhere else in the country if you put together a group of people of this youth to work on something, the competition would be insurmountable and untenable. Look what happened with Robbie and Take That. Hand in hand with that bustling self-promotion comes a corresponding awkwardness. Nobody is prepared to expose themselves if someone is ready to score a point off them. It's the hallmark of adolescence, a time - for everyone - of retreat. Teenagers stereotypically don't speak because they are terrified and awkward. Somehow, in this room, as if by magic, they are able to remove the awkwardness and everyone is prepared to put themselves on the line. And all to write about life. Somewhere there is a fundamentally reassuring aspect to this.

But then fundamentals seem to be at the centre of everything that happens in this particular session. As they discuss

Hip Hop Years, 1999

certain developments in the plot, questions of wrongdoing and evil raise their startling heads. Harry Enfield, who of course, plays Tony's father in *Skins* and appears as a guiding light in the writer's room, mentions the monstrously abject murders committed by the Wests. The writer he is talking to looks blank. It doesn't raise a flicker of recognition; they happened before he was born, and they were discovered before his memory begins. The world being created here is new, not neophile, not in love with its own novelty, but young and fresh. And yet, sitting in the corner, Brian Elsley watches what is going on and makes sure that it retains certain qualities, qualities some might be naïve enough to call old-fashioned, though they are in fact what allow *Skins* to spark with life. Brian Elsley has something of Dennis Potter about him as he sits, hidden from view every time the door opens. He doesn't confine anyone in the room to do anything, he's not there to control. He does, however, have an adamantine strength about certain things. One of the characters' actions is in debate, Cassie's in fact. People are worried that their plans for her are too outlandish, too far-fetched. But they wrote them down because somewhere they know it is the right thing to do with Cassie. They believe in it. Far-fetchedness isn't a problem for Brian; what matters to him, more than anything, is that what happens 'has a sense of truth as well'. Everything that they discuss and everything they write must feel true. That is his magic trick.

Dawson's Creek was the grandfather of teen-drama. It allowed teenagers on screen and it allowed them to have their own fantasy lives. It was the first and it was thrilling. But, my God, on reflection, what a fantasy it was. *Skins* may be the coolest show on TV, everyone may want to be in their gang but, thank God it's not in Capeside. Thank God it's true, thank God it's Bristol. Well, thank God it's true, at least.

Somehow, as if by magic, they are able to remove the awkwardness and everyone is prepared to put themselves on the line

Fourteen   Youth in its Wisdom

Oliver James, the clinical psychologist and author, chronicles the dilemmas faced by today's youth

Network 7, 1987

Too Much, Too Young

The Big Breakfast, 1992

As If, 2001

The 25 years since the creation of Channel 4 coincided with a substantial increase in mental illness among young people – depression, anxiety, eating disorders, substance abuse, violence and ADHD (attention deficit hyperactivity disorder). At times *The Daily Mail* has implied this was cause and effect, that 'Channel Filth' wrecked our youth. The truth is much more interesting: Selfish Capitalism (or Neo-Liberalism) screwed them up.

The most startling scientific illustration of increased mental illness is a study comparing the mental health of 5,000 fifteen-year-olds in 1987 with the same number in 1999. Identical questions were asked of these very large samples. Overall, mental illness had increased from sixteen per cent to 24 per cent. But most horrifying of all was that the vast majority of the increase had occurred among girls, and girls from the highest social class: up from 24 per cent to a staggering 38 per cent for girls in social classes 1 and 2 (the highest). Four factors emerged as reasons: school performance worries; fears about exam failure; weight; and family problems (like parental divorce or disharmony). It

is no coincidence that 1987 to 1999 was the period when boys and girls went from being equal in GCSE success rates to girls outstripping boys by some margin. Nor is it coincidental that this was when the pressure on women to be thin increased considerably, through role models, TV and advertising. Girls from the top social class were not just being told they could have it all, they were being made to feel like hopeless failures unless they succeeded in doing so – the grades, the body, the boyfriend, but also the labels and the lifestyle (clubbing, ecstasy and 'Wild Child' girls splashed across the press, like Amanda de Cadenet and Emma Ridley). Indeed, during this period the

Hollyoaks, from 1995

number of girls who had sex before age sixteen exceeded the number of boys (between 1984 and 1994, girls who had sex before sixteen went from sixteen per cent to 25 per cent).

But the pressures were not restricted to posh girls. As a thousand newspaper articles have chronicled (alas, with no discernible effect on the government), we have epidemics of ADHD, eating disorders and even autism. In fact, it is not completely clear that any of these have really increased in prevalence. It could just be due to more reporting and changed definitions. But there is little doubt about depression, anxiety and substance abuse (drink and drugs).

What has been driving youth mad? My two books, *Britain on the Couch* (1997) and *Affluenza* (2007), have blamed all these trends on Selfish Capitalism. This form of political economy has four core characteristics. One, a business's success is judged almost exclusively by current share price. Two, privatising public utilities. Three, massive economic inequality caused by minimal regulation of business, suppression of unions and very low taxation for the rich. Four, the

In creating <u>Network 7</u>, Janet Street-Porter rigorously applied her so-called 'rules', which set out to ensure innovation and interest

The channel's track record in the specific genre of youth programming is arguably the single greatest achievement to be celebrated on its 25th birthday

ideology that consumption and market forces can meet human needs of almost every kind. World Health Organisation surveys show that mental illness is twice as common in selfish, English-speaking nations (23 per cent), compared with relatively unselfish, mainland western European ones (11.5 per cent). Above all, the canaries in the Selfish Capitalist mine have been young women, the most screwed-up group by a long way, despite living in an era of the greatest freedoms and affluence of any females in any time.

Some critics claim that C4 has had to reflect these Selfish Capitalist realities by departing from its general remit to innovate, but this argument is least

tenable in its youth programming. Mental illness and a commercial, exploitative attitude have been forced on the viewers (and on the increasingly youthful people who both commission and make the programmes at C4) but the channel's track record in this specific genre is arguably the single greatest achievement to be celebrated on its 25th birthday.

My personal connection to Channel 4 began in 1985 through friendship with John Cummins, then commissioning editor for young people's programmes. He jumped to these heights from the most junior production job (researcher) on *The Tube*. This celebrated live music series was presented by Jools Holland and Paula Yat-

es with an invigorating informality never seen on TV today. At least in the early years, there were still numerous memorable bands – The Jam, The Smiths, Culture Club, Madonna or The Pretenders.

But as the Eighties wore on, Paula and Jools became increasingly erratic in their behaviour. Once, doing a live promo for the show at around 5.15pm, Jools exhorted the viewing children to be 'a groovy little fucker' and tune in. The C4 switchboard exploded with calls from horrified parents. In 1987, Cummins replaced *The Tube* with *Network 7*, running for two hours on Sunday lunchtimes, at a stroke inventing a new genre of programming: Yoof TV. For two series, peculiar camera-work combined with an eclectic and exotic collection of young presenters to provide a magazine programme designed by youth for youth. The programme won a BAFTA but Cummins left the channel. The channel still continued

<u>Don't Forget Your Toothbrush</u>, 1994

to be the one most watched by teenagers but this programming was reflecting an increasingly 'greed is good' culture.

Michael Jackson started work as Chief Executive at the channel on the same spring day in 1997 that Tony Blair took residence in Downing Street. He achieved the difficult feat of recovering audience share and keeping it around the ten per cent mark. A big factor was his young people's programming, of which the *Big Brother* franchise was a cornerstone. Jackson was actually quite nervous about whether it would work and surprised it became so huge. Wisely appointing the clubbable, imaginative Kevin Lygo as Head of Entertainment meant there were plenty of other youth-flavoured confections that did well, most famously *Ali G*.

The *Big Brother* franchise became a highly significant revenue source for the channel. What had begun as a serious exercise in stretching the boundaries of what can be achieved through TV became a much-imitated cash cow in a brutally competitive commercial environment. The show's development was emblematic of the wider society.

Reviewing the evolution – and huge contribution – of C4 to TV for youth, it is striking how much it has mirrored that audience. The exuberance and optimism of *The Tube* and *Network 7* were replaced by the game-playing of *Ali G* and *Big Brother*. Today's teens are primarily concerned with obtaining the car, house, iPod or luxurious foreign holidays of their parents as quickly as possible – ironically, these are now much harder to acquire. No students left university in 1982 with big debts making them afraid of dissenting from the status quo. And it was still possible to get a toe on the property ladder, whereas today's students must totally commit themselves to conventional values from their mid-teens (good GCSE grades, CV-building through holiday work experience) onwards, if they are to have any chance of solvent home ownership. Even then, it is extremely tough for those without affluent parents. Indeed, a child born in 1958 is more likely to have achieved upward mobility through the education system than one born in 1970.

When asked what they want to be when they grow up, a much higher proportion of young people answer 'famous'

than ten years ago. As the broadcaster that brought reality TV to Britain – *Big Brother* – it seems undeniable that C4 significantly contributed to the desire to be famous for being famous, by making it a real possibility.

In this, however, it has been no worse than any other broadcaster and in the end, as one C4 programme controller put it to me recently, the reason why people watch TV has changed during the last quarter century: 'People look to it to entertain much more than to inform'. As head of BBC2, Michael Jackson had felt impelled to axe *40 Minutes*, and its successor *Modern Times* did not last long. In all these cases he felt he had no choice because, quite simply, hardly anyone was watching. That was not TV's fault, it was the fault of post-1979 (and post-1997) Selfish Capitalism. Increasingly obese, substance-abusing, overworked, needy and miserable, viewers switched on their telly at the end of the day wanting bread and circuses to accompany their fast food, not information or missions to explain. This was not C4's fault. The blame wholly falls upon Thatcher, Major, Blatcher and, today, Bratcher.

June Sarpong shot to prominence as a TV presenter on *T4*. Here, she explains why it is important to engage young people in politics

Hearing Young Voices

June Sarpong

I don't personally buy the argument that politics is stale. The issues are as vibrant and vital as ever – they affect all our lives after all. No doubt there has been an erosion of trust in politicians in recent years because of divisive foreign policy decisions. But the issues, the causes and the choices in politics are still there, waiting to be taken up again by future generations.

The terms of the debate will need to change to draw young people in. The whole stuffed-shirt atmosphere of Parliament may appeal to tourists and fuddy-duddies, but if any politician alive today is serious about changing the country for the better and enthusing young people in the process, then the way Parliament is conducted must change.

Out with the tribal slanging matches, which are too often excused as 'political theatre'. In with reasoned, relevant debate which touches on real lives, explains as it goes along and allows young people to make a considered choice.

To engage the young in the first place, the political media has to expand to accommodate the young. The dull, middle-aged men in grey suits blathering away outside Number 10 need to move over sometimes for some younger journos, who know how to express politics through the language of young people. That doesn't mean dumbing down, it means sharpening up, keeping it real.

And if the faces on our screens need to change, then so too should the faces on the benches of Parliament and in council chambers across the country. Let the young people stand, to speak up for their peers. I want to see teenage councillors and eventually teenage MPs ready to speak out when young people are unfairly demonised by the media that trades on the prejudices of older people.

Let's prepare young people for those roles – or jobs in areas like teaching or the law – with debating societies in every school, starting in the last years in primary school. Think what debating skills could do to unlock the potential of so many youngsters, as well as boosting speaking and negotiation skills.

Let's encourage parents to take more interest in politics too, encourage discussing issues at the dinner table or around the TV. Parents crucially need to understand that if they bad-mouth or switch off around politics and current affairs, that sends out a very negative message to the kids. I've lost count of how many times I've heard young people say 'Politicians are all the same, they're only in it for themselves.' It's a sweeping statement and a cliché, too often trotted out by parents who came to that conclusion from the media.

Back to the media. We can do a lot to change perceptions of politics if we choose. Actually, it's more than a choice, it's a duty. If media outlets want to reflect the totality of everyday life, the missing element at the moment is politics for young people. Where are the political shows aimed at the young?

Let's see some produced to appeal to young people. Use sharp editing and music, humour and all the rest of it, but first and foremost, appeal to the sense of social justice that exists in every young person. Let's have phone-ins and *Question Time*-style debates. Let's use TV, radio and the web to allow young people their own say in putting the world to rights.

239

Advertising Executive
David Bain believes
Channel 4 has a unique
relationship with the
New Youth

<u>Hollyoaks</u>, from 1995

About the Young Idea

<u>T4</u>, from 1998

Sometimes the idea of youth is very different from the reality of being young. The idea of youth is our shared belief in the creative force and power of a mind not dulled by experience, convention or inhibited by time-tutored pragmatism. The idea of youth is our faith in the power of raw inventiveness and in the ability of fresh eyes to imagine the world anew; it is a talent to be developed; a gift that fades without diligent practise. Youth is lived most intensely by those with fewer years on the clock. But the relationship is not linear. Britney Spears may never be quite as old as she was when she burst onto the scene, the carefully choreographed and word perfect embodiment of a Disney Club domesticated young person.

So as Channel 4 hits 25, the time is right to consider its role in both nurturing the idea of youth and in serving the needs of young people. Because both have never been as important as they are today.

Yes, the young are back, having survived the great youth culture drought of the late Nineties when it seemed like they were in danger of becoming relegated into some hazy category of less affluent, less old people. They dressed and talked like grown ups, thought and bought like grown ups. A legion of middle youth had seemingly succeeded in taming the young, pulling them into the orbit of their ageless but docile tastes.

Pulp's Jarvis Cocker was the unnamed agent of this whole process, secretly undermining all youth stood for with his considered 30-something cool. Cocker invited us to abandon the idea that the young really mattered at all. Only now, in recently discovered personal papers, do we learn of his plan to invoke the mass intonation of Alan Bennett monologues, his requirement for daily tea and biscuits sacraments.

Thankfully, Cocker's scheme floundered and the young are once again unintelligible to their elders, once more the object of middle English anxiety, once again utterly alien in the eyes of their elders. We are, once again, going to hell in a hand basket and it is once again all the fault of the young.

The young are tearing up the rules of our culture again, are exacting a casual retribution on the ageing hipsters of the record and film industries, ignoring the politicians and laughing at the last century's sources of authority. But in all this magnificent disorder their relationship with Channel 4 seems only to get stronger, because Channel 4 is somehow one of them, a unifying point of identification across all the new youth tribes. Only Channel 4 seems to be a place where we can all connect with their disparate energies and unruly potential.

And I think I know why. It has nothing to do with the brand being young. Channel 4 connects with them because it is a lifelong servant of the idea of youth. It has a constitution that has to ask questions and a temperament that relishes the discomfort of conflicting ideas. Channel 4 believes the new is to be nurtured, not just welcomed. In a new century where inventiveness is society's necessity, not its ornament, we have never needed Channel 4 more. The idea of youth, that it so profoundly embodies, matters because without it we will never make sense in this bewildering new century.

Thank you Channel 4 for helping this ageing fan remember that the young are worth it and that youth, full of force and fascination, belongs to all of us.

The young novelist Rose Heiney's growing
pains were eased by the delights of Channel 4

Miquita Oliver

Growing Up

The Big Breakfast, 1992

As If, 2001

I have a troubled relationship with Vernon Kay. Or at least I used to, when he was fronting *T4*. On our good days, he was a special-haired edifice of wicked good times, carved from a plasticine brick of Cool. He hurled himself out of the telly and into my arms, offering reassurance that this violent, seething, mendacious existence is nothing more or less than one big cheeky prank. When Vernon was treating me well, all would be resolved within the hour, each contestant in the benign gameshow of life would leave the stage with a good-sport smile, every band would get their five minutes, then it'd all be over; we'd get the bus to Bolton and have some chips. I was young, life was good, and the world was my soundstage.

Then came the shame. It would come in the night, when your well-behaved *T4* viewer should be tucked up in their single bed, staring moonily but asexually at the Colin Farrell poster on the ceiling. I would dream of a twenty-foot Vernon stamping destructively through a post-apocalyptic world where all that survives is banter. I would join and leave Vernon-dedicated Facebook groups at lightning speed, terrified that

the Youth Police were going to come round and take my hard drive. 'Vernon Kay is a Twat.' 'Vernon Kay is the best thing on telly.' 'I want to have Vernon Kay's babies.' 'Vernon Kay should have been sterilised at birth.' I used to sit, whey-faced in front of a blank telly, imagining Vernon's beautiful hair growing and growing and growing until his smile was concealed and he became a six foot four Cousin It, but a friendly one, who'd give big hairy hugs and leave you smelling of serum and shampoo and man.

This wild confusion was born of shame. Not just Vernon-shame, but *T4*-shame. At the height of mine and Vernon's sado-masochistic broadcast relationship, I was nearly 21. I wasn't hormonal, I was post-hormonal. I was at the stage of life where all endocrine processes should have been cancelled out by a surplus of mid-priced liquor, where ambition ruled and the future was a land of Finals and houses and tax. No, *T4* – I can't come to your beach party. I'm off to Courchevel for a drunken yet aspirational skiing holiday with a bunch of future-centred uni chums. But still I tuned in, Sunday mornings, *Friends*, Gwen Stefani, Vernon,

June, and a pummelling sense of dangerously arrested personal development.

I still watch *T4*. Not every week, and I try not to text in as much as I used to. But now, aged 24, I will watch that damned show openly and proudly, like the mother defiantly breastfeeding her six-year-old in Waitrose.

What changed it for me, what made it suddenly OK, was Miquita Oliver. More specifically, discovering that Miquita Oliver and I are the same age. Seriously, we were born within days of each other, we were gestating together, if only we'd known it. We might have passed each other on trollies in the maternity wing, her on the way to a life of pop-tastic, sun-kissed ebullient fabulousness, me on my way to school, then university, then work, then boredom, then death (for such are the options open to those who lack the gift of telly). Knowing this, seeing my precise contemporary on screen being a bit flirty with Tony Blair, turned *T4* from a yoof-tastic guilty pleasure of a magazine show into something more genuinely, solidly aspirational. If Miquita can enjoy life that much, then so can I.

The *T4* team portray early adulthood as a sort of childhood-plus (adolescence need never come into it). We can still frolic and roll and hug like puppies, but oh, look, there's an innuendo, there's a surprisingly insightful reference to the Young Conservatives, and there's an episode of *Friends* we'd long since forgotten. We're growing up without losing the primary coloured innocence of a ten-year-old, we're paying taxes with a wink and a smile, to the sound of Gwen Stefani's latest. My dream night out involves me and the *T4* gang, who will always have the same company spirit, no matter how the cast changes. We'll romp in a ball pond for a while, then get tipsy at Nando's and make some prank calls to members of the Shadow Cabinet. It's adulthood, but not as we're forced to know it.

If *T4* eased me into adulthood with a cheery backwards glance, then it was another show which made me happy to be a grown-up, happy in a 'yes, it's a good world, I can really do something with this' sort of a way. It was the most serious, least flashy show I've ever truly loved – *Operatunity*. From the winning clumsiness of the title-pun to that final, triumphant night at the Coliseum, *Operatunity* showed the warmth, compassion and genuine hope with which reality television can be made, and so seldom is. The format rang alarm bells, of course – untrained singers do opera on telly, judges give feedback, There Can Only Be One Winner, leave your dignity at the door and let your dreams be pounded to pieces before the altar of light entertainment. But that wasn't *Operatunity*'s style. Only the truly gifted were invited to audition, the feedback was kind, and we were privileged to see hearts and voices expand before us under the passionate, profes-

sional tutelage of some real opera folk. It was a fabulous shock to see a camera cut tastefully away from a tear-stained face – a far cry from the common tactic of shoving the lens right in there like a snout, as Kate Thornton pricks the weeper with a pin and holds up photos of dead puppies. And then the finale – God, the finale. That hour of air-punching, sofa-smashing, joyful-howling transcendence when our winners, Denise and Jane, shared the role of Gilda in *Rigoletto*. We didn't really care who they were. Their supermarket jobs and young families and disabilities and very British struggles weren't even the point, they'd just done their new jobs as singers, and done them as well as we'd all hoped.

Nothing's ever matched up to *Operatunity*, either on C4 or any other channel. Even *Musicality* – a similarly-toned musical theatre talent hunt – for me lacked the *Operatunity* magic. Perhaps the musical theatre vocals threw up too many memories of *Pop Idol*, perhaps there were a few too many tears and a few too many tortured close-ups. No, *Operatunity* was a risk, and one that was very much in the spirit of Channel 4 – a show so elitist in content, populist in style, yet suffused with such goodness, went so strongly against the televisual grain that it became subversive, radical. To an extent, *T4* does the same thing. It's music hall, variety, a kids' party to which a few lucky grown-ups are invited. Shows, comedy, turns, stooges, the lightest, most youthful bits of satire. It pokes fun at itself without being knowing or snide, talks to youth (and I use the term loosely) without talking down to it.

It's a peculiar time, your early twenties. A discomfort zone between adolescence and adulthood. So I'm grateful for those programmes which ease the transition. Not just the two I've mentioned, but *Dispatches*, *Channel 4 News*, and – God help me – *Deal or No Deal*. Bite-size chunks of the world, thought provokers, a quick kick in the direction of a more universal knowledge. Let Miquita and I grow old together, consistently delighted and surprised by Channel 4.

I'm grateful for these bite-size chunks of the world, thought provokers, a quick kick in the direction of a more universal knowledge

---

Vernon Kay

A Question of Difference

If Channel 4 could choose a single word to sum up its ethos, that word would be different; different from other channels in its funding, structure and values and, most importantly, in its programme choices. Viewers of Channel 4 have always been exposed to voices and viewpoints that are different to those they find elsewhere on television, an alternative perspective offered not just for the sake of it but to promote greater understanding. This championing of difference, so deeply ingrained within Channel 4's commissioning culture, runs contrary to the prevailing tides in television. Digital technology has led to an explosion of choice, and yet most viewers are super-served with easy entertainment choices and seek out the safe and the same again and again. Hundreds of niche channels celebrate the tastes and interests that unite their audience, making a virtue of presenting a narrow menu of familiar choices and ensuring that those viewers are not challenged to sample something different. Channel 4 is the antidote to that trend, giving a mainstream platform to those who remain outside the mainstream, whether their point of difference is one of belief, physical or mental disability, sexual orientation or campaigning obsession.

Lara Masters is disabled. She is also a director, producer, and writer. She points out that significant and influential disability representation has only occurred recently as Channel 4 has pushed it out of specialist programming to enable it to forge a gradual take-over in all areas of television

Are We There Yet?

Reviewing the changes in how Channel 4 has portrayed disabled people over the last quarter of a century, it struck me that 'disability representation' is almost oxymoronic – because 'disability' encapsulates an infinite myriad of anomalies and everyone's interpretation is individual. Whilst one person just cannot get enough of their 'difference', another will feel their disability is not integral to their life. And then to try and 'represent' this deluge of idiosyncrasies onscreen? I feel quite paralysed by the mere thought (Okay, more paralysed).

Fortunately, Channel 4 was undaunted by the enormity of the task and aired *Walter* on the first night of transmission, starring Ian McKellen as a young man with learning disabilities who is admitted to a highly dysfunctional 'care home' after the death of his parents. The channel's renegade, ground-breaking future was blueprinted by showing this film. To show such dark disability content and, although Sir Ian is of course able-bodied, to cast many disabled people in the drama as 'inmates', was unprecedented at the time.

Since then, experimentation in disability programming has been an essential part of Channel 4's remit, both to reflect changes in society and as an attempt to encourage social inclusion. One prominent avenue in Channel 4's Operation Disability Visibility has been a stream of increasingly fearless and mould-breaking disability documentaries, including the recent *Born To Be Different* and *Bodyshock* strands, which take an honest look at the impact of serious disability, particularly on children who have debilitating and life-limiting conditions.

The 80-Year-Old Children focused on the Khan family in India who have five children born with Progeria, an extreme condition of premature accelerated ageing. The children are tiny and frail and struggle with arthritic problems and bone disintegration. They have been ostracised and bullied by an ill-educated society and told by doctors that their condition is incurable, yet they endure extensive medical research tests in the hope that this might prevent other children and their families from suffering in the future.

The needs of others were also paramount in the most powerful, and multi-award-winning, *The Boy Whose Skin Fell Off* (see page 253), following the last few months of Jonny Kennedy's life as he battles with a malignant skin disease (DEB). Even as Jonny becomes increasingly ill, he plans his funeral, directs the making of his coffin and visits Number 10 to secure charity support in the hope of finding a cure.

Walter, 1982

Many of these stunning and 'life-affirming' films feature exceptional people who fully engage in their lives in an awe-inspiring way. However, in order to project a more balanced image, Channel 4 has adopted a 'warts-and-all' approach to representing disability. So

John Callahan, the cartoonist whose work is published in this section, is quadriplegic and draws his cartoons with a pen clutched in both hands

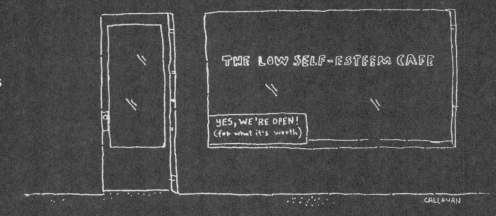

THE LOW SELF-ESTEEM CAFE

YES, WE'RE OPEN!
(for what it's worth)

CALLAHAN

where were the common-or-garden, warted variety of disabled folk? Scouring the archives, I was frustrated by several wart red herrings.

In *Crip On A Trip*, Dom, who has a fatal brittle-bone condition, interrails around Europe with his mates who, at one point, accuse him of being lazy. Eureka! I thought, a real-life lazy disabled person! Alas, on closer examination, it seems that even though Dom's friends have to do almost everything for him, including bum-wiping and manhood-washing – jobs that most 18-year-old boys can't even be bothered to do for themselves – Dom's mates actually feel he's the group's 'nucleus' and the one they rely on. Score: Lazy Crips 0, Reliable Nucleus Crips 1.

I wondered whether the diversity department at Channel 4 were deluding themselves like the beasts in *Animal Farm*? Had anyone even read this fabled 'warts-and-all' manifesto? Then, at a college for the blind (*Blind Young Things*), there was moody, aggressive Steve who refused to get up for lectures and regularly told people where to go using very colourful language. Adjusting to life on campus, Steve was confronted by the constant peril of bumping into other students and whacking whitesticks like lightsaber-wielding Jedi. Despite this, Steve didn't stay surly. In fact, he dropped the attitude, immersed himself in college life and excelled. Grrrr! Another amazing disabled person!

Now even I, a card-carrying crip who should know better, was starting to believe that people with impairments are actually superior beings and Hitler missed the main chance by exterminating us when he should have been using our genes to create a super-race. But there was one documentary that tipped

It's now 'two legs bad; one leg, no legs, a stick, crutches or wheels good' as disability becomes incidental

the balance. *Aged 12 and Looking After the Family* provoked outrage by showing the blind parents of six children heavily relying on their two young daughters to care for them and look after four younger brothers. The girls were clearly overwhelmed by this responsibility but then it was shockingly revealed that the youngest girl had even tried to suffocate herself. After the programme was aired, social services intervened.

The documentary showed it was the couple's apathetic attitude, and not their disability, that made them negligent parents. I accepted that the 'warts and all' theorem worked like exposure therapy: by flooding the airwaves with all types of disabled people and all aspects of disability until society is finally worn down to the point of acceptance and inclusion – and we'll be on that Circle Line quicker than you can say whirling dervish.

Many other programmes with disability content have pushed the viewing public's emotional triggers, at times to the point of RSI. For instance, *The Dyslexia Myth* suggested that dyslexia did not exist, infuriating parents and teachers, not to mention the branding department at the Dyslexia Institute. Further furore was created by *The House of Obsessive Compulsives*, which was attacked for showing OCD sufferers in a reality 'entertainment' format, but was highly successful in engaging and

educating large audiences about this little understood and severely incapacitating illness.

The controversial topic of relationships and learning disabilities was opened up in *Truly, Madly, Deeply*, about an extraordinary dating agency with the sole aim of bringing together people with learning disabilities for loving and sexual relationships. When Apu goes on his first date with Tamana, we see their exchange is similar to many other couples. She shares that her grandfather died of diabetes. 'Was it cancer?' Apu responds, proving he's as incapable of listening as any other man. Tamana patiently reiterates that it was diabetes that killed her grandfather and Apu says he's heard of diabetes 'lots of times', reminding us that learning difficulties make a man no less inclined to exaggerate (lie).

Essentially, these disability-orientated documentaries are more of an exercise in awareness than representation. Significant and influential disability representation has only occurred recently, as disability pushes it's way out of the confines of specialist programming and makes a gradual, at times subversive, Orwellian takeover in all areas of television. From reality TV to drama and even comedy, it's now 'two legs bad; one leg, no legs, a stick, crutches or wheels good', as disability becomes incidental.

Want to get on the property ladder? Or do your require a ramp for your ascent? Phil and Kirstie helped Laura (with mobility problems) find her perfect, accessible home in *Location, Location, Location*. Enjoy your cordon bleu extra blue? Learning difficulties won't stop Gordon dishing out generous portions of verbal abuse, as budding chef Danny (AKA 'Little Fucker') discovered in *Ramsay's Kitchen Nightmares*. And in *The Baby Race* Natalie, a wheelchair-user who needs full-time care, joined a group of single women in their mid-30s who all want children.

Make me Normal, 2005

Disabled actors are also starting to put disability talent on the map in a slew of original dramas. *Richard is my Boyfriend* deliberates whether a couple with learning disabilities should be allowed to have a sexual relationship and stars Elliot Rosen, who has Down's Syndrome. *Rush* features several deaf actors in a murky world of drugs and drive-bys and *The Spastic King*, which centres around learning-disabled Toby, has many cast members with disabilities. It was also written by the accomplished Jack Thorne, demonstrating that off-camera jobs are also increasingly the domain of the differently abled.

Just last year, 12 short films made by disabled directors in *New Shoots* included the artist Nancy Willis's quest to find a suitable retirement home for

her beloved wheelchair-adapted car after 25 years of service (*Elegy to the Elswick Envoy*).

These shifts are so significant, it looks like disability is about to stage a *coup d'etat* in mainstream TV on Channel 4, perhaps encouraged by the on-going alterations of the Disability Discrimination Act and 2005's 'reasonable adjustment' clause. Although, as Tom Shakespeare points out in *Who Stole My Parking Space?*, off-screen shifts in attitudes towards disabled people are not so tangible and many of us have to fight for our civil rights daily as we are denied access to basic goods and services. The programme emphasised how frustratingly impotent the DDA, is even to ensure a disabled person can park in their local supermarket car park. Without the law protecting our rights it may indeed be reasonable adjustments onscreen that precipitate the descent of disabled people into generic society. But with inclusivity comes anonymity; are we ready to lose our USP and meld in with the ten-a-penny able-bodieds?

It's a far cry from the time of the freak shows when audiences came to revel in difference, gloriously free from any fettering notions of inclusion, and someone with a disability could carve themselves (perhaps using their highly dextrous feet) a lucrative career purely by virtue of their 'abnormality' (*Born Freak*). Freak shows made money from

Blind Young Things, 2007

the human propensity for voyeurism, but the do-gooders shut them down, saying it wasn't nice to stare at the afflicted. However, that doesn't stop *Big Brother* audiences from tuning in. It took six years of harassment from disabled people before *BB* bosses brought in a disabled housemate, and Pete, who has Tourette's, quickly became the most popular housemate *of all time*. Well, I hate to say, 'I told you so', but... we did.

BB hit the jackpot with a winning combination of disability and reality TV – yet, this year, not even a squeak of a disability in the house. But an even more difficult area of TV for disability to inveigle than the hallowed *BB* house has also been successfully cracked: comedy. It's now officially OK to laugh about being crippled. In fact, I think it's considered un-PC not to.

Channel 4 hosts the outrageous cartoon *Quads* and its group of 'physically challenged' friends, including a man with hooks for hands and a portly, blind African-American from whose white stick no orifice is sacred. And in the notorious *I'm Spazticus*, disabled actors wreak havoc on an unsuspecting PC public with set-ups such as a blind man entering an off-licence brandishing a dildo and loudly complaining that he wants to return it, and a wheelchair-using presenter turning a music exec a whiter shade of pale by suggesting he re-make rock classic 'Stairway to Heaven' as the disability-friendly 'Stairlift to Heaven'.

Stairlifts were not built for speed, and neither was Channel 4's journey of disability representation over the past 25 years. As with any long journey, there is also the repetitive echo of 'Are we there yet?' Disabled people everywhere know the answer is still 'no'; but then we do not yet live in a fully inclusive society and the two go hand in hand (or stump in hand, prosthesis in hand, etc). However, major inroads have been made with disability's progressive invasion of Channel 4's airwaves, particularly the victories in mainstream programming over the last couple of years. Momentum is now gathering and, as disabled people become increasingly omnipresent on-screen, it's surely just a matter of time before that virtual presence is translated into an actual presence and we are welcomed into an inclusive society where everyone can experience the boundless joys of the Oyster card.

Now even I, a card-carrying crip who should know better, was starting to believe that people with impairments are actually superior beings?!

The Spastic King

Toby, a 33 year old with Downs Syndrome, discusses his dead mother. Extract from Jack Thorne's script, *The Spastic King*

The Spastic King, 2007

14
INT. TOBY'S HOUSE. BEDROOM. NIGHT.
Toby is sitting up on the side of his bed. Taking off his shoes, this is quite a difficult task. It should be just starting to become apparent how much he let his Mum do for him.

15
INT. VOX POP.

PATEL
We like Toby, very much. He puts leaflets in the newspapers for our delivery boys to post. They never do it properly – Toby does.

16
EXT. BUS STOP. DAY.
TOBY is sitting beside ANNIE again. Neither say anything to eachother. TOBY takes out his mobile phone and play's snake on it.

TOBY (TO CAM)
The secret to making sure no-one guesses your Mum's dead is to do everything the same. If you're a bastard, stay bastard. if you're always late then stay always late.

ANNIE
Have you got photos on that thing?
It takes TOBY a minute to realise she's talking to him.

TOBY
What?

ANNIE
You know how some of them have – photos you can

take pictures ...

TOBY
No. Not this one.

ANNIE
Can I have a look? Don't worry I won't nick it.

TOBY
Yeah?
He hands her the phone. She flicks a few buttons.

ANNIE
Nope, what a shame, I was going to have you take a picture of the back of my head. I have a theory that last impressions are more important than first ... I'm going to an interview. Sorry. I'll leave you be.

TOBY
No, it's ok.

ANNIE
I just think that it's pointless sitting by someone and not saying hi, if you want to. Or asking them a favour, if you need one. But maybe I'm weird.

TOBY
You were here ... yesterday ...

ANNIE
That's right, a different interview, which I didn't get. Listen, if I showed you the back of my head, would you tell me honestly if it looked odd.

TOBY
OK.
She does. Then she stands up, and walks away like a model. Then she comes back. Laughing.

ANNIE
What do you think?

TOBY
Very nice.

ANNIE
Great arse, right?

TOBY
What?

ANNIE
Oh! Saved by the bus! Wish me luck!

The 156 pulls up, she hurries to meet it, putting the mobile phone back on his lap as she does. She gets on.

TOBY hesitates, and makes as if to follow her, but doesn't. The bus pulls off. He waves it goodbye.

Walter

In 1982, novelist David Cook adapted his powerful novel *Walter* for Channel 4. In this scene, the mentally retarded Walter is discovered concealing his dead mother's body in her bedroom.

Walter, 1982

Walter's mother lies dead in her bedroom when a friend visits.

> MRS. ASHBY
> Can I see her?

The woman is staring at the pigeon-shit covering his hair and clothes.

> WALTER
> I've got a bird in here and she might escape.

> MRS. ASHBY
> I'd like to speak to your mother, please.

> WALTER
> She's sleeping ... She's not been very well ... I've had to stay at home with her.

> MRS. ASHBY
> What's she been ill with?

> WALTER
> I don't know. She won't wake up.

> MRS. ASHBY
> Can I see her?

> WALTER
> She's asleep.

> MRS. ASHBY
> Yes, you said. But she may need a woman, you know. (He clearly doesn't understand) Some shopping, or something. I won't stay long, I promise.

69
DAY. INT. SARAH'S BEDROOM.
The birds seem almost to have multiplied, and are certainly disturbed by this new presence.
SARAH's face is marked and her hair caked with droppings.
MRS. ASHBY stares in disbelief.

> MRS. ASHBY
> She's ... sleeping very soundly, isn't she?

She turns and pushes past him, through the door and down the stairs, speaking as she goes.

70
DAY. INT. HALL
She has her hand on the front door. Now with the safety of the stairs between them she screams back at him up the stairs.

> MRS. ASHBY
> They'll be coming for you, don't you worry! How could you let her go like that, covered in pigeon muck, you great mistake of a man! It's criminal, after all she's done for you. They'll know what to do to you to make you learn. They'll show you.

She goes in floods of tears, slamming the door.

Quads, John Callahan

Fifteen   A Question of Difference

Having challenged the medical establishment's view of 'mental illness' throughout his career as a clinical psychologist, Rufus May discusses the making of his latest Channel 4 film

The 'Mad' Psychologist

Leo Regan came across me when he was looking into making a film on Mad Pride. That's when he heard about me as 'this mad psychologist'.

I work with people who get defined as 'mentally ill'. But I don't see them as having faulty brains and in need of strong medication. I believe madness and distress is a result of having been on the receiving end of various forms of social injustice. Unless we deeply listen to people, we will be denying their humanity and potential for recovery. Instead of encouraging people to suppress their minds with drugs, I introduce people to alternative methods of calming the mind and expressing difficult feelings, from shadow boxing to chanting out loud. I'm coming at this from my own experience of madness and recovery. At 18, I was diagnosed with schizophrenia and forcibly given powerfully sedating drugs, which I was told I would have to take for the rest of my life. My recovery came from a good friend sticking by me and believing in me, and finding places to express myself creatively and help others. I eventually trained as a psychologist, to challenge the status quo and argue for a better approach. The modern day emphasis on brain chemicals and the prescription of psychiatric drugs is generally an obstacle to understanding and helping people to make sense of their distress and confusion and move on. However, the might of the pharmaceutical industry and the medical establishment mean it's difficult to get a debate going about the social trend of trying to drug away our pain.

So when Leo became interested in filming my work I was keen to give it a go. When he warned me I would soon be sick of him, I did not know what he meant. Eighteen months later, I now have a clearer idea! Leo always wants more. He wants to be able to get to the heart of the subjects he covers. He once turned up at my house at three in the morning. I was really worried about the safety of someone I was trying to help and he wanted to film me in that state: 'great,' I thought to myself. Making documentaries about mental health is tricky; the camera can be very intrusive and often intensifies people's sense of paranoia. This did happen in the making of this film, so I was pleased when Leo agreed to acknowledge this in the film. Usually, filmmakers never mention this. The film follows the story of a junior doctor who started to hear voices. She could not tell her doctor, or it would definitely have been the end of her medical career. So I worked with her without any medication to teach her how to live with the voices and recover so that she could get on with her medical practice. We used the actor Ruth Wilson to play the junior doctor. The use of dramatic reconstruction allows us to tell truths that otherwise would be impossible to tell. I think it's a ground-breaking film. It shows the public, for the first time, what the taboo experience of voice-hearing is really like, and the huge obstacles people face once employers find out they have had mental health problems.

Madness and distress is a result of having been on the receiving end of various forms of social injustice

Quads
John Callahan

The interviewer Ann McFerran talks to Edna Kennedy, the mother of Jonny, the inspirational *Boy Whose Skin Fell Off*

The Sun Has Come Out at Last

When Patrick Collerton's documentary about the final days of her son's life, *The Boy Whose Skin Fell Off*, was nominated for an Emmy in 2004, Edna Kennedy flew to New York for the awards ceremony. For the big night, Edna wore a sequinned purple dress and gold shoes, paid for by Lily Savage/Paul O'Grady. But when Edna and Patrick arrived at the red carpet banked by photographers, Patrick wanted to avoid the razzamatazz and sneak in the back door. 'No way!' said Edna. 'I'm not going to miss walking up that red carpet.'

Edna Kennedy laughs at the memory of striding down the carpet with 'photographers shouting to me and Patrick, "Look this way!" Although they hadn't a clue who I was! To actually be a celebrity and have people trying to take your picture all the time must be horrendous. But for me, walking up that red carpet was wonderful.'

It was as different to the previous 36 years of Edna's life as it's possible to imagine. Edna's son Jonny was born on 4 November 1966 with a rare and incurable skin condition, dystrophic epidermolysis bullosa (EB), where even the mildest touch caused his skin to blister and flake

off. Edna cared for Jonny throughout his life, changing his bandages every day, which often caused him agonising pain. 'Can you imagine what it's like picking up your newborn baby and you are actually blistering it?' says Edna, who admits that her first reaction to her son's death was relief rather than grief. 'When you're constantly watching someone in so much agony, you're willing them to be free of that pain. I wouldn't have wished Jonny's condition on Saddam Hussein.'

There's something terribly wrong. His right leg looks like cod's roe

The Channel 4 documentary won the Emmy and 13 other awards. Edna was interviewed by everyone from Richard and Judy to most national newspapers. Radio 4's Jenni Murray made her feel 'so comfortable, you forgot the microphone,' but she was a little irritated

The Boy Whose Skin Fell Off, 2004

by a photographer from *The Times* 'who had me virtually swinging from the chandelier. I said: "I'm not a glamour model. Just take the picture!"'

As well as raising nearly a million pounds for research into EB with DEBRA (Dystrophic Epidermolysis Bullosa Research Association) and for Jonny Kennedy North East, which provides welfare for people with EB, the documentary made sense of Jonny's life. The film has also changed Edna's life. Today,

"Finish your vegetables! There are children in Beverly Hills with eating disorders."

When you give birth to a child like Jonny, you're grieving from day one. I'd done my grieving before Jonny died

she fund-raises for both charities and each summer, she drives horse-drawn carriages for disabled people. Jonny also indirectly introduced her to her current partner, Colin, who was one of Jonny's carers. 'He's my crutch,' she says.

Did the film also help her to grieve for her son? Edna shakes her head firmly. 'When you give birth to a child like Jonny, you're grieving from day one. I'd done my grieving before Jonny died.'

Collerton's documentary is deeply moving, but in no sense is it a relentless misery. For at its centre is a clever, charming and often outrageous young man, Jonny Kennedy. Edna says, 'If I had £1 for all the people who've seen the documentary and said to me "I wish I'd known him!" I tell them, "If you saw the film you knew Jonny!"' It also gives a strong sense of Edna's warmth and wisdom, her gentle stoicism and constant

The Boy Whose Skin Fell Off, 2004

good humour, as well as her blacker moments. 'Once, I was crying with frustration when I was milking these goats,' she says. 'Jonathan means gift from God. I cried, "this is some gift from God!"'

Even as Edna was in labour with her second child, 'something inside me was telling me things were terribly wrong.' When Jonny was born, he was whisked away. After two days, Edna's husband

Frank confirmed her worst fears. 'There's something terribly wrong. His right leg looks like cod's roe.' When she first saw her baby son lying there with his raw, blistered skin, Edna felt huge pity and overwhelming love. A predicted life expectancy of weeks stretched to months, then years. No one ever imagined Jonny could live as long as he did.

When Jonny was a year old, his father Frank fetched buckets of seawater to bathe him in. 'An old wives' tale,' says Edna, ruefully. 'The salt water did nothing to help and must have been uncomfortable for Jonny.' Frank supported the family financially. 'But the whole Jonny situation was a total embarrassment to him,' says Edna. 'He was a big macho man, and it was as though Jonny reflected badly on him.'

Caring for Jonny was all down to Edna. Basic things often presented enormous difficulties. Even sleeping; his skin would get stuck to the bed clothes. But just as you think how appalling all this must have been, Edna regales you with stories of how Jonny led his teachers a merry dance, of his many friends, of his larger than life personality. 'He was born confident; just as I was born blushing,'

"Sorry, Mike, you just can't hold your liquor."

Quads, John Callahan

Quads, John Callahan

beams Edna, blushing. 'He always managed to get what he wanted; he could be quite manipulative. In another life, he'd probably have been an actor.'

Throughout his life, Edna tried to help him do everything he wanted to do. She even took him to New York at the height of summer. 'Now, I don't know how I did it - pushing Jonny around in a wheelchair at 90 degrees heat and 85 degrees humidity. But why not?'

In 1997, aged 62, her husband died of a heart attack. 'It sounds rather odd saying this, but Frank would have been devastated by Jonny's being diagnosed with cancer. Trying to placate Frank and caring for Jonny would have been too much.' In early 2003, shortly after being diagnosed with cancer, Jonny told his mother that Patrick Collerton would film his final days. 'I worried that the film would be too invasive and intimate; too warts and all. I didn't want Jonny getting upset. But Patrick was such a lovely chap. He'd had prostate cancer himself, and he was very philosophical and gentle.'

Jonny and Patrick instantly hit it off. Patrick stayed with Jonny - by this time living in a nearby bungalow, with Edna on call for any out of hours care. 'Jonny charmed Patrick,' says Edna, 'and the film ended up being as much Jonny's as Patrick's.' *The Boy Whose Skin Fell Off* spans the final months of an irrepressible, witty and charismatic young man. One of the most poignant moments shows Edna changing his dressings. Aged 36, he's a frail, ghostly, fragile figure, bent double with pain. 'Oh, I'm sorry. I'm sorry. It's just so painful,' he sobs. Edna remembers: 'I couldn't show any emotion at all. You have to try to absorb some of the frustration and pain.'

When the glamorous young model Nell McAndrew comes to wish Jonny well, we see Jonny chuckling conspiratorially with an unseen figure off-screen. 'Jonny had a bet with the sound man that he could make Nell McAndrew cry!' hoots his mother. 'And he does! That's what you see when Jonny gives his thumbs up to someone off-screen!'

After Jonny died in September 2003, Edna learned he'd contemplated suicide when he was 18, but he couldn't find a way to do it. 'He couldn't swallow pills because of the blisters on his tongue. But the film meant Jonny's 36 years weren't a waste. It's been a very healing film for many people.' The documentary continues to be shown in schools and Edna still receives letters and emails. Typical, she says, is one from a young woman who was plunged into depression after her baby died. She wrote: 'The baby is now sitting on a cloud next to Jonny. I can get on with my life.'

And Edna, too. 'But had it not been for Jonny, I wouldn't have done all the things I've done, and I certainly wouldn't have walked up the red carpet in New York. Every cloud has a silver lining, but sometimes you need to look for it. Life is wonderful.' Edna pauses to stare out of the window. 'Look,' she says, 'the sun has come out at last.'

Shrinking Planet

Cheap air travel and the growing ubiquity of digital communications have made the concept of the global village a reality. And yet, it's arguable that many Britons know less about the world around them than ever before. Channel 4 has always looked beyond the 24-hour news agenda of conflict, unrest and natural disasters to tell more nuanced, detailed stories about different cultures. Films like *China's Stolen Children* and *Living With Hunger* continue the tradition of documentaries like *Beyond the Clouds* and *The Dying Rooms*, while More4's *True Stories* continues to give a regular showcase to the world's best documentaries. *Unreported World* is British television's only regular peak time series dedicated to the developing world, while *Dispatches* features more international stories than other current affairs strands.

Brian Woods, pre-eminent maker of human rights documentaries, revisits the implications of China's One Child Policy

The Dying Rooms to China's Stolen Children

Ten years after the transmission of *The Dying Rooms*, we were holding a fund-raising dinner for COCOA (Care Of China's Orphaned and Abandoned), the charity that was started as a result of the film. At that dinner I was talking to Dorothy Byrne, Head of Current Affairs at Channel 4, and she suggested that we go back to China and see how things had changed. Two years later, Channel 4 broadcast the result of that investigation, *China's Stolen Children*.

In the dozen years between the two films, China has changed dramatically. *The Dying Rooms* was about an unfore-seen side-effect of the One Child Policy when it collided with the age-old prefer-ence for boys: girls were being aban-doned in their thousands at the gates of China's state orphanages, and under-resourced institutes were choosing to allow them to die of neglect to keep numbers down – 'a policy of fatal neglect' was the description Human Rights Watch used.

In 2007, we found that the situa-tion has moved on. In the interim, the profit motive has arrived in China with a vengeance, and as Capitalism and Com-munism dance around each other, we found that there is now not only a price on the heads of China's 'little princes', but also – to our surprise – on the heads of female babies.

Girls are of course worth less, around half the price of a male child the same age, but market economics have dictated that it's cheaper to buy a baby girl and bring her up to maturity and then marry her to your son, than to risk that either he may never find a wife (an increasingly likely outcome, with 40 mil-lion more boys than girls growing up in China as a result of sex-selective abor-tion) or that you will have to buy a wife at a bride auction, for ten or twenty times the price you need to spend today on a girl baby.

And where there is demand, Chinese market forces ensure there will be a supply: children willingly sold by their parents (either simply for profit, or to avoid the punitive One Child Policy fines) or children snatched from the streets (the best estimate we could find was that this is currently happening to up to 70,000 children a year).

But while the economics of China's One Child Policy have changed, other

Girls are of course worth less, around half the price of a male child the same age, but market economics have dictated that it's cheaper to buy a baby girl and bring her up to maturity and then marry her to your son

things have not: to make *The Dying Rooms* we had to enter China on tourist visas, with a small Hi8 'tourist' camera and a back-up secret camera. Twelve years on, even though the 2008 Beijing Olympics have brought 'official' journalists much greater freedom to report, there was no way we were going to be able to tell this story with official sanction. It was tourist visas again, and this time far more sophisticated secret camera technology.

For *The Dying Rooms*, the camera unit of our secret camera kit was 18 inches long – and that just provided a picture, it didn't even record it onto tape. The output from that camera (powered by a 6V lead-acid battery!) was fed into a Hi8 camcorder that took up the rest of the space in the rucksack I carried over my shoulder. We thought it was very high-tech at the time! Looking back, I'm amazed we got away with it.

Today, the secret camera recording unit is about the size of a pack of cards, with the picture and sound being recorded onto an SD card. The camera itself is also now tiny, about the size of two £1 coins, and comes ready mounted to fit behind a shirt button or a handbag rivet.

Improvements in technology also meant we could keep in touch with the team much more easily (Kate Blewett and I could not go back to China for this film, so we sat safely in London while director/cameraman Jezza Neumann

took all the risks). Back in 1995, we were pretty much on our own in China, but today there is near-universal cell phone coverage, and even small towns usually have internet cafés. As a result, we were in contact with the crew daily, either through a simple security SMS to let us know they were safe, or through emails containing editorial discussions that had been encrypted with a system that would not look out of place on *Spooks*.

But all the technology in the world can't make a good film. That comes back to elements that haven't changed since Euripides – engaging characters and good unfolding narrative.

Jezza and the team met several couples whose children had been snatched before finally being passed on to Chen Jie's parents – as soon as Jezza met them he felt sure they were the right couple to be at the heart of the film, particularly because their missing child was exactly the same age as Jezza's own son. Over the months that followed Jezza, and his British/Chinese assistant producer, Sky, spent many many days with Chen Jie's parents, sometimes filming, often just talking and giving the sympathetic ear that the couple so desperately needed. As a result, when Jezza walked into the room where the couple were sitting on a bed talking one afternoon, he just sensed that he should start filming. Sky was outside shooting GVs, so he had no way of knowing what they were saying, but he

just quietly started to film, and because he had become a friend, the couple carried on chatting completely naturally.

For the next 40 minutes, Jezza continued to film their conversation, a chat we ended up cutting down into five or six minutes, that gives an extraordinarily intimate insight into the grief that every couple who have lost a child must endure.

Chen Jie's parents were never afraid of the authorities' reaction to the film because they felt they had already lost everything that mattered in their world. In the event, it took the Chinese security services just a few days to identify them. They were asked to come to a nearby police station where they were interrogated for several hours about the team that had filmed with them. To their credit, the police also asked what they could do to help find Chen Jie, but the couple were left in no doubt that the identity of Jezza and his team was a far higher priority.

Twelve years on from *The Dying Rooms*, politics, technology, commissioning preferences and TV fashions may have changed, but some things remain the same. In China, the state machine does not like foreign journalists making films without permission. And in the UK, a good story well told remains the gold standard for everyone working in all genres of television.

China's Stolen Children, advert 2007

Rana Dasgupta, the British-Indian writer whose works include *Tokyo Cancelled*, invokes the possibilities (and paranoias) of globalisation

Beyond the Clouds, 1994

Beyond the Clouds, 1994

Surviving Globalisation

Empire's Children, 2007

Last Peasants of Europe, 2003

When the 20th century began, there was *history*. Capitalists and Socialists alike believed that time unfolded with moral purpose, leading human society through periodic crises into inevitable improvement. By the end of the century, there was *globalisation*.

Glass towers and shopping malls sprouted in the world's cities, annihilating older forms of commerce. Millions were pushed out of villages by war, drought and the global market's takeover of agriculture. In 2005, the UN said it counted 30 million refugees 'of concern' – equivalent to the total number of refugees in 1945 – as if what was previously disaster had become run-of-the-mill. Many of these fleeing multitudes lived in the era's most startling innovation: vast, rapidly expanding, slum-city-states, such as the one surrounding Lagos. Meanwhile, barricades intensified around wealthy neighbourhoods, cities and nations, and the affluent of the world were subjected to a media fantasy of universal freedom and mobility.

There was no more talk of 'progress'. The gigantic processes of the global market were their own purpose, and no one could really say what they meant, or what human end they served.

Elites of the late 19th and early 20th centuries were serenely confident about the direction their own experiments in 'globalisation' would take. In *The Time Machine* (1895), H.G. Wells warned of the ultimate consequences of the class inequalities he saw around him. But his time traveller had to journey 800,000 years into the future to detect workers and elites splitting into separate, degraded species, and *30 million years* for the effects to be complete. There was a certain lack of urgency to the prediction, and his readers could feel reassured that the mighty engine of European commerce would continue for the foreseeable generations.

The 2002 Hollywood movie of *The Time Machine*, made by Wells's grandson, Simon Wells, shrank this epic timescale dramatically. Everything had already come to an end by 2037, when a space-exploration disaster caused the moon to rain down on the earth, instantly destroying capitalist society, and turning human beings out into a ruined nature. The idea that western Capitalism would gradually decline across the millennia was now outmoded: instead, the film presented a world already stretched to dangerous limits and threatened at every moment with catastrophe.

This is a prevalent, early 21st century feeling. While 'consumers' continue to buy and sell in the global marketplace, they are stalked by the suspicion that *it cannot continue like this*. The buzzword for every industry is *sustainability*, which only reminds everyone how improbable that seems. Countless movies now show science and capitalism reaching their limits, and suffering total defeat at the hands of returning natural forces. *The Day After Tomorrow* (2004), for instance, showed the world destroyed by climatic change. Scientist James Lovelock, creator of the 'Gaia Hypothesis', prophesied in 2006 that 'billions of us will die and the few breeding pairs of people that survive will be in the Arctic where the climate remains tolerable'.

The paradox of globalisation, in fact, is that the greater possibilities it offers to its elites – the global, especially the western middle classes – comes with it an even greater increase in their paranoia and fear. Why?

By the end of the 20th century, 100 years of atrocities by the wealthy nations had swept away the West's supposed innocence, revealing a terrifying potential for violence. Environmentalism had shown that the increase in products brought

an increase in drought, deserts and poisoned landscapes. This deterioration was intensified sharply by the added appetites of new Third World consumers, and, since its burden was borne overwhelmingly by the world's poor, it was difficult to believe any longer that the consequences of the expansion of markets would be only enlightenment and harmony. No cost-benefit analysis could predict exactly how the peoples of the world would respond when rapacious global markets arrived to dictate the terms of their lives. The world seemed more threatening and more obscure at the end of the 20th century than at the end of the 19th. When stark images began to float back – sweatshops, terrorist attacks, resource wars, desperate migrants dying at borders – it seemed that some terrible catastrophe was being stored up.

The British Empire of a century ago, vast as it was, was controlled by a coterie of like-minded men from their drawing rooms, clubs and offices. The forces at play in globalisation, on the other hand, seem stern and abstract and beyond all human control. It is difficult to see who is in charge of globalisation. Even Prime Ministers and CEOs seem to be just agents of larger energies. It is as if globalisation is a great spirit, with its own dark and non-negotiable intentions. In fact, early 21st century humans have a similar relationship to the system they live in as primitive humans had to nature. And it was often hi-tech folk religion and conspiracy theory superstition that best captured the feeling of its inscrutable workings. There is widespread disillusion with the inherited systems of political control, which now seem powerless at rebuking storms and plagues. Voter turnout fell across the OECD countries, for national elections seemed parochial and superficial. Many feel they have no remaining sphere of political expression except consumption itself. *Buy Organic* has become politics. *Buy Free Trade*. But when the problem is precisely how much *stuff* is needed to run the average modern life, such *consumer power* feels suspiciously like just another marketing ploy.

But it is difficult to find alternative ways to live – which explains the sense of helplessness of people who otherwise appear so privileged. While globalisation entertains them with daily fantasies of escape and transcendence, in practice the system makes it impossible to experiment with the parameters of one's life. The flow of global real estate capital has made New York and London – historically the centres of bohemianism and counter-culture as well as of commerce – so unrelentingly expensive it is difficult to survive in either without signing oneself over to the kind of corporate mindset captured in the 1999 Lexus ad: 'Sure we take vacations. They're called lunch breaks.' These cities have ceased to be the places of anonymity and freedom that attracted independent spirits. The average Londoner is filmed 300 times a day by the city's 200,000 security cameras,[1] and, especially after the anti-terrorism laws of 2001, there is very little about city life that is spontaneous, riotous or subversive.

A vast and violent system that tolerates no alternatives, and an anxious generation with no room for ethical manoeuvre or innovation: the beneficiaries of globalisation feel harried and burdened by it. But there is still no question of any compromise to the 'western way of life' so dependent on intensive extraction from every continent. The outside seems increasingly barbaric, and the world's wealthy want no part of its disease, environmental degradation, terrorist attacks and war. Putting stern controls on the cross-border movements of refugees and economic migrants, the west is taking refuge in isolation. The shrill jamboree of marketing and celebrity provides much-needed relief from the eerie spiritual silence. The energy of the arts – 'world cinema', 'world music', novels from the 'periphery', food from the Pacific rim – supply a frisson of the strange and exotic.

In 2003 Clare Short, Labour MP under Prime Minister Blair, resigned from the Cabinet over his government's role in the invasion of Iraq. As Secretary of State for International Development, she had several times seen her own conception of justice founder on globalisation's harder edges, and her resulting anger and impotence led her to write, later: 'We will have to move to a higher level of civilisation where all people have the basics that they need, and then we must develop a new way of living which gets beyond an obsession with the ownership of more and more material goods and economic growth for its own sake. We must learn to enjoy caring for each other, nature, literature, the arts, philosophy and the spirituality for which western people in particular are yearning as they find that material plenty does not provide meaning to their lives.'

What her experiences taught her is that globalisation is not fundamentally economic – though everything tend towards economics these days – but philosophical.

For the 18th century philosophers whose conceptual architecture of politics still prevail in the early 21st century, the nation state was the highest level of political organisation. It is only within nation states that people are prepared to make an effort – and even sacrifices – in the name of creative coexistence. States might have official, top-level alliances with each other, but there are no ties of politics, empathy, or care between citizens of one state and citizens of another. When globalisation creates substantial relationships between factory workers in China, cotton farmers in Mali, tribal communities in Brazil and advertising executives in London, there is bewilderment between them.

This shows that our vision of life has become small and parochial, entirely inadequate for the scale of globalisation. Naturally, the grandiose abstract systems of finance, commerce and production seem vast and indomitable, and, in comparison, life seems weak and in decline. But human society has successfully faced up to this situation before. There was a time, after all, when the European nation states themselves seemed impossibly large and forbidding, and when it seemed implausible that such extreme human variety could be brought into common citizenship.

Now globalisation, which contains every conceivable form of living, and which has no 'outside' by which the inside can be defined, needs to be rescued from senselessness. This requires new systems of thought that accept the planet as a single intellectual horizon, and new theories of ethics and justice that do not make the national gated community the pre-eminent value. A new brand of heroics that can blend ambition with frugality and the ability to bear consequences. A new humanism, unswayed by the entrenched rationalisations of inequalities. New art forms and new sensibilities to outdo the scale and dynamism of economics, and to make the global market seem comprehensible. There is no underestimating the enterprise. But only in such a way can people emerge from their apocalyptic apprehensions, and believe once again that human society has a future.

1 'Cameras in Britain record the criminal and the banal,' New York Times, 23 July 2005

In 2004 Channel 4 aired Sierra Leonean journalist Sorious Samura's *Living with Hunger*; here he remembers its making

The Devil and the Stranger

Living with Hunger, 2004

Remembering the making of *Living With Hunger*, I cannot think of a worse way for our filming to have started. I was there as a fellow African to introduce myself to a group of poor and hungry Ethiopian farmers. I was hoping to live among them so that I could understand how they survive without food and also try to experience their suffering first hand, for four weeks eating and drinking only as little as they did.

'What are they saying?' I asked Gethu, my new deacon friend, as the crowd pushed closer, now waving sticks and threatening to beat me. 'They are saying that you are big and black and that you are a devil and that you are going to eat their children and their pregnant wives.'

Well, being no stranger to hostillities in other peoples' land, I kind of knew that this was all about the unknown and the superstitions that come out when the stranger comes. After a while, though, they calmed down. It was the head priest who turned the tide. He spoke to his congregation of Coptic Christians in front of their ancient church in northern Ethiopia. 'I have heard with my own ears that Samura eats babies, but let us give him a chance to tell us why he is here.'

'OK,' I said to Gethu. 'Just tell them that I'm one of them, the same blood, the same flesh and I'm just here to tell their story,' and I think that was the moment when we really had the chance to tell our first *Living with…* story, *Living with Hunger*.

Africans like me who live in the West know that Ethiopi-ans, Eritreans and Somalis do not like to call themselves Africans. We don't call it racism if you're the same colour, so we call it prejudice. Whatever we call it, it surprised me as much as my crew, producer Ivan O'Mahoney, director Charlotte Metcalfe and assistant producer George Waldrum.

I suppose it has always been easy for me to make what we now call 'bottom up' films, because when I started making films in Sierra Leone it was with ordinary people that I began my work. My colleague Ron McCullagh, who runs Insight News TV, the film company I work for, always gets people who come up to our small offices in Clapham to look at a photograph taken by the famous African cameraman, Mohamed Amin, during the Ethiopian famine of 1984, and the significance that it has in the

Living with Hunger, 2004

way Africa has been reported for all these years. Because when you look at that picture of thousands of starving people on the plains of Ethiopia in 1984, you can't see any faces, just name-less victims. It was very representative of how Africa has been reported by the western media over the years – just groups of

265

Sixteen   Shrinking Planet

desperate, nameless, starving Africans. In other words, victims.

So this was our challenge – to give names and addresses to people like these, to show that they are real people like all of us, just that they were living in conditions that were really challenging and, remarkably, they were dealing with it.

That first night in the village of Kirkus was when things really hit me. You suddenly realise you've left your comfort zone. No amount of preparation prepares you for this.

Brahanu, the village chairman, had agreed to host me, at least for the first few days, and on the first night he led me to my temporary bedroom, the kitchen hut. I only had a candle to break the dark, and I made myself as comfortable as I could beside the embers of the open fire. When I blew the candle out it was completely dark and I thought, one day you're watching telly, with your loved ones around you, and now you're sleeping in a cold, pitch-dark hut.

Living with Hunger, 2004

What I didn't know was that as I slept, the usual tenants of the kitchen came to take their place by the kitchen embers. Above all things, I'm scared of cats. Even now I find it hard to describe how I felt when I woke up with two cats rubbing against me and crying in the middle of the night. I scrambled in my bag for a torch and as I lit it, all I could see were eyes of different shapes and sizes, reflecting the torch light back towards me. It was like a horror movie. With me in this tiny hut were goats, and sheep, cats and cows, donkeys and dogs, and there were chickens as well, all looking at me, probably all as scared of me as I was of them.

Over the next few days I settled into the routine of life with the Brahanu family. I didn't know I was lucky until I moved in with the Alamnu family. They were much poorer. I worked with them in their fields and lived as they did, sharing what little food they had with the adults and their three children and the hungrier and more angry I got, the more my respect grew for these remarkable people.

Mrs Alamnu was so gentle, with so much power, in all the suffering of her family. She never blamed anyone for the suffering of her children, she just worked as hard as anyone could to make things as good as they could be. There was sometimes cow milk and grain for the tef, their bread, but mostly there was this horrible bitter plant they ate called wild cabbage. It had no nutritional value at all, we just ate this bitter weed because there was nothing else to eat. It just makes your stomach turn and makes you pee a lot.

Perhaps I should not be surprised at what happened next. As I became more malnourished, I began to lose it with the crew. I had become part of the people I was living with and as I got more hungry, I became more angry with these well-fed people who just filmed us. Of course, I knew they were friends and colleagues, but this hunger made me see them in a very different light.

It all came to a head when Gethu, Adesu and I walked the 40 kilometres to the town of Lalabela to find some work, make some money and buy some proper food. I'll never forget that journey. I was so pissed off with them in their car and us walking

Living with Hunger, 2004

in the rain. It seemed to me that they didn't care about me or my friends. They became 'others'.

Of course I realise now that they had to keep that separation for me to make this film, but the anger I felt at the time was very real. It's still strange to me that Gethu and Adesu felt nothing of my anger. Like everyone I lived with in Ethiopia, they took the circumstances they lived with without complaint, blaming nobody for their conditions, asking no one for aid. They just 'coped'. Every day they found some way or other to struggle through.

And so, by living with them, and filming their lives, I think we managed to show that these people are many things, but they can never ever be called victims

And so, by living with them, and filming their lives, I think we managed to show that these people are many things, but they can never ever be called victims.

Five years later, and around the world more people are hungry now than they were then. Hunger is growing at a proportionate level in that region but my friend Gethu is getting an education in Lalibela, something the crew and I helped put in place. Mr and Mrs Alamnu's daughter is also going to school four miles away from the village, while her elder brother, Desala, is kept at home to work in the farms.

For me, though, leaving them behind – saying goodbye – was tougher than anything else I experienced during those four weeks living the reality of their farming lives. Allowing us to document their reality was an eye-opening, eye-watering experience that pushed boundaries and helped prepare us for the films that followed in the *Living with…* series.

Unreported World, 2004
India's Missing Children

By tracing the journey of one girl into
sex slavery from West Bengal to Calcutta, Sam Kiley revealed the missing
children of India. According to the UN
30,000 women and girls are forced into
slavery through Calcutta every year.
One third of the girls are HIV positive.
There is little done to curb the demand
and the rescue foundations are reluctant to trust what they consider to be
a corrupt police force.

Unreported World, 2005
Congo: UN's Dirty War

The UN has an aggressive mandate
to bring peace to the Democratic
Republic of Congo. The UN army acts
in support of the government army
in East Congo. Local warlords are
scrapping among themselves for
riches in diamonds and minerals. A
Congolese army watches as the UN
soldiers destroy towns allowing the
army to steal cattle and potentially
maiming civilians. As far as the people
are concerned the army and the UN
are the enemy.

Unreported World, 2005
Iraq: On the Front Line

When Peter Oborne visited Iraq, President Bush believed it to be the front line in his war on terror. The American troops displayed a 'wonderful belief' in the process of American democracy and capitalism, advising villagers to vote against councillors they have a problem with. It is not, however, terrorists alone who destabilise security in Iraq. Insurgents attack the US and Iraqi armies (An 1,000-man strong Iraqi battalion is 200 men short from death and desertion in two months). The US strikes back. While they believe they are keeping the peace, the Americans may be taking sides in what could turn into a civil war.

Unreported World, 2005
Somalia: Al-Qaeda's New Haven

500,000 have been killed by war and famine in Somalia; civil war looms. There is only gun-rule and extortion; a hand grenade costs about ten dollars, the same as a pizza. There are 3,000 Islamist recruits in training in Somalia. Days before Aidan Hartley arrived, gunmen invaded the house of a peace activist and executed him in front of his wife. Islamist schools are the only option as the governments have been ruined in the war. Mosques spring up from the rubble, funded by the Union of Islamic Courts. The US feared Somalia would become a haven for *jihadist* Al-Qaeda and its ideology. Now that fear is being realised.

When Channel 4 screened a season of Iranian cinema, it revealed some of the world's most beautiful and hidden films. Sarfraz Manzoor, whose television credits for Channel 4 include *The Great British Asian Invasion*, lifts the veil on this filmic tradition

The Beautiful and the Hidden

The Circle, 2000

Through the Olive Trees, 1994

In the years since the Islamic Revolution, Iran has produced some of the most inventive and innovative films in the world. The success of directors such as Abbas Kiarostami, Mohsen and Samira Makhmalbaf has given cinema audiences a far more sophisticated insight into modern Iran than they would have if they only watched the television news. The critical acclaim accorded to Iranian cinema also raises intriguing questions, such as, how has a film industry been able to flourish in such a strictly Islamic state? And why is it only Iran where this is the case?

Iranian cinema stems from a particular cultural context that sets it apart from other Middle Eastern nations. Iranian films are part of a visual tradition that existed in Iran since before the arrival of Islam. This tradition was historically apparent in shrines to saints and in the striking architecture of mosques and it continues in cinema. Iranian films are also inspired by the nation's poetic tradition. Where western cinema is essentially novelistic and driven by narrative, Iranian films tend to stress the potency of specific moments and emotions rather than follow classical narrative structures. The emphasis on poetic imagery and symbolism became increasingly necessary following the 1979 Islamic revolution. With the toppling of the Shah and the return from exile of the Ayatollah Khomeini, filmmakers found themselves facing heavy restrictions. Directors were not permitted to show men looking lustfully at women. Even showing a close-up of a female face was banned. Since men and women could not appear on screen together unless they were married, actors and actresses were sometimes forced to marry in real life so that they could act together on screen.

The Circle, 2000

This strict censorship forced filmmakers to be more creative in how they made films. There was much oblique hinting of issues through symbolism. The themes of films were also affected by the restrictions. Unable to tackle love and sexual relationships, directors focused instead on social issues such as friendship and community.

In the early days of the revolution cinema was deemed inappropriate, but with time the government softened its stance as it became aware of the power of cinema to reach the masses. Cinema, declared the Ayatollah Khomeini, had become decadent and titillating and it needed to play a more helpful and educative role in building social and religious values. The restrictions remained but the government began to provide incentives for filmmakers. A film festival was established. There were tax incentives and financial support for film projects. It was in this curious climate of both censorship and support that Iranian cinema entered its golden age with the emergence of two acclaimed directors.

Abbas Kiarostami first came to international attention with the 1987 film *Where is my Friend's House?* Ten years later his 1997 film *Taste of Cherry,* about a taxi driver contemplating suicide, won him the Palme d'Or at Cannes. 'Cinema starts with D.W. Griffith,' remarked Jean-Luc Godard admiringly, 'and ends

Through the Olive Trees, 1994

1962 short film *The House is Black*, which depicted life in a leper colony spliced with her celebrated poetry, was one of the first landmarks in Iranian film.

Modern female filmmakers such as Samira Makhmalbaf and Tahmineh Milani are thus part of a female cinematic tradition that is unique to Iran. For such female directors, shooting their films often meant working with men who were reluctant to be directed by a woman; women directors would have to explain their directions to a male intermediary who would then pass on their orders. This pragmatic approach was also employed by all filmmakers to be able to operate under the restrictions imposed by the state. All films are required to be submitted to the government for approval; in reality, filmmakers routinely send out scripts which are very different from what they intend to shoot.

with Kiarostami.' Effortlessly simple and conceptually complex in equal measure; poetic, lyrical, meditative, self-reflective and increasingly sophisticated, the films of Kiarostami mix fiction and documentary in unique ways, often presenting fact as fiction and fiction as fact.

Kiarostami was not the only leading light in this new Iranian cinema. Mohsen Makhmalbaf was a working class former revolutionary who had formed an undergound Islamic militia group when he was fifteen and had served almost five years in prison for attempting to stab a policeman. In 1996, Makhmalbaf invited the policeman he had stabbed to participate in his film. In *A Moment of Innocence* the policeman and Makhmalbaf portray themselves making a film and casting a pair of young actors to play themselves as young men and to re-enact the stabbing. Later films such as *The Cyclist* and *The Silence* confirmed Makhmalbaf as a giant of modern Iranian cinema. His influence stretches beyond his own films; in 1996 he formed the Makhmalbaf Film House in which he taught film to a select group of pupils.

Amongst these was his daughter Samira, who at seven had appeared in *The Cyclist*. By the time she was eighteen Samira Makhmalbaf was the youngest director to participate in the 1998 Cannes Film Festival with her debut feature *The Apple*; two years later, her second feature film *The Blackboard* won the jury prize at Cannes. The success of Samira Makhmalbaf and other female directors indicates an intriguing paradox about the role of women within Iranian cinema. The post-revolutionary climate led to women being almost invisible on-screen. This might suggest that Iranian cinema was hostile and alien territory for women and yet Forough Farrokhzad – one of the founding figures of Iranian cinema – was a woman. Farrokzad's

Iranian cinema stems from a cultural context that sets it apart from other Middle Eastern nations

The Apple, 1998

The growth of the internet has provided another means by which filmmakers can get round censorship, as films can be shot and uploaded and viewed online without state interference. The rise of the internet highlights the final paradox about Iranian cinema – that the most acclaimed Iranian films of recent years are banned in Iran. It is only recently, with the popularity of pirate DVDs and the internet, that ordinary Iranians are finally able to watch the films which have for the past three decades been entrancing international audiences.

New Family Values

Channel 4 was the first to regularly present a le[ss] sanitised view of family life in *Brookside* – a wo[rld] of divorce, incest, domestic violence and poiso[n-] ous family disputes. Over the last quarter cent[ury] television has successfully charted the evoluti[on of] family life; the Waltons gave way to the Gallag[hers,] the 2.4 children of the eponymous BBC sitco[m] were replaced by something more complex. B[ut] drama is not the only story. Channel 4's exten[sive] documentary output has also explored every corner of family life in the UK, from the hars[h to] the humorous. This tradition is being continu[ed] in 2008 as Channel 4 undertakes its most co[mpre-] hensive study ever of family relationships wit[h the] observational documentary series, *The Famil[y]* which will seek to understand whether the m[odern] family unit really is becoming as dysfunction[al or] unorthodox as is often portrayed.

Frank Furedi, Professor of Sociology at the University of Kent, explains how *Brookside's* existence informed the intellectual elite

From Brookside to Supernanny

Brookside, 1982

In an era of rapid technological advance it is easy to overlook the speed with which family life has undergone important alterations. Back in the good old days, the happy and uncomplicated stable nuclear family seen on the American television series *Father Knows Best* resonated with most viewers. However, by 1982, when Channel 4 was launched, people were all too aware that family life was more complicated. And in the past quarter of a century those traditional ideals often seem to contradict lived experience.

Today the cornflake-packet family – white, middle class, mum and dad, two smiling children – has acquired a minority status in contemporary culture. This is not surprising since marriage has become an option, a lifestyle choice rather than an obligation of adulthood, an option that competes with 'living together', 'living apart' and 'living alone'. Look at your neighbours – some live in single households, others are cohabiting. Around a quarter of children in Great Britain live in lone-parent families. Marriage is no longer a precondition for having children. Births outside marriage have almost quadrupled since the Seventies to around forty-three per cent today. And in many parts of the country they exceed fifty per cent. Consequently a home can mean anything from a solo adult household to a single-parent family to a same-sex couple.

All this is paralleled by a growing awareness of the tension and instability that often dominates at home. Divorce is increasingly common and the Office of National Statistics says an average marriage now lasts 11.6 years. By the time *Brookside* hit the screen it was difficult to pretend that family life was unproblematic. The pivotal Grant family spoke to widely recognised social trends. Bobby and Sheila's turbulent marriage captured many of the issues familiar to viewers. However, *Brookside* did more than provide a dramatic expression to stereotypical marital frustrations. It captured the zeitgeist of the early Eighties, when discussions about the so-called 'dark side' of family life acquired an unprecedented public prominence. In the early Thatcher years the public imagination had to engage with issues such as domestic violence and child abuse. *Brookside* covered these trends.

Brookside, 1982

For soap operas 'family problems' have always been the staple plot lines. But these issues are frequently represented in a timeless manner drawing attention to their continuity with the problems of the past. This is not surprising since many of us yearn for the stability and security represented in idealised representations of the home. The success of *Coronation Street* was in part due to our search for security and belonging. Continuity and permanence are also important themes of *EastEnders*, where strongly rooted families distract us from confronting a world that is surprisingly different from the one we expected to inhabit. In contrast, *Brookside* is a community without a past. The people have moved in from somewhere else. This is a brand new cul-de-sac and the first episode represents a sort of Year Zero. It is not centred on the Queen Vic or the Rover's Return. *Brookside* characters are people on the move and constantly remind us that we are living through changing times. Unlike the equally hard-hitting *EastEnders, Brookside* appeared to be not only of the times but a tiny bit ahead of it. This provided considerable scope for experimentation with story lines that went beyond the purview of traditional soaps. Consequently, it swiftly gained a reputation for being contemporary and for dealing with topical story lines. Many of my sociology colleagues regarded *Brookside* as a dream come true. In hundreds of seminars up and down the country we could talk about change not as abstraction but through its dramatisation on a previous night's episode. I could not shut my undergraduates up when they ventured their opinion on incest, lesbian kisses, bullying and the ethics of IVF. *Brookside* was a point of reference for the national conversation and a regular focus of controversy among opinionated young social scientists. Shocking scenes of the brutal assault and rape of Sheila Grant also gave the term 'violence against women' a powerful dimension.

Critics of *Brookside* claim it lost the plot in the Nineties, that its gritty realism gradually gave way to sensationalist violence and crime. This community without a past also had no future. The demolition of Brookside Close in the final episodes underlined the transience of contemporary community and family life.

<u>Shameless</u>, from 2004

Today around a quarter of non-married people under sixty in Great Britain are cohabiting, double the figures during the early years of *Brookside*. Women are having children later – first child at twenty-nine on average, three years older than in 1971. A growing proportion of mothers are born outside the UK – 21.9 per cent in 2006, compared to 12.8 per cent in 1996. Children born outside marriage stood at around twelve per cent when *Brookside* was launched in 1982. By the time Channel 4's *Shameless* appeared in 2004 it was forty-two per cent. And marriage continued to lose its appeal. The proportion of women aged eighteen to forty-nine who were married fell from almost three-quarters in 1979 to less than half in 2002. However, 18,059 same-sex civil partnerships were formed between December 2005 and September 2006.

Change and fluidity in intimate relationships invites insecurity and the dramatisation of family life needs to reflect this. *Shameless* is not simply an entertainingly off-beat comedy, it also provides a dose of sentimentality and nostalgia to an audience all too aware of the precarious status of their personal life. The Gallaghers are a lovable criminal family bound together by a powerful bond and a sense of loyalty. Despite their chaotic and confusing lifestyle, they are capable of pulling together when confronted with adversity. They make us feel good precisely because they endow dysfunctional personal relations with meaning.

In hundreds of seminars up and down the country we could talk about change not as abstraction but through its dramatisation on a previous night's episode

But it is *Supernanny* that really speaks to the anxieties of 21st century family life. Loss of confidence in personal relations has had a powerful impact on parenting. Child-rearing has become a minefield and parenting advice is now an entertainment format. The phenomenal success of *Supernanny* indicates that reality television not soap opera best represents the drama of modern family life. This is a major sociological statement. Twenty-five years ago the vast majority of parents were depicted as adequate, if not perfect, mothers and fathers. They could also expect to get useful advice from other family members and friends. Today, parents often appear on the screen as helpless and isolated. They lack a network of support, and family life is dramatised as a lonely experience. And when things go wrong it is not grandma but Supernanny whom we expect to arrive on the scene. So where next? And how long before a Supernanny becomes the subject for a new path-breaking soap opera?

<u>Wife Swap</u>, from 2003

Rachel Cusk, the award-winning writer of *The Lucky Ones*, believes that it is the conception of self that determines family culture in any age

Family Trees

Brookside, 1982

My cousin had a family tree drawn up. This is what people do in concrete towns where families outnumber forests. And perhaps a family is like a tree, all those connected people rooted to the ground – a safe shelter or a dead weight of meaningless lumber, depending on how you look at it.

On the paternal side our family came from Riga in Latvia. Our ancestor jumped ship in Cardiff and started up a Welsh branch there. He was a stevedore, apparently, with flat Latvian cheeks and thick, peasant calves and forearms, or so I imagine, since he bestowed them so liberally among his descendents. My mother saw a television programme once where the camera panned the streets of Riga, and she claims to have jumped out of her seat in surprise, thinking that she saw her own children there. And meanwhile she was waiting for her own genteel, Irish-inflected branch to bud and grow and bud again until it produced herself. There was red hair and Catholicism and a weakness for alcohol in that arboreal segment. My great-great grandmother had a reputation on the Holloway Road for driving drunk in charge of a pony and trap, with

her flame-coloured hair flying out behind her. She was a cousin of the poet Yeats, and died of drink in her thirties leaving nine children to tell the tale. At last the Latvian link met the red-haired tendency and produced the childhood I recall with the usual mixed feelings, seeing nothing of its genetic determinism, only the blinding knowledge of individuality that was refracted through siblings and parents

A family is a community whose common object is the self, only not the same self

and grandparents, so that we all seemed to be looking at the same thing, only from different angles. Blood relationship is not the same as friendship, or love. In friendship the common object is the world. A family is a community whose common object is the self, only not the same self.

So perhaps a family is less like a tree and more like a religion, with its miracles of birth and death, its core of ritual and

belief, its reconfiguring of randomness as design. Who looks at their own children and sees them as the offshoots of the stevedore from Riga? Not I. One's children are a codicil to one's self, and so it is the conception of self that determines family culture in any given age, just as it determines our visualisations of God. The child, with the chip of infinity that is its soul, is currently our society's most highly prized artefact. It might be said that our modern lives are so unnatural that we have re-encountered our reproductive abilities as a form of genius. Having vaunted the makers of microchips, the sheep-cloners, the genome-mappers, the discovery that we ourselves have the ability to create something far more sophisticated is newly amazing to us. Never have children been so treasured, so significant, so subject to interpretation as they are now. There is no morality currently more powerful than that of parenthood. We study our Victorian ancestors with their apparently insouciant attitudes to child mortality, and though barely a century and a half separates us from these monsters of unsentimentality, they seem as remote to us as mammoths and dinosaurs.

Human beings are very good at getting themselves thoroughly oppressed, however; we like to turn doctrines into dogmas as a way of acknowledging our own ambivalence, and then watch as other people exhibit precisely the weaknesses of which we suspect ourselves. Christianity thrived for centuries on human hypocrisy, and family life, with its separation of morality from lived experience, has the same susceptibility to witch-hunting and inquisitions and cant. A dictatorship of positive thinking has got hold of family life. A new regime has entrenched itself in an old social structure; everything about the culture of the modern family suggests a reappraisal of values, a distancing from past modes of being, the rise of a new sensibility. Yet it is hardly new, to mate

watching the same branded television, buying the same Nintendos and Playstations, dressing their girls as princesses and their boys as lumberjacks, mouthing the values of dullness, of lack of identity, of anti-intellectualism, of conservatism and conformity and selfishness. The failure to go along with all this is immediately, neurotically labelled: women are called post-natally depressed; children are called autistic or aspergic; men are usually covered up for, unless they're helpful, in which case they're called house husbands. The modern British family has no sense of humour, no edge, no individuality. It's all as earnest and corporate and capitalistic as any other modern enterprise, a Microsoft of the human soul, a branding of the experience of being and becoming. Thinking of my cousin's family tree, I wonder whether this voguish document is just another bit of propoganda, a family-fetishising artefact for the twenty-first century. And I suppose my cousin must think of it as meaningful, for why else would he have bothered with it? Yet the most striking thing about it is the portrait of randomness it paints. In

tacular elopement of my uncle with a Brazilian belly dancer, and his shame-faced return some years later, to haunt family festivals in a shiny tight-fitting suit. The disability of his son, who was born with water on the brain, and the great musical talent of his daughter, a brilliant flautist who played at our grandmother's funeral and brought the reprieve of culture to that bleak occasion. The fact that one of my cousins never met her own father, an Italian whose name and dates of birth and death are entered there. She had the chance to know him, for the death-date is quite recent: my aunt, his former wife, died shortly afterwards. Though they hadn't seen each other for years, they died of the same cancer, contracted from asbestos in a house they shared in Italy when they were first married. This cancer, the bitter fruit of their love, goes unrecorded on the family tree, as do the reasons for the estrangement of their only child.

It is my ardent supposition that the evangelism of the modern family is likewise deceptive: it conceals the intricate, human reality behind. Literature has

and bring children into the world. The reinvention of these things as the node of human happiness creates a shadow-area, a doubt. Is it a new compassion for children themselves that has caused it? Is it fear of the world? Is it a long-drawn-out excuse on behalf of women, for failing to swallow the bitter pill of their social and economic independence? Is it the latest redemptive pursuit of the dualistic male nature, that perceives certain behaviours as 'good' and others as 'bad'?

But what is most interesting about modern family life is precisely its uninterestingness, its lack of texture or variation, the homogeneity of its values and its materialism. By popular reputation the modern British family is a confederacy of clones, all driving the same ultra-safe cars, shopping in Ikea and Tesco, eating and drinking the same branded products,

fact it could hardly be said to be a tree at all: it is a web of chance encounters and snap decisions woven from the common thread of human fertility. And of course it misses out every embellishment, every adornment of the bare fact of reproduction, which is to say that it misses out life itself. The meetings and marriages and the consequent putting forth of new shoots: it all seems rather fragile and blankly contiguous, until it enters the realms of things I myself have witnessed and remember. The poisonous conservatism of my grandparents, for example, which kept them married until death, in spite of the fact that they loathed one another. The departure from the clan of my father, who converted to Catholicism and married into the red-haired tribe and dreaded communication with his own mother, even on her death-bed. The spec-

always interrogated family life as the seat of a society's self-deception and of its latent virtue, too. When I was at school, our English teacher taught us to approach a literary work methodically, in a two-pronged attack. One prong was 'form'; the other was 'content'. I always shrank from separating the meat from the bone in this way when it came to books, but it seems to me that her method works well as a means of analysing ordinary life. Form and content: too much of one and too little of the other unbalances the human system. In these times, the form of family life is everywhere apparent, but its content is a blank, a mystery. I don't believe in its religious normality, its iconography of good, its corporation-like publicity. I believe that people are more mysterious and separate and anarchic than they seem. At least, I hope they are.

Gautam Malkani presupposes that it is the emotional absence of fathers that is the strongest factor in aggression among young men

Post-Nuclear Family Values

You could call it drive-by nostalgia. Whenever I visit my relatives in west London, I take a tiny detour past the three-bedroom suburban semi that I grew up in. In today's world of speed-laced instability, nostalgia usually refers to times of greater normality. But if there's one thing that house taught me, it's that there's no such thing as normality – especially when it comes to households.

Within those walls, between the early 1980s and late 1990s, I experienced life in a two-parent nuclear family, a single-parent family, a so-called 'reconstituted' two-parent family with a stepfather, a reconstituted single-parent family, a no-parent family, then some kind of surrogate-parent family, before my younger brother and I moved as far away as possible to reconstitute our no-parent family somewhere else. If the Greeks were writing about the Oedipus complex today, they'd need a Microsoft Excel spreadsheet.

My drive-by twinge of nostalgia is always for both the first and second phases of single-parent family life. The image the house front conjures up is of Friday evenings in the living room with my

brother and our late mother. My brother and I would take a break from homework on Fridays and mum would take a break from cooking. We'd have those bread-crumb-coated, oven-ready fish fillets for dinner, invariably chased down with apple strudel and vanilla ice cream which mum would have bought on the way back from work. The sole breadwinner in our house since I was seven, she was a full-time radiographer at a nearby hospital as well as full-time mother. She also developed a part-time sideline as a flower arranger. The media enjoys portraying single mothers as welfare scroungers, but I've never known anyone to work harder.

When she wasn't working or being a mother or both, she would refashion herself as our own private tutor, partly in response to the sanctimony and scorn coming from closer to home than the

media. Relatives and friends – particularly from our part of the Asian community – would typically express their disapproval of her divorce with the delicate phrase: 'It must be hard on the children'. And for 'hard' read 'harmful'. So mum sought to prove wrong all those tacit accusations that she'd failed as a mother by bringing home maths and English textbooks from the library and WH Smiths. We duly adopted something of her work ethic – which is why Friday nights were the only weekday evenings we didn't engage in some form of schoolwork or bookwormery in our bedrooms.

The community's collective disapproval of mum over the divorce was of course part of a more general misogyny and belief that wives and daughter-in-laws (and their families) should embrace their inferior standing in the world and

If the Greeks were writing about the Oedipus complex today, they'd need a Microsoft Excel spreadsheet

This is not to suggest every single-parent family works well, merely that two-parent families can work badly even when blessed with marital bliss

behave super-subserviently (again, a more delicate, if deluded, phrase is used for this: 'respectful'). Right up until her death, mum not only stood up to these more ludicrous values, she actively filtered them from our lives.

So it always amazes me how, even now in the 21st century, people still talk in near-apocalyptical terms about the tragedy of broken homes or the disintegration of the nuclear family. From what I've sometimes seen of supposedly unbroken homes, I'd rather have an absent father than one who is present but impassive. In fact, one of the most useful pop-psychological frameworks I've used in my writing to explore hyper-masculinity and aggression among young men who face neither economic deprivation nor racial discrimination presupposes an *emotional* rather than *physical* absence of fathers.

Fathers tend to serve as the primary male role model when adolescent boys are figuring out how to be men. When their dads are physically absent, boys tend to seek out alternative father figures for this. Step forward my maternal uncles and male schoolteachers. Tom Butcher from my old Boy Scouts troop, you can take a bow too. But when physically present fathers remain emotionally absent, sons cannot form a sufficiently intimate bond to help them define the parameters of their burgeoning masculinity – yet at the same time are reluctant to betray their dads with alternative father figures. So, instead, the search for a primary male role model remains within the nuclear household. According to this pseudo-Jungian framework, these sons' masculinity is therefore defined not *in relation* to their fathers, but *in opposition* to their mothers. The mother therefore becomes the primary male role model. Instead of trying to be *as* manly as their fathers, boys try to be *more* manly than their mothers. And because they define themselves in opposition to something and with no obvious parameters, there is a greater chance they will overshoot.[1]

Throw into the mix an overbearing, domineering mother – the stereotypical matriarch in many communities from Asians and West Indians to London's East End – and it isn't hard to see why some adolescent boys often exaggerate their definition of masculinity. This also explains the seemingly contradictory coincidence of misogyny and powerful matriarchs in these communities. Italians even have a word for the particular brand of machismo induced by their overbearing mothers: 'mamismo'.

This is not to suggest every single-parent family works well, merely that two-parent families can work badly even when blessed with marital bliss. I learned much about supposedly normal two-parent families not just from research, books and those around me, but also from the Friday evening television shows we would invariably watch together. It may sound trite, but television can prove a useful tool to help all families communicate with each other. The plotlines of soap operas, for example, helped me raise difficult questions with mum that I'd find harder to discuss without the aid of fictional characters living fictional lives for me to hide behind – such as sex and relationships, drugs and even family matters such as divorce. Research suggests I wasn't alone.[2]

If it was ironic that much of what I learned about other peoples' family life I learned from those evenings in front of the television, it was not nearly as ironic as the titles of the programmes we typically watched: the Australian soap opera *Neighbours* and the US sitcom *Friends.* Even another favourite, the comedy *Cheers,* featured characters who escape to a bar to get away from their families. Neighbours, friends, drinking buddies. Why shouldn't they teach us about family? Not only did these programmes' characters spend a good part of each episode reflecting on their own family dramas and headaches, each of these social relationships *was* a kind of family relationship. One of the reasons *Friends* was so successful was that it captured a zeitgeist in which friendships have increasingly become another sort of family.[3]

By contrast, I was always struck by how disastrously dysfunctional each *Friends* character's family life was. One of the funniest threads that ran through the series was the way Chandler openly wore the scars of his parents' divorce. As he once quipped when asked how he'd coped: 'Well, I relied on a carefully regimented programme of denial

Chandler once quipped when asked how he'd coped: 'Well, I relied on a carefully regimented programme of denial and wetting the bed.' Perhaps if he'd embraced the normality of his broken home rather than denied it, he wouldn't need to change his sheets so often

and wetting the bed.' Perhaps if he'd embraced the normality of his broken home rather than denied it, he wouldn't need to change his sheets so often.

While I was happy hanging around with mum, my brother and my books, it isn't difficult to see why for many others friendships have come to usurp family relationships. Families have gradually lost many of their traditional functions to other institutions – notably education, caring and work. Perhaps it was just a matter of time before advice and socialisation got outsourced too.

There are other reasons for this transformation. In a consumer society, friends are easier to disown like goods that are faulty or no longer desired. Also, friendships rarely suppress individuality the way families often seek to. For me, the transformation was driven by a modern-day value that comes from the workplace rather than the high street: meritocracy. Hierarchies no longer work if they're based on things like class, gender or age. If someone is right, they are right. If someone is wrong, they are wrong. It doesn't matter if they're a female or a family elder. Respecting your

elders remains a perfectly civil approach and often proves to be the correct one. But sometimes it doesn't. And in most families respecting your elders is more a euphemism for presuming they are always right. These kinds of familial hierarchies and prejudices are typically justified not by reason or rationale but by custom. After all, it was structural chauvinism rather than any real consideration that prompted so many to criticise mum for getting divorced.

Perhaps this is why watching *Friends* with her every Friday evening was so compelling: by using a circle of friends as a metaphor for family, the producers successfully created a family in which, like the modern workplace, the hierarchies of gender or age mum fought against no longer prevailed. Of course, the world of work conflicts with family life in a more obvious and direct way, no matter what your definition of a normal family. Maybe that was the other magical thing about Friday evenings: it was the start of the weekend. Even our mum didn't work weekends.

1 Corneau, Guy 1991 – Absent Fathers, Lost Sons: The Search for Masculine Identity, Shambhala Publishing
2 Gillespie, Marie 1995 – Television, Ethnicity and Cultural Change, Routledge Publishing
3 Wild, David 2004 – Friends Till The End, Time Inc Publishing

Camila Batmanghelidjh, Director of Kids Company, the child support charity, believes the family narrative is struggling to survive under the current social assault on its composition and values, often reflected in Channel 4's documentary strand *Cutting Edge*

Cutting Edge:
No Home For Barry,
1990

The Family Football

Cutting Edge: Just Some Stories
For Eleanor, 1990

Cutting Edge:
Family Feuds, 1996

We live in an age where the family has become a dominant intellectual, moral and political football. Everyone seeks to define it and use its structures, or lack of them, to promote their individual social narratives. Politicians talk of an 'ideal' family; the original mother and father looking after the children. The church dabbles in the family through the issues of contraception and divorce, while economists seek to redefine the role of the mother by making decisions about when she should return to work. As the centre ground of the family is scrutinised, single parents stand on the peripheries: women and men who bring up their children on their own. Then there is the reconfigured family constituted through new relationships, bringing in the dynamics of step-parents and siblings. A bit further afield are gay parents, foster carers and adoptive families. Suddenly the family map begins to look more complicated and one realises that to conceptualise the family as simply one of a father and mother and their children in the same household fails to capture the rich tapestry which is out there.

It is this rich tapestry, this individuality which the *Cutting Edge* series has picked up on, carefully dissecting the challenges and developments facing families. Nick Hull's film *Family Feuds* carefully unpicks the tensions at the heart of a family in sharp contrast to the father devotedly writing stories for his daughter as he confronts death in a the touching *Stories for Eleanor*. But these documentaries lead us on to larger questions about families, forcing us to re-approach this unsingular institution.

Every disease of the modern world is thought both to stem from the malfunctioning of the nuclear family and be cured by it, so we are told parents should have dinner with their children

in order to promote greater cohesion and reduce violence. We are educated by an array of super-nannies and their variants on how to manage the behaviour of our children. Health promoters attack mothers' shopping, for fear of children becoming obese and also criticise them for being over anxious, not letting the child play in the park for fear of being snatched. Advertisers compete for children's attention by turning them into the primary consumer, forcing the family to buy. Baby experts fight each other over whether the baby should be picked up or ignored when it cries at night. And if all this is not enough, the family is also the battle ground for a variety of air fresheners, vacuum cleaners, sofas and washing-up liquids!

In the middle of this social assault, the family is struggling to survive

Most do not recognise themselves in the simplistic narrative of two parents and the children living in one house; there is profound guilt about not being ideal; parents are afraid of falling short and, through their choices, potentially damaging their children.

Undoubtedly some families create toxic experiences for children. Sexual and physical abuse happens within the family more than by strangers. Sometimes children are forced to

My New Home, 2006

become high achievers at the expense of their natural development, as wealthy and ambitious parents compete to push them through prep school exams. At times children become almost like the extension of the handbag; they are carted around, expected to be all-performing, all-succeeding, designer-labelled from top to toe. All this is at the expense of rolling around in the mud and being allowed to evolve as a human being rather than hot housed. Such children may live in wealthy places and every break access a foreign holiday, but they are at times as desperate for thoughtful care as those born into the ghettoes of British life.

The challenges faced by children born to vulnerable parents are more visible. Poverty and sometimes destructive choices by carers can mean children are growing up negotiating drug paraphernalia and dangerous dealers who come into the house with menace. Often in these households the role of parent and child is reversed as the child is left to fend for itself and worry about the parent's wellbeing. Many of these children grow up traumatised, emotionally and physically violated and sadly sometimes repeating these patterns as they become parents themselves.

So when as a society we talk of the 'family' we could be forgiven for not knowing what we're really talking about. Often we make the mistake of describing the 'structure,' whereas what we should be focusing on is the quality of the emotional life within the household. To constitute a healthy family it doesn't matter very much what the configuration is. Of course it is more of a challenge if you are alone, taking care of numerous children, but that does not make you less of a family or less able if you are managing to adhere to some fundamental emotional rules. So to help clear up some of the confusion, I am proposing that we define the code of conduct which is required to make a family construct. And I propose that we create this code starting from the children and their needs.

Every child requires a healthy attachment in order to feel secure, cared for and loved. The identity and self-concept of a child is created through the interaction with loving adults who reflect back to the child his/her strengths, limitations and, in doing so, define the boundaries of responsibility to themselves and the wider community. In a good enough attachment the child acquires an anchor from which they can explore the wider world around them. Children are frightened by adult irresponsibility. So if a parent is not grown up enough to be the carer, the child is alarmed by being in the care of a similarly childlike individual. The whole point of childhood is that there are grown-ups who have a duty of care to you.

At times children become almost like the extension of the handbag; they are carted around, expected to be all-performing, all-succeeding, designer-labelled from top to toe

We know from brain research that the human relationship, primarily that of the parental carer, sculpts the child's brain. Neurons, which are the messaging network of the human brain, are waiting to be skilled up for use. This learning is acquired through practice of human interaction between carer and child. Capacities for control and processing emotions and energy are formed through the parent-child relationship. Brain development continues throughout a person's life with dominant phases of opportunity at three months prior to birth, up to eighteen months, at aged four, eight and fourteen being key windows where maximum brain development is taking place. So parenting must go on well into late adolescence and the skills for it need to continuously be adapted and updated. All this functions well when the adult carer is sensitively attuned to the

<u>My New Home</u>, 2006

child's needs. Part of this attunement requires the discipline of not imposing the adult's inadequacies or desires on the child. So do not try to make a child famous or force them to become a brilliant mathematician; actually this is about the adult's needs, compensating for lack of self-worth. If a child, however, has talents and skills then the adult needs to help nurture them to maximum potential.

To maintain these emotionally correct boundaries, the adult carer needs to have addressed their own issues so that as much as possible they don't pollute the child's development, imposing a distortion which is damaging. No care condition is ideal, so provided there is enough love and the intentions are aspiring, then it's good enough care and the child will do well. An illustration of this idea comes up in Polly Bide and Helena Kennedy's film *Mothers Behind Bars* which follows children in America sent back to meet their imprisoned mothers revealing a painful story of separation and loss, but the charming scenes in the playroom also reveal the need for care.

Once the task of sensitive care has been initiated and the child begins to build their internal life in partnership with the

. . . .

But as the young person focuses their development task outward, they will always need the safety net of the attachment and the nucleus of family to turn to during set-backs, crisis or simply as an encouraging witness

. . . .

carer, then there is the need to look at separation, individuation and connecting to the outside world. This is often the role adopted traditionally by a father. But so long as this task is identified and articulated it can be initiated by extended relatives, step-parents or other carers in the potential absence of the father. But as the young person focuses their development task outward they will always need the safety net of the attachment and the nucleus of family to turn to during set-backs, crisis or simply as an encouraging witness. So in many ways the role of the family and the task of the carer continues until in old age where the role of carer and child is legitimately and appropriately reversed by virtue of the fragile carer now requiring protection.

Our narrative about the family has to change. We do well not to interfere with its structure but to create psychological and moral value systems which guide the care conditions between adult carer and the child. As a society we must stop 'acting on' the family and instead 'act for it' by creating conditions which economically and practically facilitate the care task. So more childcare support, access to leisure activities, counselling and therapeutic help, better educational support, safer neighbourhoods and generally more resources; the less stressed and distressed a parent is, the better they can care for their child. Our responsibility as a society is not to define the family structure but to promote the family spirit; whether that is in a children's home, in step, adoptive or foster families, with the single parent, the gay parent or conventional parents, it doesn't really matter. The real significance of a family is the commitment a parental carer makes to a child's wellbeing and the commitment society makes to protecting the pledge to care and to nurture a child towards meaningful capacities in the community.

Our family narrative should define the family as a space where a child is cared for by an adult, enhancing both their capacities to love, feel cherished and to acquire skills and motivation to contribute positively to the community.

Shameless advert, 2004

Nuclear Family
by Gwyneth Lewis

I wed an electron in the seventies.
Talk about naïve!
I wore pyjamas to protect the sheets,
watched her striptease
of hoola-hoops force fields, an aching dance
I could never relieve
with my brushed-cotton rhythms. There
wasn't much love
and I knew she'd leave.

On the rebound I found a randy muon,
lived in sin.
Now I felt sexy and she fancied me,
so we did it
all over the house and frequently.
Mam decided to hate
the floozy. They formed an alliance, started
to plot
when we might
and might not fornicate. I split.

Let's not be literal about this, I thought.
Met a quark
who came with two sisters. On the settee
my luck
had changed – a ménage à three
or four! But like
is harder than fucking. One day my harem
went out for a bite
but never came back.

Now I'm on my tenth mother,
am doing fine.
I take kin where I find them. I have
a son
with a lesbian proton (by IVF).
We're deuteron
together. He's happy, and he knows he's mine,
for all his step nans.
We shine, we shine.

The Creative Economy

One of the greatest shifts of the last 25 years has been the rise of the 'knowledge economy,' typified by small, highly creative businesses developing unique goods and services. With its status as a publisher rather than a producer of television programmes, and therefore with no in-house studios or production teams, Channel 4 has found itself not only the principal patron of a growing network of independent producers, but the inspiration for an army of talented but previously unrecognised individuals. Channel 4 has enjoyed such success as a catalyst for new talent that it has become a leading symbol of British creativity – a power-house of the new economy, sustaining more than 20,000 jobs, generating a couple of billion pounds a year.

Chris Blackhurst, City Editor of *The Evening Standard*, applauds Channel 4's £2 billion contribution to the creative economy

Our Creative Nation

The best way to appreciate something is to imagine what life would have been like without it.

In the case of Channel 4 that would mean no *Shameless*, *Big Brother*, *Queer as Folk*, *Ali G* – the list goes on and on. Ever since it started, C4 has been different. My own personal memory of the beginning was watching *Brookside*, and for the first time seeing a soap that I thought I could relate to. The houses in which it was shot were purpose-built and entirely genuine – therefore, it felt as though their inhabitants were also real.

It was groundbreaking advances like this that set C4 apart. Always it has been pushing the boundaries, setting new standards. There's been a radicalism to its programming that even now, and despite increased competition, it has never lost.

While the on-screen formula is well known and the hits rightly celebrated, what is less obvious is the off-screen structure that has made it possible. *Brookside*, for instance, was produced by an independent company. As a result, undoubtedly, the sort of script discussions that might stifle creativity in a large corporation simply did not occur – so *Brookside* decided to show the first pre-watershed lesbian kiss on British TV, for example, and got on with it.

I once helped make a *Dispatches* for C4. It was on the arms industry and was likely to ruffle feathers. We – myself and another journalist and a small production company – pitched it to the commissioning editor at C4. He liked what he heard, agreed a budget and we made the programme – there really wasn't much more to it than that. What was striking was the absence of crushing bureaucracy, of layers of management all wanting their say – and getting in the way.

From the outset, C4's remit was to commission externally-made programmes. What this has meant, in 25 years, is the spawning of a whole new industry – one that is now a vital contributor to the UK economy.

While the channel rightly receives plaudits for its critically-acclaimed hits, what is usually overlooked is the development, behind the scenes, of something equally remarkable and of lasting economic significance. There are studios and post-production facilities at Horseferry Road, but they are there primarily as back up, in case anything goes wrong.

Nearly all of C4's output is made off-site and by an independent company. Such has been the success of C4 that 'indies' are now an established and increasingly powerful part of the broadcasting scene. Some, like Tiger Aspect, Hat Trick, Fulcrum, Diverse, Iostar, Shed, RDF Media, Shine, All3Media and Endemol, turn over substantial sums and have large staffs. Others sell very little and are not much more than one-man bands.

It's some achievement for C4: to have originated an industry we can no longer live without

In 2005, the station used 311 external suppliers of programmes. This was 50 more than the previous year. In 2006, the figure dropped slightly, to 296.

That is 296 different companies, 296 sets of employees and their families. According to PricewaterhouseCoopers, which made a study of the genre, the overall economic impact of C4's production out-sourcing policy is £2 billion a year in gross added value for the UK. In all, it supports 22,000 jobs across the country.

Other broadcasters have followed the C4 example and commission significant amounts of their schedule from the indie sector. In 2005, ITV1 used 126 companies, five called upon 132 production houses and the BBC's entire, cross-channel offering drew upon 274. But C4 remains the undisputed leader of an industry that simply would not have grown without the channel's arrival in 1982.

C4 took upon itself to kick-start and develop the industry. If it had not taken such a single-minded approach, the sector would still exist – but in much-reduced form. There were independent production companies prior to C4's arrival but they were few in number, mostly based in London and conservative in nature.

The C4 commitment to indies has involved a four-pronged strategy. Plurality is a key principle. The more independent producers exist, reckon C4 chiefs, the greater the chance of their channel receiving diverse ideas and proposals. So, while C4 obviously has main planks in its schedule that originate from a handful of major independents – such as *Big Brother* from Endemol – it deliberately engages with smaller and medium-sized firms.

It would be very easy for C4 to focus on a few, established producers while still sticking to the brief of choosing indies. Such a ploy has much merit – it's less fraught with risk and relationships are easier to manage.

But C4's bosses have set their noses against this policy. Nevertheless, as the years have gone on and those producers fortunate enough to have major properties on their hands have grown in wealth, size and stature, inevitably some consolidation has occurred.

So concerned is C4's present director of content, Kevin Lygo, about this that he has announced the channel is to spend more on the tinier operators by ensuring twenty per cent of those that make its content have annual turnover of under £2 million. 'We are heading, if we are not careful, for a replica of the USA; just the studios and a few indies,' he warns.

The current furore over declining standards and the viewers' lack of trust in television had focused attention on the small producers. There are those who

In 25 years Channel 4 has spawned a whole new industry – one that is now a vital contributor to the UK economy

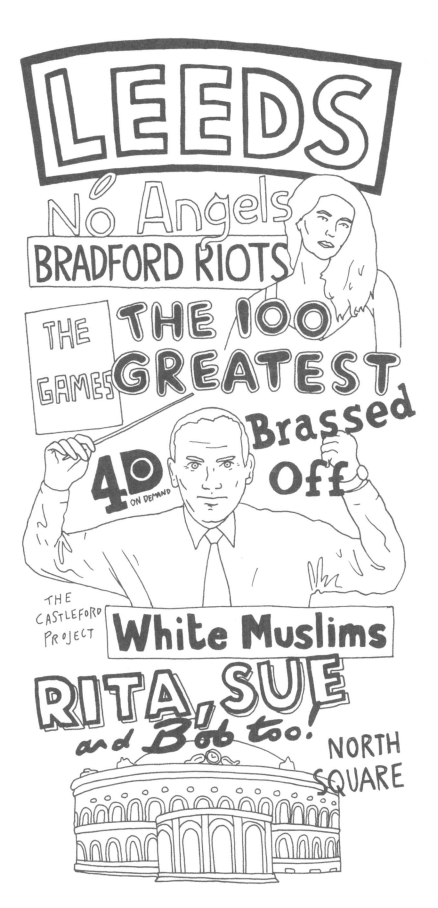

Michael Hewitt
DoubleBand

It all started with a question. 'How can a man die for making a simple mistake on the football pitch?'

It was a question that took us to Colombia in 1997 to make *Escobar's Own Goal,* our first documentary for Channel 4. This was to tell the tragic story of Andres Escobar, the Colombian footballer who had scored a costly own goal in the 1994 World Cup in America and was shot dead when he returned home just a few days later.

The documentary was not a 'whodunnit'. After all, the man who had pulled the trigger on Andres Escobar was already in jail. But it was an attempt to understand why it had happened. And to do that we found ourselves exploring the connections between Colombia's professional football clubs and its all-powerful drugs cartels.

When *Escobar's Own Goal* was broadcast in the spring of 1998, wonderful reviews were quickly followed by awards and a good number of international sales. It was all very pleasing. But perhaps most satisfying of all for my colleague Dermot Lavery and myself was the fact that something very important to us was being recognised within the Channel – that being an 'indie' in Belfast was no handicap when it came to producing international documentaries.

Other documentaries for Channel 4 quickly followed, some on a football theme such as *Maradona: Kicking the Habit* and *George Best's Body,* while others like the Grierson-nominated *Monkey Love* and *Making the Monkees* delved respectively into the worlds of science and popular culture. It has been a fascinating journey for DoubleBand, one that has allowed the company to grow and to develop some remarkable talent. And a journey that started with a simple mistake on the football pitch.

Brian Hill
Century Films

Falling Apart was a drama exploring a middle class marriage descending into domestic violence. It was an almost forensic examination of love turning ugly and banal. It was my first drama and I got to direct Mark Strong and Hermione Norris in the lead roles, which was both scary and exciting. It was also a first script for writer Anna Maloney, who happens to be my wife. I'm really proud of it because it explored an important issue in a tough and uncompromising way. It never flinched and it was sometimes uncomfortable to watch, but it got a tremendous response from the audience and from critics. I think C4 was the only broadcaster who would have let me make this film. The fact that Anna and I got a BAFTA each was an added bonus.

294

question whether they are up to the task, Lygo is dismissive of such talk, saying it's 'facile.' He adds: 'In fact, the opposite is the case. The astonishing success of the independent production sector in the last 25 years has given rise to an explosion in creativity and diversity.'

Remarkably, for someone who must put his own reputation and that of his employer first, Lygo regards it as the broadcaster's duty to help 'reinvigorate' the sector.

It's this missionary zeal that characterises another of the C4 prongs. While the channel has pledged to promote the indies, it is not that big a player – C4 does not have bottomless pockets of cash. On its own, C4 is not rich enough to sustain a burgeoning, national independent production industry.

The solution it has come up with is to spread its money more thinly – and invite others to match its funds. So whatever C4 contracts to inject into a programme, another organisation – the production company itself, a regional development agency or regional screen agency – is expected to equal that amount. This means that the total spend on independent programme-making is far higher than C4's initial outlay. Col-

Would the BBC have made *Ali G*, *Shameless* and *Big Brother*? I doubt it

lectively, the industry is therefore bigger and more prosperous than C4's limited budget allows.

There is a knock-on effect from this as well: by encouraging the regional agencies to get involved, C4 has ensured TV production is high up their regeneration agenda. Government-backed bodies that might otherwise be tempted to fall back on traditional manufacturing industries (to little positive effect) have been steered towards embracing modern change and prioritising a 'new' industry.

C4 regards it as an absolute requirement of its public service broadcasting goal to act as a catalyst for independent TV production across the whole country. Prior to C4, TV broadcasting was very London-dominant. It's worked hard to

break down this bias, setting up a 'Creative Cities' strategy to help 'spread the creative and economic benefits more equitably across the nations and regions of the UK.'

What this and C4's overall push to promote production nationwide, not just in London, has resulted in, is the emergence of regional creative clusters. Pre-C4 there were three centres in the UK where most TV production occurred. They reflected the historical shape of the BBC: London, Scotland and Bristol. But with the advent of C4, production companies have sprung up elsewhere. It makes economic sense for them, wherever possible, to work alongside each other – to pool resources and talent.

Other local businesses have been able to prosper from supplying them. Most of the main cities now have thriving indie industries. Manchester and the Northwest have been so prodigious that the region now rivals the three older centres (*Brookside*, *Hollyoaks*, *Queer as Folk*, *Shameless* and *That Peter Kay Thing* are just some of the titles to roll off the Northwest conveyor belt). The indies have become an essential ingredient in the continuing renaissance of current Manchester.

The Domesday Code

BESLAN

TSUNAMI CHRISTMAS

Unreported World

OXFORD

In fact, Manchester has much to thank C4 for. Of the £108 million spent on external programming outside London in 2005, no less than £65 million went to the north of England, with most of that heading to the Northwest. C4 has even gone so far as to persuade producers to relocate from London to Manchester.

Allied to the push around the country is the fourth plank in C4's indie strategy: the discovering and fostering of new and emerging talent. 4Talent was set up by the channel in 2002 to help young people – who might otherwise be dissuaded from doing so – to enter the creative industries. It's aimed at new, raw talent and emerging content producers and it's nationwide – a major drawback to someone going into the media can be geographical isolation.

So 4Talent applies across all regions, not only London. So far, in excess of 3,000, mostly young, people have benefited from 4Talent, with an increasing number getting their work shown across C4's range of media delivery platforms.

Another initiative, Research Centre, is located in Glasgow. It's a business development unit, organised by C4, to help independent producers make their content more sellable and to organise themselves along professional, business-like lines. Again, to date, over 100 indies in the regions have been tutored by the Research Centre.

The Research Centre also makes applications to sources of finance such as the European Regional Development Fund on behalf of the small independent producers.

This goes far beyond what C4 needs to do – but falls heavily within the bounds of what it wants to do. Similarly, C4 will help a talented producer set up in business and provide the seed money to get them going. It goes further still: C4 will supply the novice (or any other indie that needs assistance) with the full range of expertise any large TV station has at its disposal. It sees itself as much a mentor and a guide as pure financial sponsor. So the channel is on hand to offer advice on everything from marketing to law to staffing.

Far from being merely a user of the creative economy, C4 has become a proactive angel investor – identifying potential programme-makers and encouraging and nurturing them. Time-honoured barriers to entry into broadcasting and creativity – such as background and class, contacts, lack of

Far from being merely a user of the creative economy, C4 has become a proactive angel investor – identifying potential programme-makers and encouraging and nurturing them

25 YEARS OF S4C

HEDD WYN

SOLOMON & GAENOR

late night POKER

Debbie does Dallas

Human Traffic

HAY -ON- WYE

CARDIFF

For 25 years Channel 4's partner broadcaster S4C has been one of the most innovative indigenous language broadcasters in Europe

Katie Bailiff
Century Films

Towards the end of the evening, the heel of Becky's shoe breaks and she heads up to her hotel room. Steve follows her and they soon begin to kiss. But what happens next? She prosecutes for rape; he says it was consensual.

At this point *Consent* shifts from scripted drama into something very different. Everyone involved knows that this is a fictional case but the trial is conducted as if it were real. Featuring a jury of ordinary people, real barristers, solicitors, police and a judge, the film shines a light on one of today's most hotly-debated issues.

For the film to work, everyone in the courtroom had to absolutely buy into the trial process. One slip-up and the illusion would have been shattered and the film would have failed.

Watching the jury passionately debate their verdict for three hours was compelling – we knew then that we had pulled off our most ambitious project to date.

The day after the film was transmitted I received a call from York Crown Court. The Clerk told me that a man charged with rape had appeared in the dock that morning. At the very last minute the accused had changed his plea from not guilty to guilty. When asked why he replied, 'I saw a film about a rape trial on Channel 4 last night and I just can't put anyone through what that victim went through. I'm guilty'. No reviews, ratings or awards can top a reaction like that.

money, regional location – have all been broken down.

Of course, C4 has only been able to go to these lengths because of its wide interpretation of what being a public service broadcaster entails. The irony though is that from this desire to broaden and to invent, massive commercial winners, such as *Big Brother* and *Ali G*, have flowed.

PricewaterhouseCoopers said that, without C4, 'the independent sector might have been more consolidated, less diverse and more focused on London; there might also have been less new talent and fewer new entrants'.

This, to my mind, is under-stating its importance. There's no doubt that other broadcasters would have gone down the indie route. But if you take away C4 from that mix, you're left with an industry that is heavily dominated by the BBC. The corporation is everything C4 is not: large, full of levels of management between the producer and the screen and slow to respond. It is also, even after numerous relocation initiatives, heavily London-centric. As a result, it's a fair question: pick almost any one of C4's most famous shows and ask if they would have been

Without C4, the independent sector might have been more consolidated, less diverse and more focused on London; there might also have been less new talent

aired on the BBC? These weren't only programmes that proved popular – they changed the industry. Would the BBC have made *Ali G*, *Shameless* and *Big Brother*? I doubt it.

The challenge for C4, looking ahead to the next 25 years, is to maintain this remarkable record. Any cutting back on the quest for diversity, and finding and growing new talent, could have an alarming effect. Already, there are misgivings in the sector about the merging of independent companies to form 'super-producers'. Inevitably, such bigger houses are unlikely to be so willing to take risks – in either the people they employ or the shows they promote – and they're centred

on London. An industry that has taken 25 years to carefully grow, thanks to C4, remains fragile and could soon cease to yield fruit. *That* would be disastrous, on-screen and off-screen. Viewers would be denied new programming; and, critically, the economy could suffer as an increasingly significant contributor begins to wither.

That's some achievement for C4: to have originated an industry we can no longer live without.

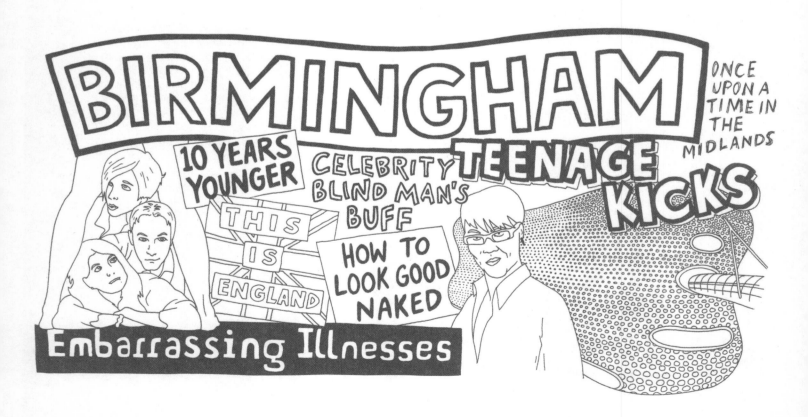

Nicola Shindler
Red Productions

All the productions I have made for Channel 4 have been really important to me, as they should be. But because it was the first and because it set the template for so much work that Red went on to make, *Queer as Folk* stands out. Russell T. Davies and I were given so much freedom by Channel 4 to create a series that – unlike so many portrayals of gay life on TV – wasn't judgemental or doom-laden. It was simply a great story of unrequited love and friendship. Gub Neal and Catriona McKenzie at the channel were brilliant at encouraging us to push boundaries, make it look as good as the aspirational American shows we loved, and never step back from being as cheeky as we wanted. *Queer as Folk* is often remembered for the sex, which is a shame because that was a tiny part of what we know in retrospect was a ground-breaking show. At the time it was really hard work, the usual madmen and schedules to deal with, but looking back now I do think it was the most fun I've ever had on a shoot because we were so free. And so young!

GLASGOW
LOCATION
LOCATION
LOCATION
FOOTBALL STORIES
SOLD
FOR SALE
HALFWAY TO PARADISE
THE OTHER BRITAIN
GAS ATTACK
THE BOOK GROUP
WHO SAYS READING IS GOOD FOR YOU?
BEAUTY QUEENS AND BLOODSHED
The Acid House
THE YOUNG PERSONS GUIDE TO BECOMING A
ROCK★STAR
The Mahabharata
THE FIRST WORLD WAR

All Change

The determination of people to re-design their homes, their relationships, their bodies, their lives – or, in extreme cases, all of the above – is a powerful and growing modern trend. Television has played a central role in inspiring its viewers towards change and Channel 4, in particular, has encouraged the attainment of aspirations in programmes as diverse as *How to Look Good Naked*, *No Going Back* and *Brat Camp*. Tuning into the dreams of the viewing public has made feature and lifestyle programmes among the most powerful and popular brands on the box – *The Times* once said of Channel 4's *Faking It* that it was doing more to shrink the class divide than any politician or party.

Cordelia Jenkins meets James Fonfe, one of the first 'brats', to discuss life during and after his time on Channel 4's *Brat Camp*

Brat Camp, 2004

From the Wilderness to the Right Track

Brat Camp, 2004

James Fonfe

When the first series of *Brat Camp* was aired in 2004, James Fonfe and his five fellow campers were billed as being abusive, arrogant, foul-mouthed and ill-disciplined. Four years later, Fonfe is holding down a full-time job, has given up drugs and become teetotal. Was the 'Redcliffe Ascent' experience responsible for this transformation, or has James got other theories about what put him back on the right track?

James is candid about his initial reactions to the idea of attending a 'wilderness programme' in Utah. 'My mum said to fill out this survey – I knew it was for a TV programme. I had regular arguments with my mum at the time – I thought I'll just fill out something and that will keep her quiet for a while. I was told I was going to be there for four or five weeks max. I thought it would be a bit like camping. I didn't know I wasn't allowed to smoke so I took 200 cigarettes with me. They let me have one outside and then they just took all my bags off me and that was it.'

Each brat came into the programme with his or her own label: the violent one, the thief, the binge drinker,

the drug addict. The leaders at Redcliffe handle the teenagers according to their perceived problems. Once the brats have completed the course, which comprises written work and physical tasks, and have shown a marked behavioural improvement, they are allowed to leave. Although James acknowledges that without the programme he would have had a more difficult time quitting his drug habit, he is sceptical about the efficacy of the counselling that was offered. 'They work out what your different issues supposedly are according to them. But I went there with a plan. My plan was: right, this'll give me four or five weeks in the middle of nowhere. I can get clean because I'm going to run out of drugs, there's nothing there, no temptation and then I'll get home and the rest is just willpower. What's the point in having therapy sessions when you don't actually learn anything from the therapy? I've been to anger management and stuff like that before, but I didn't actually learn anything from them. The way that the place works, in my opinion, is that it will only work if you want it to.'

According to James, the counsellor on the course, known as Doc Dan, had suggested to James's mother that he had a very high chance of getting back into drugs when he returned. On this subject, James is indignant. 'He tried to get me to go to this boarding school in the States, The Discovery Academy, which is owned by the same company (as Redcliffe). He tried to persuade my parents to get me sent there. And it's like a proper lockdown there, like a mini-juvie. Girls are not allowed to talk to boys, boys are not allowed to talk to girls. It's completely segregated and really strict.' The Discovery Academy bills itself as 'a clinical boarding school whose mission is to inspire each student to a quest for excellence in all areas of life'. It recommends itself as an ideal transition from a wilderness school – a sort of half-way house – back to real life for students.

One of the brats, Rachel, took longer than the others to complete the course. James suggests that there was a secondary reason that she came back when she did. 'It was because her visa expired. That's what nobody knows – nobody worked that out. You have a

90-day visa to go to the States. We didn't realise. I only worked it out after I left – I thought "hang on a minute", I never clocked it until then. It was when we were leaving and I was looking through my passport and I thought "Shit, it says 90 days." I could have just done nothing and sat there saying, "Yeah, I'm not doing it" and gone home in 90 days.' Considering their initial behaviour, it is lucky that none of the brats had the foresight to see this caveat in the supposedly strict rule that no child may go home until they have completed the course. To their credit, the course leaders – with names like Stone Bear, Black Hawk, Dancing Bear and White Winds – seemed to show tremendous patience with their young charges. While James is fairly cynical about the process, he does mention these leaders with respect and freely admits that he stills thinks about Utah and the people he met there frequently. 'It's a bit like a game when you are there. To graduate it's a bit like you have to follow this game. If I was to redo it, and I wanted to get out as quickly as I could, I'd be as bad as I could for the first week and then slowly just even out the balance.' It's obvious that the more perceptive among the teenagers figure this trick out quickly.

One of the tenets of the Redcliffe experience is that by entrusting the teenagers with the responsibility to look after themselves in the wilderness, it is empowering them to make responsible choices. James agrees with this and is keen to explain the benefits of being treated like an adult under conditions of extreme discipline and physical hardship. 'I know that if I ever needed to survive out there I'd be able to. The theory that they work on is that if you fuck the tasks up then you are going to pay for it, but if you do them well then you're going to reap the benefits. If you make a shitty shelter and it pisses it down, then you are going to get wet, if you make a good one then you are going to stay dry. They will teach you how but they won't do it for you. I did get a sense of achievement out of it, but you see each step as just one step closer to getting home and having a cigarette.'

Asked about his relationship with his parents now, James is pragmatic. 'I've just kind of grown up. Everyone says, "look how well you're doing now that you're twenty, look how you've changed." And I just think, "well you're missing the key point. I'm twenty – I've grown up."

Brat Camp, 2004

My mum isn't telling me when I can and cannot go out. She still tries. But I say, "Mum, I'm twenty." She thinks that my experience there changed me. I'm still not perfect; she still has a go at me for not eating enough and then for eating too much, but that's just the way that mothers are really. That's everyone's mum.'

His tolerance of his parents' anxiety for him extended to consenting to regular drugs tests for a year after he finished the programme. This aspect of the Redcliffe treatment seems to have really worked for him. 'At first it was every day. My mum and dad said that I couldn't live at home if I didn't agree to it.' He has since voluntarily extended his ban on drugs to alcohol and has a curiously simplistic explanation for this decision: 'It's not as good as drugs. So what's the point? It does sound bizarre, but I just think that if I'm not going to do drugs then why spend all my money on something that I don't like as much as drugs?' – it makes sense within the black and white logical and moral system of Redcliffe. Much of the success of the treatment seems to rely on the absolute isolation of the teenagers from their friends and family and the space, physical and mental, that this affords them. Anger at being abandoned by their parents quickly turns into acceptance and a new-found, goal-orientated ability to complete the task at hand. As James put it: 'You do feel trapped. But it is worth it. I am glad I did it. I wouldn't go back now, but I don't have a problem any more – if I had a problem in the future then I would go back.'

The theory that they work on is that if you fuck the tasks up, then you are going to pay for it, but if you do them well, then you're going to reap the benefits

Christa D'Souza, a columnist and *Vogue* contributor, is ambivalent to, yet can't resist, anti-ageing developments

Ageorexia

A quarter of a century ago I was 22 years old, fresh out of Brown, sleeping on someone's sofa and about to embark on a life in New York. Those were the days, cinematic in their awfulness (in retrospect, anyway). Thank Christ I don't have to live through them again. But have I really changed that much since then? A little wiser, a little gaunter, a tiny bit less, shall we say, fresh-faced if I've tied one on the night before, but otherwise essentially the same. Which is why I got such a shock when I saw a familiar-looking woman in a magazine the other day and suddenly realised it was me. That wasn't me, that was a 47-year-old, 30 months away from being 50. Me? Nearly 50? Six years older than the leader of the Conservative Party? There must be some mistake.

There may be women out there who cannot wait for middle age so workmen will stop hassling them. But I am not one of them

----

Ageorexia. Fear of getting old. It's not like this is any new cultural neurosis. D'ya think Elizabeth I, her of the arsenic face masks, wouldn't have had botox injections if they'd been around then? D'ya think Anna Karenina would have topped herself if she'd had access to a face-lift? Since time immemorial women have been lopping off the years, sitting in the seat with the most flattering light, making themselves look of more sproggable age, not just to their menfolk but to each other. It's what we are biologically programmed to do and, until men can get pregnant, it will be ever thus.

And yet. And yet. When I switched on the TV the other day and found myself watching yet another 60-something getting an anorak inserted into her upper lip (or was she getting a breast implant inserted into her bellybutton? I forget), even I wondered when and where this all might end. *Twenty Years Younger? Thirty Years Younger?* If 60 is the new 40, 40 the new 30 and 30 presumably the new ten, why not?

Twenty-five years ago, going under the knife was a whole different ball game. Now, getting your face done is like getting your kitchen done or your ride pimped. Our outer carapaces have become commodities – to be exchanged, improved, transformed, just like anything else. It worries me as I get older and wiser, not just that we have become so inured to slicing ourselves up on TV, but that it makes us think we are above nature. And it worries me that this message – anything is negotiable – is being passed on to our kids. That no lot, whether it's cancer, infertility or ageing, need be accepted. That if you don't like it then, no problem, we'll just get you another one.

But what does it do to a woman's head having the punani of a fifteen-year-old when she's supposed to be going through menopause? Wouldn't the fraudulence have to be accounted for sometime, somewhere? Isn't a society where youth is so

Tool Platter

Spinel & Diamond 'Riviera' Bracelet (Verdura)
Lipstick
Eyebrow / Eyelash Brush
Syringe
Nail File
Eyeliner
Dental Pick
Hair Thinning Shears
Corn Knife
Retractor (Skin)
Eyeliner Shavings

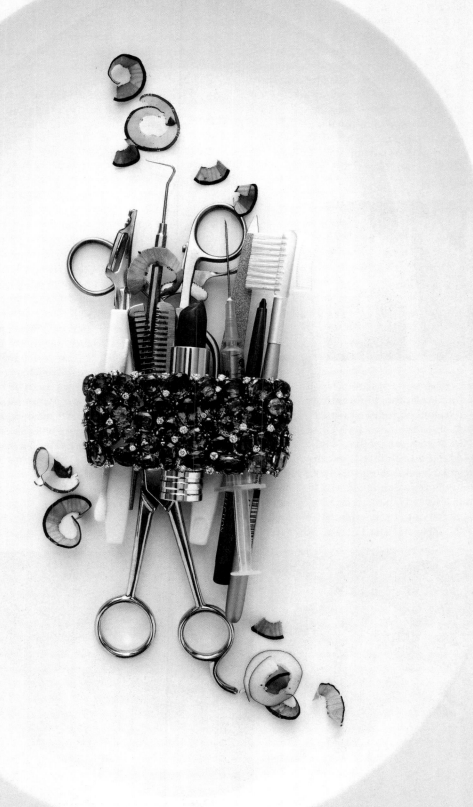

Photography by Nato Welton

fetishised and old age so reluctantly embraced a society that will eventually break down? And another thing! If babies being born now will live to two hundred if they eat enough cruciferous veg and do enough Bikram yoga – if, as that crazy professor says, the first millegenarian is already alive – aren't there just going to be too many bloody old people around?

And then, I think of *Vogue* commissioning me to test drive all the new high-tech, anti-ageing procedures. Did you know about Laser Lipo under local anaesthetic? Have you even heard of Laser Lipo under local anaesthetic? Or realised how easy and pleasant and morale-boosting it is to undergo a medical microdermabrasion combined with infra-red light therapy? Meaning, it's in the mix, it's available, you're not going to end up like that poor lady in Terry Gilliam's black comedy, *Brazil*. Or like Joan Rivers. Nature's such a mean-spirited, unfair old boot.

How to Look Good Naked, 2006

When I last wrote about the subject, you should have seen the e-lynching I got for admitting to wanting to fight middle age on the beaches, to feeling patronised rather than flattered when a scout came up to me in the glove department of Liberty's and wondered if I'd like to audition for one of those Dove commercials. How could I be so unhelpful to the cause? When our mothers (mine in particular, as one blogger pointed out) had worked so hard for us not to have to define ourselves by our looks or our age. Yeah, well, it was my mother, the tireless human-rights activist, who told me about this marvellous no-surgical face-lift thingy called CACI. Okay Mother Theresa didn't seem to worry

about her wrinkles, but so what if she secretly had? Who says God doesn't wear Prada too?

See, here's the thing. Although I acknowledge the culture of insecurity the media (yes, including me) and the anti-ageing industry (supposedly worth £43 billion by 2009) have created, this does not necessarily mean I'll exclude myself from it. There may be women out there who cannot wait for middle age so workmen will stop hassling them. But I am not one of them. Not yet, anyway.

Is this a cop out? Or is it survival? Is it about wanting to remain a sexual entity or is it simply keeping a foot in the marketplace? As the author of *Beauty Junkies*, Alex Kuczynski, puts it, 'There are two reasons people choose cosmetic surgery and cosmetic modifications: one is to ramp up sexual attractiveness and the other is to remove or reduce signs of age. I believe that among intelligent people, the second is by far the most popular reason. Why? Well, socio-economic pressures. It's a lot easier to keep yourself in the game, commerce wise, if you look young and fit.' She cites a friend of hers, an intellectual now in his late sixties, proud of his fitness and youthful good looks, who recently got bi-focal lens implants in his eyes, so he can read a menu while all of his contemporaries have to take out their reading glasses at the table. 'They all look at me and say hey, don't you need reading glasses, and I say, but of course not, I am so young and fit still!'

Is he, are we saddoes? With our knees way on show, our subscriptions to Facebook, our bi-focal lens implants, are we engaging in a battle that we will inevitably lose? Or are we merely taking advantage of what's out there, enjoying life more than ever, finally refusing to let youth get wasted on the young? Not sure if I can answer that question. But for the moment, while I am still in the old age of youth rather than in the youth of old age, I know what I will choose. They say a friend tells you when you start looking ridiculous. Well, no friend has told me that, yet…

Faking It from 1999, according to The Times, did more to shrink the class divide than any politician or party. By unearthing people's hidden talents and unleashing a whole new life, it really did transform people and show them how they could change their lives for the better

Roast Corset

Overbust Satin Corset With Ribbon (Lovehoney)
Bone Saw
Red Stones (Victoria Fergusson Collection)

Look Good Hors d'oeuvres

Wooden Spatulas (For Waxing)
Flamingo Depilatory Wax
Facial Sponge
Surgical Blades (Carbon Steel)
Cuticle Sticks
Brush On Buff (Blusher) Balls
Super Epa Fish Oil Concentrate Tablets

Dr Phil Hammond, GP and comedian, explains how to avoid dying of embarrassment

The Embarrassment Barrier

I once met a man who let his testicle swell to fifteen centimetres – larger than a grapefruit – because he was embarrassed at having a lump down below and, as it got bigger, he was worried that his GP would think he was an idiot for leaving it so long. It wasn't until it really pressed on the nerve endings that he sought help. He survived his cancer but lost a testicle that might well have been saved if he'd come earlier.

Another man asked for a visit when the pain in his testicles was so severe he fainted. The pain had been excruciating for four hours, and he had a torsion on both sides – a twisting of the tissue that fixes the testicles in the scrotum. It can lead to irreversible damage if it isn't swiftly untwisted under anaesthetic. His delay in asking for help was also down to embarrassment and he too lost a testicle. This cycle of delay caused by a recurring mixture of embarrassment, fear, stoicism and misplaced optimism is common throughout medicine. It causes huge suffering and occasionally death, and isn't always easy to predict. Some patients may be ashamed at having a sexually transmitted infection or shy about revealing a breast lump or rectal bleeding. But embarrassment is a barrier in just about every chronic disease (epilepsy, asthma, diabetes), particularly if you're overweight.

As one of my patients confided, 'I've just let a shoe assistant sell me completely the wrong shade of polish. The mistake was obvious but I didn't say anything because she'd just think, "silly fat cow, what does she know?"' If overweight patients are too shy to buy shoeshine, imagine how hard they find it to access the NHS?

Dandruff, warts, halitosis, prominent ears, acne, burst condoms, incontinence, dribbling, man boobs, excessive sweating, hairiness, impotence, cotton buds stuck in the ear… just about any illness you care to name, someone has delayed getting help for fear of what the doctor or nurse might think of them. The good news is that doctors and nurses are pretty

---

Dandruff, warts, halitosis, prominent ears, burst condoms, incontinence, dribbling, man boobs, excessive sweating, cotton buds stuck in the ear… just about any illness you care to name, someone has delayed getting help for fear of what the doctor or nurse might think of them

---

Embarrassing Illnesses,
2007

Reviewers of a squeamish disposition found some of the camera angles hard to take, but for anyone with an embarrassing illness it was a godsend

unembarrassable. We've seen it all. These days, I only turn pink after sex or if I fall asleep in the sun (hence the nickname, Salmon Hammond).

Even better news is that there are plenty of patients out there who are unembarrassable too. Back in 1996, I did a feature on erectile dysfunction for *Trust Me, I'm a Doctor* (BBC2), which included a patient demonstrating how to inject a penis with a drug called Caverject (this was in the pre-Viagra days). The BBC wouldn't let him use his own penis so he pricked a rubber one. Alas, it 'wobbled offensively' and the item was pulled. By 2002, the BBC had grown up and screened *Sex – Warts and All* on BBC3. Volunteers cheerfully displayed their warts, gonorrhoea, chlamydia and herpes to camera, and did more to destigmatise sexually transmitted diseases than I ever could.

Channel 4 picked up the baton with *Embarrassing Illnesses*, covering a vast range of ailments in eight programmes and inviting viewers to take part. I sometimes wonder about the motives of the participants – some seem genuinely keen to take the shame away for others, some seem a bit too keen to get on television and some are after a fast track to treatment. Reviewers of a squeamish disposition found some of the camera angles hard to take, but for anyone with an embarrassing illness it was a godsend.

Medicine itself isn't nearly as embarrassing as it used to be. Women can now do their own swab for chlamydia and gonorrhoea, and men just have to pee in a pot (though many remain convinced someone will jump out from behind a screen and ram an umbrella down the penis). There are tablets for erectile dysfunction, not injections, and drugs for prostate enlargement can stop you peeing all night and down your trousers without having to go near a scalpel. Surgical treatments for just about any condition are much less invasive than they used to be and can often be done as a day case. Generally, the sooner you come forward, the easier (and more successful) treatment is likely to be.

And let's not forget mental illness. It's the biggest public-health threat of this century, and millions of people don't get the help they need because they're ashamed. My dad suffered from depression and took his life when I was seven. He didn't get the help he needed because he was male and Australian, and you're supposed to be able to cope if you are. It's OK to be ill, even better to seek help. And if you're unlucky enough to get a doctor who sighs at depression, blushes at anal warts or sneers at chronic fatigue, there are plenty more out there who don't.

Implant Coulis

Breast Implant
Skin Retractor (Kiln Retra)
Coloured Contact Lenses
Catgut Chromic Suture
Bronzing Powder

Liz Jones, Fashion Editor of *The Daily Mail*,
wonders why women hate their bodies

Body Image Rules

One of the most popular shows on Channel 4 at the moment is *How to Look Good Naked* (closely followed by *10 Years Younger*). A round, middle-aged woman is taken by her chubby hand and dragged, having made several pit stops in front of full-length mirrors along the way, towards the show's denouement: the moment she appears naked in front of a camera and a live audience. This is the ultimate goal for women these days, you see. No matter what we do for a living, how nice we are, how patient as mothers, or how funny we can be, it all boils down to how we look, in harsh sunlight, without a shred of clothing. The premise of the show – and numerous others like it, not to mention all the get-the-celebrity-look features in women's magazines, the missives on how to obtain Geri Halliwell's abs or Kelly Brook's arse – is that if you are happy with your body, if you are not prepared to let nature take its course and instead opt to do the right, well-behaved, submissive thing instead, which is to pummel your body into submission, into behaving as if it hadn't given birth or put on weight or aged by even one day, then you will be fulfilled. The rest – love, money, great sex – will automatically follow.

Except it doesn't. I don't think there has ever been a time when women have been so focused on how they look, but at the same time have been so desperately unhappy. Take a look in your local gym at lunchtime: there will be rows and rows of women, not pounding the treadmill in a bid to avoid a heart attack (oh happy release), but in an attempt to be beautiful. You see them avoiding making eye contact with themselves in the mirrors, so afraid are they of what they might see. Is it progress that women are no longer spending their lunch hours shopping for food, and rushing home straight after work to prepare it (a destiny that seems positively restful in the context of what we put ourselves through today), but are instead devoting themselves to an exercise regime that is only really useful if you are an Olympic pentathlete, not to mention spending a great deal of time and money adhering to a beauty routine – Brazilian bikini wax, all-over airbrush tan, botox injections, teeth whitening, laser facial hair removal, laser brown spot zapping, eyebrow sugaring, obligatory weekend 'break' in a 'spa', blah, blah, blah – that is surely only necessary if you are about to pose naked for the cover of *FHM*.

The simple idea that, in order to enjoy your annual two weeks on the beach you just might, instead of opting

---

When my mum was in her forties and went to the beach – to the windswept sands of Frinton in Essex, to be precise – she wore a long tweed skirt, stockings, proper shoes and a sun hat

---

Hair Soup

Black Wig
Pedicure Blades
Forceps
Wax Strips
Toe Dividers

Nineteen   All Change

We are no longer urged to burn our bras, but instead to buy one from Rigby and Peller that costs more than a car, but which at least gives us great cleavage

for a tummy tuck and buttock lift and bosom enhancement, ooh, I don't know, cover up in a kaftan, is as unacceptable in today's try hard, make the most of yourself culture as saying twenty-five years ago that all you really want to do is stay home and raise your children. Or as shocking as it would have been to tell the women at Greenham Common that, actually, nuclear power might just be the environmentally friendly way forward.

Why do women (and I think it is predominantly females who do this, although men are catching up fast) hate their bodies, and want to conform so badly to some mythical, probably airbrushed extreme? When my mum was in her forties and went to the beach – to the windswept sands of Frinton in Essex, to be precise – she wore a long tweed skirt, stockings, proper shoes and a sun hat. She might, possibly, have exposed her arms in a sleeveless Jaeger blouse, but she certainly didn't worry about having 'chicken wings'. My generation of women, those now in their thirties and forties, grew up on the notion that we could have it all, and that meant owning and preserving the body of a centrefold. But just because we can all now, just about, afford a boob job, thinking mistakenly, with a toss of our Pantened, over-dyed hair, that we are 'worth it', doesn't mean we should. We have simply been brainwashed, bombarded by images of endless glossy adverts and the stupid, mindless, talentless female celebrities on red carpets smiling with their mouths but not their eyes (too much risk of crow's feet), into thinking we need to look a certain way. And, of course, if we don't all aspire to 'better' ourselves, and are content to be healthy and well fed and in possession of equal pay, the huge fashion, beauty and media industries that have been constructed on our insecurities will come tumbling down.

Do I think the pressure on women has got worse over the past 25 years?

On the cover of *Vogue* the month Channel 4 launched was a nameless model with chubby cheeks and a big smile, in a shapeless red wool Jasper Conran dress. Today, the cover girl of choice is usually a teenage eastern European with huge, vacant eyes, no breasts, and long, stick-like limbs. I think the reason we are encouraged to look like children is because we have become too powerful, and need to be put back in our place. Yes, of course I understand that Twiggy and Penelope Tree were as thin and childlike as today's 22-inch waist cadavers, but they were liberating rather than oppressive because, for the first time, they made it acceptable for us not to look or dress or behave like our mothers. If only the reverse were true today. We should remember that women in the Sixties only dressed as children for three years; by 1970, they were finding fitting into a mini skirt both tedious and demeaning and were thinking, 'Oh sod it. I'm buying a maxi.'

How much more dignified – and happy, possibly? – would we be if we could maybe wear a girdle like my mum did, rather than endure yet another endless, boring Ashtanga yoga class? Who made up these new rules? And why are grown, normal, real women being paraded in front of us as creatures in need of redemption? We are no longer urged to burn our bras, but instead to buy one from Rigby and Peller that costs more than a car, but which at least gives us great cleavage.

I am tentatively optimistic, though. I think women will tire, very soon, of being made to fixate on their bodies. I've endured a quarter century of aerobics classes and oxygen facials, of plastic surgery (I had my breasts reduced) and cosmetic dentistry, and none of it made me happy or loved. Once women realise that bald fact, the rest will be a piece of cake. Now, that is something I haven't touched in decades…

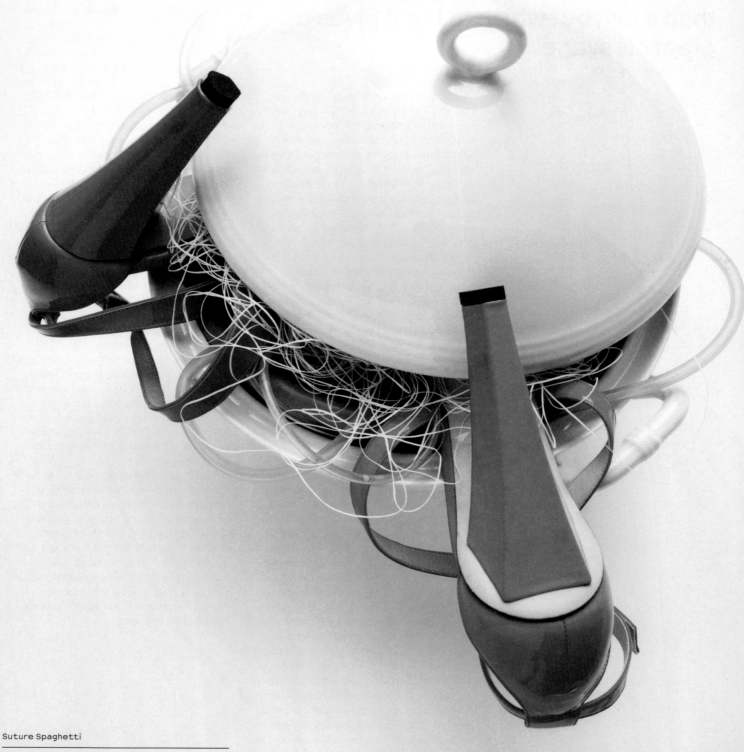

Suture Spaghetti

Shoes (Left – Biba, Right – Jimmy Choo)
Colonic Tubing
Dental Floss

Nineteen   All Change

Special Relationship

Before Channel 4 launched, the 'best of US' on British television meant *I Love Lucy*, *Dallas* and *Dynasty*. Since then viewers have enjoyed hits that give the lie to the old adage about British television being the best in the world: *Cheers*, *Frasier*, *The West Wing*, *The Sopranos*, *Sex and the City* and *Friends* – witty, nuanced and with unmatchable production values, these shows demonstrated that there are some things that the Americans do best. One thing American television lacks, however, is a tradition of serious factual programming: Channel 4 has used its own high-quality documentary skills to shine a light, often an unforgiving one, on life in the USA and the profound impact its politics and policies have on the rest of the world.

Art world insider and journalist
Anthony Haden-Guest finds that
the best US TV shows on Channel 4
map out a new reality

Television From a New World

Frasier, 1994

Brooklyn-born crime boss 'Crazy' Joey Gallo was so preoccupied with his image, he watched the movie *Kiss of Death* fourteen times to study Richard Widmark's manic giggle as he pushes a wheelchair-bound old woman down a flight of stairs. I remembered this when a young woman in Manhattan was telling me about some emotional upset or other during the glory days of *Sex and the City*.

'You know what I always wonder?' she said. 'How would Carrie Bradshaw be handling this?'

This brought home the way television has largely replaced movies as a mapmaker for our lives. It also seems relevant when contemplating the underlying factors that distinguish British television from American television, from the best on show to the gag-reflex awful.

During its early decades British television, like the rest of popular culture in this tight little island, reflected the world around it. Whether milked for laughs or melodramatised, shows of the calibre of *Steptoe and Son* and *Upstairs Downstairs*, and characters like Alf Garnett and Soames Forsyte, were founded on longstanding national, social and economic realities. In the huge, shifting demographic of the United States, however, popular culture has always had a mighty hand in actually creating the world that absorbs it. This was true in the day of the dime novels and tabloid journalism that produced Billy the Kid and Buffalo Bill. And it's true today, with FBI tapes recording mobsters discussing *The Sopranos*. This distinction has been much broken down, though, by the ping-ponging of Anglo-American cultural relations: as with the Brits inventing Pop Art, then the Americans doing it more coolly, more famously; or the way

New York came up with Punk rock, then along came Malcolm McLaren to scope the acts at New York's CBGB. Television has been a two-way highway in this process. The tangled family tree of sophisticated TV humour bears witness to this. Rowan and Martin's *Laugh-In* broke the ground for a sort of vernacular surrealism. *That Was The Week That Was* imported satire. These two begat *Saturday Night Live, Monty Python, National Lampoon, Spitting Image*, and much more. It used to be a commonplace Brit prejudice to say that our ingenuous American cousins don't 'get' irony. Indeed, you can still hear this today, if only from crusty folk who have never caught, say, David Letterman, a talk show so drenched with irony that it could drown a litter of kittens. Then there's *The Daily Show*.

The half-hour *The Daily Show*, which opened in 1996 with Craig Kilborn, who was replaced by Jon Stewart a couple of years later, has a clear lineage. It began with David Frost. Then came SNL's *Weekend Update*, of which the original anchor was Chevy Chase, HBO's *Not Necessarily the News* and Channel 4's *The 11 O'Clock Show*. And it confirms the role of American TV in shaping popular culture, rather than reflecting it, that whereas

Cheers, 1983

Friends, 1994 © Warner Bros. Television, a division of Time Warner Entertainment Company, L.P.

318   Twenty   The Special Relationship

David Frost could have been confident that his viewers would be familiar with his source material – newscasts, the papers – a Pew Research Center poll in 2004 discovered that 21 per cent of Americans between 19 and 28 cited the trenchant humour of *The Daily Show* and *Saturday Night Live* as their principal source of political news.

Newsday duly named Stewart as the most important political commentator for that year's elections. 'I'm not sure what we're dealing with out there,' said Stewart when he heard. But a poll released by Pew earlier this year showed that regular viewers of the show were usually more knowledgeable that those who got their news elsewhere. Indeed, according to *Time* magazine, Jon Stewart was under serious consideration to take over from Dan Rather, the venerated news anchor at CBS.

A couple of years back, *Broadcast* magazine asked several of British television's heaviest hitters to name their favourite show. Their overwhelming answer was *The Sopranos*. At least some of the power of the TV series lay in the way the storylines married the familiar and the unfamiliar. Yes, the mob thrives in suburbia and, yes, a Tony Soprano may suffer from panic attacks. Nobody seemed much surprised when, one by one, five *Sopranos* cast members were arrested for real-life crimes.

NYPD Blue, 1994

Just so, the wondrously over-the-top narratives of *Desperate Housewives* submerge viewers in the dark side of a different suburbia, a soapily gothic one. Or there's *Sex and the City*, which began as a series of columns by Candace Bushnell in the *New York Observer*, being thinly disguised accounts of the amorous adventures and misadventures of herself and various friends and acquaintances. They did for her generation what Helen Gurley Brown did for hers when she published *Sex and the Single Girl* in 1962.

Aaron Sorkin's superlative creation, *The West Wing*, has not been the only attempt to turn the inner workings of democratic politics into television. The BBC's *Yes Minister*, succeeded in due course by *Yes, Prime Minister*, came ninth on the British Film Institute's list of 100 best British TV programs, while *House of Cards* was 84th. But the one was broad satire and although the other was adapted from a novel by Michael Dobbs, former chief of staff at the Tory party HQ, it was a thriller. Ian Richardson, who played Francis Urquhart, initially as chief whip, towards the end of the Thatcher regime, is a wondrously velvety villain but unimaginable actually stalking the corridors of power.

The characters in *The West Wing* inhabit a reality, if a heightened reality, zippily New Journalistic, fast-talking, crisis-prone and sludge-free. Like *The Sopranos* it was an ensemble show. President Bartlet is played by Martin Sheen, who has unusual hair – it looks as if it is either landing or taking off – but no more so than Reagan, or Clinton before he had the bouffant tamed. Sheen is part of a core group of about eight, with a further three or four important satellite characters. Much of the energy of the show comes from their personal interplay.

Where *The West Wing* differs from most real-world-based TV product is that the global issues it dealt with were treated as if they mattered. True, the strokes were sometimes broad. But, with its rapid weaving between White House scandals and highly charged political issues, such as right-wing attempts to defund the National Endowment for the Arts, and global crises, such as an immediately impending war between India and Pakistan (defused by a rakish British aristocrat, vaguely reminiscent of the late Lord Lambton), the show created its own sharply knowing reality, and left one feeling better acquainted with what might actually be going on.

The last series of *The West Wing* was in 2006. And that period when British TV-land seemed at times like an American colony has, for now at least, drawn to an end. *Friends*, *Frasier*, *Sex and the City* will now swirl endlessly through the otherworld of syndicated re-runs, where they will shortly be joined by *The Sopranos*. *Lost* has been a giant but, that apart, no successors to these greats have appeared. Reality television reigns. The likes of *American Idol* there, the progeny of *Big Brother* here.

Which brings me to my second distinction between American and British television, which supersedes the first and which is the offspring of our celebrity culture. People have always gone to the United States to re-invent themselves, so celebrity culture is taken for granted there. Its ballooning in the UK has been another story. Celebrities here used to be curious anomalies, somewhat disdained by the powers-that-be. The young Winston Churchill was disapproved of by his fellow aristocrats as a showboat. Half a century ago there was a menagerie of 'celebrities' – Lady Docker, Sir Gerald Nabarro, Screaming Lord Sutch – who kept the viewers entertained while power was operating behind the scenery.

But the system was already mutating and the media had grown claws by the time pop convulsed the social landscape. A whole new class – not just pop stars, but models, photographers and hairdressers – was born. Mick Jagger became a social pet, and two generations of young toffs adopted a protective sonic colouration by affecting mockney – Mayfair Cockney. From there to Princess Diana was easy.

The upsurge of public grief at Diana's death was the grand climacteric. The stiff upper lip grew moist and pulpy. A star was being mourned, not a royal. The old order had lost its hold on the popular imagination, along with its values. And television was ready with replacements. So far as reality TV goes, the distinction between the British and the American precisely reverses the original distinction. American reality TV reflects the reality of that culture. British reality TV creates it.

That seems to be where we are now. But things are evolving with a bewildering speed. And new revenue streams perhaps with them. Bill Gates has predicted that viewers watching *Sex and the City*, say, on the internet will be able to use the remote to click onto one of the character's shoes and be instantly whisked to the manufacturer's website. The technology is apparently already in place.

Twenty The Special Relationship

The photographer
Gregory Crewdson's
images of suburban
America offer a
different and haunting
view of alienation

Gregory Crewdson
<u>Untitled, Summer 2003</u>
Digital C-print
64 1/4 X 95 1/4 inches
(163.2 X 241.94 cm)
(Merchant's Row)

Gregory Crewdson
Untitled, Summer 2003
Digital C-print
64 1/4 X 94 1/4 inches
(163.2 X 239.4 cm)
(Clover Street)

'Yesterday, the President met with
a group he calls the coalition of the
willing. Or, as the rest of the world calls
them, Britain and Spain.'
Jon Stewart

Former British Ambassador to the US Christopher Meyer takes a look at our historic, and present, attitude to America

US and Them

The Daily Show with Jon Stewart, from 2005

I remember as a child hearing my parents talk about Americans. They had both been in uniform during the Second World War. They had come into close contact with the US military. The experience left them strikingly ambivalent about Americans. I heard them describe GIs – American infantry – as 'Russians with creases in their trousers'. This referred to the fearsome reputation for brutality that the Red Army had acquired as it advanced through Europe.

After the war, my stepfather commanded the RAF station at Duxford, just outside Cambridge. Battle of Britain day was always marked by a public aerobatics display, first by venerable British Meteor jets and then by the ultra-modern, swept-wing American Super Sabers from one of the nearby US Air Force bases. The aerobatic style was very different. The Meteors were slow-moving and balletic as they wheeled and swooped in the summer sky. The Americans announced themselves by hurtling towards us low and loud from over the horizon.

I jumped up and down with excitement. But there was much sucking of teeth by my parents and their friends about the flashiness of Americans and their preference for show and brute force over skill. Fifty years later, not a lot has changed in British attitudes: Meteors v. Super Sabers; British Greeks versus American Romans; softly, softly in Basra versus surge in Baghdad; and even small, sweet, curly Caribbean bananas, favoured by Europeans, versus large, straight, coarse bananas from US plantations in Latin America, the antagonists in the ludicrous banana trade war of the late Nineties between Europe and America.

There is something disagreeable in this mix of British condescension and envy. The acerbic wartime British quip about Americans in Britain – 'over-paid, over-sexed and over here' – says as much about us as them. In some ways it got worse after the war. It was bad enough to suffer food rationing and a giant national debt, mainly owed to the Americans, while travellers returned from the US with tales of wealth

Watch *The West Wing* and, say, *The Thick of It* or *Yes, Minister* – and marvel at American reverance and British cynicsm in the representation of our political leaders

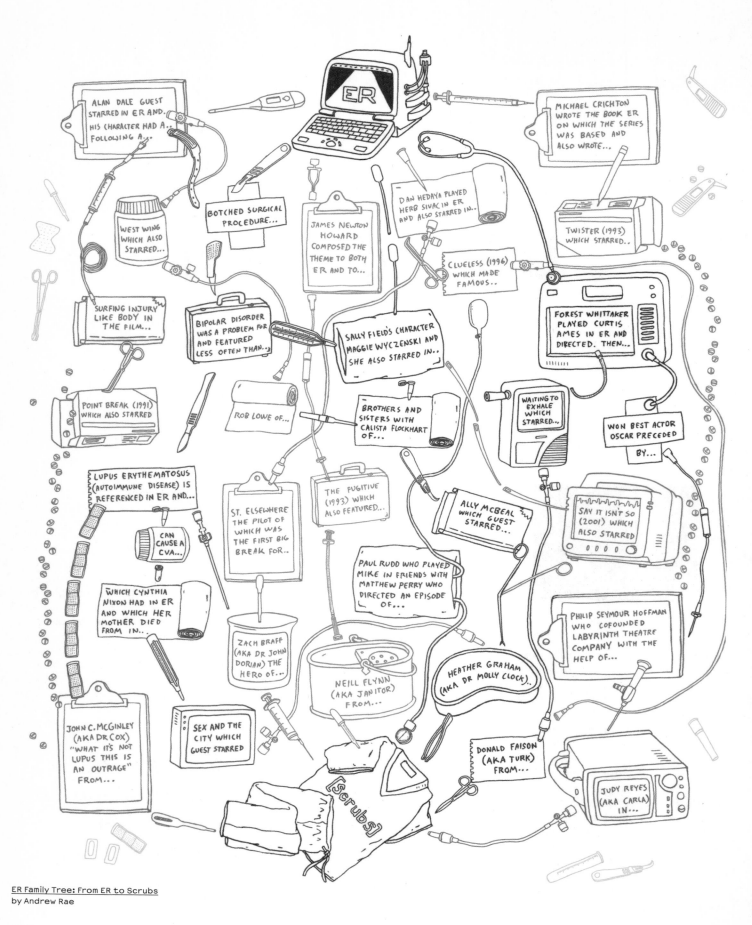

ER Family Tree: From ER to Scrubs
by Andrew Rae

Twenty   The Special Relationship

I heard them describe GIs – American infantry – as 'Russians with creases in their trousers'

The West Wing
advert, 2006

and plenty. But, after all our sacrifices, to have them seize the credit in movies for winning the war single-handedly stuck painfully in the British craw.

The irony was that my parents adored America. During mealtimes as a child we were often regaled by my stepfather's stories of his time in the US after the war, as an exchange pilot flying bombers. He loved it, and not just because he had escaped Britain's postwar austerity. I heard about American openness, friendliness and hospitality. After he died, my mother visited the US repeatedly because she liked it so much. She often told the story of finding herself, a seventy-year-old grandmother, lost – God knows how – alone, and standing at a bus-stop in a black ghetto in New Orleans, where she was rescued by a jolly group of African-American women who set her on her way.

I have never found this ambivalence odd or hard to explain. With America, it is the reality behind the overblown rhetoric of the Special Relationship; and it works both ways. I was at the Comedy Store in Las Vegas recently, watching a series of stand-up acts. As is the way in America,

there was lots of audience participation. One of the comedians picked on me. His discovery that I was British unleashed a stream of waspish observations about *Mary Poppins*, the Queen, butlers in American movies, the British class system, pubs, our accents and so on. The audience were convulsed; he was actually very funny. But it was all the more effective for being genuinely felt, as he revealed in the brief exchange we had after the show. It was a salutary antidote to all that 'we love your accent, Queen, policemen...' stuff that you hear from Americans from time to time.

We have an ambivalent relationship with America for the same reasons that we have ambivalent relationships with

The Daily Show with Jon Stewart, from 2005

Morgan Spurlock's 30 Days, 2005

France and Germany. These are the three countries with whom our history is most closely entwined. The ties of ethnicity and culture, leave aside business, are rich and centuries old. They are allies and partners. Yet we have fought brutal wars against each of them. The defining features of our mutual histories are intimacy and enmity. Today, this produces all kinds of contradictory reflexes in British attitudes towards them and in theirs to us.

When I was Ambassador in Germany, the Germans repeatedly complained to me about their being lampooned and stereotyped in the British press (they still

DEATH OF A PRESIDENT
GEORGE W. BUSH 1946 – MONDAY 9TH OCTOBER, 9PM
BRAND NEW DRAMA, EXCLUSIVELY ON MORE4
channel4.com/more4

do). Were we ever going to get over the war? How on earth could we make a TV comedy, *'Allo, 'Allo*, about the French resistance to Nazi occupation. There were various answers to these complaints. One of them was to point out that Jürgen Klinsmann, after a brilliant season at Tottenham, had been voted Footballer of the Year. Another, which I gave to Chancellor Helmut Kohl, was that, despite my father being shot down and killed by the Germans in the war, my mother and stepfather always felt comfortable in Germany. It was a complicated equation.

As to France, being married into a French family offers a fine observation point on the ancient love-hate relationship between the Frogs and the Rosbifs. We come to live and work in each other's countries in the tens of thousands, in search of something admirable and absent in our own societies. Yet our capacity for mutual mockery, respect, disdain, admiration and rivalry is boundless. My former father-in-law, also an RAF pilot, was eternally grateful to the chain of courageous French men and women who had sheltered him for almost a year as he escaped the Nazis in France. One of my grandfathers hated France because of his time in the trenches with a French regiment in the 1914-18 war. My French brother-in-law still berates me for our sinking of the French fleet at Mers-El-Kebir in 1940. My mother thought my education incomplete without my going to school in Paris, which I duly did.

Take the very notion of a Special Relationship. Today it distorts any rational debate about how Britain should conduct its relations with the US. Is America our single most important bilateral ally and partner? Absolutely. Does this mean that our respective national interests will always coincide? Absolutely not. Should we stand up for our interests when they diverge from the American? Absolutely. Will having rows with the US from time to time undermine the fundamental comity between our two nations? Absolutely not. The Americans have no hesitation in reading the riot act to us if they think we are treading on their interests.

These propositions are so self-evident, and so often demonstrated over the last fifty years, that one marvels at the addiction of today's politicians and commentators to the notion of a Special Relationship, which brooks no mention of disagreement in public and discourages plain-speaking in private. This not only damages the British national interest, which risks going by default, as

Take the very notion of a Special Relationship. Today it distorts any rational debate about how Britain should conduct its relationship with the US

Is America our single most important bilateral ally and partner? Absolutely. Does this mean that our respective national interests will always coincide? Absolutely not

happened when Blair was Prime Minister; it actually damages the relationship with the US by raising wholly unrealistic expectations of what it can achieve.

British-American relations have had a highly chequered history since the Revolutionary War. We went to war again in 1812. The two countries came near to fighting each other at least twice more in the 19th century. The idea of a Special Relationship was unknown before the Second World War. Since 1945, relations have passed through alternating extremes of coolness (Eden/ Eisenhower, Wilson/Johnson) and warmth (Thatcher/Reagan, Blair/Bush). Brown/Bush seems to be settling somewhere in between, though differences over Iraq could yet plunge relations into a new ice age.

Behind these ups and downs lie profound cultural differences between the two sides of the Atlantic. Sure, American movies sell like hot cakes over here; and British popular music would be stuck in the age of Dickie Valentine and Matt Monro without rock'n'roll and rap. But watch *The West Wing* and, say, *The Thick Of It* or *Yes, Minister* – and marvel at American reverence and British cynicism in the representation of our political leaders.

When in Washington, I used to tell new arrivals to the Embassy and their families to think of the US as a foreign country, like France or Germany. Then they would be pleasantly surprised by the many things they would still find in common with this most hospitable, generous, idealistic, and optimistic of peoples. Think of America as Britain writ large and they would come to grief. American attitudes to crime, religion, patriotism, education, the outside world could be very different from ours.

But let's not go overboard. The big ethnic groups in the United States can all claim something special about their links with the old homeland. As Miriam 'Ma' Ferguson, the first woman Governor of Texas, once said, 'If the King's English was good enough for Jesus Christ, it's sure as hell good enough for the children of Texas.'

Gregory Crewdson
Untitled, Summer 2004
Digital C-print
64 1/4 X 94 1/4 inches
(163.2 X 239.4 cm)
(trouble with Harry's)

32

Film and documentary maker Julien Temple discovers just how much or little Joe Strummer, singer/songwriter of the legendary Clash, really thought of America

Clash of Personalities

Songs by The Clash are rumoured to be among the music blasted out 24/7 to inmates of Guantanamo Bay. But it's not known if the playlist includes *I'm So Bored with the USA*. The US military has a bizarre history of turning Clash songs on their head with a certain blunt humour, in support of its own operational imperatives. General Noriega learnt the words to *Should I Stay or Should I Go* the hard way – as it shook the foundations of his Panamanian bolthole. Joe Strummer's prophetic *Rock the Casbah* lyrics have provided the pumped up soundtrack for both of America's Iraq wars and are still painted on the bombs dropped 'between the minarets' today.

The flipside of using The Clash in America's global 'War on Terror' is that you can get into trouble when listening to them at home. A guy who played Clash songs in a taxi to Heathrow recently made headlines when he was reported by the driver and physically removed from his flight as a potential terrorist.

It is 25 years since they broke up, so this contradictory desire to co-opt their music, while simultaneously seeking to demonise it, demonstrates the continuing relevance of The Clash: shedding light on America's ongoing love-hate relationship with the group and also the Clash's love-hate relationship with America.

The source of this deep-seated ambivalence to all things American lay in Joe Strummer himself. Public school renegade, teenage Beach Boys fan and Punk Rock voice of a generation, he was driven by the contradictions which defined him. Slightly older than other leading figures of the punk moment, Joe had, crucially, lived a whole series of other lives before joining The Clash.

The son of a left-wing British diplomat, Joe spent time growing up in Egypt, as well as in Turkey, Mexico, and West Germany. Eventually sent back to England by his globetrotting parents, he found himself trapped in the repressive surroundings of a minor public school in suburban Surrey while swinging London kicked off twenty miles up the road. One day, he heard the Stones' version of *Not Fade Away* thumping out of a huge wooden radio in the day room. Joe's life was transformed in that moment.

Yankee dollar talk
To the dictators of the world
In fact it's giving orders
An' they can't afford to miss a word

I'm So Bored with the USA – The Clash

Gregory Crewdson
<u>Untitled, Summer 2004</u>
Digital C–print
64 1/4 X 94 1/4 inches
(163.2 X 239.4 cm)
(summer rain)

It was not the Stones that did it for Joe – rather, the American zeitgeist that inhabited that Bobby Womack song. American rock 'n' roll and the folk blues of Woody Guthrie and Bukka White weren't just music to him, they revealed an entire attitude, a directness, a way of feeling and a code to live by, to which he dedicated the rest of his life. The mythic American landscape of the songs, their unfailing sympathy for the underdog and the outcast, the lost highways and endless railway tracks, fuelled his dreams of escape.

But Joe was also part of the hippie counter-culture generation that came of age in 1968. Fiercely opposed to America's war in Vietnam, the growth of multi-national corporations and the consumerism of American culture, Joe was there in Grosvenor Square. Leaving school, and everything it represented, behind him after the suicide of his brother, Joe, now known as Woody, reinvented himself in the persona of a penniless hobo-like Delta bluesman, who initially couldn't play the guitar! Having hitchhiked and busked his way around the festivals of the early Seventies, he gravitated to the squats of west London where he put together his first important band. The 101ers were a shambling, speed-driven tribute to gritty, no-frills American R&B. Fronted by Joe, in blues-shouting, human-dynamo mode, they pumped out ferocious covers of Roy C, Bo Diddley and Chuck Berry songs, transcending their squatting roots to become one of the biggest draws on London's live pub-rock circuit. But one night in early 1976, just as they were beginning to break out, an unknown act opened for the 101ers at the Nashville. By the end of the gig, Joe had seen the future: the Sex Pistols had just consigned everything he was doing to history.

Spat out in an ear-splitting Dickensian whine, Rotten's words brutally dismembered the bland transatlantic chart music of the time and took deadly aim at the fag end of American Sixties counter-culture. Transforming their boredom and alienation into a Pandora's box of incandescent rage, the Pistols celebrated what a new, disaffected generation of kids were feeling and the clockwork noir London of decaying council estates and unrequited dreams that had spawned them. Joe wanted in – but in the Year Zero atmosphere of the time becoming a punk meant burying all the incriminating baggage he carried with him.

One of the first things Joe did after joining The Clash was to change the title of a Mick Jones song from *I'm So Bored with You* to *I'm So Bored with the USA*. Of course, he was also giving voice to the anti-American feeling of the post-Vietnam and Watergate era, but in typically Joe fashion he managed to rasp the lyrics to *I'm So Bored…* with such a raw enthusiasm that you were left in no doubt about his deep and contradictory affection for the subject of the song.

Right from the beginning, Joe and The Clash secretly loved America. They just hated the people who ran it. Mick Jones had also grown up on American music. They both always wore this bittersweet relationship with the USA on their paint-splashed sleeves. I filmed them on the Edgware Road on a freezing winter night in late 1976. They were daubing the words 'I'm so bored with the USA' in ice cream across an American ice-cream parlour. But even then Joe and Mick were keen to point out that the song was not anti-American in a general sense, but specifically anti- what American consumer culture was doing to us over here. They liked the idea of pizza, cowboys and Kojak in America, but didn't want to see it gobbling up the rest of the world.

At the height of the punk terror, when you could be lined up against a wall and shot for going off-message, The Clash boldly announced their fascination with America by covering the rebel Texas anthem, *I Fought the Law*. They hired an American heavy-metal producer to do the second album and got an endless amount of flak from their hardcore fans for selling out. Then compounding sacrilege with sacrilege, they started hanging out with outlaw country singers, wearing cowboy shirts and hats and flicking their hair back into big rockabilly quiffs. But this was not about sucking up to the American market, they were simultaneously waging

a public war against the corporate greed of their US record company, and had the audacity to blast off their first-ever American gig on the tour which broke them wide open in the States, with a rebel-rousing rendition of – you guessed it – *I'm So Bored…* Joe had never been more excited in his life. His own personal *Mission Impossible* was to break the punk thing big over there, as if by doing so he could reconnect with his own interrupted musical journey. He just couldn't get enough of actually being in the USA, making lifelong friendships, driving Kerouac-style across the States, losing himself, first-hand this time, in the myths and meanings the music had always held for him.

Never mind the stars and stripes
Let's print the watergate tapes
I'll salute the new wave
And I hope nobody escapes

I'm So Bored with the USA—The Clash

The Clash bade farewell to the Kings Road and never looked back. Re-imagining punk rock in a mythic American context, Joe began to bring the beat poet, rockabilly and R&B influences of his past back into the ever-expanding music, combining snarling punk attitude with his old respect for its cultural roots.

Writing songs like *Washington Bullets*, *Know your Rights* and *Rock the Casbah*, Joe's lyrics took on the oil politics of the Middle East, individual liberty, and the dirty war against the Sandinistas in Nicaragua. Confronting suburban American kids with ideas of social injustice, global consciousness and freedom of speech, as well as visceral music, The Clash were able to turn them on to what their own government was up to around the world. Talking to them directly, making them reassess their lives and turn them around, meant that Joe could finally have his cake and sublimate it. All at the same time he could hate and love – and change – America.

Gregory Crewdson
Untitled, Winter 2005
Digital C-Print
64 1/4 X 95 1/4 inches
(163.2 X 241.94 cm)
(man in living room
with hole)

Alastair Campbell:
I know the position on Iraq, and I
know that maybe you're not in the
same position as I am on that, but
I think you've got to understand…
Jon Stewart:
Are you in the debacle camp?

Uncensored

The instincts of the channel's editorial and legal and compliance teams has never been to sanitise and to censor but to find the appropriate context in which to give voice to actions and viewpoints that might be thought of as unacceptable elsewhere. While they have always worked in close adherence to the regulatory codes, these have – on occasion – been tested to the limit. This philosophy has consistently placed Channel 4 in the court of public opinion and, from time to time, in real life courts of law. The channel has fought some landmark legal battles over freedom of speech, not least the infamous *Damned In The USA* trial in Mississippi. These hard-won victories are amongst the foundation stones of the more liberal regime that television enjoys today

Documentary director Paul Yule and Channel 4 fought for free speech in Mississippi, winning a landmark court case against the Christian right

Free Speech in the USA

Benefit premiere in Los Angeles presented by Alec Baldwin and Kim Basinger

Damned In The USA, directed by Paul Yule and produced by Berwick Universal Pictures, was conceived in 1990 as the centre-piece of Channel 4's *Banned* season – an initiative of the new Director of Programmes, John Willis.

The documentary was an attempt to look at the simmering controversy in the US over federal funding of the arts by the National Endowment for the Arts, and in particular examined the recent cases of 'censorship' by the religious right, aimed at artists like Robert Mapplethorpe, Madonna, Andres Serrano and The 2 Live Crew.

In 1990, Paul Yule approached the reclusive Rev Donald Wildmon, President of The American Family Association and instigator of many instances of so-called censorship, asking for a wide-ranging interview at his Tupelo, Mississippi headquarters. Wildmon agreed to be interviewed by Yule and became a central character in the documentary, excoriating the artworks he had done his best to ban.

Damned In The USA was shown with great critical success in Channel 4's *Banned* season, and subsequently went on to win the International Emmy for

The Channel 4 defence team in Mississippi
L–R John Willis (C4 Director of Programmes),
Don Christopher (C4 lawyer), Paul Yule
(defendant), Russell Smith (defending lawyer), Jan
Tomalin (C4 lawyer), Jonathan Stack (defendant)

Wildmon, through his attorney Benjamin Bull, sought a permanent injunction against the film's release in the US, and $8 million in damages

First Amendment legal specialist, Martin Garbus

Paul Yule and Jan Tomalin in New York at the first court hearing. They were attempting to move the jurisdiction of the proceedings from Mississippi to New York

Best Arts Documentary of 1991.

The film was screened for the first time in the United States on 11 September 1991 at The Margaret Mead Film Festival in New York, after which Wildmon brought a lawsuit against Paul Yule, Yule's production company, Berwick Universal Pictures, his co-producer Jonathan Stack, and Channel 4, claiming that he had the right to control distribution of the film.

Wildmon claimed that his reputation was injured by the film because it juxtaposed interviews with him (conducted by Yule in Mississippi) with images of the artworks that he had tried to censor.

Wildmon, through his attorney Benjamin Bull, sought a permanent injunction against the film's release in the US, and $8 million in damages.

The documentary was effectively pulled from release pending the trial's outcome, because Wildmon threatened suit against any distributor or exhibitor who picked up the film.

A three-day trial was held in August 1992 in front of US District Court Judge Glenn Davidson in Aberdeen, Mississippi. At stake was the claim by the Rev

Donald Wildmon of The American Family Association that he had the right to block the distribution of the film because of its graphic content.

Defending Channel 4 and the filmmakers was Martin Garbus, renowned First Amendment specialist, his assistant Russell Smith, and Channel 4's lawyer Jan Tomalin.

In effect Garbus and Channel 4 argued that by filing the lawsuit, Wildmon had already achieved much of what he hoped for in that distribution of the film had effectively ceased.

The Rev Donald Wildmon, head of The American Family Association, was the first witness on the stand during the trial, and was followed by the filmmaker Paul Yule.

Yule testified for over four hours about to his intentions when planning, shooting, editing and displaying the film, which was eventually titled *Damned In The USA*. Yule explained his reasons for including the material that Wildmon would find offensive by saying it was impossible to understand the heated controversy over 'obscene' art without seeing the actual images being discussed. 'They

Right: Paul Yule in front of the New York Court House during the proceedings to move the trial from Mississippi

Below: Paul Yule being interviewed outside the court house in Aberdeen, Mississippi

Below: Martin Garbus and Jonathan Stack

Conference between Jonathan Stack, Russell Smith and Kieran in Aberdeen, Mississippi

And Channel 4 itself – for a time in the early nineties – became a beacon of free speech in the USA

Top: Paul Yule in front of posters in New York for the release of <u>Damned In The USA</u>
Below: <u>LA Times</u> article

are there to show what the controversy is all about,' he pointed out.

The trial ended with a sensational courtroom viewing of the film itself.

Two weeks later the decision came down from Judge Davidson – Channel 4 and the filmmakers had won since the Judge ruled Wildmon had no right to control the distribution of the film.

Damned In The USA went on to be released theatrically in sixty cities across the USA – another example of what the film itself had demonstrated, that Wildmon's attempts at censorship often had the effect of promoting those works he tried hardest to bury.

And Channel 4 itself – for a time in the early nineties – became a beacon of free speech in the USA.

During the trial, a National Support Committee for *Damned In The USA* was put together, and benefit screenings and performances were held in New York, Los Angeles and elsewhere, which included a wonderful Lou Reed re-recording of his classic *Walk on The Wild Side* as follows:

Left: Jan Tomalin, Channel 4's lawyer in Tupelo, Mississippi, Elvis Presley's birthplace

Right: Jonathan Stack (l) and Paul Yule (r), the co-defendants in the Damned In The USA trial held in Mississippi

Top: Jan Tomalin, Channel 4's lawyer in Tupelo, Mississippi, on her way to court

Donald Wildmon was Damned In The USA
Tried to get Channel 4 to pay and pay
A little lie here a little lie there
He thought Mississippi was the place where
He could Hey…
Take a Walk on the Legal Side
Thought a home-town Judge would rule on his side
And all the fundamentalists go…
Sue Sue Sue Sue Sue Sue Sue Sue
Sue Sue Sue Sue Sue Sue Sue Sue…
And he lost!

Lou Reed rewrote Walk on the Wild Side for the Damned In The USA benefit screening

341

The legal and social aftermath of
Gunter von Hagens' public autopsy,
conducted on television

The Autopsy

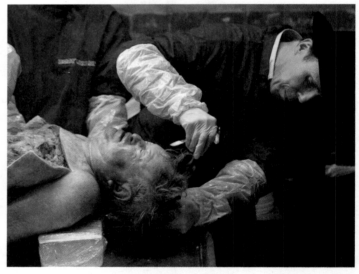

The Autopsy, 2002

When Dr Gunther von Hagens brought over his *Body Worlds*
exhibition to the UK in March 2002, the Department of Health,
after some considerable debate in correspondence, accepted that
a licence was not required under the Anatomy Act in force at that
time and the exhibition went ahead. When Dr Gunther von Hagens
conducted his public autopsy on 20 November 2002, the first in
the UK for 170 years, the relevant authorities maintained that it
was unlawful. Dr Gunther von Hagens and his legal representatives, together with Channel 4, disputed this, arguing that what
was intended did not fall under any of the relevant legislation at
that time. The autopsy duly went ahead unchallenged and the
programme recording the event, *The Autopsy,* produced by Nick
Curwin, was broadcast that evening on Channel 4.

Under s.16 Human Tissue Act 2004, which came into force
on 1 September 2006, both the *Body Worlds* exhibition and the
autopsy may now require a licence being granted by the Human
Tissue Authority as being an 'anatomical examination', a 'post-
mortem examination' or 'the use for the purpose of public display
of the body of a deceased person'.

In the early stages of consultation, the Human Tissue Authority's Code of Practice relating to Public Display was very widely
defined to include television programmes. However, after the
consultation and lobbying by Channel 4 and Nick Curwin, the final
version of the Code now expressly states under paragraph 12, 'The
HT Act does not provide for the licensing of the display of photo-
graphic or electronic images whether moving (e.g. in a broadcast
or transmission) or static (e.g. in a text book).' Television has been
responsible for many social changes, but to change the British
autopsy rules is clearly a cut above the average.

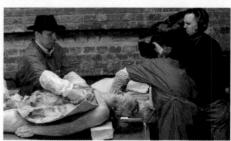

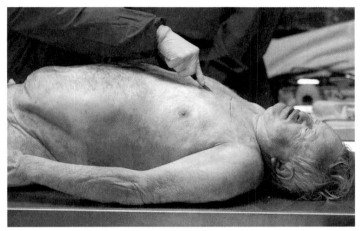

Television has been responsible for so many social changes, but to change the British autopsy rules is clearly a cut above the average

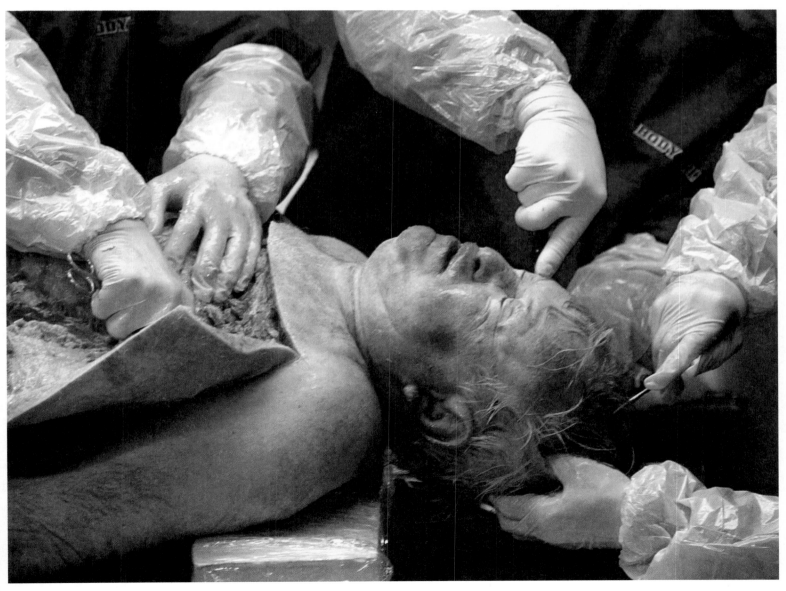

In June 2005, Pamela Edwards, who suffered from dissociative identity disorder, won the right to tell her story in the Channel 4 documentary *Being Pamela*

The Sunday Times, June 2005

Being Pamela

Being Pamela advert, 2005

Pamela Edwards, 32, is one of the few people in Britain known to suffer from dissociative identity disorder (DID), formerly known as multiple personality disorder.

St Helens council, the local authority in Merseyside responsible for her care, and the official solicitor, a government legal officer, sought a High Court injunction preventing the publication of any details of her life.

Being Pamela gave a unique insight into Pamela's rare disorder. She spends much of her time lost among the four characters who inhabit her mind. She is always surrounded by two or three carers who say 'Pamela? Where's Pamela?' – calling to her, although she is standing in front of them.

They do not know which of her characters – Sandra, Andrew, Susan or Margaret - is present. Unlike with other DID sufferers, the personalities are aware of each other's existence and often interact.

The documentary was broadcast on Channel 4 at 9pm on 8 June 2005.

From The Sunday Times, June 2005

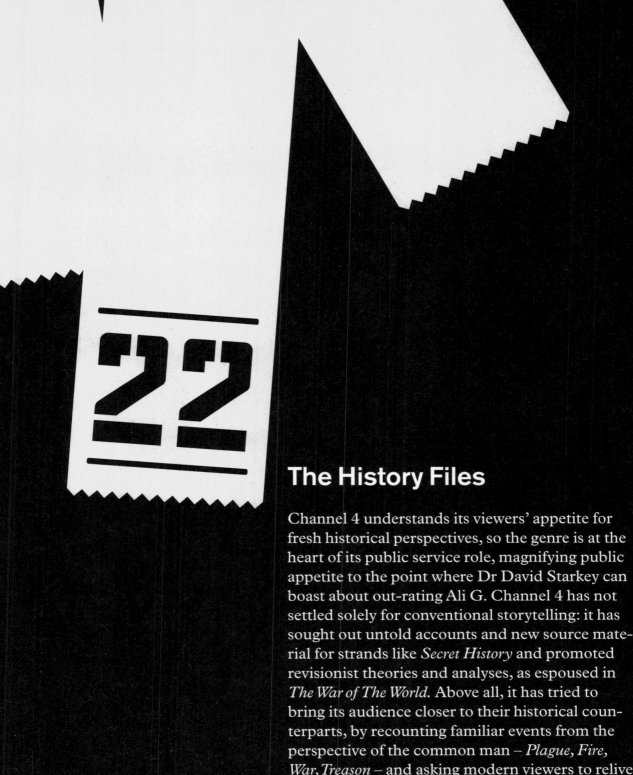

22

The History Files

Channel 4 understands its viewers' appetite for fresh historical perspectives, so the genre is at the heart of its public service role, magnifying public appetite to the point where Dr David Starkey can boast about out-rating Ali G. Channel 4 has not settled solely for conventional storytelling: it has sought out untold accounts and new source material for strands like *Secret History* and promoted revisionist theories and analyses, as espoused in *The War of The World*. Above all, it has tried to bring its audience closer to their historical counterparts, by recounting familiar events from the perspective of the common man – *Plague, Fire, War, Treason* – and asking modern viewers to relive the experiences of their forebears through living history experiments such as *The 1900 House* and *That'll Teach 'Em*.

The Future of the Monarchy

Dr David Starkey

King Charles III or King George VII? Charles has already teased us about his possible choice of royal name. But his record as Prince of Wales also suggests that he will be the most radically reforming monarch since his great-grandfather, George V, who changed the monarchy's surname, marriage customs and values in one fell swoop in the single year 1917.

The clearest indication has come in Church-State relations. Charles has famously said that, as King, he would like to be Defender of Faith, rather than Defender of the Faith. One word, but a world of difference. The Defender of the Faith is, as the Monarch has been since Queen Elizabeth I, supreme governor of the Church of England, but the Defender of Faith would be patron of many competing and conflicting religions. Whatever Charles hopes, he can't be both.

Is it now time for the monarchy to throw over the Church of England, just as it earlier and very successfully detached itself from the peerage? After all, the sometime national church, despite the splendours of its architectural inheritance, is now in fact weak, divided and fast shrinking into a mere sect; if religion still has strength in this country it lies elsewhere, in evangelical Christianity and radical Islam. Neither is very promising material for royal ceremony. In these circumstances, will it be possible for Charles to have a coronation at all? Is it even desirable? Might it be better instead to do the unthinkable and follow in the footsteps of Oliver Cromwell and have a civil inauguration?

It is not unthinkable. The regalia of crown, orb and sceptre could be used, but a new cast of characters and a different form of words would take account of the tumultuous changes of past decades. But will there still be a King to be crowned,

or will the monarchy follow so many other English [ ] into oblivion? History suggests that monarchies ra[ ] pear, save as a result of defeat in war or revolution, [ ] seems in prospect in Britain.

Instead, the real dangers are indifference and [ ] For the settlement of 1917, which established the H[ ] Windsor, is manifestly played out. Finally shorn o[ ] power, the monarchy created by George V was left [ ] strings to its bow. First, as the family monarchy, it [ ] of our morality, the focus of national sentiment an[ ] ian of the British way of life. Second, as the font of [ ] and modernised honour system, it was the patron [ ] mover of public service and the voluntary sector.

Now, 90 years later, very little, frankly, is left [ ] The family monarchy was wrecked by the Diana af[ ] most of the second half of the 20th century, the vo[ ] was in full scale retreat before the burgeoning welf[ ] Health, schools and the arts were given state fundi[ ]

subject to increasing state control. Punitive tax rates all but destroyed the Victorian tradition of charitable giving. Altruism, which the new honours system of 1917 existed to reward, had been nationalised, just like coal or steel.

But at least the welfare state preserved the distinctive not-for-profit ethos of public service. At least it did until Margaret Thatcher. She was in love with business, the bigger the better, and tried to impose business values on the public sector. New Labour, with its love affair with markets, PFI, targets and managerialism, has only followed in her footsteps. The result has been to kill off the not-for-profit ethos of public service. Instead, in our world, business values and the cash nexus rule all.

Nevertheless, it remains as true as it always was that human beings are not only motivated by money. They may even, as with increasing numbers of our new rich, want to give it away in prodigious quantities. But if the government and Civil Service won't recognise this, who will? And who will encourage and honour those who do, and shape, co-ordinate and inspire their efforts? Here, surely, there is a role for the monarchy?

It is a role which, even as Prince of Wales, Charles has begun to fulfil. More is involved than in 1917. Then, the new Honours system only recognised an existing tradition of public service and charitable giving. Now, it's a question of re-inventing the wheel. Voluntary action must be revived, money, lots of it, found, and public opinion led.

'I don't want my children and grandchildren, or yours for that matter, saying to me, "Why didn't you do something when it was possible to make a difference and when you knew what was happening?"' Prince Charles has said.

With Charles, we have for the first time since Prince Albert in the 19th century, or the young George III in the 18th century, a royal patron who does aspire to lead the voluntary side of social life, who dares to talk of real, intellectual effort and eminence and, above all, who puts his money where his mouth is.

···

If the Prince's Trust can do all this, only imagine what the King's Trust could do

···

A recent example is the rescue of the Georgian time capsule, Dumfries House, a noble Georgian mansion, still furnished with the fixtures and fittings that were designed and made for it by the most eminent cabinet makers of the day. The state-funded heritage bodies were unable to save it, then, at the eleventh hour and only weeks before a sale that would have broken up the collection forever, Charles cut the Gordian knot. He saved the house and its contents by setting up an innovative mechanism to provide finance. A loan of £20 million will be paid off by the development of a model village in the Scottish lowlands. Conservation and high culture will be combined with the economic regeneration of a depressed area.

Charles has also brought a similar combination of high ideals and low cunning in the raising of money to the problems of the inner city and its benighted kids. It is a world a million miles from elegant Georgian interiors and one even more in need of the Prince's innovative approach.

<u>Trafalgar Battle Surgeon</u>, 2005

A leading member of the Prince's household describes this as charitable entrepreneurship. At its heart, there is a group of charities known as the Prince's Charities. The Prince raises their funding, some £110 million a year, and determines their principal area of activity. Most of them are leaders in their field. They venture into areas that others dare not and they blaze trails that other organisations, in particular state funded ones, willingly follow.

The outstanding example is the Prince's Trust. This helps disadvantaged young people into employment, becoming worthwhile members of society. Most of its clients have done badly at school, are poor or come from broken homes. Above all they are poor in aspiration. The Prince's Trust uses a variety of methods, from individual mentoring to outdoor adventure activities, to give them the confidence to help themselves. Its rate of success is striking and politicians, New Labour and newish Tory alike, strive to emulate it and to learn from it.

If the Prince's Trust can do all this, only imagine what the King's Trust could do. Is this the new role for the monarchy under Charles as it changes direction yet again in its 1,000-year-old history? Once the monarchy was the state, then it became the symbol of the state. Now, there is a moral vacuum left by the sell-out of the state to business values. Will King Charles step into the breach to nurture a new kingdom of the mind – spirit, culture and values? It is a destiny not unworthy of a 1,000-year-old throne.

Since my eight-year-old self watched the coronation of Elizabeth, the monarchy has managed to survive against the odds by doggedly sticking to tradition and duty. But now, as the state surrenders to big business and the cash nexus rules all, something new is required. Altruism, neighbourliness, the fruits of the spirit are as important as ever. Who will speak up for them, if not the Crown? Who indeed?

History teacher Jonty Ollif-Cooper, having spent some time in Channel 4's *The Edwardian Country House,* wonders how alike we are to the Edwardians

Dancing Towards the Icebergs

The Edwardian Country House, 2002

At first glance, Britain in 2008 could not differ more from the Britain of 1908. Our perception of Edwardian society is clear. Socially, Edwardians were laughably formal. Explicit rules of etiquette governed all situations an Edwardian lady or gentleman might encounter. They wore distinct clothes for every activity. Ladies spent up to five hours a day just changing, and to be seen outside without gloves and hat was quite unconscionable. In circles, old-fashioned even then, chair legs would be covered to avoid arousal (very sensible if you ask me). Edwardian pastimes, too, seem rather quaint. Backgammon was preferred to Pokémon. Their idea of a good time was tapestry making, croquet, or perhaps a stroll around the grounds of one's house. That is pretty tame compared with 'happy slapping' your class mates, and then posting the results on YouTube.

Politically too, Edwardians seem a world apart. Despite some reform, the electoral franchise was still tightly restricted to men of at least a little property. Political correctness was entirely alien to them: indeed discourse was openly racist, sexist and quite bombastically colonial. Many educated people were social Darwinists, arguing that Africans' poverty was proof of their genetic inferiority. Governing natives was, frankly, a bit of a chore: what Kipling bemoaned as The White Man's Burden.

Edwardian Britain's economy was also radically different. Heavy industry dominated: coal in Wales; steel in Sheffield; shipping in Scotland. In 1900 the Clyde built one in every five ships launched in the world. In the countryside, traditional farming predominated. Horses, not tractors, still drew bales along country lanes. This was a society without iPods, or BlackBerrys, space flight or atomic power. Most people lived in crowded tenements or rotting cottages without running water, electricity, or that mark of proper civilisation, the indoor lavatory.

Modern society is a million miles away from all that. Television, celebrity gossip, advertising and health and safety regulation mark our culture. Old codes of conduct have been swept away. Whalebone and starch are long gone. White tie and morning dress have all but disappeared. Instead we flaunt casual wear to all occasions, eschewing even suits and ties in favour of pre-distressed denim and scuffed trainers. We are self-doubting, organic, fairly traded, rainforest friendly, sustainably harvested softies. Edwardian Britain was ebullient, confident and successful. We, it seems, are not.

However, upon closer inspection, these rather crude stereotypes of our two societies do not stand up. There are some genuine differences across the century, of course. Technology has had an impact, obviously. The media holds more power in our society. We are genuinely much less formal, at least by traditional codes of etiquette. However, our two societies' similarities outweigh their differences.

For one thing, class persists. You do not have to be on Facebook to know that we mix with people of remarkably similar backgrounds to ourselves. Everyone is friends of friends. Although Edwardian society was socially ossified, so is ours. It remains the case that a clique of largely Oxbridge educated, southern grammar or public school alumni control today's society, just as they did in 1908 – even if,

Unlike Lord Salisbury, you are unlikely to become Prime Minister today with a fourth-class degree in classics. We too have servants, though perhaps we prefer to call them secretaries, cleaners or au-pairs rather than maids or footmen.

Moreover, we are infatuated with Edwardian culture. We delight in its novels, art and architecture. Just ask Merchant and Ivory. And politically, we are similar. Lloyd George would surely recognise today's issues of devolution, ter-rorism, the reform of the House of Lords, migration, overstretch of the armed forces and housing shortages on a 1912 order paper. Clearly we share more with the Edwardians than we might at first think.

However, equivalent parallels could easily be drawn with the late Victorians or Georgians, or indeed Elizabethans. Surely it is a truism to point out that all societies are both substantially different, and fundamentally the same. So, what was distinctive about the Edwardians?

What sets the Edwardians apart is what they were not. Edwardian society was curiously sandwiched between two great eras: the Victorian age and the First World War. Both cast a shadow: the first on the Edwardians' perception of them-selves; the other on ours. Lasting a mere decade, Edwardian society appears to us either as simply the bookend to the much grander 19th century, or as the last hur-rah of the old order before Paschendale: a joyous confection of extravagance, glory and innocence.

This fiction has entirely subsumed real Edwardian society. In fact, like post-war Britons, Edwardians shared our strong sense of following a British society greater than their own. Edwardians did not share that most Victorian value of progress'. Instead, unlike our rose-tinted retrospection, Edwardian society was uncertain, in flux, with a *fin de siècle* edge.

Just like us, Edwardians suffered terrorism (though theirs was Irish and feminist, not Islamic). Feminism and

Socialism led them, too, to bemoan the collapse of deference and antisocial behaviour. Like us, Edwardians thrilled to royal gossip or music hall performers who would now be equally at home on the sofa with Ant and Dec. They too had their Pete Dohertys and Tracey Emins in Oscar Wilde, or the Symbolist painters. They were as excited and terrified by Ruther-ford and Currie's atomic discoveries as we are by GM crops or cybernetics.

Just like us, Edwardians were entangled in Afghanistan and mired in their own expensive counterinsurgency, complete with its own moral outrages, against the Boers. South African concen-tration camps were their Abu Ghraib. The war left a nation obsessed with its physical collapse brought on by modern lifestyles, although for them the problem was not obesity, but physical deterioration. Forty per cent of volunteers for the Boer War

were rejected as unfit to serve. Far from the bombastic confidence of our memory, Edwardians actually saw themselves as enervated by luxury, fearful and over-stretched: in other words, rather like us.

No surprise then that perhaps the most famous event of the Edwardian era was the sinking of the *Titanic*. Sinking ships are not unusual. However, somehow the *Titanic* has lived on in the modern imagination, because it embodies what we now see as most distinctly Edwardian: a stratified society, encased in mighty tech-nology and incredible opulence, gliding obliviously towards calamity.

If the defining characteristic of the Edwardian era was of something on the turn, a society heading towards calamity, it may be that we have more in common with them than we can imagine. Perhaps future generations will look back on our long decades of post-war peace, prosper-ity and technology, and think of us as showing the same exuberant, wanton lack of foresight about our own impend-ing calamities, be they Chinese power or climate change. Perhaps, like the Edward-ians, we too are dancing gaily towards our own iceberg. But never fear. By the time we get there, all the icebergs will probably have melted.

You do not have to be on Facebook to know that we mix with people of remarkably similar backgrounds to ourselves

The Edwardian Country House, 2002

Jan Morris, the historian and travel writer whose work includes the seminal trilogy *Pax Britannica*, asks if we have overlooked the real cost of the British Empire

Paying the Price of Empire

The War of the World:
A New History of the 20th Century, 2006

Empire, 2003

'So long as we rule India,' declared Lord Curzon, surveying the kingdom of Great Britain in the early years of the 20th century, 'we are the greatest power in the world. If we lose it we shall drop straight away to a third rate power.' He was a prescient imperialist, and he was right. Half way through the century India gained its independence from Britain, and almost at once the immense construction of the British Empire disintegrated. One by one the imperial colonies were emancipated, and the self-governing dominions became states of their own. The legendary imperial fleets were dispersed, the imperial kings and captains lost their almost magical potency, and the British would never again be supreme among the Powers.

It was an object lesson, pundits declared, in the meaning of hubris – the condition of insolent pride that often preceded, so the ancients believed, the calamity of nemesis. But in my opinion the pundits were mistaken. Heaven knows there was insolence enough in the British pride of Empire, but it was tempered by the miseries of two world wars and if hubris necessarily preceded nemesis, it hasn't happened yet. The British have paid the price of Empire in subtler, sadder ways.

Even in the heyday of British imperialism there were those who doubted if the Empire was economically worth having – the command of resources had to be balanced against the cost of acquiring and protecting them. Far-flung colonies, too, were debatably profitable, and the expense of maintaining garrisons around the world and fleets in every ocean would become more burdensome as the decades passed.

As it turned out, the sceptics were half-right. There was a time, certainly, when the possession of the Empire had made

Britain rich, but the time was long ago, and by the end of the 20th century it was apparent that without an Empire, Great Britain Inc was at least as profitable as Pax Britannica. Other countries had overtaken Britain in an age of new technology and the kingdom was decidedly no longer 'The Workshop of the World', as it had loved to call itself. But the British found compensatory profit in intellectual, financial and service industries, and by then almost nobody attributed national problems to the decline of the Empire.

Anyway, the British public as a whole had never been hubristic. Empire was essentially an enthusiasm of the middle classes. Except at moments of heady triumphalism (Queen Victoria's jubilee, say) or dramatic poignancy (Rorke's Drift, the death of General Gordon), toffs and workers alike generally found the Empire rather a bore. A national joke said that King George V's reported last words, 'How goes the Empire?' were really, 'What's on at the Empire?', and by the time it all ended, with the handover of Hong Kong in 1997, there were few who shed sentimental tears over its passing.

So nemesis it certainly was not, as it seldom had been hubris. All the same, almost without knowing it, the British would pay heavily for their loss of Empire: for beyond all the flummery, the complacency and the self-deceit, the imperial experience really had made them, for a few generations, unique in the world. It was not the loss of power or prestige, not the Last Posts or the furling of the flags that affected this people. It was the subliminal realisation that they were no longer special.

In the 1930s most Britons thought they were best. They did not particularly want to rule the world, and many of them were embarrassed by imperialism's pomp and brazen pageantry; but on the whole they vaguely thought that their dominance of affairs was good for humanity, and was merely a reflection anyway of their organically superior qualities. Their laws, they were brought up to believe in those days, were the fairest and most just. Their countryside was the most beautiful. Their politicians were the least corrupt, their sportsmen the most athletic, their ships the biggest, their machines the most efficient, their customs the most interesting, their beliefs the most logical, their gardens the loveliest, their systems of government the most enlightened. Shakespeare was British, and so was Lord Nelson. In short, they generally assumed, they were *sui generis*.

They ruled, at that time, nearly a quarter of the world's land mass and a quarter of all its people, but the possession of Empire was not the direct progenitor of these delusions. They sprang, perhaps, from the island condition of the British, necessarily making them different from other nations. Empire was certainly no dampener, of course. They may not have thought much about it, but the merest glimpse of a world map, then so much of it emblazoned with the red of Britishness, was a fillip to their conceit. Their world-view was loaded with comforting assumptions. It occurred to few of them that German machinery might be just as good as theirs, French railways just as efficient, American industry far more productive and even Japanese scientists just as inventive.

The War of the World:
A New History of the
20th Century, 2006

It took time, and history, to persuade the British that they were only another European people after all, not particularly special, good at some things, poor at others, and relatively rarely the best.

For it is not the penalty of Empire itself that the British are now paying, but the penalty of imperial disillusionment. If this people was not generically imperialist, it had become intuitively imperial. The sensation had been instilled in them for generations – perhaps since the seminal Battle of Trafalgar, which gave them a command of the seas not merely strategic or commercial, but powerfully symbolical too. Nemesis never reached the British, but they were visited by that other destiny of the ancients, pathos – all too often blending with its parodic equivalent, bathos.

So their legacy of Empire has been a profound national disenchantment – with glory, with power, with success. The existence of the British Empire had been so subliminally

pervasive that when it died, there died with it a national instinct. Whether they were imperialist in their views, or radical pacifists, the British were sustained by a profound self-assurance which had undoubtedly sprung, whether they liked to admit it or not, from their nation's once pre-eminent status in the world – the red on the map, the flag that flew across a quarter of the globe. Even the most dedicated anti-imperialists among them were subject to its allure. Even the poet Wilfred Skawen Blunt, virulently opposed to the very idea of it, found himself moved by the majestic Britishness of Gibraltar:

At this door
England stands sentry. God! to hear the shrill
Sweet treble of her fifes upon the breeze,
And at the summons of the rock gun's roar,
To see her red coats marching from the hill!

When it all went, when the redcoats marched no more, the grand confidence of the British went too. It had been the enviable wonder of foreigners, but nowadays there is probably no country more neurotically unsure of its place in the world, of its very identity indeed, which had seemed so unassailable in the days when the sun never set upon its pastures. Open any British newspaper now, any day of the year, and you will find it abased in self-criticism. Where everything once seemed best, now nothing does. In half a century, since the last tragic splendours of World War II, which were the last splendours of the imperial spirit, too, the British have lost their belief in themselves.

It is their penalty for having had an Empire, and for giving it up. More debilitating still, perhaps, part of their penalty is guilt. Deeply ingrained in the British consciousness now is the assumption that their Empire was altogether bad. It is a blot on their escutcheon, they have been conditioned to think, like the blot of the Holocaust on the arms of Germany. The benevolent, diligent and creative aspects of Empire are forgotten: what is drummed into the heads of children and newspaper readers is the evil of it. The historical record of the British, which used to seem to their grandfathers so clean and so kind, is besmirched by an inescapable sense of shame, so that the historical story is told at best in satire, at worst in self-reproach.

This, then, is the profoundest forfeit that the British have paid for their imperial enterprise, and if it is a just forfeit in some ways (for who could now argue for the ideological merit of imperialism?), it is unjustly debilitating in others. The great good works of the British Empire have been largely forgotten, overwhelmed by knowledge of its faults – for example, the British role in the slave trade is constantly emphasised, the British role in its extinction scarcely understood.

And more subtly, as confidence has been sapped by the end of power, and self-esteem whittled away, so too has faded any sense of the Empire's grandeur. Part of the power of Empire in its heyday – which was also the heyday of the British nation itself – was its incongruous beauty. For better or for worse, the imperial experience could be inspiring: when the sad fascination left the bugle-calls of Empire, when there was no longer a thrill to the grey warships at sea, or the great trains speeding across the Indian plains, when the spectacles of British mastery could no longer excite the British themselves, some sense of purpose and fulfilment left the British psyche, and in long, tired instalments the price of Empire is paid.

Tony Robinson, actor, political campaigner and presenter of *Time Team*, recalls the creation of an unlikely hit and relishes putting out more post-dig reports than all the archaeology departments in all the English universities put together

Digging Deep

Time Team, from 1997

Time Team, from 1997

Sixteen years ago a conversation took place in the Little Chef on the Honiton bypass between Tim Taylor, an ex-school teacher turned video producer, and archaeologist Mick Aston from Bristol University. It went something like this:

> *Tim Taylor:* The trouble with archaeology is that it takes so bloody long.
> *Mick Aston:* Not necessarily. Nowadays archaeologists can run their gadgets over a field, and locate stuff it used to take us months to find.
> *Tim: (eagerly)* So how long would it take to do a little dig for television – a month?
> *Mick:* Less.
> *Tim: (beginning to twitch)* A week?
> *Mick:* Probably even less.
> *Tim: (slavering)* Three days?

And that is how one of the legendary Channel 4 programme proposals was born – archaeology in just three days! And as an afterthought…

> *Mick:* My mate Tony Robinson could be in it.
> *Tim:* What, Baldrick? Are you mad?

I can't imagine any other TV network responding positively to such a pitch, but this was Channel 4 in its early days, when it relished making quirky programmes for minority audiences and being a bit daft. It touted the idea round its various departments; even light entertainment tinkered with it for a few months. Eventually it landed on the desk of Karen Brown, who ran continuing education. Predictably the channel's education budget wasn't huge, but Karen took the plunge and commissioned a pilot.

The most successful Channel 4 factual programme at the time was *Treasure Hunt,* and our pilot attempted to be *Treasure Hunt II.* Clues written in wobbly, ancient writing were discovered nailed to church doors or shot unbidden out of photocopiers; archaeologists struggled furiously through cobweb-strewn tunnels; the presenter, with his long lank hair swirling round his head like a drug dealer in a storm, gasped with wonder at every rusty nail that appeared from the spoil heap. But despite this inauspicious start Channel 4 decided to commission a whole series.

Two fairly bloody years followed. Tempers flared, fists were banged on tables, geophysicists cried with frustration at the hotel bar. The basic problem was that there were two camps, the archaeologists and the programme makers; all perfectionists, all stubborn and all with different priorities. The archaeologists only ever wanted to shoot a scene once, the programme makers insisted on shooting it five or six times. The archaeologists wanted to dig slowly and carefully, the programme makers wanted action, excitement and a good story.

Over time though, these rows began to diminish. The two camps gossiped with each other, drank with each other and slept with each other – all deep, bonding experiences that helped them see the other side's point of view. Eventually we managed to create a mode of operation that still exists today. When we arrive at a site we genuinely don't know what we're going to find, we really do the archaeology in three days and we

Time Team, from 1997

don't bury anything in advance. The work is done to the highest standards, everything's properly recorded, and any finds are given to the local museum or county archaeologist.

Time Team was an unlikely hit. There was no sex or drugs or rock 'n' roll – at least not on screen. The participants were mostly middle-aged, and the few younger ones looked like they spent the rest of the week selling *The Big Issue* outside Tesco with dogs on string. Nevertheless, a hit it was, and a hit it still is. We have gone from four shows a year to six, then to eight and now thirteen. We've been commissioned to make spin-off series, peak-time documentaries, and to dig up the Queen's back garden. Yet though it has proved so consistently popular – indeed last year's was the most successful run yet – the response from the professional archaeology community has often ranged from lukewarm to ice-cold. I've never quite understood why. It's reliably reported that applications to universities to read archaeology have risen significantly because of its influence. It has kept major archaeological issues in the public eye, and our documentary strand – dealing with subjects like Iron Age hill forts, the 18th century English landscape and global warming in the Bronze Age – has regularly aired pretty arcane archaeology-related subjects in front of large audiences. Over the past fifteen years, we've also produced more than 150 full post-excavation reports about our sites, more than all the archaeology departments in all the English universities put together. But maybe that's part of the reason there's been antagonism from some academics, who've been a bit tardy producing reports of their own digs.

But is *Time Team* 'real'? Does it genuinely reflect what happens on an archaeological site? I think the current argument about authenticity on television is a pretty absurd one. Television is, by its nature, visual sleight of hand, every shot is deliberately constructed in order to fool the eye. You might as well criticise a conjurer for not using proper magic. Nevertheless, *Time Team* is closer to everyday reality than any other programme I've been involved with. We admit our cock-ups, air our disagreements and express our frustrations, all under the ruthless scrutiny of the television camera.

More important than authenticity though, is the pro-

Yet though it has proved so consistently popular – indeed last year's was the most successful run yet – the response from the professional archaeology community has often ranged from lukewarm to ice-cold

Our archaeologists aren't interested in looking good on television – as you can tell from their choice of clothes. Their only objective is to share with the public their excitement for digging around in old rubbish and making up stories about it. The programme may look like a shambolic romp involving half a dozen middle-aged hippies poking around in a big field not finding much, but a huge amount of thought, heart-searching, research and love is poured into each episode.

Last year our secret dread became reality when, after digging for three days in a field outside Manchester, we'd found absolutely nothing. But we did what we always said we'd do if such an eventuality arose; we brazenly transmitted the programme along with all the others.

As I came out of a sound studio in Berwick Street the morning after it had been shown, a bloke on one of the fruit and veg stalls called out that he'd seen it the previous night. My heart sank. Was he about to slag it off in typical cockney fashion in front of the entire market? 'What did you think?' I asked nervously. 'Lovely!' he replied. 'But we didn't find anything,' I insisted. 'I know,' he said, throwing me an apple. 'You buggers!'

Having taken part in Channel 4's *That'll Teach 'Em*, Henrietta Haynes talks to Daisy Leitch about life in a 1950s school, and draws some startling conclusions about our present-day education system

Henrietta's Teachings

That'll Teach 'Em, 2003

Now: Aged 20, student at the Trinity Music College, Greenwich

Daisy Leitch: How did you first find out about the show?

Henrietta Haynes: My mum found out about the show in the *Radio Times* and she really wanted me to do it. I was enthusiastic from the very start, as I'd never been that into normal school. Even though I had good grades, I hated it. I was sporty and creative and at my school it was all about exams, exams, exams. You just didn't learn that much. When I did my application form for the show I did it by hand and made it all creative.

Were you at all apprehensive before the show?

The auditions were really scary, there were hundreds of sixteen year olds all staring at each other thinking 'I want to be on telly.' Most of the interviews lasted five minutes but I was in there for half an hour talking to the producer. They got us down to 30 girls and 30 boys and then they had to wangle it down to fifteen. When I got told that I had got through I was happy and scared. I was like, 'what have I got myself into?' They told us a

list of what we could and couldn't bring but there was not that much information about what it would be like.

What things couldn't you have?

We weren't allowed to dye our hair, we had to all look the same. You were allowed to take in one extra item. I took a teddy bear but later they took it away because they found out I had hidden things in the bear's dress and knickers!

What were your first few days in the 1950s school like?

At the time I was going out with a boy called Chris. It was upsetting not being able to see him. We'd been going out together for maybe about a year at that point and I'd seen him every day, so I missed him. He was my best friend really. The most upsetting thing was not being able to ring home. We were only allowed letters once a week. My mum had thyroid cancer at the time so that was hard. She was having operations while I was in there and that was very hard. It was isolating not knowing anyone or what was expected of you.

What did people find the hardest being in the 1950s school?

People missed the home comforts. We were only allowed one shower a week. You know for a girl at a certain time of the month it's just not too nice. They were really long days, because you never stopped, you were never alone and it was physically a very small place. One classroom, one hall. It was physically intensive.

How different was the school from your grammar school?

For me the experience wasn't of a reality TV show. To me it was historical and accurate and about education. We worked very hard. I've never worked so hard in my whole life! School work went on from eight in the morning until seven at night after prep. I went to a grammar school normally so I was used to school being quite strict. But the King's School was stricter, for example we had 'the six inch rule'– that you could never be closer than six inches to a boy! But at my grammar school you would still get sent home if you had the wrong shade of blue socks. I found that trivial. At KS at least they gave you the uniform and you didn't have to worry about that kind of stuff.

Did you learn a lot in the four weeks at the 1950s school?

I think I learnt more than through the whole rest of my education! I learnt so much, and lots of the other people who did it say the same.

Education today doesn't link up. Now you get detailed knowledge about a few things, but in the Fifties you had to learn around the subject, they always asked, 'Why?'

Today we are too focused on exams and there's no thought involved. You can be stupid and still get four As at A-Level. I know lots of people who've done that. In the Fifties you had to read between the lines and apply your learning. That's definitely the case in English and history, but it was even true for maths. It was much more a visual type of learning and more thorough. I felt really motivated at KS. The teachers were so inspiring and I had lots of respect for them. The lessons were engaging.

That'll Teach 'Em, 2003

Do you think your experience was authentic 1950s schooling?

I felt like I had literally time travelled! I really couldn't cope with normal life when the four weeks were over.

Do you think the experience has had a lasting effect on you?

When I started back at normal school in September I wasn't ready for it at all. It must have taken six months to get back to normality. I refused to watch TV. I didn't want to sleep in my room with all my things. Today sixteen-year-olds have too many things. I was so materialistic before I went to the Fifties school.

I'm definitely a different person now. I'm less selfish and more motivated; I realised that you have to do things for yourself. At my normal school I felt that I was learning things just for the school's reputation. It was like a sausage factory for A-grades. The Fifties school was stressful and you did have to work hard, but you really appreciated your time off, and felt like you had actually achieved stuff.

We had half an hour of free time before bed, when we reverted to being about ten, playing snakes and ladders and other games. In the Fifties you didn't have to be adult-like at sixteen, you could still be a child. It made me realise that at sixteen you are still a child, you still like childish things.

I think now that designer clothes and that kind of stuff don't matter so much. It really changed me. Actually it made me want to take over the country. I feel cheated by the government and this country, I feel cheated out of an education. We're so confined by assessment goals, the teachers are miserable and that makes them uninspiring. If the teachers work hard, you work hard back. I think I would have gone off the rails if I hadn't done it. Most sixteen-year-olds only care about their own self-image and how other people see them. They don't care about themselves, only about the media. They are not rounded individuals.

What did you think of it when you watched the show?

I haven't watched the show. For me it's real. I know that TV's all edited and skewed. I want to remember it myself. My friends watched it and thought it was really funny, and that I was just myself. There was some jealousy at school, there was some bitching after I came back. That's just girls. Going back to school was a real reality check back to 21st century sixteen-year-old life. I loved boarding at King's School, it was so safe and so warm. When I got back I just wanted to have my parents come and tuck me in. I could have gone to boarding school, my brother and my dad did, and I wish I had now.

Were there some things that you thought your grammar school should have learnt from the Fifties education system?

There were lots of sports at the Fifties school, I felt so fit and healthy. I lost about half a stone. We played hockey, did cross-country running and swimming. The days were so long. I think that education today lacks the element of competing against one another. Some people are better at things than others. I don't see what's wrong with that. Things are too politically correct today; everyone has to be too equal. Competition brought us together at KS, rather than just playing to the lowest common denominator, and waiting all the time for the people who are not getting things in the classroom.

Tony Blair tried to get rid of grammar schools – but why can't we have clever people and not so clever people? Some people tried to say that all the participants on the show were 'posh' – but they weren't, they were just clever. It seems like you can't excel at anything today. The teaching level was much higher in the Fifties; the way they spoke to you made me see what I could do. If you didn't understand something in class you had to go and figure it out yourself afterwards. It helped me to see my potential.

What do you think we should do to improve our education system?

I think they should raise the bar tenfold. People who can't do the exams shouldn't do them; what's the point in always lowering the bar? Out of 120 girls in my year at school no one got a C at A-Level. There are so many more things on the syllabus, like carpentry GCSE. It's as if everyone has to have the same qualifications. I'm not saying there's anything wrong with doing carpentry, but maths GCSE and carpentry GCSE are not the same thing.

The consensus on the show was that our real education was disappointing compared with the Fifties one. There are too many assumptions made about students and they aren't treated as individuals. In our system you get stuck too soon in one path. You have to choose GCSE subjects at thirteen or fourteen and A-Levels at fifteen or sixteen. It's too quick. In the Fifties at least your personal life could develop more slowly, even if the pressure was intense at school. You were allowed to be a child for longer. Today there are just so many pressures on a sixteen-year-old. Family is much less important and you have to rely more on your friends.

In the Fifties science was so fun, the learning was much more visual. They showed you: this is a liver, this is a heart. Yeah, art and music were not the main focus of exams, but exams weren't the main focus either. It was about education.

That'll Teach 'Em, 2003

The Pink Triangle

Society's view of homosexuality has changed so
radically in the last 25 years, it's almost impossible
to credit the seismic shock of TV's first lesbian kiss
on *Brookside* or the outrage triggered by the brazen
Queer as Folk. Where once Channel 4 was alone in
urging its audience to be *Out on Tuesday* now every
soap has its gay story line. There is still debate
about negative stereotyping of gay men and wom-
en on television – witness the response to Kevin
Elyot's film, *Clapham Junction,* or the row about
the use of the word 'poof' in *Big Brother* – but it is
conducted within a supportive mainstream consensus which television, and Channel 4 in particular, has been instrumental in informing.

A Box at
the Opera?
Patrick Gale

Patrick Gale

A Box at
the Opera?
Patrick Gale

Brookside, 1993

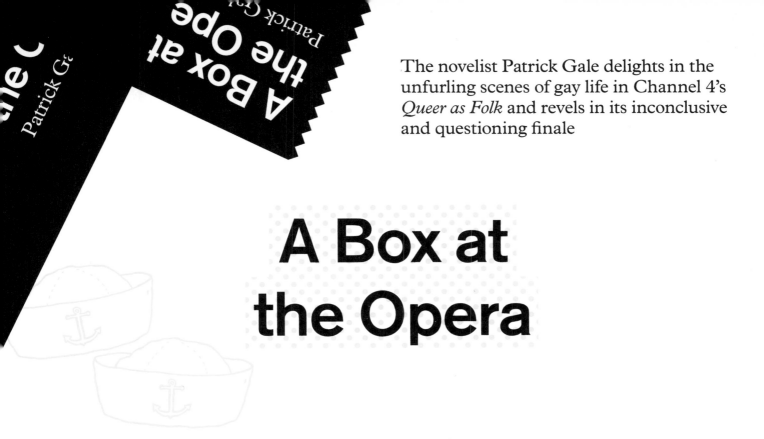

A Box at
the Ope
Patrick G
A Box at
the Ope
Patrick Ga

The novelist Patrick Gale delights in the unfurling scenes of gay life in Channel 4's *Queer as Folk* and revels in its inconclusive and questioning finale

A Box at the Opera

Being a gay television viewer can be a twitchy experience. Most of the time you find yourself so unrepresented on the small screen that you lurch between being pathetically grateful for any gay programming that comes along (and feeling honour bound to watch it lest your ungrateful lack of interest halt any gay programming in future) and being indignant that said gay broadcasting is distorted, unrepresentative and/ or embarrassingly crap. Gay television viewers, like generations of gay filmgoers before them, become adept from childhood both at projecting themselves into the unremittingly hetero scenarios before them and at hungrily falling on and analysing-to-death the merest suggestion that some situation is not quite as straight as it seems. Such is even the average level of skill at this kind of codified viewing that above-the-parapet programming for and about gay people can strike its target

Queer as Folk was more celebratory than erotic

audience as tasteless. There's also an old established tradition of gay claiming: seizing on and claiming a product that wasn't perhaps meant for us initially. Thus one finds a show that is merely camp, like the (marvellous!) Stephanie Beacham vehicle, *Connie*, being cherished by gay and lesbian audiences at the expense of shows overtly aimed at them.

I was lucky enough to grow up in the Seventies, when terrestrial channels still screened several subtitled films a week and thus shooed in all manner of gay and lesbian material by Fassbinder and friends under a late night, highbrow, parents-safely-asleep banner. Without scrabbling for my gay broadcasting encyclopaedia, however (yes there is one, *Broadcasting It* by Keith Howes, hot pink, published by Cassell, riveting stuff), I can remember only a handful of overtly gay programmes before *Queer as Folk*.

First the dramas. As early as 1977, the surreal ABC comedy series, *Soap*, featured Billy Crystal as a wildly confused (now he's transgender, now he's bi) young gay father. So what if he had bad hair and no boyfriend? He was shown in the centre of a more or less loving family and was cuter and considerably less camp than John Inman. At the opposite

dramatic pole were two one-offs, *The Naked Civil Servant* (1975) from Thames, in which John Hurt was saintly and safely effeminate (and single) as Quentin Crisp, and the BBC's *Coming Out* (1979) which offered Anton Rogers and Nigel Havers in the least sexually-compatible romantic pairing since Rock Hudson and Doris Day. Altogether more cheering, if marginal, were the nice gay couple who lived upstairs from the Anna Raeburn character (played by Maureen Lipmann) in the LWT sitcom *Agony*. These actually made it through three series from 1979 to 1981 before one of them lost his teaching job, got depressed and killed himself and even then, hey, his bereaved partner found a nice, blond Australian replacement. One does not mention Stephen in *Dynasty*.

As for the non-fiction, those brave attempts to cover gay current affairs, all that sticks in the mind are LWT's *Gay Life* (1981), whose two series were aired on weekend slots so late that no-one with friends or a sex life saw them (I had neither at the time) and whose straight commentary smacked unfortunately of the nature documentary (young, radical lesbians in their natural habitat etc) and *Gaytime TV* (1995-9).

Gaytime, BBC's outrageously tardy acknowledgment of its gay and lesbian licence fee payers, was a great improvement, having toothsome gay and lesbian presenters (Rhona Cameron, the improbably named Bert Tyler-Moore and Richard Fairbrass) and a tongue firmly in its cheek (fitness workouts with porn star Mark Anthony and a live torch song to play out each episode). However, its dayglo palette and relentless cheerfulness verged on Teletubbydom.

scabrously working class gorgon and a no less egotistical, permanently 'resting' gay actor. Where Harvey's West End success, *Beautiful Thing*, had been heart-warming in its portrayal of a gay teenager finding his way, *Gimme Gimme Gimme* was deliriously cruel, and so wilfully offensive as to make *Absolutely Fabulous* look thoughtful. The other 1999 show was Channel 4's *Queer as Folk*. Comparing them is pointless, since the formal conventions of studio-based sitcom make it a dramatic

ITV detective show, *Touching Evil* and period drama, *The Grand*), *Queer as Folk* set out to shatter gay stereotypes and to shake up liberal complacency as much as tabloid homophobia. (That the impossible working title, *Queer as Fuck* should have been rounded down into the cosily northern *Queer as Folk*, as in there's nowt so, was a neat indication of the limits set on Davies' trailblazing.)

Queer as Folk is about two men and a schoolboy on the gay scene in Manchester. The men, Vince and Stuart, have known each other since they were fourteen and are now nearly 30. Stuart, played by Aidan Gillen and a quantity of hair wax, is a puckish, Irish man-whore in PR, consumed with a self-love that can only be bolstered by his ability to have any man he wants, of whatever persuasion. His best mate, Vince, a delicious performance by Craig Kelly, is a type all gay men recognise yet which had never received much publicity: the gay man who is actually rather crap at being gay, who doggedly goes clubbing because that's what everyone does but who only ever manages to pick up weirdos because of his social awkwardness, and who would actually rather spend a quiet night in with his encyclopaedic collection of *Doctor Who* tapes.

In 1999, like the proverbial buses, two assertively gay series came along in quick succession

In 1999, like the proverbial buses, two assertively gay series came along in quick succession but could hardly have been more different. One, written by playwright Jonathan Harvey for the BBC, was a sitcom as conventional in its format as it was unconventional in its material. *Gimme Gimme Gimme* gave us Kathy Burke and James Dreyfuss as the loveless flat-sharers from Hell, a deluded,

closed circuit, as far removed from a character-led drama series as Punch and Judy is from Ibsen. But in their way each raised the benchmark for how much gayness could be screened in our front rooms without moral disorder ensuing?

Written by Russell T. Davies (now a national treasure, thanks to his ballsy resuscitation of the *Doctor Who* franchise but then known only for his work on the

Hollyoaks, 2007

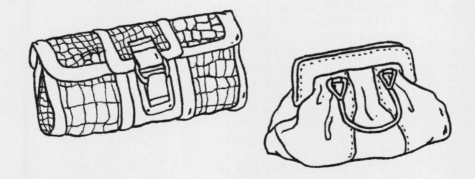

The schoolboy, Nathan, is erupting out of the closet and onto Canal Street at fifteen and manages to lose several different kinds of virginity to Stuart on his first night out. Nathan confuses hormones with attachment and convinces himself he's in love with Stuart; while Vince, of course, is in love with Stuart but is never going to find the assertiveness to do anything about it. Davies also throws into the mix a lesbian couple who have just become a family, thanks to Stuart's sperm donation, Vince's outrageous single mother, who's as much a fixture on the scene as her boy, and the fact that Stuart isn't out at home, Vince isn't out at work and Nathan is hell-bent on outing himself at school and running away if his parents won't accept him.

By ticking so many issue boxes Davies ran the danger of political correctness – but not for long because he thumbed his nose at just as many liberal expectations. There was no cosily middle-class gay couple, apart from the outrageously respectable suburban lesbians. At least which even my mother would have learnt that rimming has nothing to do with teacups, the tabloids worked themselves into a lather and made it sound as though the series was darkly pornographic.

In fact, as made clear from the outset by the perky marimbas of Murray Gold's theme music, *Queer as Folk* was more celebratory than erotic. Certainly it celebrated the ease with which any gay man in a city of any size can get laid, but it also celebrated gay friendship. Gay men *are* good at friendship, historically they've had to be to help themselves and their networks survive. This series dared to suggest that the non-sexual friendships between gay men are perhaps more to be prized than any pseudo-hetero domestic bliss they might find with a steady partner. It dared to suggest that sex, rendered freely available through a commercially regulated scene, might be pursued as a kind of sport, liberated from any ideal of emotional fulfilment. And it portrayed steady relationships as inherently middle aged and unsexy.

but as the series unfurled and Sarah Harding's more intimate direction took over from Charles McDougall's brasher approach, it emerged that Stuart and Vince's hedonism was not being defended but questioned. Triumphalist at first, Stuart emerges as a victim of the scene, his good qualities muffled by superficiality and easy narcissism. Both he and Vince are challenged by the plot, the one to recognise how much his friend means to him, the other to have the courage to be who he is and say what he wants. And yes, it's a bit depressing that they should finally come together on the podium of some naff club rather than daring to grow up and move on. But where else to go? A quiet table for two? A box at the opera? I hardly think so.

Superficially there was no searching for love. There was not even a whiff of high culture. These were three gay blokes looking for a shag

superficially there was no searching for love. There was not even a whiff of high culture. These were three gay blokes looking for a shag. And then perhaps another one. There was anonymous sex in loos, but no mention of Aids or even STDs. Somebody died, with shocking suddenness, from taking drugs, but plenty of others took them and simply had a good time (and more shagging) as a result, and one of them even got himself (briefly) a boyfriend at the funeral.

The two strongest female characters, Vince's mum, Hazel, played with relish by *Coronation Street* veteran Denise Black, and Donna, Nathan's best friend at school, played like a latterday Rita Tushingham by Carla Henry, personified the show's generous ethos, understanding all, forgiving (nearly) all and giving the little shaggers their blessing with just a glint of envy. Goaded by the deliberately shocking first episode, by the end of

The most realistic portrayals of gay men tend to be in British soaps where, like most gay people, they live lives of supreme ordinariness, vastly outnumbered and overshadowed by their straight neighbours. Adam and Ian on *The Archers* are perfect in their imperfections and dullness (and now that I'm civilly partnered with a Cornish farmer, I can at last find my life reflected in at least a small bit of the BBC's output.) Who-buys-the-cat-litter realism and the faithful representation of minorities are not the stuff of post-watershed entertainment, however, and the abiding achievement of *Queer as Folk* was to entertain and intrigue even while raising urgent questions – like homophobia in schools – that have yet to receive adequate political solutions nearly a decade later.

The show's gaudy mythologising of Manchester's gay scene might have seemed smugly unquestioning at first,

Queer as Folk, 1999

It Started
With a Kiss

Bidisha

The novelist and critic
Bidisha analyses lesbian
love on television

It Started With a Kiss

When it comes to sex objects, we all have our type. Mine's tough, cheekbones, deep voice, wiry with muscles and a ton of primal gym-toned rage. Think Linda Hamilton as the ultimate avenging warrior mum in *Terminator 2*, who made my heart pound obscurely fifteen years ago (and still does).

<u>Out on Tuesday</u>, 1989

So a small-screen smooch by two Laura Ashley models called Beth and Margaret near the UPVC front door of a standard semi was never going to do it for me. Still, that famous *Brookside* kiss broke the unspoken anti-dyke TV injunction and achieved the stunning victory of letting straight people know, (a) that lesbians existed, and (b) they were even quite nice, sympathetic and not offensive to behold. And for that patronage the lesbians of the world are humbly thank-

ful to the men who wrote, produced and directed the scene. That kiss was going to herald a new age in mainstream TV, when lesbians would be depicted as ordinary people living ordinary lives on ordinary streets, above the rotting remains of their abusive dads.

Brookside pointed out something simple yet fundamental: that lesbians are human beings, not monsters, castrators, hysterical self-haters, twisted sisters or sadistic matrons

Brookside pointed out something simple yet fundamental: that lesbians are human beings, not monsters, castrators, hysterical self-haters, twisted sisters or sadistic matrons. Which is hardly radical; we shouldn't be grateful to writers for finally showing the respect they ought to have been showing in the first place. And yet where else in the mainstream is lesbianism freely available? Porn, actually. In mainstream pornography, pseudo-

lesbian moves are performed obediently by straight women for the pleasure of a male watcher. In straight porn, lesbianism is a way for women to get men's attention; porn lesbians are men's geishas. *Brookside's* simple depiction of a relationship between two average women was,

though a long time coming, a humane and socially integrated enterprise. Apart from the surprise value of the kiss/realisation itself, these fictional women's lives weren't exploited for further titillation – or no more than any new young soap couple's.

But that was thirteen years ago. It turned out that the kiss was an isolated point in the development of straight viewers' consciousness and lesbians' recognition within the mainstream.

Sugar Rush, 2005

requirements for superheroism already mark out a character as rare, set apart, not ordinarily found in society. Where are the lesbians with jobs, families, thoughts, ambitions, feelings, challenges, daily joys and triumphs, going about life just like anyone else? How far have we really moved from the limitations of yore?

make ideal popcorn viewing. And yet the thinness of the conceit and the cheapness of the look are saved by Julie Burchill's signature bite and fearlessness, her affection for her characters and the sense that the plot could tip towards Sapphic anarchy at any moment. It's a far cry from the neurotic, masochist self-sacrifice of the

Where are the lesbians with jobs, families, thoughts, ambitions, feelings, challenges, daily joys and triumphs, going about life just like anyone else?

None of this, you could say, particularly matters; if there's a thriving and specifically lesbian artistic community, history and culture, then who needs the validation of a white, male, patriarchal, heterosexual (etcetera) dominant culture? Yet it's surprising, given the way society itself has developed, that we haven't seen a corresponding, non-stereotypical mainstreaming of lesbianism within televised culture. We have the brightness and talent of Rhona Cameron and Sue Perkins in reality – and yet, perversely, fiction is still playing catch-up.

Out on Tuesday, 1989

Viewers looking for decent lesbian characters in TV and film are still reduced, as so often, to reading between the lines, snatching at the odd hint, clue, moment, glance – even Agatha Christie's splendid Miss Marple has undergone a lesbian re-reading. With the honourable exceptions of Willow and Xena, the iconic, larger-than-life dykons – Ripley, G.I. Jane, Trinity, Janeway, whoever – are not actual lesbians within their narratives. They're lesbian icons, but only subtextually; and they are straight women's icons at the same time, possessing strength, intelligence, charismatic power, independence and resourcefulness. You could say that it's easier to create a sci-fi/action/fantasy lesbian superhero because the

The answer is, not far. Lesbians are discriminated against in the way that women have always been discriminated against: by being frozen out. When they do feature, the characterisations used commonly to demean women in general are intensified further when writers depict lesbians in particular. It cuts a few different ways:

First, there's Demon Dykes: The Dark Side. Here, lesbians are penis-envying, bitter, randy, mad, predatory, jealous bitches (if not actually full-on killers as in *Single White Female*) and becoming one is a sure route to brutalisation, violence and a coarsening of the psyche. Think Zoe in *Emmerdale* or Judi Dench rewritten as the ultimate emotional leech in the adaptation of *Notes on a Scandal*. None of these stray far from the dour nightmare scenarios of *Prisoner: Cell Block H* and *The Killing of Sister George*.

Second, there's Girls' Girls: Fluffy Fun, in which the objectifying porno-depiction of lesbianism is brought to the fore – hello, Sharon Stone in *Basic Instinct*. Female homosexuality is a pretty, delicious, minor thing to be nibbled experimentally like a cherry on a passing fruit plate, easily discarded when the meaty main course comes along – think Naomi in *Eastenders*. In *Footballers' Wives* the Girls' Girl is camp, fab and ultimately meaningless, while teen Girls' Girls are powerless sex objects for wanking men to enjoy, as in *The O.C*, for instance. *Sugar Rush* is an interesting show to mention here, because on the surface it seems to conform to this kind of template. The pocket-sized cuteness of the actresses and their picturesque, apolitical adventures

ultimate lesbian self-realisation text of yesteryear, *The Well of Loneliness*.

Finally, there's Don't Bother Me, I'm Busy: The Administrative Lesbian, with her sensible hairdo, good degree, pleasant face and elegant wardrobe. The Administrative Lesbian is a brilliant role model for women everywhere, but there's one catch: a high-flying job, demeanour, education and outfit are all attained at the expense of simple, sexy enjoyment. The Administrative Lesbian might run a mega-million-pound company but, poor thing, she never has a laugh. Remember that early series of *Bad Girls*, where the clever new governor battled sexual harassment and her own burgeoning lesbian feelings? Remember the po-faced professional lesbian couple in the otherwise brilliant *Queer as Folk*? It's unlikely that you do; they were the ones having babies and dutifully marrying volatile migrant workers for visa purposes while the boys got to have a lot of actual cocksucking fun. You wouldn't want to meet those lesbians, except to get a recipe for a tofu salad off them, because they were so boring.

Out on Tuesday, 1989

<u>Sugar Rush</u>, 2005

At the risk of sounding like the dullest social worker ever (dull enough, perhaps, to be given a role in *Queer as Folk*), much still remains to be done. The mistake *Queer as Folk* made was to think that 'positive representation' meant that lesbians must conform to a policeman's idea of the ideal plaintiff in a rape trial: professional, teetotal, upstanding, a woman who pays her taxes, contributes to charities, never steps out of line and finds total fulfillment in motherhood. What it *really* means is that characters are depicted with integrity, authenticity and completeness. To achieve that, lesbians must take up the pen and producers must employ them. None of the mingled misogyny, homophobia, voyeurism and sheer giggling puerility will go away unless the people who create the roles are themselves operating from a position of political awareness, respect for women, respect for lesbians and a good old-fashioned insight into what they're writing about, leavened with the TV virtues of wit, concision and fluidity. The foregrounding of lesbian desire and lesbian relationships only has validity when it is described by someone who's experienced it. That is why the adaptations of the novels *Oranges are Not the Only Fruit*, *Portrait of a Marriage*, *Tipping the Velvet* and *Fingersmith* have been such achievements: they recreate the work of supremely gifted authors who write with insider confidence and mastery.

In a way, America is leading the movement towards the belated establishment of lesbian power in film and TV. Films like indie classic *Go Fish*, *Watermelon Woman*, the lesbian-lite *Desert Hearts* and *But I'm a Cheerleader*, *Boys Don't Cry* and *High Art* and series like the overwhelmingly successful *The L Word* (although that too is problematic given the sheer wealth, vapidity, glamour and femininity of the cast) have given creators like Rose Troche, Guinevere Turner,

For reasons of finance and the organisation of the industry, among other things, these achievements would be hard to replicate in Britain. But it's not impossible. Those at the top of the UK television and film industries themselves – the execs, the moneybags, the commissioners – must dump their bigotry and realise that there's a unified will among audiences for decent viewing and a pool of talent determined to find an outlet. It's a change worth forcing, and for that we need a generation of lesbian creators to step up and serve. There's no glory in being a token joke in someone else's storyline; it's time for a revolution.

The Administrative Lesbian might run a mega-million-pound company but, poor thing, she never has a laugh

Ilene Chaiken and Lisa Cholodenko dominion within the mainstream. Ditto the success of Ellen De Generes and Rosie O'Donnell. They took a while to come out, against real opposition, but it didn't slow them down.

Nicky Haslam, international decorator and social columnist, parses the past and present language and culture of camp

Notes on the New Camp

So Graham Norton, 1998

So Graham Norton, 1998

In the beginning, it was the 'thing', rather than the 'word'. So when, how, why, did this near-indefinable phenomenon become more than a concept and get given a handle? How strongly was anyone aware of its presence? Had it existed for centuries? Susan Sontag suggested in her seminal essay of 1961 – when camp, as we think of it, was a mere debutante in its flamboyant life cycle – that Louis XIV's Versailles, by dint of its elaborate taming of nature, was camp. If so, it opens up the possibility that agriculture itself is camp; and that maybe for first turning the wilderness and forests into Campo di Fiori or Champs Elysee, the Romans or Goths should be handed the palm for camp's nomenclature.

It would follow therefore, that buildings are camp, as are clothes, religion, science – in fact, all human life, all art, all thought, all intellect, is camp. Well, I wouldn't be surprised; except for the fact that the Complete Oxford English Dictionary gives, baldly, and long before any reference to rows of tents, the word's first meaning as 'All-masculine'. Do admit, as Nancy would say.

William Gaunt, writing *The Aesthetic Adventure* in 1945, never uses the word camp, even though reminding us that Oscar Wilde's lectures in America were entitled *The Value and Character of Handicrafts*, and *House Decoration*. Janet Flanner, Paris living-and-loving columnist for *The New Yorker* in the flamboyant inter-war years doesn't hint at camp's self-evident prevalence, even when sublimely portraying such icons of the genre as Elsie Mendl, Josephine Baker, and Mlle Schiaparelli.

As late as 1954, Cecil Beaton, in *The Glass of Fashion*, a kind of *catalogue raisonne* with knobs on by and about the epitomes of campness, seems utterly unaware of the existence of the word, the 'thing', the attitude, though Antonia Fraser, who ghosted the book for Beaton, tells me that the first time she came across the word was in Angus Wilson's novel, *Hemlock & After* written a couple of years earlier.

This jibes with my earliest memory of campness, the waiters at the Bicyclette in Lower Belgravia and La Popote d'Argent in Marylebone whom, being moonlighting chorus boys to a man, behaved as much as possible like the two Hermiones, Gingold and Baddeley in their *echt* camp revues. These revered ladies' barbed brilliance was soon to be manfully mirrored by the two most magical drag artistes ever, Rogers and Starr, whose new shows, staged in a tiny theatre in Notting Hill, were as eagerly awaited as the openings of *My Fair Lady* or *West Side Story*.

Within months, such subtle nuances had broadened, encouraged by the nasal twangs of Hugh Paddick and Kenneth Williams, or the sultry slur of Fenella Fielding in *Valmouth*, Sandy Wilson's exemplary camp musical, into that *lingua franca* of vadas and riahs and ecafs, perfected by that weird assortment of 'girls' – Scotch Agnes, The West One, The Fabulous Vous, Carlotta and Babs – that peopled the court of Geoffrey Bennison, doyen of Pimlico Road antiquaires whose drag was made by Eddie (The man with the Golden Trumpet) Calvert's mother.

But what is sent up must come down. So, rare, refined, camp has come down with a thud, to be joined at the hip to her common ugly sister Kitsch. The trouble, as with anything once rare and refined, is that it's gone mainstream; almost everything

So Graham Norton, 1998

Pockets of true camp still exist
Newly created peers choose the campest names; you can't beat Lord Adonis
A.N. Wilson's lightness of delivery, so subtly camp you hardly notice it, has a genuine whiff of Beardsley
A.A. Gill deeply yearns to be camp; he's never out of a tent in some far-flung hell-hole, churning out sentences of more complex campness than Gertrude Stein and Ronald Firbank combined
Bread and Butter letters are camp, cream laid by Samantha Cameron
Is knowledge camp now?
Is camp now equated with gay? It shouldn't be, necessarily
Camp is antithetical to fact
Tea is camp, but heavens! How camp was Camp Coffee
Rugger is camp, though the Beautiful Game isn't
Cricket stopped being camp with the end of the Eton vs. Harrow match
Cliff Richard and Cilla Black are National Trust camp sites
Memorial services are camp, especially with an address by Christopher Gibbs
Wags were camp, but then so is all sport, provided we lose
This is the camp of camps! Princess Michael has just rung me up to ask me to tea with Madonna!

is quasi-camp, with banal double entendres, bad enough in the actually gay but far worse when taken up by heterosexuals.

The media, blameworthy as always in making everything déclassé, has unleashed a host of neo-camp presenters; first there was Brucie, then Dale and Graham, and Stephen Fry – horribly smugly camp, but right in noting that modern German is very camp, a mobile is a handi, pronounced hendi – and now Russell and Walliams. But even these seemingly straight ones purposely talk and act – and not just on the box – like, as Dominic Dunne would put it, pink hair nets.

Magazines print reams of pictures of people who aim at iconic campness. Posh, with her relentless lack of humour in any photo, her aggressive leg pout, has none of that essential wry charm that constitutes camp, while the evident self-belief that she is a stylish beauty makes Nancy Del'Olio a parody of it. Camp and Kitsch are sometimes joined by Dainty. Rita Konig suggests you buy an antique teacup to measure your washing powder.

The established echelons of camp are changing. Art is no longer camp, but a business, featuring taut-featured hedge fund wives grimly stomping around Freize snapping up 'pieces'. Rock stars used to be subtly camp, but now it's rappers with their crotch rather than tit emphasis, their real bling rather than rhinestones, who are the camp showgirls of the moment. In the past, English bishops were camp if somewhat dour. Now, Rowan Williams positively takes the camp out of Cantuar though one hears that, when in Rome rather than the Vatican, *il Papa* wears Prada, the little devil. And a few weeks ago, in New York, the charming young Hassidic Jew at whose counter I was buying a camera, started asking me out of the blue about Diana Vreeland. Courtiers used to be sexlessly camp, but now they make *marriages blanches*.

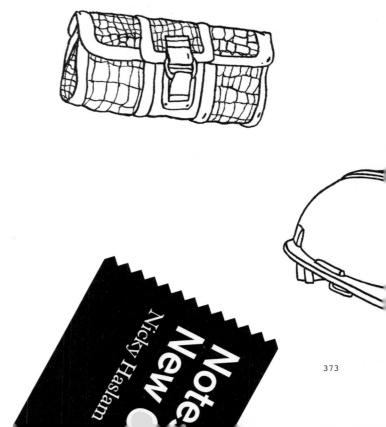

Tales of the City, 1993

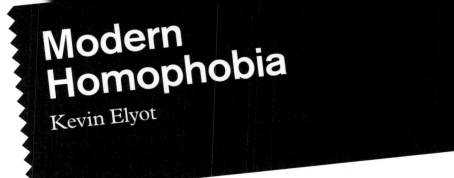

Kevin Elyot illuminates some of the darker issues surrounding his 2007 Channel 4 drama *Clapham Junction*

Modern Homophobia

At the reception after the civil partnership ceremony in my play, *Clapham Junction*, Will (played by Richard Lintern) tells the guests how he and Gavin met one summer's night sixteen years before on Hampstead Heath. 'But now,' he says, 'we've stepped out of the shadows and into the light, declaring our love for all to witness.' Although this was cut from the film in the last few days of the edit, it stands as a simple statement of fact: that in the past few decades, huge progress has been made in society's stumbling acceptance of its large gay minority.

I was brought up in Birmingham in the Fifties and Sixties, yet had a relatively

Queer as Folk, 1999

easy time of it as far as my sexuality was concerned. I can't remember ever having suffered at the hands of bullies, and by the age of fifteen I was enjoying sex with boys and men. This was about a year prior to the 1967 Sexual Offences Act, which partially decriminalised homosexuality, but our law-breaking libidos weren't deterred.

I arrived in London in the Seventies. At that time there were still a few gay establishments, in upper rooms around Soho, I seem to recall, leftovers from a more repressed age where you'd have to ring a doorbell to gain access. But these were fast being superseded by the brazen cockiness of clubs such as Heaven, a regular haunt which, on many nights, in so many ways, lived up to its name. Gay London, with its clubs, cottages, commons and heath, was a playground. Then in the 1980s, with a sickening, deadly thud, Aids brought the party to an end.

It took several years, and much pain and grief, for gay society to regroup, but regroup it did, with perhaps more confidence and a more positive outlook than ever before. The appetite for excitement tinged with danger prevails once again, to the extent in some quarters of even shunning the notion of safe sex.

With the advances in HIV/Aids treatment, undreamt of in the mid-Eighties, and the great legislative strides that have been made towards equality since the 1967 Act (the gradual equalisation of the age of consent, the repeal of Section 28, the Civil Partnership Act), together with a less covert presence in the media, there is no doubt that we have come out of the shadows and into the light. All would seem to be rosy – and there are some in the gay community who resent any suggestion to the contrary.

Clapham Junction, 2007

When producer Elinor Day (of the independent production company Darlow Smithson) approached me early in 2006 about writing a film for Channel 4, she sent me a research document entitled *Queerbashing*. It made grim reading. As well as providing a potted history of

375

Jarman and the Red Triangle

Channel 4 was the first to show Derek Jarman's film *Sebastiane*, a retelling of the story of Saint Sebastian and his crucifixion. Premiered as part of the Red Triangle Season, a series of explicit, worldwide art-house films, it was a film of peculiar boldness, expressing latent homosexuality in its depictions of Roman soldiers. It was also entirely in Latin and has the rare position of being an English film which requires English subtitles. Its provocative subject and bold beauty were the aspirations of the season, Jarman's unerring eye producing a sensual high as well as an exciting 'gay moment'. Far from being a warning, the Red Triangle may well have exposed *Sebastiane* to an even wider audience.

gay legislation, it also included details of homophobic incidents, from murder and assault to harassment and playground bullying. In London alone the gay community has to contend with, on average, over twenty homophobic crimes a week and, according to a Metropolitan Police report, 90 per cent of such incidents go unreported. Whatever progress we make towards tolerance and acceptability, homophobia still bubbles beneath the surface, and occasionally, alarmingly, breaks through. This is hardly surprising; the higher the profile, the more the homophobes are fired up. This, it was suggested, is what the film should explore.

Common and what might be happening to one of their sons back home. 'You don't want to end up lonely,' warns Terry's nan (June Watson) earlier in the film, 'We all need someone.' But each character, even those with partners or spouses, seems destined to be alone. Faithful, loving, lifelong relationships are for many, perhaps, a romantic illusion, and maybe marriage itself isn't all it's cracked up to be: an unrealistic contract that can too often slip into antipathy and a sort of entropy. Perhaps a more promiscuous lifestyle is a truer reflection of human sexuality, certainly of the male.

Perhaps a more promiscuous lifestyle is a truer reflection of human sexuality, certainly of the male

The multi-stranded structure, concentrated into a 36-hour time-frame, kicks off with Danny (Jared Thomas), a twelve year-old with aspirations to be a classical violinist, emerging from the shadows of an underpass into the blinding light of a hot midsummer's day. We gradually meet the other seemingly disparate characters and, as the film moves into night, everything appears possible as they all in their own ways strive to take control of their lives, only to find such delusion thrown back in their faces time and again; lost souls crisscrossing a stifling London, having accidental encounters in the muddle of a heartless metropolis, some inconsequential, some with devastating results, but all drawn towards a single incident – the murder of a stranger on Clapham Common – and each one, to a greater or lesser extent, affected by it. They chance their arm, they push their luck, then in the cold light of day they are forced to face the consequences. The film ends back in the shadows of the underpass, Danny's violin smashed to pieces, the price he pays his peer group for daring to aspire, daring to be different.

At the Clapham dinner party, over the road from where the murder is taking place, the men instinctively bond in an attitude of *laissez-faire*, whilst the women are restless and proactive; they're the ones who get it right about the assault on the

The film was originally intended as a one-off, but some months after I'd finished the script, Channel 4 decided to build a small season around it to coincide with the 40th anniversary of the 1967 Act. This was a mixed blessing, the downside being that, in a few instances, the agenda for discussion was the film as polemic rather than drama.

On *Forty Years Out*, a discussion programme on Channel 4 transmitted a few days after *Clapham Junction*, gay journalist Matthew Parris upbraided the film, with the patronising half-smile of a disappointed aunt, for being stuck

<u>Clapham Junction</u>, 2007

Clapham Junction, 2007

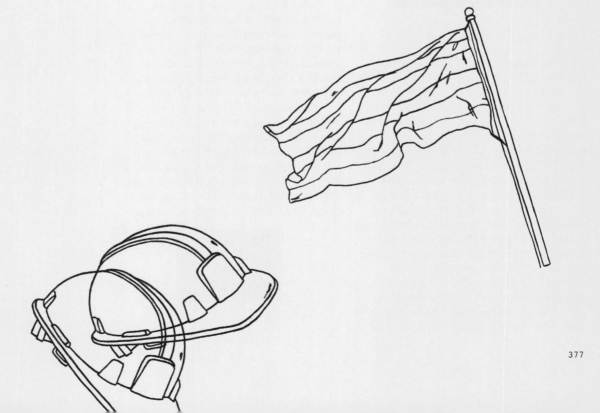

in the Eighties (as if cottaging, *al fresco* sex, queerbashing, infidelity and bullying are as outdated as shoulder-pads and big hair, indeed, as if human nature itself has somehow transformed since Thatcher's reign). It was time for us to 'stop moaning' and time to feel positive, but it seemed he was in denial about the full picture, as was writer Mark *Metrosexual* Simpson on the same programme. Simpson delicately proposed that homophobia nowadays was more probably a question of 'distaste'. This was blown out of the water by the response of former Metropolitan Police Deputy Assistant Commissioner Brian Paddick, who pointed out that decades-old prejudice was still rife and that there had been 'two clearly homophobic murders' in London in the past two years. Fairly 'distasteful' by anybody's standards! It would appear that there are those among us who cannot bear very much reality.

Queer as Folk, 1999

In the past few decades television censorship has eased up; the shock-waves caused by Kenneth Tynan saying 'fuck' during a live debate in November 1965 now seem as ridiculous as Victorians covering up piano legs. Nonetheless I was still prepared for a few problems with *Clapham Junction*, but the sequences I thought might be most vulnerable surprisingly didn't end up on the cutting-room floor.

Penises were a hot topic of discussion from the start. Erections were strictly forbidden, but director Adrian Shergold nonetheless had the art department make several prosthetic penises in various stages of tumescence. All glimpses of the prosthetics were eventually deemed unacceptable; the real penises, however, with one exception, survived – the penis that

was cut was a shot of Terry (Paul Nicholls) urinating over the camera during the sequence in which he attacks a pick-up (Johnny Harris). Before shooting began we had a run-in with the Royal Mail. Again Terry was the problem. He's a mailman, but they refused us permission to use the Royal Mail logo, not because they didn't wish to be associated with a violent, dysfunctional character, but because there's a shot of Terry driving one of their vans listening to his iPod. This they regarded as a slur on the professionalism of their drivers.

The word 'cunt' caused much debate. In the original script there were six 'cunts', but we were advised that 'cunt' would only be defensible after 10pm, and originally the film was due to be transmitted at 9pm (this was later changed to 10pm). So all the 'cunts' went – almost.

Most disappointing was the fracas with the Pet Shop Boys. I've always been an admirer of theirs and was keen to use one of their songs. Channel 4 duly got clearance on *I'm With Stupid,* which played in the background during the above-mentioned queerbashing scene, but during the violence Terry makes a comment about them and I believe this is what caused offence. After seeing the transmission, the Pet Shop Boys insisted that the song be cut from the film, that Terry's offending line be taken out and that we write them a letter of apology. We of course complied with their wishes, so now, sadly, *Clapham Junction* is *sans* Pet Shop Boys.

As suspected paedophile Tim (Joseph Mawle) tells his fourteen year-old admirer (Luke Treadaway), 'People are scared of being different and I can understand that. It takes a lot of courage. But if you can be what you are and not what you think you should be, you'll be happy enough. Understand yourself, and you can face anything.' Many people now accept us, albeit some with a degree of unease, and there are those who will never accept us at all. But as long as we're not complacent, and as long as we don't kid ourselves, then we'll continue to rub along, and all will be pretty well okay.

Clapham Junction, 2007

Access All Areas

UGC is a buzzy new concept to most media organisations, but the principles enshrined in this digital acronym have long been at the core of Channel 4's editorial mission. From the outset, Channel 4 opened its doors to its audience, encouraging them to participate through early interactive experiments such as *Right to Reply's* Video Box. Channel 4 remains the only mainstream broadcaster that gives regular airtime to TV newcomers and up-and-comers, through strands such as *3 Minute Wonder, First Cut* and *Coming Up.* It has also embraced the UGC revolution online, recognising that digital technology has made every viewer a potential content creator and that radically different relationships are called for.

Russell M Davies, new media aficionado,
looks to an all-access future at Channel 4

Age of Abundance

WEDNESDAY, DECEMBER 05, 2007

Skins Series 2
Well as you can see our lovely Skins
MySpace page has had an update and new
look! We hope you like it as much as we
do. What's that you ask? Well no idea! Oh hear you
ask? Series II of course. The new series
will be hitting E4 in February 2008! We
can't tell you much yet [as much as we'd
love to!] but keep your eyes peeled here
on MySpace and at www.e4.com/skins to
hear the latest news.

2:55 - 12 Comments - 14 Kudos -
Add Comment

ELECTROGIRL
waheyy:D
Posted by electrogirl on Wednesday,
December 05, 2007 at 3:39 AM
[Reply to this]

xX_CHAOS
can't wait for the new series [:
yayyyy.
xxxxxxxxxxx.
Posted by xX_Chaos™ on Wednesday,
December 05, 2007 at 4:47 AM
[Reply to this]

YEONJU
oh my!!!!!XD
I can't wait!!!!!
Posted by YeonJu on Wednesday,
December 05, 2007 at 5:13 AM
[Reply to this]

JADE BABES!
Wit woo :}! xo
Posted by Jade Babes! on Wednesday,
December 05, 2007 at 5:37 AM
[Reply to this]

BREN.
yummm
Posted by Bren.
December 05, 20
[Reply to this]

JADE BABES!
Wit woo :}! xo
Posted by Jade
December 05, 20
[Reply to this]

I was on *Right to Reply* once. Remember *Right to Reply*? There were these strange video-boxes around the country – basically a box with a video camera and a big button in which you could vent your spleen about televisual matters. Some of them would then show up on the programme, along with viewers complaining about this and that and programme makers doing that half-stonewalling, half-apologising little dance they've become so good at. It's a measure of how far the world has changed that these dribbles of audience voice felt revolutionary and special. Amateurs on the telly! And not just on *Candid Camera* and *Game for a Laugh*. It all seemed part of Channel 4's mission to challenge the orthodoxy. The BBC would have a jolly programme like *Points of View* with viewers' letters filtered through the reassurance of RADA-modulated accents while Channel 4 let actual real people appear on the box.

You have to give Channel 4 credit for a history of doing this kind of stuff. When television bandwidth was a scarce resource they were probably more generous with it than anyone. Various little programmes and initiatives let real lives leak onto our TV screens, relatively unmediated by the received wisdom of the broadcasting experts. As well as *Right to Reply* there was *The Slot* – a chance for people to express themselves. Now replaced with *3 Minute Wonder*, another platform for the unexpected and unregarded. And if you're talking about the conventional world of UGC they probably led the way with things like *E-stings* – an open competition allowing people to create promotional stuff for E4. It wasn't exactly for your average viewer but it broadened the definition of who was 'allowed' to create TV content. They breathed life into and nurtured the independent

sector; more people than ever before were making television; a more diverse, different bunch of people. This seemed to me a central part of what made Channel 4 different and interesting. They had a broader view of what and who should be on television and they let it happen.

But then, all of a sudden, everything changed. The thing that had been difficult and scarce – access to television – suddenly became easy and free. (And by access to television I don't mean the sort of access that David Starkey or Basil Brush have, I mean the ability to film yourself and let millions of people watch it, if they want to.) This wasn't something television did, it wasn't Ofcom or Hat Trick or Michael Grade, this was something technology did. A bunch of engineers and coders just invented a way that everyone could make and receive video whenever they wanted. Some of them called it YouTube, others called it other things, but it didn't matter. It changed everything.

And what is this UGC that everyone's so het up about? It's real people, using video as a way to talk to each other, to entertain each other, to piss each other off, to have a laugh. It's nothing more complicated than that. What confuses matters is comparing it to the stuff that gets made in the world of televisual scarcity, that's what gives telly folk the impression that UGC is all crap, but they're missing the point. YouTube isn't about virals and talent discovery and programme-makers earning a buck from pilots they can't get made. It's personal TV. If you upload some footage of you and your mates getting drunk and having a laugh in a bar then to you and your mates that's the best telly in the world; cleverer than *The West Wing* and funnier than *Green Wing*. It might look like rubbish to everyone else but

E-stings

E4's annual <u>E-Stings</u> competition, run in
conjunction with <u>Creative Review</u> magazine offers
young graphic designers the opportunity to win
a commission to produce E4 on-air idents, and
has attracted some remarkable entries since its
inception in 2003.

From top left:
Fraser Croall & Chris Hall
Marcus Chaloner
David Johnson
Gregg & Miles McLeod
Yannis Konstantinnidis & Christos Lefakis
Susanne Rostosky

There are all sorts of interestingly generous things bubbling under – things like FourDocs and all the online education initiatives

it doesn't matter, that's what televisual abundance does; it creates personal TV. And it's really hard to fight for eyeballs against something that intimate. How do you make a programme that's more compelling to a granny than watching her little angel in the school play?

That's the challenge for the next twenty-five years of Channel 4. How can they be as generous in an age of abundance? If their mission, and a lot of what makes them different and interesting, comes from giving voice to the disenfranchised, the unheard and the unexpected, what happens when they've got all the access they could ever need? We've already seen how phonecams and YouTube are changing presidential elections and news, what will they do to sports coverage and chat shows? What's now precious and scarce that Channel 4 can be generous with? Clearly their cultural nous is valuable; they've got a good ear for the zeitgeist and a sense of the stories people will love. So I'm excited by the channels they'll curate when every-

one is creating. And there are all sorts of interestingly generous things bubbling under – things like Four Docs and all the online education initiatives. Things that don't necessarily assume the broadcast moment is paramount.

I suspect the big contribution will be their sense of spectacle; that ability to get lots of people watching and even more people talking. That's something that personal TV can't do, that's content that users can't yet generate; the big, mouth-watering, you-had-to-be-there moments of cultural history. That's going to be the new scarcity, the ability to get lots and lots of people all looking at the same thing at the same time and that's valuable. Not just economically, but to our sense of self as a nation. I'd love to see Channel 4 being generous with that scarcity, offering new people opportunities to be at the centre of those rare, delicious national moments.

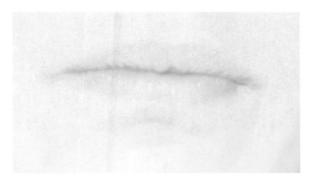

From top left:
<u>3Minute Wonder New Sensations: Mark Melvin</u>, 2007
<u>3Minute Wonder New Sensations: Sarah Maple</u>, 2007
<u>3Minute Wonder North Circular Stories:</u>
<u>Toil and Trouble</u>, 2007
<u>3Minute Wonder North Circular Stories:</u>
<u>Them Sort</u>, 2007
<u>3Minute Wonder North Circular Stories:</u>
<u>Toil and Trouble</u>, 2007

<u>3 Minute Wonder</u>
<u>3 Minute Wonder</u> broadcasts first time directors'
three-minute films in the middle of the channel's
weekday primetime schedule. It offers first-
time directors and assistant producers the
opportunity to air their work to a large audience
and, in doing so, to take a first step into the
competitive UK film industry.

The Garage Wars

Dance

A Blind Perspective

 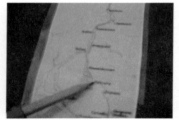  

The Midge Lion

FourDocs
FourDocs is the pioneering online documentary
channel from Channel 4. It's the place to watch,
share and make four minute documentaries. It's
the first time a major broadcaster has offered
this kind of opportunity to everyone for free.

Charles Leadbetter, an independent writer and advisor on technology and creativity, outlines a technological future of collaborative creativity founded in the ethos of folk art

You Are What You Share

A video of Dan Dunn, the young performance artist who paints with both hands at the same time, has attracted 8.5 million views on YouTube. Lasse Gjertsen, a 22-year-old from Larvik, Norway, has become an international star by making intricately cut home videos that have reached an audience of more than 2 million. Innovation and creativity, long the preserve of the professional, is now also for Pro-Ams who do it for the love of it but to very high standards. Distributing, sharing, rating, ranking, borrowing, amending, copying and adapting this material is also spreading, out of the hands of mainstream publishers into the web's social networks.

Everything is getting scrambled up by the way the web is enabling more people to participate and collaborate in producing culture. At times it feels like an explosion of everyday creativity, with more ideas coming from more sources. Often it feels like a descent into cacophony, confusion and chaos, the only escape from which is to submerge oneself in social networks of people and ideas that are already comfortably familiar.

The cast-iron categories of industrial-era media are breaking down. Demand can generate some of its own supply, if it has the tools. Spectators, at least some of them, some of the time, can become producers. For some people – Lasse Gjertsen toiling away in his bedroom – leisure looks suspiciously like work; while many companies clumsily attempt to make work look like leisure by turning offices into cafés. Professionals, it turns out, do not have all the answers, in a world in which television news bulletins can be led by footage from camera phones. But then who do we trust to provide us with fact and truth, when Wikipedia with its five employees attracts more web traffic than the BBC with its hundreds of well-trained journalists?

The motto for the generation growing up with this capability to participate and collaborate, culturally and creatively, is 'We Think Therefore We Are'. It is *by* the masses not just for them. This is raising difficult issues about controlling quality when the traditional gatekeepers have been overrun.

We used to know where new ideas would come from: special people in special places; the writer in their garret, the designer in their studio, the boffin in the lab. The century just gone created a society of mass production for mass consumption – creativity and cultural expression was mainly for an elite. In the century to come, new ideas will come from many people and places. Collaborations to create new ideas, games, software programmes, scientific theories, will also become more common. As more people share ideas and collaborate, it will become more difficult to work out exactly who had which idea. We like to think that each and every new idea has a sole author and a eureka moment. That romantic ideal will become more difficult to sustain.

One way to make sense of this is to look back not forward. We are recovering older ways to organise and express ourselves that were sidelined in the industrial era. Such as folk culture. The growth of an enormous vernacular culture over the next few years will be more democratic than what went before but also more raucous and out of control. Many of the themes of folk culture recur in current discussions about the growth of social networks, blogging and YouTube. Folk has always rested on a cult of authenticity: the self-taught singer-songwriters armed with just an acoustic guitar; self-taught artists making sculptures from driftwood.

Now we have the self-taught garage band, their music published on MySpace, their videos on YouTube. Nothing is fresher in our manufactured and commercialised culture than raw, untutored talent, untouched by training, academic theories or the lure of commerce.

Folk has always been art for people outside and at odds with the mainstream culture industry. Folk artists are not in it for the fame but the pleasure of producing good art, using a vernacular, everyday style rather than the formal, self-conscious and fancy styles taught in art and music colleges. By making tools of cultural production ever more widely available, Web 2.0 and its successors have unleashed new waves of authentic talent – pensioners on YouTube, bloggers like Salam Pax or internet performers like Ze Frank and Ask a Ninja – who can find audiences without succumbing to the cookie-cutter marketing of the mainstream culture industry.

The wave of digitally enabled folk culture is presented as an antidote to the plastic, celebrity-obsessed and contrived culture of mainstream television heavily reliant on so-called reality TV. The more

The spectacle is the opposite of dialogue. It is the sun that never sets on the empire of modern passivity

shaky and grainy video looks the more real it must be; professional advertisers and agencies crave the raw and fresh. The everyday digital folk and the trendy avant-garde find common ground in their shared search for outsider, rebel status. In the 1960s Guy Debord, the anarchist founder of Situationist International, argued that all art should be regarded as a situation in which people would live out the action. Debord denounced modern society as no more than a 'society of spectacle': 'The spectacle is the opposite of dialogue. It is the sun that never sets on the empire of modern passivity.'

The 1960s avant-garde imagined that as spectatorship gave way to participation so people would become more social and collaborative; they become more egalitarian and engaged with one another. Collage and pastiche, recombining the ingredients provided by others, was central not just to Situationism but to Futurism, Cubism, Dadaism and Pop Art. The rip, mix, burn generation of Apple iPods and YouTube videos are the heirs of Debord's manifesto. YouTube is a bastard offspring of Debord's call for a society of participation: it is creating a society in which anyone can make a spectacle of themselves.

The 'you are what you share' ethic of modern digital culture echoes folk's shared approach to creativity. Folk music, for example, is self-consciously anti-commercial and anti-celebrity. It is a self-styled communal creative culture: songs and tunes, borrowed and passed on for generations. Claiming sole author-ship, pushing yourself forward, is frowned upon in folk. The point is to rework material created by others, to pay homage to those who went before. Authorship is lost in the mists of collective creativity.

Ten4 Magazine
Put together by first time designers, writers
and producers, Ten4 Magazine, launched in 2005,
showcases and celebrates new creative talent.
Later it will evolve into 4Talent Magazine.

Ten4 magazine covers (from top)
Issue 3: Clusta
Issue 6: Ross Gilmore, Christian Zebitz
& Anke Weckmann
Issue 4: Dave Remes
Issue 1: Dave Remes
Issue 2: Temper
Issue 7: Stephen Earl Rogers
Issue 8: Empty Creative

in the mists of collective creativity. Folk artists encourage others to borrow from them rather than protecting their rights as authors. As Woody Guthrie's copyright notice put it: 'This song is Copyrighted in U.S., under Seal of Copyright 154085, for a period of 28 years, and anybody caught singing it without our permission, will be mighty good friends of ours, cause we don't give a dern. Publish it. Write it. Sing it. Swing to it. Yodel it. We wrote it, that's all we wanted to do.' This could be a rallying cry for the file-sharing We Think generation.

Professor Dorothy Noyes, a leading US folklorist, points out that epic poems such as the *Illiad* and *Odyssey* developed over many years through the contributions of probably several hundred poets and performers all over the Greek world. Many people worked on them, some specialising in particular scenes or episodes. There was no 'fixed' master text until much later, when the poems became attributed to Homer. Noyes says Homer is the name we give to what was a collective process of creativity involving many people over a long period. The founding myths of our culture set out in classical drama, drawn upon time and again by subsequent writers, were created by highly collaborative social process.

Before the mass-produced book, for most of human history most culture and art was folk based. In many developing-world societies it still is. In Ghana, for example, designs of traditional adinkra and kente cloths are owned by communities that include craftsmen living and dead, royal patrons and entire communities. Much the same is true for Aboriginal stories.

Modern popular culture, the culture of YouTube and World of Warcraft, is a mutant offspring from the marriage of folk culture and digital technology. Much of the time the many contributors with the tools to think, act and experiment work independently and in parallel, often reworking elements of a core central product. They come together through festivals, websites, bulletin boards, carnivals and wikis. The product grows through accretion, mutual criticism, support and imitation. Most take part because they get intrinsic pleasure from the activity and they want recognition from a community of peers. Social creativity is informal but nonetheless structured. It is not enough for people merely to participate, to have their say; they have to find ways to collaborate to build on what one another does. When they can pull off this trick, which is by no means always, they can create complex, valuable, reliable products: encyclopaedias, software programmes, computer games, news reports, scientific theories. Whether we can make the most of the potential for participation and collaboration to spawn new forms of creativity is the question we are all now trying to sort through.

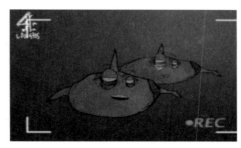

4Laughs

Channel 4's user-generated comedy site 4Laughs has been providing a platform for new young comics to develop their work in as near to a work professional environment as possible. In the last year the 4Laughs community has provided sketches for Justin Lee Collins and Alan Carr on Friday Night Project, appeared on 4Radio, and written for The Secret Policeman's Ball.

From top left:
Mr Mantis by Mvstott
Off the Coast of Cornwall by Allyn Lawson
Peter Crouch by Green and Gray
Jackie Ass 3 by 3 Girls in a Boat
The Second Annual Comedy Event by Yielding
David Bussell by Professional Punographer

Comedy Lab

Comedy Lab is Channel 4's unique televisual experiment which unearths the comedy stars of tomorrow. Since its launch in 1997 it has unearthed major comedy talent including Peter Kay, Jimmy Carr, Dom Joly and Russell Brand, and is open to anyone with a good idea.

From top left:
The Services, 1998
Modern Toss, 2005
Meet The Magoons, 2002
Jimmy Carr, 2001
Trigger Happy TV, 1998

Cordelia Jenkins tries to uncover the
web world's most popular person

Who Is Tom Anderson?

'Tom is at work…workin' on plans' says the status bar of his MySpace page. Tom is good looking, smiley-faced, slightly creepy. A virtual maître d', the nice-guy host that offers you his friendship from the first minute of your MySpace membership, along with some 'helpful hints' on how to use the site. More an emoticon than a representation of actual flesh and blood, his profile picture has become an iconic internet image (he is 9th on *VH1*'s Greatest Internet Superstars poll). His mood is set as 'calm'. He is 31 years old, from Santa Monica, California. He currently has 197,533,987 friends, though he claims to want more, and he is one half of the double act that founded the third most popular website in the world. Or is he?

Until recently, the received wisdom has been that 'President' Tom, and his business partner 'CEO' Chris De Wolfe, set up MySpace as an ingenious joint venture- in the same vein as the Google boys did their revolutionary search engine. Many MySpace users believe in the attractive story of two twenty-some-things, working out of their bedrooms or from a garage and accidentally setting

up an internet phenomenon, which has grown so famous that it has recently been bought up by Rupert Murdoch's burgeoning News Corporation. The kind of dotcom 'rags to riches' success story that has become so familiar. Then, in September 2006, Valleywag (a Silicon Valley gossip blog) published an article by Trent Lapinski, which claimed that the whole Tom Anderson story was a PR stunt and that MySpace had actually been developed by a team of marketing gurus at a company called eUniverse.

'Tom Anderson has served as an exceptionally convincing distraction', said Trent, 'the mascot designed to give the friendliest feel to a site created by a marketing company.

In interview Tom is vague about the early days of MySpace. He alludes to a group of other 'guys and programmers' who helped him set the site up and sticks to the line that the site was aimed at the creative community of actors, artists and musicians living in LA. He also suggests that his major in English and Rhetoric at Berkeley and his attendance at UCLA Film School was a form of rebellion against his entrepreneurial

father and claims that he was 'planning to be a lifetime student' when he met Chris De Wolfe. Which all sits well with the 'nice guy who got lucky' version of events and chimes nicely with the aspirations of MySpace's target market.

Whatever the case, with 230,000 new registrations a day, MySpace is an advertiser's dream, and its genius lies in the fact that none of its members seem to realise it. On the other hand, there is something disturbing about the vitriol with which some people have attacked the MySpace team. When the question of Tom's real age was raised recently, the idea that he may have been misleading MySpace members about any of his personal details (despite the fact that many members are far from honest about themselves on their own profiles) caused a surprisingly strong reaction. 'Tom is not my friend' t-shirts have started appearing on the internet, as have fake Rupert Murdoch profile pages with titles such as FUQ RUPERT or BILLIONAIRE TYRANT. Whatever your personal views about News Corp, it must be acknowledged that MySpace still upholds many of the ideals it set out with. Musicians still

love to!] but keep your eyes peeled here
on MySpace and at www.e4.com/skins to
hear the latest news.

2:55 - 12 Comments - 14 Kudos -
Add Comment

ELECTROGIRL
waheyy:D
Posted by electrogirl on Wednesday,
December 05, 2007 at 3:39 AM
[Reply to this]

XX_CHAOS™
can't wait for the new series (:
yayyyy.
xxxxxxxxxxx.
Posted by xX_Chaos™ on Wednesday,
December 05, 2007 at 4:47 AM
[Reply to this]

YEONJU
oh my!!!!!XD
I can't wait!!!!!
Posted by YeonJu on Wednesday,
December 05, 2007 at 5:13 AM
[Reply to this]

JADE BABES!
Wit woo :)! xo
Posted by Jade Babes! on Wednesday,
December 05, 2007 at 5:37 AM
[Reply to this]

BREN.
yummm
Posted by Bren. on Wednesday,
December 05, 2007 at 7:32 AM
[Reply to this]

'Tom is not my friend' t-shirts have started appearing on the internet

feel overwhelmingly positive towards it as an effective marketing tool. De Wolfe claims that the site will never charge bands to promote their music or use pop-up ads as long as he is in charge and, although both men's contracts expire this month, the rumour is that they have signed a two-year extension to say on as CEO and President, so that could be for a long time.

Tom still has his fans. According to an article by Patricia Sellers in Fortune magazine, he is intimately involved with the company, 'the soul of MySpace', scouring the profile pages for unsigned bands for hours at a time, looking for promising new talent to sign up to a new venture, MySpace records. The company have announced a partnership with Skype, enabling its members to make free internet phone calls even when they are not online. Tom discovered *kSolo*, an internet karaoke service he thought

would be perfect for MySpace users and bought it up; it is clear that he has the common touch. De Wolfe sums up the MySpace ethic in a series of well aimed catch phrases, but ones that ring true to the site's many fans, 'We're not deciding what's cool. Our users are', he says, 'MySpace is all about letting people be what they want to be'. With that in mind, it's not surprising that Tom's function on the site is to be both ever-present and two-dimensional. His blandness as the face of MySpace is entirely appropriate to a site which advocates self-promotion through re-invention, and his assertion that, 'I'd like to do this as long as it's fun, and that could be a long, long time', is not incompatible with the self he promotes online. As Peter Chernin of News Corp points out 'Tom lives inside the product'; whether he invented it or not, Tom Anderson is MySpace.

First Cut
Since its launch in November 2007, First Cut showcases an eclectic mix of surprising and distinctive documentary films by up and coming directors, offering a new generation of film-makers the chance to make their first prime-time film for the channel

From top:
First Cut: Karaoke Soul
First Cut: Mr Average
First Cut: Mr Average

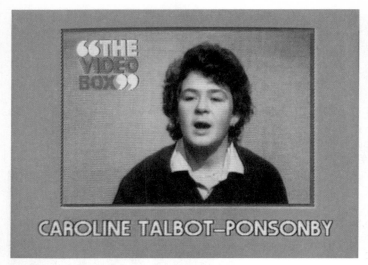

CAROLINE TALBOT–PONSONBY

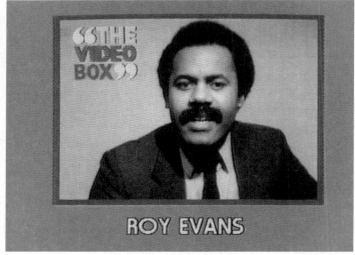

ROY EVANS

NANCY ALLUM–DRAPER

DAVID WHITEHOUSE

JOHN HEIN

Right to Reply
Running from 1982 to 2001, Right to Reply famously allowed viewers to voice their complaints or concerns about TV programmes, not only through the traditional telephone and letter, but also through a third way… the Video Box.

Filmspotting

The story of Channel 4's relationship with film is best told through the filmmakers it has supported – Ken Loach, Stephen Frears, Mike Leigh, Danny Boyle, Kevin Macdonald, Sarah Gavron and Shane Meadows to name just a few. Channel 4 has championed British independent filmmaking, helping to secure the widest possible distribution for dozens of iconic titles including *My Beautiful Laundrette*, *Trainspotting*, *The Madness of King George* and *East is East*. They've all been shown on the small screen as well, creating a real distinction from the soaps-and-serials which dominate the schedules of other broadcasters. The tradition has continued to today as Film4 develops and funds acclaimed British films for cinema release, such as *The Last King of Scotland* and *This is England*.

Filmmaker and writer Hannah Rothschild talks to leading directors of the British film industry, which had new life breathed into it by Film4, resulting in contemporary British cinema becoming the centre of our creative and cultural life

East is East, 1999

Labour of Love

My Beautiful Laundrette, 1985

The Motorcycle Diaries, 2004

It's hard to imagine the fate of British cinema without the birth of Channel 4. The advent of its film department offered a life-saving transfusion to an ailing industry and led to a renaissance in filmmaking. In 1981, the year before the channel launched, only 24 British films were made and audiences had dropped to an all time low of 86 million. Scarcely two decades earlier, in 1963, 113 films were released and seen by a staggering 350 million cinemagoers. The Sixties boom, kick-started by the Bond franchise, fluffed up by the *Carry On*s, sharpened by Stanley Kubrick and romanced by David Lean, resulted in the UK bringing home four best picture Oscars that decade. However, the following decade (some notable exceptions aside), the Seventies, saw a drop in quality and production on both sides of the Atlantic. In Britain, production fell to levels not seen since 1914.

Jeremy Isaacs, Channel 4's first Chief Executive, agrees. 'In those days the industry was in a moribund state and its heart was mortgaged to US money.' In his letter of application for the job, Isaacs promised to put money into 'films of feature length for television here, for the cinema abroad'. He'd seen the extraordinary success in Italy and Germany, where public television quotas funded the work of talented directors. If Europe could nurture the likes of Bertolucci, Fellini, Wim Wenders and Fassbinder, Isaacs reasoned that Britain should do the same.

The most passionate argument in favour of film production came from an assorted bunch of filmmakers that visited the newly formed Channel 4 executive at its temporary offices. Stephen Frears, David Hare, Richard Eyre, Ann Scott and Simon Relph pleaded for their films to have a cinema release before being shown on television. Having worked for years to nurture an idea from script to screen, why shouldn't they enjoy the fruits of their labour with a live audience?

At that time, British filmmakers and television executives were locked in a stalemate. The film industry argued that TV got their movies at a fraction of their real cost. Television, apparently, cherry-picked the best products and avoided the high risk of investing up front.

Television countered that the film industry's refusal to show anything aired previously on the box hampered its own attempts to generate original film. And how could any company afford to delay screening a drama for up to three years after a cinema exhibition? Given that this attitude had been entrenched for years, and was supported by many unions, how did Isaacs and Justin Dukes, the Managing Director, break the stalemate? 'Simple,' Isaacs says. 'We told them that if we paid for it, we'd bloody well show it when we wanted to.'

Channel 4 allocated six million pounds a year to original drama. This was separate from the fifteen hundred straight acquisitions that the station bought before it launched. David Rose was appointed as its first Head of Drama (or Senior Commissioning Editor, Fiction) and decided to spread this money in chunks of £300,000 over twenty films. Rose came straight from BBC Pebble Mill and, in his own words, 'just transferred the BBC in

Rose, the inventor of the docudrama format and part of the original team at *Z Cars*, had spent years creating partnerships with gifted writers, directors and actors. Talent such as Judi Dench, Alison Steadman and Joss Ackland had had guest roles in Rose's shows and he'd collaborated with luminaries such as David Hare, Ken Loach, Alan Clark, Bill Kenwright, Colin Welland and Alan Plater.

Many of these people followed him to Channel 4 and enjoyed the relative autonomy of this new unit. Rose reflects that these days everything has to be referred to middle management and focus groups. That's the quickest way to lose the trust of any writer or director.' Stephen Frears also points out that favoured writers and directors were paid to develop ideas in general and not just for specific projects.

Channel 4, freed from the shackles of production, had the advantage of speed. The BBC, hampered even in those days by its unwieldy bureaucracy and programme-making requirements, took eight years to set up a rival film operation and often lost films to rivals through indecision. Mike Leigh gives the example of *Career Girls*, which was originally commissioned by the Beeb. It just dragged on and on and nobody took any responsibility for it and the producer at the BBC messed about. And finally for a wheeze we went round the corner to Film4.' They took one look at Leigh's script and gazumped the corporation.

This ability to act quickly netted other great successes. Isaacs was given 24 hours to decide whether to make a film about a gay inter-racial relationship set in a west London laundrette for double their normal budget. The rest, of course, is history. *My Beautiful Laundrette*, directed by Stephen Frears, and starring Daniel Day-Lewis, became one of the defining films in the history of British cinema.

Howards End, 1992

The list of Film4's successes grew thanks to a twin track policy of breaking new talent and nurturing the greats. Frears went on to deliver three more Film4 productions. A call for help with last-minute funding on a film called *The Draughtsman's Contract* by the unknown Peter Greenaway led to a long-term, fruitful collaboration. John Boorman recommended his young untried assistant called Neil Jordan, which resulted in three classics, *Angel*, *The Crying Game* and *Mona Lisa*. Rose spotted the genius of Alan Clarke at *Z Cars* and Isaacs remembered Terence Davies from his days at the BFI.

With the exception of *Wish You Were Here* by David Leland, most of the channel's investment could be measured in critical acclaim rather than box-office receipts. This included some of the investments in foreign films, which the channel saw as part of its commitment to international film culture. It's a startling statistic that over 80 per cent of all foreign films shown on television have been shown on Channel 4. No one expected Tarkovsky's *Sacrifice* or even Wim Wenders's *Paris, Texas* to set the tills jingling. This kind of investment in either foreign directors or languages paid off with Oscars for *Solomon and Gaenor* in the Best Foreign Film category.

Touching the Void, 2003

However, even when films were hits, the investment was rarely recouped. The channel never made a penny out of Merchant Ivory's productions including *A Room with a View* and the legendary *Howard's End*, which packed the Curzon Cinema for a whole year, from which the channel, according to David Aukin made nothing.

Six years after its birth, every single one of Film4's twenty productions that year were at Cannes either as part of the competition, or in the Directors' Fortnight or in the market. What, one wondered, was David Rose's magic formula? Jeremy Isaacs credits Rose with 'the best eye for a script in history'. Rose says it's to do with nurturing talent and adds mysteriously, 'Well, you know a film is a film is a film and that's all there is to it.'

His successor, David Aukin, is equally elliptical on the subject of spotting winners. 'It's a bit like yoga,' he says. 'If you aim, you miss.' He took over the department just as the British film industry was once again sliding into a recession. There were few sources of funding and all of Film4's theatrical releases had failed to recoup their investment. The new Chief Executive, Michael Grade, and director of programmes, Liz Forgan, gave Aukin six months to prove there was any point in keeping open the window for theatrical release and, to add to his problems, they capped spending at £8 million.

However, Aukin credits Grade with the inspirational remit 'Your only sin will be to commission something you don't believe in passionately.' Few would have foreseen that *Shallow Grave*, a cheap anarchic first film starring an unknown Ewan McGregor, would become the saviour of Film4. Director Danny Boyle, who'd never dreamed of breaking into features, spotted its potential as it 'shared a sense of humour, a morality, or lack of it with pop music' – which Boyle considers the nation's greatest talent. The film became the first in Channel 4's history to make money and was quickly followed by *Trainspotting*, which united the same team, and brought home an estimated $70 million.

These films are the exception. Tessa Ross, the present head of the newly retitled Film4 points out that the BBC has only very recently earned anything from its investment in the hugely lucrative *Billy Elliot*. The same is true of the vast majority of Film4 productions. However, the ratio of money spent to brilliance of outcome doesn't tally. 'The more resources that are available don't necessarily throw up greater talent,' Aukin says, 'and even with a little money, cream always rises to the top.'

What is the universal appeal of some of these small budget success stories? Danny Boyle puts it down to the channel clearly setting out 'to embrace and challenge British taste and include exciting sexy, dangerous British movies.' Did Stephen Frears know that he was making a smash hit with *Beautiful Laundrette*? 'No, I just thought it was good fun,' he replies. Asked the same question David Aukin stops, thinks and then laughs, 'It's down to a lot of luck.' As if to prove the randomness of success, Aukin maintains that he commissioned Neil Jordan's *The Crying Game* (nominated for six Oscars) because he was missing a film from his slate, and that the success of *Four Weddings* was as much of a surprise to him as it was to the rest of the universe.

Ironically, some claim that it was Aukin's success that led to the death of the old Film4. In the Nineties, there was a sea change in the perception of what the British film industry should and could deliver: if America could have major studios, why shouldn't Britain create mini varieties. In 1997, Channel 4 suddenly enjoyed a financial windfall from being able to sell its own advertising. The then Minister for Culture Chris Smith insisted that more money in return should go to film production. Michael Jackson, the new Chief Executive, and a film fanatic, believed the channel could create a commercially lucrative enterprise and masterminded the creation of a new British 'Studio' supported by Film4 and the Arts Council.

The budget was increased to £30 million, swanky new offices were procured in Charlotte Street and a commercially minded producer, Paul Webster, was brought in to run the venture. However, for the first time in its career, Film4 seemed to have lost its magic touch: the films flopped and floundered. 'The problem,' said one insider who asked not to be named, was 'that £30 million might sound like a lot in this country but

Career Girls, 1997

it buys you very little bargaining power in the US.' Webster also points out that, 'the relationship between the television company, broadcaster and film company was extremely difficult. It was OK when you had a film buff like Michael Jackson but after his departure, people only cared about the economics.'

Gurinder Chadha, another director to get her first break at Film4, took Webster a script for a low budget picture about two young girls who wanted to play football. 'I actually gave it to him twice,' she remembers, 'and he said, oh we have already done it (a reference presumably to the highly successful *East is East*). I said you are making a big mistake really… are you sure

you don't want to look at it? And he was like, No, No, No.' *Bend It like Beckham* made over $32 million dollars in the US alone. But then everyone has a story about the one who let the one get away. Unfortunately for Webster, two of the most notable films out of the 70 he commissioned, *Touching the Void* and *Motorcycle Diaries*, came out after he'd left. Webster is sanguine about the experience. 'My predecessors, David Rose and David Aukin, were allowed to fail. Things changed.'

In 2002, Paul Webster was the last person to leave the building in Charlotte Street. He locked the door behind him and with it Channel 4's dream of being a studio. Sixty-six employees were laid off and in one hour, 55 projects in development were given away.

Michael Jackson's successor Mark Thompson reinstated a slimmed-down department back at HQ in Horseferry Road,

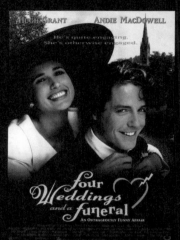

Four Weddings and a Funeral, 1994

led by Tessa Ross. She inherited a few of Webster's projects, including *The Lovely Bones*, a book soon to be filmed by Peter Jackson, and *The Motorcycle Diaries*. Her entire budget is £10 million.

As controller of both film and drama, Ross sees both as great places to cross-fertilise talent. 'I'm interested in authorship and television is a great place to enable authors.' One of her protégées, the ridiculously talented Peter Morgan, wrote his first short for the channel, but it was *The Deal* that really put him on the map. Morgan describes Film4 as 'impecunious but inspired' – a sentiment echoed by Barnaby Thompson (Ealing Studios) and Peter Cattaneo (*The Full Monty*), who were respectively the producer and director of that same Oscar-nominated short that launched these important careers. Martin McDonagh, who won the Academy Award for his short, has just completed his first feature for Film4. Andrea Arnold, whose short, *Wasp*, also won an Oscar, chose to make her first feature, *Red Road*, for the rivals at the BBC.

Ross spreads her net wide in the search for new talent. One offshoot is Warp X, an ultra-low-budget drama unit specifically designed to make micro-budget films with a younger generation. Film4's tentacles reach out to theatre companies, film school, and there's even a new online film with MySpace, *Faintheart*, chosen by MySpace users. 'The important thing is that there are avenues for talent to come into the building,' she says. The importance of creating opportunity in the film industry can't be underestimated. Barnaby Thompson, who started his career when Channel 4 was born, says, 'For my generation it opened up the opportunity to be in the business at all. Before then, it was a small group of people most of whom seemed to be born into families connected with the business.' Nor is television just a waiting room for the lucrative world of cinema. There is still a great respect for the tube. Director Ken Loach, who works in both mediums, adds, 'The odds are that if you don't have a big name your film will get a very short print run… [and your film] kind of fades away. So every few years we have a first run on television… you get a new audience.'

Ross's belief in authorship extends to taking obsessional care to match the right director to the right project. 'You can make a *successful* film without a great director's vision but its impossible to make a *great* film without a great director's vision. My ambition is to find and enable that authorship.' Ross also believes in giving her directors room to breathe. Asked how involved she's been in the new Mike Leigh film, she laughs, 'I look forward to seeing his cut.' First timer Sarah Gavron, chosen by Ross and Alison Owen to direct *Brick Lane*, is clearly something of a perfectionist. She spent over a year with the writer working and reworking the script. Only then did she announce that she was ready to go. Wasn't there pressure from Film4 to get on with it? Absolutely not.'

Perhaps it's this kind of supportiveness that lures the established directors back. Like salmon working their way back up to the pools in which they were spawned, many of the early protégées, now the grand men of cinema themselves, are still making films for the channel. Danny Boyle has just started *Slumdog Millionaire*. Mike Leigh is struggling to come up with a name for his newly completed opus.[1] Ken Loach recently completed a TV film. Kevin Macdonald, who cut his teeth there with *Touching the Void*, is shooting a big Hollywood film but can't wait to get back to Horseferry Road to start on 'a cowboy movie set in Roman times filmed in the wilderness of Scotland'. Shane Meadows, who made his first film back in the days of Paul Webster, returned to the channel to make *This is England*. It looks like Tessa Ross's dream – 'to make films that people want to keep in their DVD collection rather than films that come and go' – is well on course.

The Last King of Scotland, 2006

However, one doesn't have to look further than the 2007 Oscars to appreciate what an extraordinary contribution this department has made – not just to Channel 4, nor only to broadcasting, but to Great Britain and World Cinema. The nominees included many whose talents were discovered, honed and refined and nurtured by Film4. These included two nominees for best directors Stephen Frears and Paul Greengrass. Forest Whittaker netted his gong for Best Actor with Film4's *The Last King of Scotland*, whose screenwriter Peter Morgan was nominated for best original screenplay for his other film that year, *The Queen*. Peter O'Toole lost out yet again in the Best Actor cat-

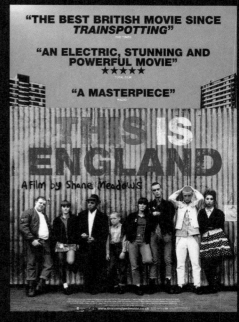

This is England, 2006

egory, but all agree that his translation of Hanif Kureishi's Maurice was a *tour de force*. Best Actress Helen Mirren is an *habituée* of many Film4 productions. Given that the Academy Awards is broadcast to over two billion people worldwide, given that the whole department is run on less than a major studio's travel budget, the thank-yous to Film4 that night brought incalculably valuable publicity and fully endorsed not just its own work but the astonishing talent found in Great Britain.

The golden age of film and television, we're often told, has passed. The newspapers are full of sanctimonious observations about re-runs, about failing standards and dodgy ethics. The fact that revenue is falling, that everyone is struggling to adapt to the digital era where rules and formats change on a weekly basis, is not mentioned. Nor is television's equally important second role; it's as much about training as it is about product. There isn't a single job in either the film or television industry that doesn't require skills and it's the publicly owned stations in particular, Channel 4 and the BBC, which offer the greatest training in this craft. You only have to look at the CVs of British directors, actors and technicians to see evidence of vital experience learned from working for the small screen. The influence of television extends like a fantastic coral reef, a unique interdependent biosphere. It's no coincidence that Sarah Gavron

THIS FILM IS
EXPECTED TO
ARRIVE...

Trainspotting

:02:96

From the team that brought you Shallow Grave

#1 RENTON

#2 BEGBIE

#3

#4 SICK BOY

#5 SPUD

Trainspotting, 1996

was taught by Stephen Frears, who in turn was taught by Carol Reid. Or that the BBC's Nick Fraser gave Kevin Macdonald his first break in documentaries. Or that James McAvoy and Anne-Marie Duff spawned both a wonderful love affair and a career in *Shameless*. Or that Richard Eyre and Mike Leigh owe a debt to the theatre, Ridley Scott and Ken Loach owe one to *Z Cars* and Mike Radford and Co came out of *Coronation Street*.

The national benefit of television isn't just measured in couch-potato hours. Our creative industries are worth £60 billion a year and employ nearly two million people. This doesn't include by-products such as the £800 million earned last year from film-related tourism.

Tessa Ross admits, 'If I went to my bosses and said you could make back your investment, I'd be lying.' But Film4 has never been about financial returns or audience profile. It's been a labour of love; it's been about providing a platform for the most talented writers, directors, actors, cinematographers, production staff and technicians. It's produced a fair share of honking turkeys, films that don't even deserve to make it to DVD, but by keeping its focus resolutely on filmmaking not money-making, Film4 has given us a significant proportion of the films and the talent that have defined British cinema over the last 25 years. Film is now back at the heart of our creative and cultural life and British talent is recognised all over the world.

Operating on a micro budget, it offers one hell of a return. Twice in its history it rekindled the dying flame of an industry; many of its films have set fire to the box office worldwide. Mike Leigh, now acknowledged as one of our greatest directors, had to wait seventeen years between his first film, *Bleak Moments*, made in 1971, until the creation of the channel to make his second feature, *High Hopes*. Like many of his contemporaries he spent that time honing his skills in theatre and in television, but he's in no doubt that Film4 saved the British cinema. 'This is a non-negotiable, historical fact of life and anybody who suggests that this isn't the case is simply either suffering from some kind of ignorance or has got some terrible chip.'

1 Mike Leigh's film is now called Happy Go Lucky
FilmFour evolved into Film4 when Tessa Ross became
head of Film4 and Channel 4 Drama in 2004

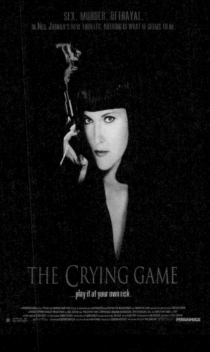

SEX. MURDER. BETRAYAL.
IN NEIL JORDAN'S NEW THRILLER, NOTHING IS WHAT IT SEEMS TO BE.

THE CRYING GAME
...play it at your own risk.

MIRAMAX

The Crying Game, 1992

Stephen Frears

Hannah Rothschild: How did you come to be involved in *My Beautiful Laundrette*?

Stephen Frears: It came in a slightly dodgy way. There was this boy who put a script through my door. I read it and said, 'This is wonderful and we should do this now.' I'd recently worked with Tim Bevan and Sarah Radclyffe at Working Title on a pop video. So I said to Tim, 'You had better produce this.' He arranged a cash flow and then I rang up Channel 4 and said, 'I want an answer in 24 hours.' At 5 o'clock David Rose rang me on the Tuesday and said OK. So it worked.

You make it sound very easy.

Now it does. I am not even sure I dare to tell you this but actually it was only afterwards I discovered that they'd actually approached another director first but Hanif Kureishi insisted on me.

How many years later did you find that out?

Ten to fifteen. Just think, somewhere there's a man who had his hands on it but it was snatched away.

How did you spot Daniel Day-Lewis? It was his first film.

I didn't spot him! The women around me did. They told me to cast him because they fancied him.

Is that how you normally do your casting?

Of course. It works.

How experienced were your producers?

Tim Bevan had never made a film and ran around asking for advice. Sarah Radclyffe had made films with people like Derek Jarman so she was fine, but Jane Fraser, who is a wonderful line producer, said she went home every night and cried.

When did you realise that *Laundrette* might be a hit?

It was chosen for the Edinburgh Film Festival and I saw that the trades had put a film that Ridley Scott made called *Legend* with Tom Cruise at the top and us right down at the bottom of the list. And I thought, I will take you [Ridley] on any day [laughing]. I went up and I took a taxi from the airport but I hadn't any money and I went to the box office, said who I was and asked to borrow the fare. They looked at me and said, 'You can have whatever you want.' So I knew we were going to be OK. Initially Romaine Hart offered us six weeks in her cinema but having read Derek Malcolm's review said 'What do you want?' It had an enchanted life really.

Did you always know there was something rather magical about the film?

Well I knew it was good. I never had any doubts about that. Really I just thought it was good fun and an extension of what I'd been doing in TV for fifteen years.

My Beautiful Laundrette, 1985

You had to wait fifteen years between your first film *The Hit* and *Laundrette*. Mike Leigh had to wait seventeen? And many of your contemporaries had to wait longer. Was that frustrating for your generation?

We were doing really good work on the television, largely at the BBC. And also at the theatre. But we were also childish and jealous of each other. No bad thing really.

Many people like working with the same crew, the same team and often the same actors again and again. Why are you always changing the team?

Well if you are going to be iconoclastic you have to go the whole hog don't you.

I can't imagine you waking up saying, 'I am going to be an iconoclast today'?

I like to irritate people [laughing].

Would you say your main motivation in life is to irritate people?

No absolutely not! But if you are going to be iconic you must decide to make a piece of provocation.

Did you always know you were going to be a film director?

I just wanted to work. I liked the theatre but then when I started working at the BBC. I just thought this was paradise. And then Channel 4 came out of the BBC.

Theatre and television in particular in this country seem like the training ground for film.

Absolutely, and if you look back at the debates about starting BBC2 you'll see that it was set up like a job scheme for graduates. All the clever people wanted to work there, as you were sheltered from capitalism. There was never any inducement from my generation to go into business. Then politics became a sort of mocked profession because of *Beyond the Fringe*, which started the lack of respect. So entertainment or the news became a very intoxicating option. Most of the people I knew at Cambridge went into some branch of television or the theatre. Cinema was like a sort of closed shop. When I made *Gumshoe*, it wasn't much fun because the old guard resented me, then a young gun, just as they always do.

Why are each of your films so different? What makes you so different from your contemporaries such as Ken Loach or Mike Leigh, whose films are recognisably theirs?

I have a very low boredom threshold I suppose, or perhaps they are more committed to what they do. Or maybe they are proper artists or something. But it's not really for me to analyse. I do it because doing the same film all the time doesn't interest me. But it clearly interests Mike and it clearly interests Ken. I don't know, what do they say?

I didn't ask them that question.
I would go mad with boredom, but they find it very, very interesting. I have no idea why.

<u>Walter</u>, 1982

Do you think film has the power to change the way we look at the world?
Well *Laundrette* changed the way people thought.

Any others?
When Ken made *Up the Junction* and then *Cathy Come Home* it sort of changed everything. I mean you had never seen stuff like that before and we were brought up to envy a man who had done something that original. That was the spirit of the time but it isn't the spirit of today. One of the reasons I wanted to make *The Queen* was because no one had ever done it before; the subject matter had never been touched before. But it is harder to do now. It's hard to find fresh material.

And people to fund fresh ideas?
Well that was always one of the points of Channel 4.

To be radical?
Yes, except now I have to admit that it's Mrs Thatcher who should be given all the credit for Channel 4. We started making films when what she was doing was beginning to de-regulate and she even created the first form of tax relief for cinema. The truth is that *Laundrette*, which was plainly an attack on Mrs Thatcher, was actually a perfect Thatcherite model. We the filmmakers became small businessmen and we were making a film about small businesses – the route of Thatcherism!

Why do you think you were chosen to do *Walter*, the film made for the opening night of Channel 4?
I made it and then Jeremy chose it. It was

incredible. He said it was the best night's programming that ever was on television. When David Rose came into the office at the end of the first week at Channel 4, the whole company stood up and clapped.

When did you realise what a great thing it was?
I'm a professional moaner and complained endlessly about Channel 4, but when I went to Cannes and saw *Paris, Texas* with a Channel 4 credit I thought, 'My God, if they put money in that they are a really good organisation.'

Why were you moaning about it until then?
Just because. What else do you do? What else is there to do? On long winter nights you moan don't you.

What do you think will happen to film in the future?
I haven't a clue.

But you still teach a younger generation at the film school so you must have hope?
If I had my way, there would be a law that all people of a certain age should be forced to teach.

Why do you think more people don't?
They are not Jewish, I don't know!

Shall I put that in?
Put in whatever you like.

What is it that makes you want to put something back into the industry?
It would be a rabbinical tradition wouldn't it? I don't know. I don't know why people don't go and teach, it is really good fun and rather good for me.

Because you get ideas?
My ex-wife used to say people over 30 are rogues and sort of dead. Young people are sparky.

Do young people make better films?
I hope not! I don't know. Sometimes you see a very early film you have made and you just think, I can't do that any more. You don't have a choice, this game thickens your skin and in the most dreadful way because it is such a bruising business. And you can't lose your virginity twice.

Perhaps you make different kinds of films all the time to try and recapture that innocence?
Yes, that moment of panic, that emotional spasm is very energising. And I have to say, it's been a lark!

Danny Boyle

Hannah Rothschild: What was your first association with Film4?

Danny Boyle: I got sent a script, *Shallow Grave*, and had to go in to describe my ideas on making it to David Aukin. He then said you can make it, here's a million pounds!

Had it always been your ambition to make a movie?

Oh God yes. But from the kind of background I come from, you couldn't get into the film industry. So I went into the theatre and then into television. In America TV and theatre tends not to be a route to movies. But here virtually all the directors you will talk to have come through TV.

Was *Shallow Grave* a typical Channel 4 film?

Very much so. The Channel clearly set out to embrace and challenge British taste and this included exciting, sexy, dangerous British movies.

Did you realise that *Shallow Grave* and *Trainspotting* were going to be such successes?

No, definitely not. But the scripts did share a sense of humour, morality, or lack of it, with pop music.

I don't understand the connection between films and pop music?

We hardly produce any decent movies, but we revive and reinvigorate pop music constantly. This is where our culture is triumphant in my opinion, and it explains people's loyalty is to music and *Shallow Grave* and *Trainspotting*. But then a lot of it is accidental, and you set out to make [each movie] even better than the previous one.

Do you think you achieved that? Do you feel each movie you have made is better than the last one?

[laughs]

You led me into asking that!

I am certainly not going to be led into answering it.

You seem to be able to switch easily between low budget, high budget, working in the States, working here with Film4.

I wouldn't really agree with you. I think I am better at slightly lower budget films. Really big budget films bring a different set of problems. The problem is making a good film and a budget is all dress-ing. Nobody turns up at a multiplex and thinks, 'Now which one of these costs the least?' when they are considering choosing a movie. So what you have got to do really regardless of your budget is just make something compelling and good. And the money thing is slightly peripheral to that in a way.

Earlier in this interview you said you still feel you don't know anything about making films.

My philosophy is you should try to make each film as differently as possible so that you set off in innocence. It's a fake of course, like your virginity, once it's gone it's gone. But that's why I like to do films that are very different to each other.

After a long break, you're making another film for Film4. How did this come about?

Film4 picked up the book called *Slumdog Millionaire* and got Simon Beaufoy to adapt it. It is very exciting to be able to work with them again. (Set in Mumbai the comedy is centered around, an illiterate kid who looks to become a contestant on the Hindi version of *Who Wants to be A Millionaire* in order to re-establish contact with the girl he loves, who is an ardent fan of the show.)

Tessa Ross said you could make a successful film with a good writer, but you can only make a great film with a great director. Do you agree?

Perhaps her skill is to find the right directors for each film.

How different would the history of film be without Film4?

It had this kind of confident, young, intelligent, snappy attitude there to challenge and to shock people. And whatever *The Daily Mail* writes up, people do want to be shocked. They want to see men kissing in *My Beautiful Laundrette*. Cinema should shock you and disturb you and amaze you and all that.

Do you think that Hollywood and filmmaking in general has lost the ability to shock and disturb?

Well Hollywood can't be an engine of that because it is too much of a business and can't take those risks. Some of the Film4 triumphs and failures are unpalatable in some ways and so they should be.

But is there really an appetite for so called difficult films?

Well the British prefer to go and see Hollywood movies. Because they work hard in a hospital or school and are knackered at the end of the week and their brain is on fire with boredom so they want to go and see Tom Cruise running around blowing up things that are impossible. Film's just not taken seriously here. In France, films are in their blood. Ordinary people go virtually every week to the movies. We go twice a year.

Does that mean we should subsidise film or let it live or die on its merits?

When you work in an industry and you see the way people behave and take taxis everywhere and lunches everywhere you ask is this right that we should be spending a million pounds (which is nothing in US terms), on any film. A million pounds. Should people be paying out of their taxes for these kinds of people to be running around spending money like this? It just seems wrong to me. What's brilliant about Channel 4 is that it's not subsidy, but it's actually paying for itself.

If you had to nominate one film or one scene that sums up Film4 for you?

I think there are a couple of things. The guys kissing in *My Beautiful Laundrette* and the change of the woman into a man in *The Crying Game*. Those really sum up Channel 4 for me.

If you had to give Channel 4 or Film4 any advice on its 25th year?

I wouldn't presume to give advice to somebody half my age.

If you had a present what would you give it?

I know the one it wants! *Trainspotting 2*.

Shallow Grave, 1994

Sarah Gavron

Hannah Rothschild: You've just made your first feature, *Brick Lane*, for Film4. How did it come about?

Sarah Gavron: It was one of those bizarre coincidences. I'd been looking for a project which dealt with themes of outsiders and women when Tessa Ross and Alison Owen approached me. I felt such an emotional connection with this story about an immigrant woman finding her voice and managing to reconcile her past with her present. Like her, I am a woman, a mother, I am a Londoner, I'm married and though I'm not from Bangladesh, I have immigrant grandparents. *Brick Lane* is a universal story.

Was it hard to get the script right?

Yes, but you have to get it right. Not least because each film takes such a lot out of you. After many drafts, we came up with this idea of having something contained in this one year of this woman's life, starting with spring and ending with winter and using 9/11 as the catalyst when the outer world started to impact on [the heroine's] inner life.

How important was going to film-school for your career?

I am a great believer in going on every course that is on offer, because you meet people and you get an opportunity to make things and make mistakes. Film-school allowed me to try things out.

And imagine having people like Stephen Frears in your cutting room! What more could you ask for. I definitely wouldn't have been able to get to the point of making a first film without having gone through that process of making lots and lots of shorts.

Your style is very painterly.

I wanted to be an artist and am very interested how images connect to story modes or emotions. I didn't know about filmmaking until I saw Terence Davies' film when I was about seventeen. I realised he had a particular perspective on the world. And I suddenly thought I have a particular view of the world too.

Have other British directors influenced you?

Loach, Frears and Mike Leigh have hugely influenced me. They made me think, we don't just have to make films about pretty women. We can make films about the world around us. Another influence is the female filmmakers like Jane Campion, who put emotion on the screen, and Lynne Ramsay and Gurinder Chadha for making me think.

But why is it so hard for women to make it as directors?

There are many factors. One is the system of filmmaking, the hierarchy of the crew. I don't think women would have ever invented it in that way. For example, in Denmark filmmaking is more collabora-

tive and there is no gender divide at all. Here, unconsciously or consciously, you do feel it. Also, the working hours in film make it very tough to have a family. Inevitably the stage in your career, when you are at the point of making films, which is in your 30s and 40s when you have done enough training and ground work, is the time when you are bringing up young children.

Would making a film with large resources be a dream?

I am material driven and really think that how you make a film should suit the film that you are making and the material. I would feel really uncomfortable having a huge budget for something that didn't merit it. The money has to go on screen. But time is so precious when you are making a film and time costs money. So for that reason having more a generous budget is a good thing.

Is it right to have a subsidised film industry?

Because we share a language with America and run the risk of being swamped by American films, we have to subsidise our film industry and make sure that stories that would not otherwise be told are told.

Can you nominate one Film4 film that particularly inspired you?

My Beautiful Laundrette made a huge impact on me in my formative years.

What advice would you give Film4 on its 25th year?

Keep going, because Britain really needs you to keep making films that others don't dare to.

Brick Lane, 2007

Mike Leigh

Naked, 1993

Secrets and Lies, 1996

Hannah Rothschild: How did the advent of Channel 4 change your working life?

Mike Leigh: Before then you couldn't get an independent film together. I'd had a seventeen year break since my first film, *Bleak Moments*. Then Channel 4 came along and suddenly the landscape changed. I made my second film *High Hopes* for them.

Seventeen years is a long time to wait. Had you given up believing you'd make another feature?

Absolutely. And if you'd told me then that I'd go on to make eight or nine more feature films, get a number of Oscar nominations, two Oscars, a Palme d'Or and a Golden Lion at Venice, I simply would have said, go whistle.

Wasn't it heartbreaking to spend seventeen years not doing what you really loved – making movies?

It was much more painful then than it is in retrospect because within that period of time I was still working all the time and developing my filmmaking skills. I had done quite a number of some very

successful plays at the theatre and, apart from that, grown up somewhat.

You sound remarkably sanguine about it.

Things happen and life is meant to be that way you know. A little bit of Zen about the whole thing. It is what it is. And actually, it couldn't have worked out better than the way that it has.

So how did Channel 4 contribute to your second film?

I'd worked with David Rose [the first head of Film4] a lot at the Beeb and did *Nuts in May*. And it was him who commissioned *Meantime*. Sadly, it was just a bit early to be a feature film, but six to nine months later it would have been. But we got on and did what's now an obscure but very popular underground film. It is now out on DVD. Then I did, consecutively, *Short-and-Curlies*, *High Hopes*, *Life is Sweet* and *Naked*.

Naked, 1993

High Hopes, 1988

Did you make *Career Girls* for Film4?

The BBC commissioned us [originally] to make the film. But then the contracts department lost the paperwork or didn't sign things. Then there was a letter that my producer Simon Channing-Williams

sent from our completion guarantor that also got lost. It just dragged on and on and nobody took any responsibility for it and the producer at the BBC messed about. And finally, for a wheeze, we went round the corner to see David Aukin at Film4 and said, 'look why don't you do this?' He said okay and for exactly the same budget. They processed it in ten days, when it had taken eighteen months for the BBC to wank about. When they heard, the BBC were furious. They said, 'You can't do that.' We said, 'You can't do what?' So that is how *Career Girls* happened.

Life is Sweet, 1990

Based on your experience, would you say that Channel 4 resuscitated the British Film Industry?

This is such a non-negotiable, historical fact of life fact and anybody who suggests that this isn't the case is simply either suffering from some kind of ignorance or has got some terrible chip.

Do you feel a sense of camaraderie with contemporaries such as Stephen Frears, Ken Loach and Terence Davies who also did great work with Film4?

What is interesting is how different we are, but I would acknowledge that fraternity and I think they would too.

You're just finishing post on a new movie for Film4. How did it come about and what is it called?

It is not called anything. That Roget's Thesaurus on the desk over there is a sign that I am under pressure to decide what it is called.

What's it about?

I am not talking about it at all. You'll have to see it. I can tell you every frame if I want, but I am not going to because you will see it when it is finished.

Are there any particular favourites amongst the Film4 productions?

I don't know. There are lots.

What about one of your own?

I can't answer that question, neither in the context of my films or anybody else's.

Gurinder Chadha

Bhaji on the Beach, 1993

Hannah Rothschild: How did you get into making films?

Gurinder Chadha: I made various documentaries and shorts but my first film was a short called *I'm British But…* which I made with the BFI and Channel 4 in 1989 as part of a scheme which allowed people who had no film experience, but had a voice to kind of say what they wanted to say. I then got together with Meera Syal and Karin Bamborough at Film4 and started developing *Bhaji on the Beach*. Channel 4 definitely gave me my break for features.

Why was *Bhaji on the Beach* so significant?

It was the first British film which had a large Asian female cast, but had its feet firmly in the roots of British cinema. It had a British sensibility although there were Indians in it, but most importantly people really related to it all over the world.

Why didn't you bring your next films, including *Bend it like Beckham* to Film4?

I actually gave it to Paul Webster twice. And he said, 'Oh we have already done it.' I said, 'You are making a big mistake really.' And he just said, 'No. I have seen that, I don't want to see it again.' I even accosted him at an airport; I caught him at Heathrow airport once and said to him, 'Are you sure you don't want to look at it?' And he was like, 'No, No, No.'

Are you always so sure?

I knew *Beckham* was going to be a hit obviously, I just felt it had to be. It was hitting the right marks in terms of British society at that time; the Beckham thing, the girls, it was just the thing to do it.

Quite a lot of people claim to have had an input into *Bend It like Beckham*.

Only two qualify. John Woodwood and Simon Terry. This film shows how easy it is for history to change. If Paul Webster had backed me at the time there would still be a FilmFour rather than a Channel 4 Film, as it is now. Put that in your book.

Did the shorts and documentaries provide necessary training?

Filmmaking is technical, and you need to know technical facts. But it's also about storytelling, and television drama is a good training ground. To some degree you can do this in commercials, but shooting objects doesn't necessarily give you the right background.

Unlike many people, you produce, direct and write.

I didn't want to be a writer. I was a director but I turned to writing because I couldn't find the scripts I wanted to make, and then I turned to producing because people did not necessarily want to finance the sort of films I wanted to direct.

Doesn't it require a huge amount of energy and very different skills to switch between writing and directing and producing?

Yes, but sometimes it is easier directing a scene that you've written as you know where all the beats are. And then if it's not working for one reason or another, you can adapt and change the script quickly to get the beats that you need. So in that sense it is good. But at other times it takes all your energy just to do one thing, and I can't say I am always good at doing all three things all the time.

Do you imagine going back to making small budget films or are you more interested in larger productions with bigger scope?

I am not averse to small budgets. I mean I am not averse to doing anything that tells a story. As long as the script is good and it is a good story you are telling. I think you can do shorts, you can do television dramas, you can do features. I think they all have their own good points and bad points. Some are easier to shoot, some are harder to put together financially. I mean a big budget film has its own problems because you have so many people you have to please all the time. And a lot of it becomes filmmaking by committee, whereas the smaller and shorter lower budget films you can have a lot more control over. It is horses for courses actually and I am lucky enough to have had a taste of all of it.

Did you have any mentors at the beginning or now, or do you feel you have always had to do your own thing?

I have had to rely on myself and learn on the job. I didn't know anyone in the business and came up through being a journalist really. That's how I slotted into that British, human way of telling stories.

Do you feel it is harder for women to be film directors?

I think it is hard for everyone to make features, to get that break, which is why I come back to say it is about storytelling and really being the person with the voice. Having a voice or having a vision is the only way to get things made.

What would you give Film4 for its 25th year?

Another *Bend It Like Beckham*!

Bhaji on the Beach, 1993

Ken Loach

Riff-Raff, 1990

Riff-Raff, 1990

Hannah Rothschild: Can you tell me about your history with Channel 4?

Ken Loach: I've had very mixed experiences with Channel 4, some brilliant and some horrific. I did *The Band* for them [which] was banned in what was straight political censorship, and Channel 4 was politically inept and cowardly. That took two years out of my life and a lot of senior people just hung me out to dry. But there were good experiences, such as working with David Rose and Film4.

Do you think that without Film4 your career would have been very different?

Yes. The critical things for me were that Film4 wholly financed three films in the beginning of the Nineties. *Riff-Raff*, *Raining Stones* and *Ladybird Ladybird* and they really were the turning point for me. Before that I was really struggling and after that it was much easier, so I owe Film4 a huge debt.

Would you agree that for many British directors, television is their training school?

Yes, people either come [to film] through television, fiction or the theatre and commercials. Television is one industry with films. It is not separate. I mean you work in the same way. All the issues you have to deal with are the same. Whether the film is going on television or in the cinema.

You've just made *It's a Free World* for Channel 4. Why did you decide to do it for TV and not film?

Television is still a very important medium; that's the reality for British film. And the odds are that if you don't have a big name your film will get a very short print run and therefore not much advertising and therefore not many people will see it. And it kind of fades away. So every few years we have tried to do one that has its first run on television. And then you might get a new audience.

What are the figures like between something shown at the cinema and on telly?

The biggest success we have had in the cinema was probably *The Wind that Shakes the Barley* and we had 40 prints in Britain for that. In France they had 350, in Ireland they had 70 because it was an Irish film, so there is a massive difference.

What's the average print run for a big movie here?

In Britain you would probably get two hundred to three hundred prints for a popular commercial show. But in terms of audience I would think we could maybe look at, if we were lucky, between half a million people coming, whereas in television it should be several million I would hope. And then there is the DVD at the same time.

Is there an archetypal Film4?

There should not be an archetypal Film4; it should be a really broad range shouldn't it?

Should Film4's remit be to nurture new talent or support the old masters?

It has got to do both. But it's often more difficult after the first film. It is the ones doing their third and fourth who need support. Because producers and executives have this idea that filmmaking's a craft you don't need to learn and that somehow you can be a first time filmmaker and do something marvellous. Well you might, but it is very hit and miss. It is like anything. I mean it's like journalism; you do learn it through experience. I think it is no bad thing if Channel 4 helps to re-establish the primacy of writers. Because there is a whole heresy grown up I think, partly fostered by the film schools, that directors should write their own scripts – it's pretentious really. So I think Channel 4 should cherish the writers and directors who have maybe made two or three films.

Do you feel part of a fraternity with contemporaries such as Stephen Frears and Mike Leigh, or are you completely independent; people who happen to be British?

No, it is neither one nor t'other really. Mostly we all know each other and are good friends. And enjoy each other's work. But I think beyond that it is not helpful to see yourself as a collective. Because you know everybody has got to plough their own furrow and arrive at what they do through their own experience and preoccupations.

It's a Free World, 2007

Shane Meadows

Hannah Rothschild: How did you get into film in the first place?

Shane Meadows: I was a bit like Madonna. You know these people who do really badly at school and left with no qualifications and went for a job as a clown's assistant at Alton Towers. Then I got on a photography course in Nottingham and exposed every loophole and got about eighteen student loans and would use fake names with the gas board and stuff. I had all these names with different gas bills in different names and had to leave because I got into a lot of trouble. They said I had to pay all the money back. I was on my way home from having that meeting with the head of the photography course when I saw a film crew, and the thing that attracted me was there were about eight girls. There was this guy, Graham Ford, a black guy and I was saying, 'How did you get on the course?' He said, 'Well unless you are black or a lesbian or single parent or disabled,' he said, 'you have absolutely no chance, because it is for minorities.' This guy took me under his wing and at weekends he would lend me camcorders and cameras and things like that. It was the holidays and everyone was away, so I made this film by myself where I played like four to five characters in the house, just to amuse myself. By the time they had all come back from their holidays I had made three films. So within twelve months I had self-trained myself as it were and gone through my own kind of condensed film course if you like.

Then your career took off very quickly didn't it?

I sent *Where's the Money, Ronnie?* off to a short film competition and got a call from Steve Wooley. And then within I think two to three months we were basically going round having meetings about *24/7* and Stephen knew Bob Hoskins from *Mona Lisa* and said, 'Who do you imagine playing the part?' And it was like at every turn I said, 'I would love to work with Bob Hoskins,' and he knew him and arranged all these meetings and I realised if you have got a key to the door in those things, having the right person who knows these people makes all the difference. That was kind of how that transition from making a load of films with my friends and one phone call from someone senior in a film competition, and everything accelerated at an incredible pace.

So becoming a director was accidental?

Yes completely. Now I am directing I have that passion and I have that vision and I can't imagine doing anything else and it almost scares me sometime because I think to myself it would have been so easy not to have found it.

Are you telling stories that no one else could tell?

It's not the story; it's the way of telling it. Lots of working class dramas are the same on paper, but what sets me aside is the fact that I kind of grew up within it. I was a small time thief, I was a gambler and I was a hustler. A lot of films about that kind of subject matter seem to be observational and so rather than sympathising with people, I am empathising with people.

Can you imagine another company that would support you as wholeheartedly as Film4?

No way. For example, I just found out that my granddad is very poorly and he lives in Thailand. I very briefly spoke to Peter Carlton and Tessa Ross at Film4 and said, 'I don't know quite what I am going to do, but I am thinking about going over to see my granddad and making a documentary. It isn't a feature film but it could be like a short film.' So Tessa sat me down and said, 'We want you to travel the world and see things.' They give me true artistic freedom. It is almost embarrassing to say, but it is like being home. With Tessa there was always an undying belief that at some point my films would hit and that takes a lot of pressure off your shoulders because as a filmmaker, it is like in any job, if someone says to you, you have got to sell twenty cars by the end of the week otherwise you haven't got a job, who wants to work under those conditions?

You said you started on *Small Time* when you were in Nottingham. Had you seen films when you were growing up?

We had a Hell's Angel who lived two fields away from us in a little housing estate and I used to walk over these films and he had a massive pirate video collection. So I watched a lot of stuff like *The Warriors*, *Texas Chain Saw Massacre*, a lot of the cult stuff that was around. My dad was a long distance lorry driver and away a lot of the time, so when he got back we used to sit down on a Sunday afternoon and watch four or five westerns back to back. Two of my favourite films I had seen were *Raging Bull* and *Taxi Driver* and I didn't have any idea it was the same person that directed them.

Would you say Scorsese is a hero, or not really like that?

The fact that Scorsese had made a film about the mafia but the absolute bottom rung of the ladder, you know, inspired me to make a film. You have to make films about things that are personal to you. I used to hustle you know and I got caught pinching chicken tikka sandwiches with raspberry crush. I had pinched a high quality snack because I thought if I am going to get done for it I might as well eat really well. There is no point getting done for egg and cress. And so I made films about that because that was true to where I was from.

But as your career gets more established, as you earn more money and gain more acclaim, will it remove you from source material and change what you do?

It could do. But tonight I am going to a beard shaving competition in Uttoxeter where I am from. I stay very much in touch with the local gossip and stories and I go and play in the darts team that is still in the area. So I still mix with a lot of those characters.

What's happening next?

I have just signed a new deal with Film4 for the next three years. I am just about to start developing a story about the bare-knuckled gypsy fighter who was actually the King of the Gypsies for about twenty years. I also have two or three lower budget things in mind too. So at the moment it couldn't be better.

This is England, 2006

Kevin Macdonald

Hannah Rothschild: How did you get into filmmaking?

Kevin Macdonald: I was writing a book about my grandfather, the filmmaker and screenwriter Emeric Pressburger, an Eastern European Jew who came via Prague and Berlin to London and formed a partnership with Michael Powell. And the book became a documentary. It was my first experience of working with Channel 4 and what was great was that they were happy to give someone who was very inexperienced a shoot with £120,000, which is more than you probably get these days for a one off documentary film.

What was your next film with them?

I was sent the book *Touching the Void* and I loved it and felt we should make this not just for TV but also for cinema. Film4 was then under Paul Webster and had a lot of film money. It was pretty much the last production that Film4 made before it collapsed. There'd been five years of flops and then along came *Touching the Void* and *The Motorcycle Diaries*.

Did you always see documentaries as a stepping stone to features?

Nothing in my life is planned; it's all been accidental. I actually used to really quite despise filmmaking and was evangelical about documentaries. But then I made *Touching the Void* and experienced a little bit more of the control that you can have as a director in terms of controlling the performances of the actors and the special effects and realised that documentary can be a bit limiting sometimes. There are things you can do in documentary that you can't do in any other form and it is the spontaneity and the intimacy and all those things, but there are also great limitations. But I wanted to stretch myself technically as a director and drama allows that.

The Last King of Scotland has a fresh and documentary feel at times. Is this down to your training in that field?

We could only make that film in eight weeks because I was a documentary film

maker. If I'd been a trained dramatic filmmaker I'd probably have been there four months later still trying to get the shots. Nothing went according to plan in Uganda. You would be promised X, Y & Z and it wouldn't show up or you couldn't start shooting until-mid day because of such and such. And the extras were traumatised soldiers from the war in the north and weren't able to act. But if you come from a documentary background you are used to working, making the most of that and using accidents and embracing accidents rather than to trying to control absolutely everything. We shot a lot on two cameras to cover everything.

The Last King of Scotland cost around five million pounds, your latest film is rumoured to cost over 80 million dollars. Presumably you wont be shooting on the hoof this time.

I don't know. I am hoping that the Director of Photography and I can find a way of having a certain spontaneity and we both agree that we never want to use cranes and be hand held most of the time. Certainly it is different from *The Last King of Scotland* in that here you can have whatever you want. And so I don't know what effect that is going to have. I am curious. The important thing for me is you have to retain a certain degree of anarchy. But I am not sure how easy it is to retain anarchy when you are working with that amount of money!

Have you tasted the apple in the Garden of Eden? Will you ever go back to low budget British films?

I would like to carry on doing everything you know. For me doing this Hollywood film is really an adventure but I am not sort of embracing a Hollywood career at present. But if somebody says to you, 'Do you want Ed Norton and Helen Mirren and to do a movie for a huge amount of money in a studio and we will build a huge set?' I said, 'Well of course, who wouldn't.' You would be mad not to try it once wouldn't you? So that's the way I see it. And we will see what happens.

Are you nervous?

No, because it's all magic and it is out of your control. My grandfather used to say that you build the best nest you can and have to hope that the magic is going to come and flutter down and reside in the nest that you have created. You can prepare as much as you like and it can all go wrong.

How did the magic come about with *The Last King of Scotland*?

I read Peter Morgan's script and got very excited and saw the way to mix fact and fiction and a way to make a film that is both, you know, horrific and comedic. You get a surge of excitement when you get the feeling you know how to make it work or you understand the tone of something and it is an indefinable thing. You kind of grasp what the story is to yourself without putting it into words. The producer Lisa Bryer had been battling for ages to make it and it was fully supported and nurtured by Film4.

You are steeped in a tradition of film. Can you imagine the history of British Film for example without Film4?

Film4 came at an absolutely crucial moment and with an attitude. That was in the 1980s, when it started making films which were an extension of what it was doing as a television station at that time. It started making films that had some relevance to people's lives and young people's lives in particular and reflecting British subculture.

Should Film4 be commissioning first timers or supporting existing masters whose films are hard to finance?

The bottom line is that you know there aren't many good people around, not many good scripts around and the consequence of that is there aren't many good films around. Film4 has a duty to support people like Loach and Leigh because they are the masters in our country and they make very low budget films and are an important part of British cinematic culture. However, I was supported by Film4 and I was a first time director.

You mentioned Loach and Leigh, do you have specific mentors?

I admire the three elder statesmen of British cinema, Loach, Leigh and Stephen Frears. I don't like every film they have made but they've all made great, great movies and they all have a specific way of going about things. They are all flies in the ointment of the establishment.

What are you doing next?

I have got a film I very much want to make with Film4 called *The Eagle of the Ninth* which is set during the Roman occupation of Britain, based on a children's book. It's like a cowboy movie but set in Roman times in the wilderness of Scotland and it's mostly just figures in landscape, about a boy going to look for his father who has gone missing with the Roman legion in the north of Scotland.

The Last King of Scotland, 2006

Contributors

Niall Ferguson is the author of *War of the World* and a specialist in economic and financial history. He is Professor of History at Harvard Univeristy.

TWO
Making The News

Edward Docx is a British newspaper columnist, broadcaster and writer. His second novel *Self Help* was longlisted for the 2007 Booker Prize.

Stewart Purvis is a British broadcaster and the former Chief Executive and Editor in Chief of ITN.

Jon Snow is the presenter of the *Channel 4 News*.

THREE
Provoking Debate

Nick Broomfield is a documentary film maker, whose films include *Aileen, Kurt & Courteney*, and *Ghosts*. His latest film is *The Battle For Haditha*.

Molly Dineen is a broadcaster and documentary maker whose work includes *The Ark, The Company of Men* and, most recently, Channel 4's *The Lie of the Land*.

Michael Gallagher is the head of the Omagh Support and Self Help Group.

Tony Harrison is an English poet: in 2004 he won the Northern Rock Foundation Writer's Award.

Lucie Willan is a Bombay-based journalist and editor.

Peter Morgan is a writer; his screenplay for *The Queen* was nominated for a 2007 Oscar. In 2006, he won a BAFTA for *The Last King of Scotland*.

Peter Oborne is a journalist and commentator. He writes for *The Daily Mail*, as well as being a contributing editor of *The Spectator*. He has written and presented a number of documentaries for Channel 4, including *Iraq: On the Front Line* for *Unreported World*.

FOUR
Our Multi-Culture

Diran Adebayo is the author of *Some Kind of Black*, which won the 1996 Saga Prize. He has worked for *The Guardian*, *The Daily Mail*, and Britain's biggest black newspaper, *The Voice*.

Alkarim Jivani was formerly the TV editor of *Time Out*. He has published *It's not Unusual: A History of Lesbian and Gay Britain in the Twentieth Century*.

Hanif Kureishi is an author and writer whose work includes *My Beautiful Laundrette, The Buddha of Surbubia* and *Intimacy*. His latest book is *Something to Tell You*.

Daljit Nagra won the Forward Prize for Best Single Poem 2004, for his poem *Look We Are Coming To Dover*.

FIVE
Laughter

Stephen Armstrong is a comedy writer for *The Guardian, The Sunday Times, GQ, Wallpaper** and the *New Statesman*.

Alan Carr is a British stand-up comedian and TV presenter, currently presenting Channel 4's *Friday Night Project*.

Tamsin Greig is best known for her comedy performances, which include two Channel 4 television parts: Fran Katzenjammer in *Black Books* and Dr. Caroline Todd in *Green Wing*.

Jessica Hynes is an English actress and writer, as well as one of the creators and stars of Channel 4's *Spaced*.

Martin Parr is an internationally celebrated British documentary photographer and photojournalist.

Father Seed is a Catholic Priest and Ecumenical Officer at the Archdiocese of Westminster. His published works include *Gift of Assurance, Letters from the Heart* and *Will I See You in Heaven?*

SIX
The Drug Deal

Horatio Clare has written for *The Guardian*, *The Sunday Times*, *The Daily Telegraph* and *Vogue*. His book *Running for the Hills* won the Somerset Maugham Award in 2007.

Nick Davies is an award-winning journalist who won the 2004 Europe Prize: Journalism for a Changing World. He wrote and presented the Channel 4 documentary *The Drug Laws Don't Work: The Phoney War*.

Mario Hugo is a New York-based artist and designer.

Simon Moore wrote *Traffik;* his work on that mini-series was the basis for the Oscar-winning film *Traffic*. Other credits include the 1991 film *Under Suspicion*.

SEVEN
Adventures in Art

Rupert Christiansen is the chief opera critic for *The Telegraph*, and has contributed to *The Spectator*, *TLS*, *Harpers & Queen*, *Vanity Fair*, *The New Yorker* and *Talk*.

Paul Daniel is the former Director of Music at the ENO. In 2009 he will take up the post of Principal Conductor of the West Australian Symphonic Orchestra.

Sir Christopher Frayling is a writer on popular culture, critic, Rector of the Royal College of Art and Chairman of the Arts Council. His books include a biography of the Spaghetti Western director Sergio Leone.

Howard Goodall is a composer of musicals, choral music and music for television. He has presented the *Choir of the Year*, *Chorister of the Year* and *Young Musician of the Year* and six award-winning series of television programmes on musical history.

Waldemar Januszczak is a British art critic, a contributor to *The Sunday Times* and a maker of television arts documentaries. He has also worked at Channel 4 as Commissioning Editor for Arts.

EIGHT
The Food Fight

Tamasin Day-Lewis is a food writer and author. Her books include *Tarts with Tops on: Or How to Make the Perfect Pie* and *Simply the Best* and most recently, *Where Shall We Go For Dinner Darling?*

Hugh Fearnley-Whittingstall is a writer and broadcaster whose books include *The River Cottage Meat Book*, and *The River Cottage Fish Book*. He presents *The River Cottage* for Channel 4.

Rose Prince is an author and columnist for *The Daily Telegraph*. She is the author of *The Savvy Shopper*. Her latest book is *The New English Table*.

Gordon Ramsay is a chef and TV presenter whose programmes include *The F Word*.

Boo Ritson is an artist who coats objects and living people with household emulsion to transform them into new characters. Her work is an amalgam of sculpture, paint and photography.

NINE
Earthly Powers

Phil Agland is the award-winning director of *Fragile Earth*, *Beyond the Clouds*, *Baka: People of the Rainforest*, *French Affair* and *Shanghai Vice*.

Andy Goldsworthy is a sculptor, photographer and environmentalist who produces site-specific temporary or permanent sculpture and land art situated in natural and urban settings.

Mark Lynas is the author of several books on climate warming. *Six Degrees: Our Future on a Hotter Planet* will be published in 2008.

Richard Mabey has written on countryside and art issues for *The Times*, *The Sunday Times* and *The Sunday Telegraph*. A selection of these writings were compiled as the book *Country Matters*.

Marcel Theroux is a novelist and a broadcaster. His most recent novel is *A Blow to the Heart*. He wrote and presented the Channel 4 documentary *The End of the World As We Know It*.

TEN
The Female Equation

Michelle Hanson writes *The Age of Dissent* column for *The Guardian*. A collection of her journalism has been published as *The Age of Dissent* by Virago press.

Rita Konig is the author of *Domestic Bliss: Simple Ways to Add Style to Your Life* and *Rita's Culinary Trickery*. She is a contributor to British *Vogue*.

Serge Seidlitz is an artist who lives and works in London. He has created illustrations for MTV, VH1, Honda, Volvic, Orange, JWT, John Brown Citrus Publishing, *The Guardian*, *NME* and Scarlett

Zoe Williams is a columnist for *The Guardian*: she writes political commentary, interviews and reviews.

ELEVEN
Oh My God

Karen Armstrong is a former nun turned author who writes on Judaism, Christianity, Islam and Buddhism. Her books include *A History of God: The 4,000-Year Quest of Judaism, Christianity & Islam* and *The Battle for God*.

Professor Richard Dawkins is an evolutionary biologist and author. He has also made documentaries for Channel 4.

Gwyneth Lewis is the first National Poet of Wales. She is an Honorary Fellow of Cardiff University.

Michael Morpurgo has written over 100 books. He was Childrens' Laureate in 2006.

Lee Mawdsley is a London-based photographer whose work includes both commercial and art projects.

Ivo Stourton is an author and lawyer, whose book *The Night Climbers* was published in 2007

Kevin Toolis is a writer and filmmaker whose work includes *The Cult of the Suicide Bomber*. He has reported on conflicts in Africa, Ireland and the Middle East.

TWELVE
Reality Check

Terry Eagleton is Professor of English at Manchester University. He writes regularly for the *New Statesman*, and *The Guardian*.

Gautam Malkani is a *Financial Times* journalist and author of *Londonstani*.

Andrew O'Hagan is a writer and winner of The Somerset Maugham and The People's Choice awards. His books include *Personality*, *The Missing* and *Our Fathers*. He is a contributing editor of the *London Review of Books*.

Snowdon is one of Britain's most prominent and respected photographers. He also makes documentary films.

THIRTEEN
Home Sweet Home

Leon Chew is a London-based photographer. He gained a PhD in Fine Art/ Aesthetics from Goldsmiths College. In 1989 he was awarded life membership of the Society of Chinese Artists.

Nigel Coates is an English architect and interior designer known for his futuristic, avant-garde designs. He is Professor of Architectural Design at The Royal College of Art.

Alain de Botton is a writer and television producer. He is the author of *Essays in Love*.

Daisy Leitch is a writer and researcher. She has written for *The Daily Mail*, *Art Review* and *Varsity*. She has most recently been working on *The Channel 4 Political Awards*.

Kevin McCloud is the writer and presenter of *Grand Designs* and *Grand Designs: Trade Secrets*.

Angela Moore is a London-based photographer who specialises in still life and interiors. She has worked extensively for *Wallpaper**, *The Saturday Telegraph* and *The New York Times*.

Peter York is a British management consultant, author and broadcaster best known for co-authoring *Harpers & Queen's The Official Sloane Ranger Handbook* with Ann Barr. He is also a columnist for *The Independent on Sunday*, *GQ* and *Management Today*.

FOURTEEN
Youth In Its Wisdom

David Bain is a Partner at BMB Advertising Agency.

Jody Barton has worked as an illustrator and animator for MTV, Greenpeace, Glastonbury Festival, Amnesty International and *The Big Issue*.

Edward Behrens is a writer and editor of *Christie's Magazine*. He has also directed several plays, including Booker Prize-winning author Alan Hollinghurst's translation of Racine's *Bajazet*.

Rose Heiney is an actor, novelist and writer. Her work has appeared in *The Times* and her first novel *The Days of Judy B* is published in 2008.

Oliver James is a clinical psychologist, writer and television documentary producer who has written columns for *The Sun*, *The Sunday Telegraph* and most recently, *The Observer Magazine*.

June Sarpong is a TV presenter who shot to prominence on T4. She is an ambassador for The Prince's Trust and also campaigns for the Make Poverty History movement.

Miranda Sawyer is a feature writer for *The Observer* and *Esquire*. Her work also appears in *GQ*, *Vogue*, and *The Guardian*.

Ewen Spencer is a freelance photographer who has worked with magazines such as *The Face*, *Sleaze*, *Details* and *I-D* and bands such as The Streets, The White Stripes and Doves.

FIFTEEN
A Question of Difference

John Callahan was rendered quadriplegic by an automobile accident in 1972 at the age of 21; he draws his cartoons by clutching a pen between both hands. Two animated films have been based on his cartoons: *Pelswick*, a children's show on Nickelodeon; and *Quads*, a Canadian-Australian co-production subsequently shown on Channel 4.

David Cook is a novelist and playwright.

Ann McFerran is an interviewer who regularly contributes to *The Sunday Times Magazine's Life in the Day* columns.

Lara Masters is a disabled director, producer, writer, researcher and actress.

Rufus May is a clinical psychologist who teaches at the University of Bradford.

Jack Thorne is a playwright whose work includes *Skins*.

SIXTEEN
Shrinking Planet

Rana Dasgupta is a British-Indian writer whose works include *Tokyo Cancelled*, which was shortlisted for the 2005 John Llewellyn Rhys Prize. He is currently writing a novel about the history of daydreams in Bulgaria.

Christopher Herwig is a Canadian travel and anthropological photographer based in Monroe, Liberia.

Sarfraz Manzoor is a writer, broadcaster and documentary filmmaker. He is a columnist for *The Guardian* and contributes to *The Daily Mail*, *The Independent*, *The Observer*, and *Uncut*. His television directing credits include *The Great British Asian Invasion* and *Death of a Porn Star* both for Channel 4.

Sorious Samura is an award winning Sierra Leone journalist and documentary maker whose work includes *Living with Hunger*, which was shown on Channel 4.

Brian Woods is a documentary filmmaker, who founded the independent production company True Vision, which concentrates on human-rights issues. He has been awarded or nominated for several international awards, including six Emmies and a BAFTA. His documentaries *The Dying Rooms* and *China's Stolen Children* were shown on Channel 4.

SEVENTEEN
New Family Values

Camilla Batmanghelidjh is the head of the children's support organisation Kids Company.

Rachel Cusk is an award-winning writer and author whose books include *The Lucky Ones* and *Arlington Park*

Frank Furedi is Professor of Sociology at the University of Kent. He writes regularly for *Spiked Online*.

EIGHTEEN
The Creative Economy

Chris Blackhurst is City Editor of *The Evening Standard*. He was formerly deputy editor of *The Independent* and *The Daily Express*.

Adam Hayes is a designer and illustrator. In 2006 he formed his own studio in east London where he works and collaborates on projects for himself, his friends and various clients worldwide.

NINETEEN
All Change

Christa D' Souza is a columnist for *The Observer* and *The Times* and a regular *Vogue* contributor.

Dr Phil Hammond is a medical doctor and a comedian and commentator on health issues. Although he still works part time as a GP he is best known for his humorous commentary on the National Health Service.

Cordelia Jenkins has worked for *The World of Interiors* and *House and Garden* magazines and is currently an editor at *Christie's Magazine*.

Liz Jones is an English writer and journalist. She writes regularly for *The Daily Mail*.

Nato Welton is a London-based photographer who previously studied as a clothes designer and stylist. His work has appeared in a variety of international publications.

TWENTY
The Special Relationship

Gregory Crewdson is an American photographer best known for elaborately staged, surreal scenes of American homes and neighbourhoods. His work has been shown in New York at the Luhring Augustine Gallery and in London by the White Cube Gallery. He is Professor of Photography at Yale University.

Anthony Haden-Guest is a writer, reporter and cartoonist. He has published in leading magazines in Britain and America, most recently in *Esquire*, *GQ* and *The Observer Magazine*.

Sir Christopher Meyer is a former British Ambassador to the United States and the current Chair of the Press Complaints Commission. In 2006 he published his memoirs *DC Confidential*.

Julien Temple is an English film, documentary and music video director. His best known work featured the Sex Pistols in *The Great Rock & Roll Swindle*.

TWENTY-ONE
Uncensored

Paul Yule is an award-winning documentary filmmaker, specialising in directing and producing controversial documentaries, often on political themes. For Channel 4 he wrote and directed the documentary *Damned in the USA*.

TWENTY-TWO
The History Files

Dr. David Starkey is a Fellow of Fitzwilliam College, Cambridge and a pre-eminent TV historian.

Jan Morris is a history and travel writer. Her work includes the seminal Empire trilogy *Pax Britannica*.

Jonty Oliff-Cooper is a history teacher who also took part in *The Edwardian Country House*.

Tony Robinson is an English actor, broadcaster, political campaigner and presenter of *Time Team*.

Raqib Shaw is a London-based Kashmiri-born contemporary artist whose *Garden of Earthly Delights X 2004 series* was exhibited at Tate Britain in 2006.

TWENTY-THREE
The Pink Triangle

Bidisha is a writer and a novelist. Her work has appeared in *I-D* and *The Big Issue*. Her novels include *Sea Horses* and *Venetian Masters*.

Kevin Elyot is a playwright whose work includes *My Night with Reg*, winner of the 1994 Olivier Award for best comedy. His most recent play *Clapham Junction* was shown on Channel 4 in 2007.

Patrick Gale is a novelist whose work includes *Facing the Tank*, *The Aerodynamics of Pork* and *Ease*.

Nicky Haslam is an interior designer and social columnist. His autobiography is due out in 2008.

TWENTY-FOUR
Access All Areas

Russell M Davies is a writer, blogger and advertising strategist.

Charles Leadbetter is a writer and adviser on technology and creativity. In 2005 Accenture ranked him as one of the top management thinkers in the world.

TWENTY-FIVE
Filmspotting

Hannah Rothschild makes documentary features including portraits of Frank Auerbach, Walter Sickert and RB Kitaj. She has written screenplays for Working Title and Ridley Scott and articles for *Vanity Fair*, *The New York Times*, *W* and *Vogue*.

Alastair Thain is a British photographer whose imaginative and often subversive portraits have appeared in *Vogue*, *The New York Times*, *Vanity Fair* and *The Face*.

THE SCRIBBLER

Andrew Rae is an illustrator and member of the Illustration Collective Peepshow.

Credits

Credits for images in order
of appearance

ONE
TWENTY-FIVE YEARS ON
Channel Four Ident, Lambie-Nairn, courtesy of Channel Four Television © 1982
Channel Four Diner Ident, 4 Creative / director Brett Foraker, courtesy of Channel 4 Television © 2004

TWO
MAKING THE NEWS
Michael Heseltine, Female Prisoners, Alastair Campbell, Jon Snow, Serbia image courtesy of ITN, producer of Channel Four News since 1982
Miners' Strike, Martin Shakeshaft

THREE
PROVOKING DEBATE
The Mark of Cain photograph by Nick Wall 2007
Bremner, Bird and Fortune image courtesy of Vera Productions Ltd
GBH © 1991
Dispatches – Beneath The Veil a Hardcash Production for Channel Four, courtesy of Channel Four Television © 2001
Hamburg Cell photographs by Phil Fisk
Iraq: The Bloody Circus Advert, 4 Creative / Polly Borland © 2006
Lost for Words Advert, 4 Creative / Tim Simmons © 2007
9/11 Falling Man Advert, 4 Creative / PA Photos / AP
Dispatches: The Hurricane that Shamed America, 4 Creative / Jim Watson / AFP / Getty Images
Omagh photographs by Patrick Redmond courtesy of Element Pictures
Lie of the Land photographs by Glenn Dearing © 2007
Class in Britain Advert, 4Creative / Marc Aspland / NI Syndication
The Deal photographs by Chris Terry / Contour by Getty Images
Legless Advert, 4Creative / Alan Mahon / Horton Stephens
The Government Inspector Advert 4Creative / Bruno Vincent / Getty Images
The Government Inspector photographs by Laurie Sparham
Dispatches – Mad About Animals Advert, 4 Creative Hans Reinhard / Zefa / Corbis
Ghosts Advert, 4 Creative, George Kavanagh / Alex Howe / Green Dog © 2007

FOUR
OUR MULTI-CULTURE
My Beautiful Laundrette images courtesy of Film Four Ltd © 1985
Screen grab from 100% English courtesy of Wall to Wall Media Ltd © 2006
Bandung File © 1985
Screen grab from Britz courtesy of Daybreak Pictures © 2007
East is East images courtesy of Film Four Ltd ©
Britz Advert, 4 Creative / Gavin Evans

Caribbean Summer Flag Advert, 4 Creative / Rapier
Screen grab from Caribbean Summer courtesy of ECB / Channel Four
Cricket Supporter image, courtesy of Julian Finney / Getty Images
Summer Sessions Advert, 4 Creative / Blue Source
WG Grace Advert, 4 Creative / David Purdie / Mutton Bones
Indian Summer Advert, 4 Creative
Young Black Farmers photograph by John Hurst
White Teeth photographs by Alex Bailey
Desmond's © 1989
Screen grab from Hajj: The Greatest Trip on Earth an ITN Ltd production for Channel Four, courtesy of Channel Four Television © 2003

FIVE
LAUGHTER
Friday Night Project photograph by John Wright
Phoenix Nights photograph by Ken Loveday
The Comic Strip Presents © 1982
Ali G photograph by Amanda Searle
Saturday Night Live © 1985
The 11 O'Clock Show © 1998
Screen grab from Brass Eye a Talkback Production Ltd production for Channel Four courtesy of Channel Four Television
Star Stories photograph by John Wright
Screen grabs from Green Wing a Talk Back Thames production for Channel Four courtesy of Talkback Thames, Victoria Pile and Channel Four Television
Green Wing Advert, 4 Creative / Jim Fiscus
Screen grabs from Black Books an Assembly Film and Television Limited production for Channel Four courtesy of Channel Four Television
Spaced cast photographs by Jason Joyce
Father Ted photograph courtesy of Hat Trick Productions Ltd

SIX
THE DRUG DEAL
Screen grabs from Equinox: Rave New World a McDougall Craig Ltd production for Channel Four, courtesy of Channel Four Television © 1994
Trainspotting images courtesy of Film Four Ltd
Going Cold Turkey Advert, 4 Creative / Alastair Thain
Screen grab from Dispatches – Drugs The Phoney War a RDF Media Ltd production for Channel Four, courtesy of Channel Four Television © 2001
Pot Night © 1995
Screen grabs from Cocaine courtesy of October Films © 2005
Screen grabs of Without Walls: An Interview with Dennis Potter a London Weekend Television

Ltd production for Channel Four, courtesy of Channel Four Television © 1994
Traffik images © 1989
Screen grabs of Traffik a Picture Partnership Productions Ltd production for Channel Four, courtesy of Channel Four Television © 1989

SEVEN
ADVENTURES IN ART
The Big Art Project image courtesy of Dan Holdsworth, Art Direction by YES
Peter and the Wolf images courtesy of BreakThru Ltd & Se-ma-for © 2006
Grayson Perry photograph courtesy of Dave Benett / Getty Images
Ballet Changed My Life photograph by Stuart Wood
Screen grabs from Ballet Boyz a Landseer Film & TV Productions Ltd production for Channel Four, courtesy of Channel Four Television © 1999
Andy Warhol Street Map courtesy of Daniel Eatock
Howard Goodall – How Music Works photographs by Brian Sweeney
Andy Warhol Billboards, 4 Creative / Daniel Eatock / Carlo Draisci / © 2008 Andy Warhol Foundation for the Visual Arts / Artists Rights Society (ARS), New York / DACS, London
Screen grab from The Turner Prize an Illuminations Television Ltd production for Channel Four, courtesy of Channel Four Television © 1995
The Samuel Beckett Film Project: Breath courtesy of Blue Angel Films Ltd
Screen grabs from The Death of Klinghoffer a Blast! Films Ltd production for Channel Four, courtesy of Channel Four Television © 2003
The Big 4 photograph by Michelle Sadgrove, Mike Smith Studio
Screen grabs of Operatunity a Diverse Ltd production for Channel Four, courtesy of Channel Four Television © 2003

EIGHT
THE FOOD FIGHT
The Big Food Fight, 4 Creative / Tim Gutt
Screen grab of Grow Your Greens a Wall to Wall Television Ltd Production for Channel Four, courtesy of Channel Four Television © 1993
Screen grab of Dispatches: Hot Potato, A Granada Television Ltd Production for Channel Four, courtesy of Channel Four Television © 1999
Screen grab of Nigella Bites a Flashback Productions / Pacific production for Channel Four, courtesy of Channel Four Television © 2000
Jamie's School Dinners Advert, 4 Creative / Harry Borden © 2005
Jamie's Return To School Dinners

Advert, 4 Creative / Lorenzo Agius
The F Word Advert, 4 Creative / Tim Bret-Day
Hugh Fearnley-Whittingstall photograph by Des Willie
River Cottage image courtesy of River Cottage

NINE
EARTHLY POWERS
Beyond the Clouds, Fragile Earth, Baka – People of the Rain Forest, images courtesy of Phil Agland / River Films
Ali image courtesy of Lisa Sidcock
Screen grab from The End of the World As We Know It courtesy of October Films © 2005

TEN
THE FEMALE EQUATION
Sex & The City, Tom Kingston / WireImage / Getty Images
A Woman of Substance image courtesy of Southern Star / Portman Productions © 1985
Smack the Pony photographs by Jason Joyce
Sex & The City, HBO / Newsmakers / Getty Images
Screen grab of Shere Hite interview on Channel Four News courtesy of ITN © 1998
Screen grab of The Big Breakfast a Planet 24 Productions Ltd production for Channel Four, courtesy of Channel Four Television © 1992
Screen grab of Divorce Iranian Style a Twentieth Century Vixen Ltd for Channel Four, courtesy of Channel Four Television © 1999
Desperate Housewives, 4 Creative / Ellen Von Unwerth
Desperate Housewives, 4 Creative / David LaChapelle
Ugly Betty 4 Creative / Ellen Von Unwerth © 2007
Sisters in Law photograph by Mary Milton

ELEVEN
OH MY GOD
Cult of the Suicide Bomber, 4 Creative Dmitry Nikiforov / News Team / Reuters / Corbis © 2005
Cult of the Suicide Bomber II, 4 Creative/Reuters/Corbis © 2006
Screen grab from Shariah TV a CTVC Productions for Channel Four, courtesy of CTVC Productions © 2006
Screen grabs from Children of Abraham a 3BM Television Ltd Production for Channel Four, courtesy of Channel Four Television © 2004
Priest Idol photograph by David Marsden / Page One
Screen grabs from Kumbh Mela Rex Mundi Ltd / Denis Whyte Films 2001
God is Black photograph by Christopher Sims
Imagine A World Without Religion Advert 4 Creative / Frank Labua / Getty Images

Screen grab from The Week They Elected the Pope courtesy of Map TV © 2005

TWELVE
REALITY CHECK
Big Brother Logo, Daniel Eatock
Big Brother Human Eyes, The Creative Partnership
Guardian Article courtesy of Guardian News & Media Ltd 2000
Guardian Article Illustration courtesy of Jonas Hendrik
Screen grabs of Celebrity Big Brother an Endemol production for Channel Four, courtesy of Channel Four Television © 2005
Celebrity Big Brother Photographs by Tim Anderson © 2005
Big Brother Housemates featured in the Times article photographs by Amanda Searle
Big Brother House featured in The Times photograph by Michelle Sadgrove
Times Article courtesy of The Times, 2000 / NI Syndication
Big Brother Billboard courtesy of 4 Creative / Daniel Eatock / Carlo Draisci

THIRTEEN
HOME SWEET HOME
Screen grabs of Location, Location, Location courtesy of IWC Media
The Perfect Home photograph by Phil Fisk
Property Ladder photographs by John Carey

FOURTEEN
YOUTH IN ITS WISDOM
Screen grabs from The Word a Planet 24 Productions Ltd production for Channel Four, courtesy of Channel Four Television © 1991
Screen grab of Max Headroom a Chrysalis Visual Ent production courtesy of All3Media International & Matt Frewer ©1985
The Tube © 1982
Skins, 4 Creative / Ewen Spencer
Dawson's Creek courtesy of Getty Images
The Hip Hop Years © 1999
As If images courtesy of Nick Briggs / Carnival Film & Television Ltd © 2001
Screen grabs from Network 7 a Sunday Productions production for Channel Four, courtesy of Channel Four Television © 1987
The Big Breakfast photographs by Sven Arnstein
Don't Forget Your Toothbrush photograph by Sven Arnstein
June Sarpong photograph courtesy of Ray Burmiston / Shoot
Hollyoaks images courtesy of Lime Pictures
Miquita Oliver photograph courtesy of Ray Burmiston / Shoot
Vernon Kay photograph courtesy of Ray Burmiston / Shoot
T4 photographs courtesy of

Ray Burmiston / Shoot
FIFTEEN
A QUESTION OF DIFFERENCE
Walter screen grab, a Central Television Production for ITV, courtesy of ITV plc © 1982
Screen grab from Make Me Normal courtesy of Century Films © 2005
Blind Young Things photograph by Phil Fisk
The Spastic King courtesy of IWC Media ©
Screengrab from The Boy Whose Skin Fell Off courtesy of Yipp Films / DEBRA © 2004
Image from The Boy Whose Skin Fell Off courtesy of Yipp Films / DEBRA © 2004

SIXTEEN
SHRINKING PLANET
China's Stolen Children 4 Creative / Glowimages / Getty/ Green Dog
Screengrab from Beyond the Clouds a DJA River Films Ltd production for Channel Four courtesy of Channel Four Television © 1994
Screen grabs from Empire's Children courtesy of Wall to Wall / Illumina Digital Ltd © 2007
Screen grabs from The Last Peasant of Europe an October Films production for Channel Four courtesy of Channel Four Television © 2003
Living with Hunger images courtesy of Insight News TV Ltd
Screen grab taken from Unreported World: India's Missing Children courtesy of Mentorn Media
Screen grab taken from Unreported World Congo: UN's Dirty War courtesy of Mentorn Media
Screen grab taken from Unreported World Iraq: On the Front Line courtesy of Mentorn Media
Screen grab taken from Unreported World Somalia: Al-Qaeda's New Haven courtesy of Mentorn Media
The Circle, Winstar / Everett / Rex Features © 2000
Through the Olive Trees Tristar / Everett / Rex Features © 1994
The Circle Winstar / Everett / Rex Features © 2000
Through the Olive Trees Tristar / Everett / Rex Features © 1994
The Apple Everett Collection / Rex Features © 1998

SEVENTEEN
NEW FAMILY VALUES
Shameless Before and After, 4 Creative / Jim Fiscus
Brookside images courtesy of Lime Pictures
Wife Swap photograph by Stuart Wood
Screen grab of Shameless a Company Television production for Channel Four, courtesy of Channel Four Television, © Channel Four Television
Wife Swap photograph by Darren Gerrish
Friends images © Warner Bros.

Television, a division of Time Warner Entertainment Company, L.P.
Screen grab from Cutting Edge: No Home For Barry an Adventure Pictures Ltd production for Channel Four courtesy of Channel Four Television © 1990
Screen grab from Cutting Edge: Family Feuds a Clark Television Production Ltd for Channel Four courtesy of Channel Four Television © 1996
Screen grab from Cutting Edge: Stories for Eleanor a John Gau Production Ltd for Channel Four courtesy of Channel Four Television © 1990
My New Home photographs by Phil Fisk

NINETEEN
ALL CHANGE
Photography Stylists: Chloe Brown and Astrid Joss
Plates courtesy of Wedgewood www.wedgewood.com
Implants courtesy of The Hospital Group, www.thehospitalgroup.org
Contact lenses courtesy of www.contamac.co.uk
Screen grabs from Brat Camp courtesy of Twenty Twenty Productions Ltd
Brat Camp James Fonfe image courtesy of Twenty Twenty Televison
Brat Camp photograph by Lance W Clayton
How to Look Good Naked photograph by Adam Lawrence
Faking it Before photograph by Matt Squire
Faking it After photograph by Dave King
Embarrassing Illnesses photograph by John Wright

TWENTY
THE SPECIAL RELATIONSHIP
Frasier courtesy of Gale Adler / Paramount / Getty Images
Cheers courtesy of NBC Televison / Fotos International / Getty Images
Friends © Warner Bros. Television, a division of Time Warner Entertainment Company, L.P.
NYPD Blue courtesy of Vince Bucci / Getty Images
The Daily Show Jon Stewart courtesy of Scott Gries / Getty Images
The Daily Show Jon Stewart close shot courtesy of Frank Micelotta / Getty Images
West Wing Advert , 4 Creative / Walcott Henry / Getty Images
Morgan Spurlock image courtesy of FX
Death of a President Advert 4 Creative / Dean Williams
West Wing © Warner Bros. Television, a division of Time Warner Entertainment Company, L.P.
ER, © Warner Bros. Television, a division of Time Warner Entertainment Company, L.P.
Joe Strummer courtesy of Dave Hogan / Hulton Archive / Getty Images

TWENTY-ONE
UNCENSORED
Los Angeles Times, © 1991,
Los Angeles Times reprinted with
permission
Autopsy courtesy of Scott Barbour
/ Getty Images
Being Pamela Times Article
courtesy of The Sunday Times, 2005
/ NI Syndication
Being Pamela images courtesy
of David Modell © 2005

TWENTY-TWO
THE HISTORY FILES
Dr. David Starkey photograph
by Ranald Mackechnie
Trafalgar Battle Surgeon
photograph by Phil Fisk
The Edwardian Country House © 2002
War of the Worlds photographs
by Dewald Aukema
Empire © 1990
Screen grabs from Time Team
courtesy of Time Team
Time Team photograph by Mark Thomas
That'll Teach Them photographs by
Dave King

TWENTY-THREE
THE PINK TRIANGLE
Screengrabs from Brookside a
Mersey TV production for Channel
Four, courtesy Lime Pictures
and Channel Four, © Channel Four
Television
Screen grabs from Hollyoaks
courtesy of Lime Pictures
Screen grabs from Queer as Folk
a Red Production Company Ltd
production for Channel Four
courtesy of Channel Four Television
© 1999
Out on Tuesday photographs
by Fara Furfe
Sugar Rush photograph by Phil Fisk
Screen grabs from Sugar Rush
courtesy of Shine Productions
Graham Norton photograph against
yellow Background by Barry J Holmes
Graham Norton photographs by
Andrew Williams
Tales of The City a Working Titles
Films Limited production for
Channel 4 courtesy of Channel Four
Television © 1993
Queer as Folk photograph
Jaap Buitendijk
Clapham Junction photographs
by Jack Barnes
Sebastiane photograph courtesy
of Gerald Incandela / Disctac Ltd
Screen grabs from Clapham Junction
courtesy of Darlow Smithson
Productions
Queer as Folk 3 Characters,
photographed by Nicky Johnston

TWENTY-FOUR
ACCESS ALL AREAS
E-Stings courtesy of E4
Screen grab from 3 Minute
Wonder New Sensations:
Mark Melvin courtesy of
Tiger Aspect Productions
Screen grab from 3 Minute

Wonder New Sensations:
Sarah Maple courtesy of
Tiger Aspect Productions
Screen grab from 3 Minute
Wonder North Circular Stories:
Toil and Trouble courtesy
of Uproar Productions Ltd
Screen grab from 3 Minute
Wonder North Circular
Stories: Them Sort courtesy
of Uproar Productions Ltd
4 Docs courtesy of
channel4.com/4docs
4 Laughs courtesy of
channel4.com/4laughs
Screen grabs from The Services,
an Open Mike Productions Ltd
production for Channel Four
courtesy of Channel Four
Television © 1998
Screen grabs from Modern Toss,
a Channel X Communications
Ltd production for Channel
Four courtesy of Channel Four
Television © 2005
Comedy Lab: Meet the Magoons,
a Tiger Wark Clements Ltd
production for Channel Four,
Courtesy of Channel Four Television
© 2002
Comedy Lab: Jimmy Carr's World of
Corporate Videos a Talent Shed
Com production for Channel Four,
courtesy of Channel Four
Television © 2001
Comedy Lab: Trigger Happy TV
an Absolute Productions Ltd
production for Channel Four,
courtesy of Channel Four
Television © 1998
First Cut: Karaoke Soul image
courtesy of Raw Television
First Cut: Mr Average images
courtesy of Century Films
Screen grabs from Video Box
a Channel Four Production,
courtesy of Channel Four
Television © 1999

TWENTY-FIVE
FILMSPOTTING
My Beautiful Laundrette poster
courtesy of Film Four Ltd.
The Motorcycle Diaries poster
courtesy of Pathe and Film Four Ltd.
East Is East poster courtesy of Film
Four Ltd.
Howard's End poster courtesy of
Merchant Ivory Productions Ltd.
Touching the Void poster courtesy
of Pathe and Film Four Ltd.
Career Girls poster courtesy of
Thin Man Films and Film Four Ltd.
Four Weddings and a Funeral poster
courtesy of Polly Gram and Film Four
Ltd.
The Last King of Scotland images
© 2006 Twentieth Century Fox. All
Rights Reserved.
This is England poster courtesy of
Optimum Releasing.
Trainspotting poster courtesy of
Film Four Ltd and Universal.
The Crying Game poster courtesy of
Film Four Ltd.
My Beautiful Laundrette images

courtesy of Film Four Ltd © 1985
Screen grab from Walter, a Central
Television Production for ITV,
courtesy of ITV plc © 1982
Shallow Grave images courtesy
of Film Four Ltd © 1994
Brick Lane courtesy of
Ruby Films © 2007
Naked images courtesy
of Film Four Ltd © 1993
Life is Sweet images courtesy
of Film Four Ltd © 1990
Secrets and Lies images
courtesy of Film Four Ltd © 1996
High Hopes images courtesy
of Portman Productions and
Southern Star © 1988
Bhaji on the Beach images
courtesy of Film Four Ltd © 1993
Riff Raff images courtesy
of Film Four Ltd © 1990
It's a Free World courtesy
of Sixteen Films © 2007
Touching the Void courtesy
of Film Four Ltd © 2003
This is England courtesy of Warp
Films & Optimum Releasing © 2006

Thanks to the Channel 4 Archive for
their help in sourcing many of the
images included in this book.